Making the Bible Belt

Making the Bible Belt

Texas Prohibitionists and the Politicization of Southern Religion

JOSEPH L. LOCKE

OXFORD
UNIVERSITY PRESS

OXFORD

UNIVERSITY PRESS

Oxford University Press is a department of the University of Oxford. It furthers
the University's objective of excellence in research, scholarship, and education
by publishing worldwide. Oxford is a registered trade mark of Oxford University
Press in the UK and certain other countries.

Published in the United States of America by Oxford University Press
198 Madison Avenue, New York, NY 10016, United States of America.

© Oxford University Press 2017

First issued as an Oxford University Press paperback, 2020

Library of Congress Cataloging-in-Publication Data
Names: Locke, Joseph (Historian), author.
Title: Making the Bible Belt : Texas prohibitionists and the politicization
of southern religion / Joseph Locke.
Description: New York : Oxford University Press, [2017] |
Includes bibliographical references and index.
Identifiers: LCCN 2016053531 (print) | LCCN 2016055369 (ebook) |
ISBN 9780190216283 (hardcover : alk. paper) | ISBN 9780190216290 (Updf) |
ISBN 9780190216306 (Epub) | ISBN 9780199780197532911 (paperback : alk. paper)
Subjects: LCSH: Prohibition—Texas—History. | Texas—Religion. |
Religion and politics—Texas—History. | Religion and politics—Southern
States—History.
Classification: LCC HV5090.T4 L63 2017 (print) | LCC HV5090.T4 (ebook) |
DDC 277.64/082—dc23
LC record available at https://lccn.loc.gov/2016053531

For Dad

Contents

Acknowledgments

THIS PROJECT COULD not have been completed without the help of countless scholars, staff members, friends, and family members. Funding from the Rice University Department of History, the Rice University Humanities Research Center, and the Dolph Briscoe Center for American History at the University of Texas at Austin facilitated much of my research. Staff members at several archives and libraries, including the Carroll Library at Baylor University, the Roberts Library at Southwestern Baptist Theological Seminary Baylor University, the Bridwell Library at Southern Methodist University, and especially the Dolph Briscoe Center for American History assisted me throughout the early stages of this project. Staff members in the Rice University History Department and the School of Arts and Sciences at the University of Houston–Victoria likewise provided invaluable administrative aid.

Howard Miller and Gary Keith at the University of Texas at Austin shepherded this project in its infancy. My doctoral advisor at Rice University, John Boles, not only shaped much of my thinking about southern history but also provided an enduring model of professionalism, scholarship, and collegiality. He, together with Allen Matusow, Caleb McDaniel, and Michael Emerson, offered extensive feedback on the manuscript. I benefited immensely from the academic community at Rice University. Drew Bledsoe, Allison Madar, Carl Paulus, Jim Wainwright, Ben Wright, Andy Lang, Wes Phelps, Blake Ellis, Luke Harlow, and others all helped refine my thinking on this topic and many others.

Terry Bilhartz, Walter Buenger, Mike Campbell, Gaines Foster, Paul Harvey, Charles Postel, Eddie Weller, and other scholars at various institutions also read and offered feedback on particular chapters or sections. At Oxford University Press, Susan Ferber, Alexandra Dauler, and several anonymous reviewers provided invaluable substantive and stylistic feedback. But of course, I owe the most to my family. No words of mine will ever capture the love and appreciation I have for them.

Making the Bible Belt

Introduction

ON AN AUGUST afternoon in 1885, several thousand Texans crowded into a park in Waco to hear the state's Democratic establishment decry prohibition and excoriate the "political preachers" who were championing it in that county. Between speeches, brass bands, and barbecue, Senator Richard Coke rose and addressed the crowd. "Ah, my fellow-citizens," he said, "whenever your preachers go into politics, scourge them back!" The crowd cheered. "Our forefathers were driven to the country seeking freedom of conscience against the persecutions of state religion and shall we now combine church and state?" No! cried the crowd. "The worst sign of the times that I can perceive is to be found in the delivery of stump speeches on the holy Sabbath day from God's pulpit." The crowd roared. The senator continued on about the pure gospel, good government, and all the widows, orphans, and bloodshed wrought by alliances of church and state. The crowd cheered even louder. They were well-versed in Coke's brand of anticlericalism and the tropes and images and fears came all too easily to mind. The prohibition campaign collapsed, the senator remained in office, and public opinion continued to muzzle "political" religion.[1]

Whatever those Texans called their world, it was not the Bible Belt. H. L. Mencken coined that term later, in the 1920s, to capture what he saw as the South's peculiar alliance of region and religion. Mencken used the label, he later recalled, "to designate those parts of the country in which the literal accuracy of the Bible is credited," and also, he said, where the "clergymen who preach it have public influence."[2] "The Bible Belt" described not just a geographic bloc of biblical literalism, but an entire culture enthralled to religion and religious authority.[3] In other words, it marked a region where evangelical religion was not only pervasive but powerful, too. The Bible Belt itself had its "origins" and its "beginnings" in the evangelical ferment of the early nineteenth century, but it was this new and aggressive aspect of southern religion that proved so attention-grabbing in Mencken's time—and in ours.[4] Today, the South's pervasive religiosity bleeds so heavily into American life that the melding of region and religion seems inevitable, foreordained, and automatic. Political prayer rallies, school-board battles, and faith-based politics seem natural and native, even timeless. But everything has a history. The reality that Mencken described was only the closing chapter of a long historical process—and the beginning of something else entirely. Like the label itself, the Bible Belt was something new. And this is the history of its making.[5]

Few who witnessed Richard Coke so profitably condemn prohibitionist clergymen in 1885 could have anticipated that the South—and Texas in particular—would eventually capitulate to prohibition and its clerical champions. Yet a generation later, another Texas senator, Morris Sheppard, would often lecture on "Christian citizenship," pray with anti-liquor demonstrators on the steps of the US Capitol, and tell the United States Senate that "a Christian nation cannot tolerate the liquor traffic."[6] In 1917, when Sheppard cemented his reputation as the "Father of National Prohibition" by successfully introducing a constitutional amendment to prohibit "the manufacture, sale, or transportation of intoxicating liquors," nine of the eleven former Confederate states had already legislated statewide liquor bans, and the southern states raced against one another to be the first to ratify what would become Eighteenth Amendment.[7] Baptist and Methodist ministers stalked southern statehouses lobbying legislators to support the amendment, and when it was formally ratified in 1919, ministers congratulated themselves for the work they had performed. Churchgoers marched in parades and evangelists held mock funerals for John Barleycorn. It was "the advent of a new day," Senator Sheppard declared.[8]

The southern embrace of prohibition marked the destruction of a venerable anticlerical tradition and the emergence of a new and powerful clerical alternative. Issues ranging from education to Sabbath-breaking to disfranchisement consumed religious activists, but none matched the alluring, world-in-the-balance intensity surrounding the legal proscription of alcohol: prohibition. Building on a long-standing Protestant commitment to temperance, southern religious leaders increasingly regarded alcohol as the age's greatest malady. They scoured their vocabularies to communicate their unmitigated hatred of alcohol. But they also used the issue as a political battering ram, and the impact from each blow burst the lingering barriers to the full flowering of political religion in the South. Prohibition not only criminalized liquor, it ripped apart a culture of anticlericalism and offered evangelicals a clear path into the heart of the South.

Whereas southern anticlericalism relied on the general rejection of religious interference in public life, Christian activists constructed an alternative around the convictions that religion deserved a larger role in the world, that ministers should be heard and heeded, that politics should bend before morality, and that history bowed before God. Articulated most vocally by the region's religious leaders, this new clerical vision inspired generations of religious southerners to successfully articulate a noble Christian history, justify a new aggressive faith, and reconceive the relationship between religion and politics. Over several decades, religious leaders built an intoxicating and empowering ideology, assembled the organizational resources for mass mobilization, and rallied the religious behind the banner of moral reform.

By focusing on the decades-long controversy surrounding prohibition in Texas and the broader American South, *Making the Bible Belt* advances three basic arguments. First, that instead of bowing blindly before religious authority, and despite some ministers' unprecedented activism in championing slavery, promoting secession, and bolstering the Confederacy, most late-nineteenth-century southerners subscribed instead to what might accurately be called a culture of anticlericalism: in and out of the churches, a very real and potent fear of political religion scrubbed many public issues from the pulpit and cast scorn on "political preachers." Put another way, appreciating the novelty of the Bible Belt requires understanding how and why Richard Coke could say what he did on that summer day in 1885. Although the contentious politics of prohibition and other moral issues marked a truly radical break in the southern religious tradition, these campaigns also culminated a broader and more fundamental transformation in the cultural and organizational resources of southern evangelicals—clerical activists marshaled newly constructed denominational structures and championed revolutionary new ideas about the role of religion in public life, ideas propelled by a burst of new, usable histories and potent notions of Christian nationalism. Finally, clerics leveraged these new innovations into a decades-long battle to realize the Bible Belt. Never hidden, this conflict was consciously waged, conspicuously fought, and frequently commented on. The struggle filled newspaper columns, sermons, political contests, private conversations, and personal reflections. If the present-day power of the Bible Belt veils the reality that the American South once struggled to define the proper bounds of religion—and at times stifled those who favored its expansion—it need not. Beyond assumptions of the South as a tranquil region united in religion lurks the roaring, culture-splitting turbulence from which the Bible Belt was made.

In the hope that a narrow geographic focus may allow a fuller and more intimate accounting of this pivotal transformation, the following pages largely confine themselves to the understudied experience of Texas. Just as Senator Sheppard's political ascendance reflected the broader cultural fortunes of a politicized southern religion, the history of Sheppard's home state reveals the dynamics of the Bible Belt. By narrowing the scope of inquiry to Texas—only one theater in a much wider conflict—clerical activism and its anticlerical counterpart come immediately into focus. "Texas," wrote sociologist Robert Wuthnow, "is America's most powerful Bible-Belt state."[9] The present-day potency of its faith-based politics alone would seem to suggest the state as a proper area of historical study, but Texas's outsized religious influence is only the capstone to a story that began more than a century ago, when a new breed of aggressively political religious leaders first pushed the issue of prohibition into the public sphere.

"Prohibition is as perennial as it is paramount as an issue to our politics," the *Dallas Morning News* reported in 1916. "It determines most other decisions and influences all of them, until it would hardly exaggerate to say that no question is considered on its own merits."[10] Prohibition dominated Texas politics. Political races divided between "wet" and "dry" factions, and elections became referendums on the proper place of religion in public life. Texans could hardly open a newspaper without reading some clergyman's thoughts on the separation of church and state or some politician's opinions of "political preachers."

Prohibition's shifting political fortunes reflected a newly ascendant clerical culture. Beginning in the late nineteenth century, insurgents in the South's white evangelical churches amplified a vibrant religious subculture, conquered the major denominations, set their sights on public life, and manufactured the materials they needed for a popular movement. In Waco, the fiery oratory of a six-feet-four, 260-pound Baptist preacher named Benajah Harvey Carroll inspired a generation of religious leaders to organize within their denominations and pick political fights in the public arena. His followers, such as James Cranfill, a doughy faced, yarn-spinning neurasthenic who cultivated the power of the religious press, churned notions of history, race, gender, morality, and religion into a broad and powerful crusade that, through the politics of moral reform, crushed a popular anticlericalism and wed southern white evangelicals inextricably to public life and political issues. Clerics such as Carroll and Cranfill supported prohibition, but they also redefined the mission of religion in American life. These changes began with the making of the Bible Belt—and the unmaking of a culture of anticlericalism.

To most white southerners of the nineteenth century, a minister's place was his pulpit, and his focus was spiritual. Many northern evangelicals chased social and political reforms; southerners demurred. The region's prevailing sentiment, in and out of the churches, demanded that "political preachers" be condemned. Southern preachers rarely needed to be, of course, for "politics" was a dangerous game that few churchmen dared play: anticlericalism pervaded the pulpit and the pew no less than it did the public square. Conscious of the limitations of such seemingly all-encompassing terms to capture complex historical phenomena, this book nevertheless employs the dictionary definition of *anticlericalism*: opposition to the interference or influence of the clergy in secular affairs.[11] Deployed periodically by contemporaries, *anticlericalism* captures the popular attitudes of many white nineteenth-century southerners. Sustained by a veritable culture complete with its own mythology, symbols, histories, and codes of proper conduct, fears of clerical authority oriented generations of American southerners, regulated political preaching, and stunted the birth of the Bible Belt. It was in this context that Texas senators and congressmen could tell adoring audiences to "scourge" preachers and assure them that "hell was full of such political preachers."[12]

Anticlericalism is not synonymous with irreligion, anti-Catholicism, or any other anti-religious sentiment, nor is it incompatible with religiosity. Many contemporary preachers touted its principles, and prominent scholars, such as Rhys Isaac and Nathaniel Hatch, long ago noted anticlericalism's role in the widespread appeal of American—and southern—evangelicalism.[13] Anticlericalism often shared much with what a previous generation of southern historians had called, after a Presbyterian construct, "the doctrine of spirituality" or "the spirituality of the church," but southern anticlericalism was perhaps less narrowly theological and more broadly cultural, concerned particularly with the power and authority of ministers, and reinforced by external cultural expectations as well as self-imposed theological pretensions.[14]

Still, the word *anticlericalism* typically evokes European intellectuals or Latin American revolutionaries, if it evokes anything at all. It recalls priests and Catholicism and state churches: the vestiges of the Old World and its old order.[15] "The United States has never had a clerical or an anticlerical tradition," one scholar of religion and American life recently argued.[16] The word simply fails to stir up relevant images of the United States, let alone that den of religious fervor known as the Bible Belt.[17] But it should. Fierce opposition challenged the South's clerical insurgency at every step. Freethinkers, traditionalists, secularists, and jealous politicians all manned the battlements to crush the crusade.

Before religious leaders could earn Mencken's derision, before the cynic could coin the term "Bible Belt" and have it mean anything at all, religious activists conquered greater obstacles at home. The triumph of prohibition signaled the destruction of a venerable anticlerical tradition, but of course anticlericalism is merely a negative formulation. What then of its opposite? What of clericalism itself? Over the course of several decades, a complex but shared commitment to religious empowerment transformed southern evangelicals' self-conscious timidity into an aggressive, self-assertive, and unapologetic activism. In Fort Worth, a fiery young fundamentalist named J. Frank Norris, despite indictments for arson and murder, picked headline-grabbing fights with mayors, gamblers, governors, and saloonkeepers on his way to building the largest congregation in America. In Dallas, an ambitious, vitriolic Methodist minister named George Rankin wrote political editorials for the *Texas Christian Advocate* that inspired Austin's First Methodist Church to remove the sitting governor, an anti-prohibitionist named Oscar Colquitt, from its membership. Methodist Bishop Edwin Mouzon purged the governor from the denomination altogether. Across Texas, zealotry trampled moderation and cloaked the clerical insurgency in the aura of inevitability. But the creation of the Bible Belt was never predestined—it had to be fought for and won.

As it explores this radically transformative moment in the history of religion and American public life, this study emerges from the historiography of southern religion. Born amid the civil rights movement, the field's pioneering works emphasized constraint. In the mid- to late-twentieth century, scholars—often native southerners—grappled with the easy acquiescence of southern white churches to a culture of white supremacy. Samuel Hill, reflecting on his path-breaking *Southern Churches in Crisis*, admitted that "the crisis of those years provoked the study." How could southern churches, he asked, "miss the ethical demands of their black southern neighbors and of the region's historical opportunity to set right what had been so oppressive for so long?"[18] Amid such a momentous controversy, these southerners looked on, dumbstruck, as their churches stood idly by. Consumed by this moral failure, early scholars, such as Hill, John Boles, and Donald Mathews, found the roots of paralysis in a distinctly regional religion. Southern evangelicals, they argued, privileged an otherworldly individualism and could never develop the social ethic necessary to challenge the prejudices of their culture. Southern religion (usually, white evangelicalism) was, and had been, in "cultural captivity."[19]

The captivity thesis survives today mostly as a foil for new scholarship, but its parameters offer one last, shining beacon for a study of the Bible Belt. For if religion can be captive to culture, it can also capture a culture.[20] This is part of the pattern of clericalism in Texas. The burden, therefore, is to rediscover that long, difficult quest for religious authority and to recapture the creation of the culture that compelled it.

The new imperatives of southern religious history, meanwhile, stress the varieties of regional faiths and a spectrum of beliefs and practices belied by such seemingly static monikers as "evangelicalism" and "the Bible Belt."[21] By breaking apart "southern religion," scholars found various manifestations of southern faiths around which developed dozens of new historiographies.[22] The exposed fault lines of the fractured field reveal that conflict and controversy—not stability—distinguish the history of the region's religion. But by foregrounding the tensions and entanglements of rival traditions, a new religious history can move beyond questions of definition and division and seek unity in a shared—if often contentious—experience.[23] It can reconcile contending religious cultures, incorporate the religious with the irreligious, and arrive at a fuller and truer understanding of southern religion.[24] Religion transcends pulpits and pews. Texas churchgoers, for instance, weren't Baptists or Presbyterians only on Sundays. Everywhere and always the sacred and the secular moved together, intertwined and inseparable. The making of the Bible Belt did not happen in an isolated religious world but in a life-and-death struggle between competing cultures of clerics and anticlerics. By emphasizing the interplay of the sacred and the secular, this study recaptures the intensity of partisans and repopulates the past with the pressing concerns of those who lived it.

In reconstructing the religious conquest of public life in the post-Reconstruction South, *Making the Bible Belt* details how religious identity intensified, muscled its way to the fore, reoriented lives, battled anticlerical assumptions, and changed the way white southerners saw the world. It seeks to understand what compelled so many churchgoers to wage unceasing war on a new host of imagined enemies. The imperatives of religion awoke many to culture, politics, and public life. Clerics so Christianized ideas of history, race, family, and education that such disparate subjects suddenly became the proper targets for sacred warfare.

But as the dreams of activists outpaced reality, religious southerners comprehended a widespread spiritual crisis. Clerics, even as they carved out a larger role for religion in culture and politics, nevertheless saw themselves as marginalized and powerless. They felt exploited by politicians and besieged by popular culture. Judging even their congregants to be apathetic and list-less, they struggled to find meaning in the "old-time religion." A nagging sense of worthlessness preyed on their labor. Abstract theological debates and the mundane, day-to-day duties of pastoral work suddenly rang hollow. Newly ambitious clergymen dreamed of doing great things, but they lived their lives shackled by the chains of anxiety. And they hated it. Lost to emp-tiness, they yearned for the visceral and ecstatic touch of the divine. So they plotted against their newfound spiritual void and schemed strategies for its destruction. Activists decided that human agency, not grace or providence, would release them from spiritual calamity. Thereafter, they found liberation in action, exertion, and conscious purpose. In short, they found it in the mak-ing of the Bible Belt.

Much of what follows depicts that discovery. Long before William James urged Americans to unite in common purpose by finding the "moral equiv-alent to war," southern clerics found that purpose in their moral crusades. Religious activists channeled new aims through denominationalism, a rein-vigorated spirituality, and politics. Within a generation or two, southern cler-ics transformed a freewheeling conglomeration of clashing traditions into a powerful, self-assured, and efficient crusade of righteous conviction. Soon the imperatives of religious reform trampled across denominational lines. White evangelical southerners applied their morality to the world, developed the standards with which to judge a nation, and assembled the materials they needed to construct the Bible Belt.

Making the Bible Belt begins in Texas in the late nineteenth century, when, with one foot planted in the Old South and another in the New, the state leaped headlong into decades of growth and development. Farmers chased cheap land, industry stalked easy profits, and by 1900, nearly ten thousand miles of rail lines had stitched together the far-flung corners of the state. Texas's population exploded, from over one-and-a-half million in 1880 to more than four-and-a-half million in 1920. The state nevertheless maintained its south-ern identity. "So many Texans have come out of the South," two prominent Texas writers explained in 1916, "that Texas is predominately Southern in thought and feeling."[25] Although Texas's historical memory would later privi-lege cattle and cowboys over cotton and sharecroppers, few Texans at the turn of the twentieth century would have thought to question what one historian would later call their "essential southernness."[26]

Public life in Texas therefore reflected southern political patterns. Conservative Democrats dominated state politics after the "redemption" of the state from Reconstruction in 1874. In the 1880s, farmers across the state, fighting against falling prices and failing crops, found solace in the cooperative vision of the Texas-born Farmers' Alliance and, beginning in 1892, its political offshoot, the People's (or Populist) Party. The Populists' political revolt threatened to shatter the Democratic Party's control over the state, but the charismatic Democratic governor James Hogg maintained a measure of political unity in the 1890s by advocating a reform platform of railroad regulation and antitrust legislation. Regulatory schemes aimed at railroads, insurance companies, corporate landholders, and "foreign" (out-of-state) corporations consumed state politics.[27] Then came prohibition.

The dominance of the "liquor question" in Texas politics testified to the potency of a new clerical worldview born of worldly ambition and a perceived spiritual crisis. As the nineteenth century closed, the New England aristocrat Henry Adams observed that machinery had supplanted God in the American mind, and in his autobiography, he famously wondered what it all meant. America was being remade, but in whose image?[28] Religious Texans anticipated Adams's anxiety. Although they welcomed industrial progress, murmurs of a New South nevertheless unsettled them, and in their churches they came to speak a shared language of crisis. Some succumbed to their worries, but others used the materials of crisis to build the vehicle for professional advancement. Activists preached the doctrine of clericalism, the notion that religious leaders should engage public life and reshape the world in their own image. The apostles of a new clerical culture crafted histories that privileged religion and religious leaders, developed new schemes for public education that emphasized religious principles, and pushed new ideas of government grounded in religious authority. They spoke, too, of a Christian nation. Their expansive new visions reoriented southern religion. Clericalism took on the churchless population, the skeptics, the critics, the politicians, the weak-kneed preachers, the indolent congregants—everyone—and declared war on their decadent, diseased world.

As clericalism's aggressive faith shoved its way to the fore, it instilled in its hosts a fighting faith. Clerics innovated weapons of spiritual warfare. The language of "crusades" and "insurgencies" that runs through these chapters is their language. The clerical conquest marched to martial music. Its soldiers believed themselves to be locked in mortal combat with a vicious malignancy. Clerics' aggressive willingness to deploy the uncompromising language of warfare won them converts. Their rhetoric raised the stakes of their faith. The movement depended on it. Under the terms of the clerical culture, if Christians weren't fighting, they were losing. But if the infidels would never yield, then neither could good Christians relent. Vigilance demanded defense.

When the clerics sallied forth, deep-seated fears and suspicions united their opponents. Public figures denounced them, church elders castigated them, and the nameless masses—farmers. bankers, publishers, and intellectuals—stifled them. When the clerics protested, their critics mocked them, newspapers pilloried them, and politicians urged adoring crowds to "scourge them back into their pulpits." But they persevered. They spoke as God's emissaries and refused to unlearn their new clerical language. The logic of their nascent worldview reinforced them in defeat and taught them to harness their embattlement for gain. As Senator Morris Sheppard said of his pursuit of moral reform, in 1911, Texans could be "crowned with the confidence and approbation of Almighty God."[29] Could there be a more fulfilling engine of activism? The greater the resistance, the more vivid their struggle, the deeper their commitment and the more inevitable their victory.

By turning religious leaders into politicians and politicians into religious leaders, prohibition redefined what it meant for white southerners to be religious.[30] As Senator Sheppard put it, "there can be no society and no citizenship disassociated from the idea of God."[31] Anticlerical political barriers crumbled all across the South. In Virginia, Methodist bishop James Cannon leveraged his leadership roles in the Anti-Saloon League and the Methodist Church to become not only a veritable political boss in Virginia, but one of America's most powerful political voices (H. L. Mencken said that he was, at the peak of his influence, "the undisputed boss of the United States."[32]) Ministers even rushed into political office. In Florida, for instance, a race-baiting, Catholic-hating Baptist minister named Sidney Johnston Catts won the governor's seat in 1916 on the Prohibition Party ticket.[33] Revivalists such as Sam Jones and Mordecai Hamm, meanwhile, barnstormed the South saving souls by preaching prohibition, muddying the distinction between traditional politics and religious practice.

As religious Texans quested for righteousness, they manufactured an all-encompassing, us-and-them division between saints and sinners, the secular and the sacred. Intractable and oppositional caricatures emerged. While anticlerics defamed the crusaders as Puritans and cranks, reformers cast their opponents as immoral and debauched. Antiprohibitionists, the clerics said, were foreign, un-American, and the embodiment of everything a holy citizenry should struggle against. The fighting prohibitionist came to represent a beacon of manhood, whiteness, honor, godliness—of everything that white religious Texans held dear. The culture of clericalism imbued provincial narrowness with the uncompromising righteousness of a fighting faith.

And yet rigid social boundaries sometimes buckled beneath the clerical crusade. Clerics were more than race-baiting brutes obsessed with Lost Cause fantasies and rape myths. White evangelicals certainly shared in the racial antipathies typical of their caste and, in their own way, contributed to the region's tragic descent into Jim Crow. But clerics' notion of a "better sort" and a "worse sort" could sometimes subsume regional racial and gender divides. Black religious leaders found unexpected pathways to respectability in prohibition, while many working-class whites, clinging to their saloons, found themselves exiled from the clerics' moral republic. Even as prohibitionists promoted race-based voting restrictions, they courted black voters, denounced lynching as the perverted crime of whiskey-mad rabble, and occasionally integrated their campaigns.

Small and subtle challenges to the received culture marked the creation of clericalism, but in defining a new, "better sort" standard of citizenship grounded in morality and politics, clerics paved their own unique road to prejudice. Clerics, more than anyone else, made the case that their bigotries rested on moral choices, not immutable laws. It was because black and Hispanic Texans supported the saloons, they said, that they should be disfranchised. It was because poor whites clung to whiskey that their votes should be taxed. Clerics veneered division with the appearance of malleability. And they had proof: morality could be measured in votes. Clerics could therefore publicly embrace the minority of "better sort" black prohibitionists, for instance, yet still urge a blanket disfranchisement to expunge the more numerous "worse sort." Moral outlaws, discredited by God, would remain forever targets of a perpetual culture war. As southern religion spread, this vision flourished, another of the many legacies of the Bible Belt.

The following pages recount the long construction of the Bible Belt from the end of Reconstruction in the 1870s to the ratification of the Eighteenth Amendment in 1919. Roughly chronological chapters recount the development of a unique clerical culture, the triumph of a broad religious movement, and the shifting political fortunes of prohibition. The story begins in the chaotic religious world of the 1870s and 1880s, when unorthodox faiths flourished, rival theologies warred, and freethinkers filled meeting halls. As religious leaders struggled to impose order in their churches, most Texans, born into a culture of anticlericalism, defeated prohibition's first political forays in the 1880s by scourging prohibitionist clergymen back into their pulpits. But over the coming decades, a new generation of ambitious religious leaders cultivated a sense of widespread spiritual crisis, built up their denominations, rewrote the past, and, after capturing much of the region's cultural high ground, organized politically to battle in the public sphere during the first two decades twentieth century. The Bible Belt was made in distinct though overlapping phases by activists who, chafing at anticlerical restraints, launched an insurgency within their churches that propelled southern religion head-long into politics and public life. Their unrelenting crusade not only imposed prohibition across the South, it heralded the marriage of electoral politics and southern religion, a union that would transform not only the region but the entire United States.

From their time to ours, Americans have increasingly lived in the world the clerics made. Ambitious religious leaders created a new and flowering world of fulfilling images, tropes, and arguments; convinced anxious suf-ferers to seek salvation; and taught disenchanted believers to find the satis-factions of righteousness in moral quests. In their political pursuits, clerics communed with the divine. In their moral embattlement, they *became* the sacred. Sustained by the logic of their convictions, clerics declared unceasing war upon their enemies. They sallied forth into the world and shocked con-vention. Armed with the issue of prohibition, religious partisans broke the long history of political detachment in the South. Prominent clerics dared to challenge traditional anticlerical constraints—and they triumphed. Their uncompromising efforts injected them forever into public life. Soon their voice was loud, their power manifest. "We have come to the consciousness of our power," Methodist bishop Edwin Mouzon wrote in 1913, "and we have just discovered what we can do: We can do anything that ought to be done."[34] This is the history of that discovery.

I

Heretics, Infidels, and Iconoclasts

THE FREEWHEELING RELIGIOUS WORLD OF
THE LATE NINETEENTH CENTURY

H. L. MENCKEN ONCE described the American South as "a cesspool of Baptists, a miasma of Methodism, snake-charmers, phoney real-estate operators, and syphilitic evangelists."[1] Scholars of the Bible Belt have returned to that quote as historical evidence of the region's reigning religiosity. But there is something else within it, too: Mencken—acidly—acknowledged the region's unregulated religious culture.[2]

Far from flat and static, the region's religious history, as Mencken suggested, brimmed with dynamism, diversity, and discord. Nineteenth-century Texans did not inhabit a bastion of orthodox evangelical religion; they lived in a freewheeling religious world run rife with heretics, infidels, and iconoclasts. Texas was no evangelical paradise: evangelicalism was neither universal nor uniform. Nor was it unchallenged. Texans and other southerners instead blazed many spiritual paths. Often winding, overlapping, or dead-ending, most paths were designed haphazardly and trafficked variously, but such a scattered spiritual life represented the logic of a freewheeling American religion.

As disestablishment and spiritual democracy bred innovation and diversity during the nineteenth century, a religious landscape of variety, range, and pluralism triumphed. Religious upstarts rejected theological and institutional conformity. Heterodoxy rivaled orthodoxy, diversity stifled uniformity, and a cacophony of competing voices drowned out harmony. Disagreements, confusion, and competition, for instance, ruptured the Baptist, Methodist, and Christian denominations. Meanwhile, outside the denominations, spiritual rebels innovated their own beliefs. They saw visions, spoke to the dead, and communed with the Holy Spirit. Skeptics rebelled against all religion—freethinkers found fertile ground in Texas. Infidel "churches," speaking halls, magazines, and organizations washed over the state. But others stood by, indifferent to it all.

This chaotic religious world suppressed the creation of the Bible Belt. Later, a brewing clerical vanguard would demand that the state's wild religious traditions be tamed, routinized, and marshaled into a vast enterprise of spiritual and moral warfare. The spiritual paths would be consolidated, and after decades of struggle, religious activists would finally unveil a new religious highway, a clear path running from the earth to the heavens, from a democratic world of spiritual diversity to a narrowly circumscribed world of politicized evangelical religion. Given the depth of the nineteenth century's religious disunity, the rise of the Bible Belt becomes that much more remarkable. To Texans emerging from the Civil War and Reconstruction, nothing seemed less likely.

The Civil War wrecked religion in the South. Economic disruptions and demographic dislocations shattered congregations and set many religious southerners adrift.[3] In Texas, the decade of the 1860s was an unmitigated disaster. Although the state's population swelled, from a little over 600,000 in 1860 to almost 820,000 in 1870, organized religion actually receded. According to census enumerators, only 843 religious organizations (meeting in 647 church buildings) served the state. If on any given Sunday, every Texan had chosen to attend church, three-quarters of them would not have found a seat.[4] Of course, Texas sat on the frontier of Anglo settlement and had never been a bastion of organized religion. As one prominent Texan put it in 1836, "I am afraid the way from Texas to Heaven has never been blazed out."[5] Religious adherence in the state always trailed national averages. As late as 1887, Texas Methodist leader Homer Thrall labeled the state "unoccupied territory," calling it wild and with "children as ignorant of Christianity as though they had been born heathens."[6]

Religious authority requires some basic measure of religious strength and unity. Texas had neither. Available data for 1850, 1860, and 1870 suggest that the state had stunningly low rates of religious adherence.[7] Even in 1890, several years into an aggressive church-building crusade, only 30 percent of Texans formally belonged to any religious body.[8] But numbers tell only half the story. The state's religious infighting tells the rest. Internal conflicts, rejections of orthodox creeds, and resistance to institutional bureaucracies set the denominations against themselves. Factions and dissenters were at odds with each other, efforts to cooperate could not surmount conflict, and religious heterodoxies confounded authority. The cauldron of religion boiled over.

As denominational leaders struggled to police their members, many Texans rejected the denominations altogether. Several unorthodox creeds implanted themselves among that majority of Texans who resisted formal religious affiliation. Hostility and apathy leveled their own attacks, too. Alongside the various orthodox and heterodox faiths stood liberals, agnostics, freethinkers, and atheists, who built sturdy organizations and quickly became a presence in the state's wild religious landscape. Confronted by these obstacles, traditional religious leaders could hardly have been expected to maintain public influence, manage an "informal establishment," or recognize anything resembling the Bible Belt.

If some late nineteenth-century religious Texans pursued public ambitions, internal challenges checked their efforts. Although the paucity of organized religion limited the scope of religious authority, a motley assortment of heretics, infidels, and iconoclasts threw up three key religious barriers to the making of the Bible Belt: theological nonconformity, denominational dissent, and freethinking criticism. Individually, some of these critics challenged orthodoxies from within religious institutions; some challenged them from afar; and some rejected them altogether. Together they prevented the emergence of anything approximating a powerful and politicized nineteenth-century faith.

Widespread spiritual innovation constrained the construction of the Bible Belt. "I am amazed to see how many Christians want only novelty in order to recommend a thing to their confidence," the national divine, Thomas DeWitt Talmage, said in one of his widely disseminated printed sermons. He proclaimed the age "full of new plans, new projects, new theories of government, [and] new theologies."[9] Texas bore out his observation. Although the impact of religious dissenters was perhaps the least enduring of the three obstacles to the clerical triumph, a brief look at a few admittedly exceptional spiritual innovators can nevertheless illustrate the era's expansive spiritual possibilities.

The strange religion of the famed prohibitionist and celebrity "hatcheteer" Carrie Nation best illustrates the many spiritual options open to Texans. Nation lived in the Lone Star State for twelve years, from 1877 to 1889. There, she fostered her own peculiar brand of Christian faith and received her first visions and a "Baptism of the Holy Ghost."[10] Although she later won fame for picking up the hatchet in Kansas, she learned to pick up the Bible in Texas.

In Texas, the thirty-year-old Carrie found herself bedeviled by a loveless marriage and the state's unforgiving cotton economy.[11] She despaired. "I began to see how little there was in life," she would later write.[12] Her work managing a small hotel freed her from the farm, but her emotions continued to weigh on her, and in her gloom she turned to God, to the "one brigh[t] glow amid the darkness."[13] In 1880, the Nations moved from Brazoria County to Richmond, Texas, where her husband David found professional work and Carrie operated a new hotel. Nation involved herself in the city's spiritual life. She taught Sunday school and joined in organized benevolent work. Neglected by her husband, she devoted herself to the church. "Oh if I can do any good in this life let me do some good," she wrote in her diary.[14] As her marriage disintegrated, her faith consumed her. In 1884, a Methodist minister's reading of a chapter from the book of Isiah at a conference meeting confirmed her understanding of God as an immediate spiritual presence. She felt "wrapt in ecstasy," she recalled, and committed herself then and there to Christian service: "From henceforth," she wrote, "all my time, means and efforts should be given to God."[15] She joined aid societies, doled out what personal charity she could, and turned her back on social and physical frivolities. She had been baptized in the spirit, she said, and she had a mission.

Nation's faith was both vivid and immediate. She *felt* God.[16] "I have had visions and dreams that I know were sent to me by my Heavenly Father to warn or comfort or instruct me," she wrote. At times, she dreamed of snakes, fire, and darkness. She dreamed of God as a glowing and comforting light.[17] In 1879, she recorded two visions in her diary: the first, a dead and depressing silent darkness and the second, some weeks later, a bright and rapturous communion with the divine.[18] She claimed to have foretold a major fire in Richmond in 1889, and during a brutal drought in 1886 and 1887, Nation organized a citywide prayer meeting to plead for rain.[19]

As Nation dedicated herself to God, she clashed with formal church doctrines. Raised in the Campbellite tradition—an early-nineteenth-century movement to restore a more "primitive" form of Christianity—she was forced by circumstances to join the Methodist church and then, later, the Episcopal church (the only two options available in her town). Her supernatural beliefs clashed with their staid God, and Nation bristled under their limited theological imagination. "It is torture to attend the cold, dead service of most of the churches," she later wrote.[20] She longed for a more vibrant and personal religion. She explored other faith traditions. She praised certain Orthodox Jewish beliefs and consulted with Catholic priests, but no organized religion could satisfy her demanding spiritual needs.[21]

Nation's neighbors began to see her as a fanatic. According to Nation, a local merchant and a Methodist, a Mr. Blakely, confided in her, "Your friends are becoming very uneasy about the state of your mind. You are thinking too much on religious subjects, and they asked me to warn you."[22] She supposedly replied, "If I have a religion that the world understands, it is not a religion of the Bible." She sought out extremes. "I like to go just as far as the farthest," she wrote. "I like my religion like my oysters and beefsteak—piping hot!"[23] In church, she defied religious authorities and never resisted a chance to challenge the church elders, even in the middle of a service. A Kansas church would later declare her "not sound in the faith"[24] and a "disturber of the peace." Her unorthodox beliefs rankled traditionalists. In Richmond, both the Methodist and Episcopal churches banned her from teaching Sunday school.[25] Church officials removed her from their service when she spoke out and eventually revoked her membership when she claimed to receive her visions.[26]

Local racial and political violence eventually forced David and Carrie out of Texas. In 1890, they liquidated the last of their Texas holdings before moving north, to Kansas, a prohibition state where Carrie found fame for attacking illicit saloons with her hatchet. Although the Nations had left the tumultuous religious world of Texas behind, Carrie (now spelling her name "Carry," as in "Carry A. Nation") forever clung to her unorthodoxies. When her "hatchetation" gained national attention and she began describing herself as "a bulldog running along at the feet of Jesus, barking at what He doesn't like,"[27] Carry was drawing from the heterodox faith she had cultivated in Texas. She was not alone. Many Texans were embracing unorthodox faiths.

In the 1880s and 1890s, the Populists' ground-shaking agrarian insurgency channeled the state's wild religious landscape. The Populists, historian Charles Postel argued, embraced modern beliefs, trafficked in spiritual innovations, and rejected tradition. "It would be difficult," he said, "to define a norm within a spectrum of religious belief that was so diverse, adaptive, and iconoclastic."[28] Within the movement, Postel identified strands of "Free religionists, Christian socialists, agnostics, spiritualists, Theosophists, Swedenborgians, occultists, and mental scientists."[29] Among many prominent Texas Populists, Eben Dohoney best captured the unorthodox strain of Populist faith.

Ebenezer "Eben" LaFayette Dohoney embodied heterodoxies in all walks of life. Born in Kentucky in 1832, he graduated from the nearby Columbia College at the top of his class, earned a law degree from the University of Louisville, briefly practiced law there, and moved to Paris, Texas, in 1859. He opposed secession but fought for the Confederacy and become a district attorney, an opponent of Reconstruction, and a two-term state senator. During the 1870s, Dohoney supported economic reform, women's suffrage, public education, and the Greenback Party. A fixture in the state's public life, he was instrumental in the maturation of the Populist movement in Texas and in the formation of the People's Party in 1891.[30]

Dohoney, like Carry Nation, was a committed prohibitionist. He established the state's local option election system as a delegate to the 1876 state constitutional convention, stood in as the Prohibition Party's candidate for governor in 1886, and supported statewide prohibition during the disastrous 1887 campaign. As with Nation, Dohoney's heterodox beliefs isolated him from potential allies, stunted any unified religious embrace of prohibition, and prevented the formation of anything approximating a "movement."

Although he was raised a Cumberland Presbyterian, Dohoney became an elder in the Paris Christian Church as a young man. Before long, though, his penchant for heterodoxy lured him away from conventional faith.[31] He indulged in Spiritualism and sympathized with Swedenborgianism, brands of belief that rejected orthodox creeds in favor of belief in the presence of an immediate and directly accessible spiritual world. "The paramount issue of the ages is Spiritualism vs. materialism," Dohoney said. He slammed the "host of materialism headed by the gifted [Robert] Ingersoll and the majority of the so-called scientists, backed by part of the medical profession, some religionists and a considerable per cent of the common people." But he rejected the orthodox Christian denominations as well. He praised instead the "well informed Christians, Christian Scientists, Theosophists, and Spiritualists proper, who maintain and demonstrate spirit return." He posited a living spirit world occupying a distinct sphere between the physical world and the next, and believed that "disembodied spirits have had communication with those in the flesh."[32]

Spiritualism was not entirely outside the mainstream.[33] The star of the Women's Christian Temperance Union, Frances Willard, admired many of its tenets. Eben Dohoney, in fact, communicated with Willard and received correspondence from her in 1899—despite her death a year earlier (Willard had sent her correspondence through a California medium).[34] Dohoney was not alone in believing such things. While nineteenth-century revivals attracted large numbers of the rural, unchurched population with spectacle and spirituality, they often peddled something other than evangelical orthodoxy. In Central Texas, for instance, Spiritualists drew large crowds to camp meetings at which working mediums preached the tenets of Spiritualist beliefs.[35]

Dohoney had adopted the brand of spiritualism developed by the Swedish scientist Emanuel Swedenborg. Albert Francisco, who worked as a missionary for the state's Swedenborgian New Church, traveled through Texas and reported that "there is a great revolution going on here."[36] Indeed, a number of Texans embraced Swedenborgianism. One of the state's most respected

Populist leaders, gubernatorial candidate Thomas Nugent, moved in Swedenborg's direction. Nugent had been raised a Methodist, taken an interest in Christian theology, and even studied for the ministry. But several incidents in his life—including receiving a religious admonition against violin playing—caused him to turn away from organized religion and toward the spiritualism of Swedenborgianism. At a meeting outside San Marcos, in 1893, Nugent publicly rebuked organized Protestantism for imposing a "tyranny of opinion." He declared himself a "free religionist," "outside of creed or denomination." Only by rejecting orthodoxy, Nugent insisted, could true faith flourish.[37]

But the freewheeling tradition perhaps manifested itself most clearly, not in the few cases of spiritual innovators, but among those who chose to undermine theological and institutional orthodoxy from within the denominations themselves. Internal struggles wracked the major evangelical denominations and played a large role in the emerging clerical movement. Baptists and Methodists, the evangelical denominations destined to dominate the state's spiritual life, evidenced all the era's disorganizational impulses and struggled to exercise institutional control over a landscape of widespread factional rivalry and deep-seated theological differences.

Church historian Leon McBeth depicted Baptist life in the years after Reconstruction as "a jigsaw puzzle with its pieces scattered."[38] Across the state, Baptists stewed in cauldrons of discontent. Theological diversity, institutional rivalries, and organizational disunity suppressed the power of the denomination. Unregulated by an empowered state general convention, a unified editorial voice, a stable denominational college, or even a common sense of purpose, the Baptists limped through the nineteenth century as a loosely confederated alliance of independent churches riven by rivalry and competing religious visions.

Part of the Baptists' institutional weakness derived from the denomination's historical democratic commitments.[39] Individual churches jealously guarded their independence and, indeed, reveled in their isolation. "There could certainly be no complaint concerning Baptist liberty at this time," the Baptist historian Benjamin Franklin Riley later remembered, "for it was supreme. Scattered over a practically boundless region of country were churches and so-called organizations, hundreds of miles apart, each pursuing its own course, exercising to the fullest its own liberty, and each recognizing itself as equal, if not the superior of every other."[40] Baptists treasured autonomy and localism and refused to concede authority to distant denominational bodies. Any promise of combined effort, Riley lamented, was "lost in empty oratory about soul liberty and freedom of conscience."[41] Tradition tugged too strongly on the state's Baptists. "Nothing short of a marvelous providence,"

Riley wrote, "would extricate so independent a people from a condition so precarious and bind them in to indissoluble oneness. At this time, nothing seemed more remote."[42]

If localism stunted denominational growth, competition thwarted collective effort. In the late nineteenth century, Riley wrote, "men clung sullenly to their views, localities were vehement in their assertion of their respective claims, and none of the disagreement was tempered by gentleness."[43] Church historian Joseph Early declared the period a time of "rivalry, anxiety, and distrust."[44] Texas Baptists clashed over theological orthodoxy, institutional loyalty, and proper denominational boundaries. At points in the nineteenth century, as many as five general conventions, two newspapers, and two universities each vied for the affection of state Baptists.[45] Divisions fractured the denomination at every level. In 1883, Benajah Harvey Carroll, the rising pastor of Waco's First Baptist Church, wrote that "district associations have been divided in council; some rent asunder; churches have been torn by faction; brethren alienated and strife engendered."[46] Dissension defined the denomination. Nineteenth-century Baptists did not cooperate; they competed.

The strife-ridden First Baptist Church of Dallas embodied all the clashing impulses of the late-nineteenth-century religious world. Divided denominational loyalties upended the congregation. One faction, supported by the church's pastor, James Curry, and the editor of the *Texas Baptist and Herald* John Link, favored the Baptist State Convention (BSC). A rival faction, led by Robert Buckner, editor of the *Texas Baptist*, supported the Baptist General Association (BGA). In 1878, the festering rivalry finally split the congregation in two. Church councils and resolutions failed to quell the dispute, which eventually bled into the public when letters and gossip reached the city's newspapers. Buckner slandered the church leaders in his own paper, while in its official minutes, the church dismissed him as a "cantankerous old fool." But the old fool had supporters, and the rift deepened until Buckner hatched a plan for a coup, in December 1879—his faction would claim to legally represent the one true First Baptist Church and thereby win control.[47]

No association or general body had clear authority to settle the matter. Buckner took his case to the Baptist General Association, despite critics who blasted the body for subverting localistic Baptist principles. After a botched trial, Link warned the church's supporters that pro-Buckner BGA leaders would "erect the General Association into a judicature higher than a sovereign, independent church."[48] Baptist preacher I. M. Kimbrough proclaimed that the BGA "had no right to interfere in the matters of a church, which recognized no higher power than itself to its own troubles."[49] He was right: the

BGA exercised no real authority. Pastor Curry tended to the remnants of his fractured congregation; Buckner took his exiles and, in May 1880, founded a cross-town rival, the First Baptist Church at Live Oak Street.[50]

Baptist leaders across the region surveyed the field and lamented the terrible toll denominational strife was taking. "What a power the Baptists might have been, could their forces have been allied at this time!" B. F. Riley wrote.[51] Throughout the following decade, he wrote, "men, churches, communities, and even entire sections, were taken up with denominational disagreements, and the sacred work lagged, in consequence."[52] In Waco, even one of the denomination's leading pugilists, Baylor University president Rufus Burleson, bemoaned the infighting. Although Burleson marveled at Baptist gains in the state, he still wondered what might have been. Late in the nineteenth century, he noted, there were three hundred thousand Texas Baptists. "But for the strife and division especially among preachers," he said, "I firmly believe today there would be 600,000 Baptists in Texas, and a Church in every important neighborhood. When I see how these divisions hinder the cause of Christ and open the wounds of my precious Saviour afresh, I would gladly lie down and die, if it would only bring love and harmony."[53] Unfortunately for Burleson, love and harmony were in short supply.

Despite his pleas for peace, Burleson feuded publicly with his cross-town rival, B. H. Carroll. Burleson denounced infighting but later had to "answer certain charges made against me that I have always 'been mixed up in strife.'" He said that he fought against his Baptist brethren not "for personal honor [but] for the defense of the ordinances, doctrines, and vital interests of my Redeemer's Kingdom." Conceding that, he called for peace. "I wish to say that I am now willing to sacrifice any things on earth, except my convictions of truth and duty to restore peace to our beloved bleeding Zion."[54] He would, in fact, sacrifice much: peace came only when rivals purged him from the denomination.

When the Baptists threw themselves at one another, their denominational rivalries became zero-sum struggles. "Thus were arrayed against each other the ablest men of the denomination, each party with its organ and organization," B. F. Riley wrote. "The battle waxed hot from the outset," he reported, and "from the Panhandle to the Gulf, and from the Sabine to the staked plains, Texas was the battleground of contending Baptists." Riley lamented the lost opportunities of an era in which "passion was supreme to judgment."[55]

As denominational factions fought each other for power, many Baptists rejected the denominational machinery altogether: dissenters rebelled against the denomination-builders and declared independence from bureaucratic oversight. Entrenched in their church fiefdoms, these rebels defied denominational centralization. When a bureaucratic denominational establishment began to form in Waco, Samuel Hayden's *Texas Baptist and Herald* pilloried the organizers and targeted their leaders. Hayden accused James B. Cranfill of embezzlement, B. H. Carroll of autocracy, and Carroll's brother, James Milton Carroll, of profiteering. He attacked these champions of consolidation and centralization, accused the board of the newly formed Baptist General Convention of Texas of foisting an episcopal hierarchy—an "episcopacy"—on Baptists, and derided the BGCT's partisans as "pontiffs."[56] He criticized the skyrocketing salaries being paid to the denomination's new professional caste and, citing examples of egregious mismanagement, accused various leaders of financial improprieties.[57] Anxious Baptist "disorganizers" rallied around Hayden and his paper and maneuvered to check the BGCT's growing power base in Waco.[58]

"A stormy period had now been reached," B. F. Riley later reflected. Just when the Waco leaders seemed to be exerting some modicum of institutional control, new attacks erupted. "So far from growing better," Riley wrote, "the situation was growing worse. The Baptists of Texas were not unused to upheavals and stormy distractions, but nothing ever approximated the turbulence of the present."[59] In the face of resistance, the rising denominational powers moved against their critics. J. B. Cranfill and an associate bought a rival newspaper, renamed it the *Baptist Standard*, and relocated it to Waco, where it parlayed its journalistic power into an assault against Hayden's *Baptist and Herald*.[60]

A tenet of the state's peculiar religious history is that Texas Baptists drew strength from four bedrock institutions: Baylor University, the *Baptist Standard*, Southwestern Baptist Theological Seminary, and the Baptist General Convention of Texas. But well into the late nineteenth century, two of those did not yet exist, and the remaining two, Baylor and the *Baptist Standard*, competed against rivals and struggled for financial solvency. For most of the nineteenth century, Texas Baptists had no official general body, no official university, and no official paper. For years, critics and rivalries blocked unification. As one concerned Texan wrote in reference to the various denominational newspapers, "to have a Baptist newspaper monopoly would place the denomination constantly at the mercy of one man, who would be pope, boss and supreme dictator at will."[61] One in ten white Baptist churches weren't even Southern Baptist. Those that were remained divided in their loyalties and split on their commitments to denominationalism.[62] Such divisions crippled the denomination. Universities struggled with enrollment. Newspapers wrestled with financial stability. Baptists fought against one another.

As part of the nascent clerical crusade, activist champions eventually emerged to tame the Baptists' disorderly world. The assimilation of rivals under a single banner marked an epochal transformation, not only in the denominational history of Texas Baptists, but also in the larger effort to achieve the

Bible Belt. Under the guidance of B. H. Carroll, J. B. Cranfill, and others, professional religious leaders built a vast and powerful religious bureaucracy that could be leveraged against secular opponents. Behind the power of several important pulpits, these leaders transformed Baylor University, the *Baptist Standard*, and the Baptist General Convention of Texas into a powerful religious establishment. These denomination builders would drive the clerical culture and stand with the vanguard of the clerical movement. "Consolidated into formidableness, with wisdom ripened by painful experience," Riley reported "there was born a sturdy and resistless resolve to rescue the denomination from the disrepute into which it had been dragged against its will."[63] These organizational efforts were an important chapter in the story of the construction of the Bible Belt, but, meanwhile, recurring struggles to purge the denomination testified to the lingering power of the state's freewheeling faith.

As they fought bureaucratic battles within their denominations, clerics also battled against theological dissenters. The Baptist commitment to congregational autonomy had fostered many unorthodox faiths. Pastors Henry Renfro, Matthew Thomas Martin, and George Fortune best captured the raucous religious world lurking beneath the denomination's organizational struggles.

Henry Renfro attended Baylor University (then located in Independence, Texas) in the 1850s, pastored the Independence Baptist Church, led revivals in Cass County, and tended Baptist pulpits in Johnson and Tarrant Counties in the 1870s and 1880s. Although he also farmed, raised livestock, and traded land, he threw himself into his religious work. He read, researched, and participated in Baptist associational life. In the decades after the Civil War, he became a respected and learned voice among the state's Baptists and among its citizens. When Johnson County dedicated its courthouse, it was Renfro who spoke at the ceremony.[64] And yet, slowly, he began to drift away from orthodoxy. He corresponded with the Waco freethinker James Dickson Shaw. He read controversial texts, from Spinoza to Paine to Ingersoll, and soon they began creeping into his sermons. By 1882, rumors had spread among state Baptists that Renfro had drifted into infidelity. Many of his congregants suspected that he was a freethinker.

In the fall of 1883, the conference meeting of the Alvarado Baptist Church brought charges against Renfro. Renfro admitted to "doing a little independent thinking," but he denounced the "religious fanatics" arrayed against him and professed his loyalty to religious faith. A committee met with Renfro and rescinded its charges. But Renfro thereafter began to openly denounce religious creeds in favor of a new works-based faith. Baptists recoiled. Another church conference met and leveled "the charge of Infidelity in not believing in the inspiration of the Scriptures." Renfro admitted to doubting orthodox belief. When presented with a specific passage of scripture, he denied its veracity. On February 2, 1884, Baptist leaders condemned him for "advocating and preaching the doctrine of infidelity" and revoked his certification as a Baptist preacher. According to the church, he was no longer a Baptist. His requests to address the Baptist assembly one last time were denied.[65]

Renfro despaired. The Baptist Church, he said, "is a noble church, and I love her still."[66] But as he explained that summer in Waco's *Independent Pulpit*, his conscience compelled him to dissent. "I have learned this fact," he said, "that to read is to think, to think is to investigate, to investigate is to doubt, and to doubt is to be damned by orthodox churches."[67]

Exile hurt, but it was also liberating. "I am free," Renfro said, "and can express my sentiments untrammeled. I must confess that this consideration is somewhat refreshing, as I had felt so long that my utterances had rendered me obnoxious to the church." He used his newfound freedom to spread his new gospel of freethought. "The time will come," he said, "when men will be controlled less and less by blind faith, and follow more and more the lamp of reason." He continued to express his preference for a "religion of deed rather than the religion of creed." He lectured to large crowds in Alvarado, Texas. His first meeting, the *Alvarado Bulletin* reported, drew "perhaps the largest audience ever assembled at the opera house." Citizens wrote to the *Bulletin* in praise of Renfro. Shaw congratulated him in the pages of his *Independent Pulpit*. "Who will be the next to come from under the galling yoke?" he wondered.[68] In the religious world of the nineteenth century, it could have been anyone.

In the 1880s and 1890s, several Baptist preachers challenged theological orthodoxy by adopting a set of beliefs known as "Martinism," named after Matthew Thomas Martin, a Baptist pastor from Waco. Martin preached a doctrine of "absolute assurance," an exaggeration of Baptist beliefs about conversion and the evidence of God's salvation. Martin believed that having any shred of personal doubt undercut an individual's alleged conversion experience: the converted, assured of their faith, would never doubt their own salvation. To doubt, therefore, indicted the converted. Martin's charisma seduced many followers, including prominent preachers and laymen.[69] "His personality was great," J. M. Carroll recalled. "Martin himself was an able man, and no ordinary man could have swept so many good men and women off their feet."[70] The state's freewheeling religious world encouraged such theological diversions. B. F. Riley slammed Martin's "freakish diversion from scriptural principles" but admitted that in nineteenth-century Texas, "doctrines as absurd, even, as those of Mr. Martin were destined to gain headway."[71]

B. H. Carroll called a church council in 1889 and indicted Martin for heresy. After four conference meetings, officials revoked Martin's license. In response, the Marlin Baptist Church, thirty miles away, relicensed Martin, and he resumed preaching, "unsettling the faith of not a few," as Riley put it.[72] Carroll charged Marlin Baptist with heresy and orchestrated its expulsion from the Waco Baptist Association. The BGCT condemned Martin and resolved that none of his adherents would be seated at its regular meetings. The Marlin Baptist Church ignored these declarations, and Martin withdrew to Mississippi of his own accord some years later.[73] Martinism manifested itself intermittently in the years afterward. Among Martin's followers, Rev. E. R. Carswell cut the tallest figure. "As a preacher," denominational historian J. M. Carroll recalled, "he was a remarkably strong man. He was attractive in appearance and rather unusually eloquent."[74] He carried forth the banner of heterodoxy into the 1890s and joined others who were busy challenging denominational dogma.[75]

Baptist pastor George Fortune also spurned Baptist orthodoxies. From 1891 to 1897, Fortune preached a very loose theology from his pulpit at the First Baptist Church of Paris, Texas. He dismissed the doctrine of atonement (the idea that sinners are reconciled to God only through Christ's sacrifice); discounted the ideas of Satan, hell, and original sin; and denied the divine inspiration of scripture.[76] He converted many in his congregation to his views. They adored him and voluntarily broke all ties with the denomination, declaring their support for "Fortunism." But an alienated core of church members challenged Fortune's checkered past and suspect theology. Meanwhile, the Lamar Baptist Association, of which First Baptist had been a member, wanted their church back. With the support of the church's discontented minority, the association tried Fortune, and a committee, led by the denomination's organizational policemen Rufus Burleson and B. H. Carroll, found Fortune guilty of "a candid, outright, downright, audacious attack on the central, vital doctrines of not only the Baptist faith, but the faith of evangelical Christendom."[77] In 1895, the BGCT condemned Fortune for rejecting the Baptist Articles of Faith and resolved that none of his adherents—or Martin's—would be seated at regular meetings. The convention declared a blanket injunction against the followers of Fortune, Martin, and any other heterodox Baptists. Fortune's church ignored these rulings, and he continued to preach in Paris until he withdrew to Oklahoma, of his own accord, in 1897.[78]

These brief but illustrative examples of Baptist diversity testify to both the wide range of possible Baptist beliefs and to the newfound willingness of emergent clerical energy to rein in such diversity. The Baptists were not alone in struggling to stifle theological strife and institutional resistance. The

Methodists, too, wrangled with heretics and dissenters. Heterodox preachers, including John Kennedy Street, Leonidas Lantz, and J. D. Shaw, chafed under Methodism's theological strictures, and others, most notably the apostles of the Holiness movement—a collection of dissenters who, among other tenets, typically emphasized a post-conversion "sanctification"—fractured the denomination, further testimony to Texas's disorganized religious landscape.

Methodist minister J. K. Street embodied the era's rejection of orthodoxy. In the 1870s and 1880s, Street began to preach a universalist brand of Methodism in Waco. As his thoughts evolved, he moved ever further away from orthodox Methodist doctrine. "He was mercenary," contemporary Methodist minister Rev. James Mackey said.[79] Street later spoke openly before J. D. Shaw's freethinking Religious and Benevolent Association Gradually, Street's preaching moved fully toward the tenets of universalism. He began to savage Methodist orthodoxy. "He has long been considered beyond its pale," the *Dallas Weekly Herald* declared, and at their regional quarterly conference in the summer of 1883, the Methodists expelled Street from the ministry and from the membership rolls of his Methodist church.[80] Although he himself was silenced, Street would see others challenge Methodist doctrine.

At their quarterly meeting a few years later, in 1889, the Waco Methodists expelled Leonidas Lantz from the ministry. Lantz had embraced some of Emmanual Swedenborg's teachings on spiritualism, the trinity, and atonement. He urged a rereading of scripture: "The day will come," he declared, "when Christians, divested of all prejudice, and studying the truth for truth's sake, will drink at the fountain of the word's rich, spiritual meaning and have their souls refreshed and see in its sacred teaching beauty and harmony and grandeur and glory which the letter cannot reveal." The *Dallas Morning News* called Lantz a prominent and influential figure in Central Texas, but his heresies defied Methodist doctrine. He was purged from the ministry and from church membership.[81] So, too, were others.

J. D. Shaw bridged two of the clerics' great obstacles, denominational rebellion and freethought. Shaw became a Methodist minister in 1870, taught at Marvin College in Waxahachie, worked on the *Texas Christian Advocate*, and tended several pastorates before taking over the Fifth Street Methodist Church in Waco in 1878. But as a Methodist minister, educator, and editor, Shaw drifted from orthodoxy. "A long and critical study of the claims of Christianity has forced me to reconstruct my religious beliefs to some extent, and how far this may go I am not now able to say."[82] Soon, he rejected all orthodoxy. He questioned the scriptures, atonement, and the divinity of Christ. A September 1882 sermon scandalized congregants with its rejection of basic evangelical doctrines. Visitors to his Waco church began describing him as an agnostic. In November 1882, the Methodists' Northwest Texas Conference met in Cleburne and moved to try him for heresy. Shaw offered a forty-five-minute defense of his beliefs, but the conference officials declared his wayward thoughts to be "detrimental to religion and injurious to the church." Thus repudiated by the church, Shaw helped plant the seeds of freethought in Central Texas. He formed the Religious and Benevolent Association that December; established a monthly paper, the *Independent Pulpit*; and began to war against organized religion.

Despite these expulsions, Methodists continued to struggle with dissidents. Whereas the democratic organization of the Baptists produced a pattern of power-hungry rivalries, the relatively ordered nature of the Methodist hierarchy inspired mass departures instead. As a pure reflection of the nineteenth century's freewheeling religious world, the Methodists saw fractures within fractures: Holiness advocates had to defend themselves against church officials while simultaneously condemning their own separatists. With its plots and counterplots, the Holiness movement reflected the Methodists' spiritual wrangling.

Holiness preachers shocked Texas Methodism in the years after Reconstruction. While proclaiming a kind of primitive, renewed Methodism and drawing especially on founder John Wesley's doctrine of perfection, they preached "entire sanctification," the notion that the redeemed could be baptized in the Holy Spirit and purged of carnal sinfulness dwell fully in God's love. They preached against all "carnality," tobacco, ornamentation, and all the popular sins of the world. Such doctrines first reached Texas in the 1870s. Revivalists brought the promise of perfection to several sustained camp meetings in such places as Corsicana and Ennis. Although many Holiness advocates spread their doctrines within the confines of the denomination, others were lured away by more startling spiritual innovations.[83]

The "Corsicana Enthusiasts" in Central Texas, introduced faith healing and speaking in tongues to the state. Some of the enthusiasts said they had received visions. The staunchest believers took the notion of "perfection" to its end and claimed that sanctified Christians could not be tempted and could not sin. The revivalists began to advocate separation, warning their audiences that hell awaited those stuck in the "Babylon" of the organized churches: they said it was the duty of sanctified Christians to exile themselves from the corruption of the churches.[84] The Holiness message soared and its preachers tended growing crowds. The Free Methodist and self-avowed moderate Holiness minister, George McCulloch, claimed that thousands attended meetings in Ennis and the surrounding area and that many churchgoers were fleeing the denomination for these newer, purer institutions.[85] The Northwest Texas Holiness Association was founded in 1883 to shelter these renegade

groups.[86] Robert Haynes, an erstwhile Presbyterian minister now preaching
Holiness doctrines in Corsicana and Ennis, was one of the preachers shocking
Methodists with Holiness heresies. He laid hands upon the sick; claimed to
be the harbinger of a new biblical dispensation; and, citing scripture and his
self-proclaimed total spiritualization, declared that he had abolished death
itself. Another Holiness preacher, William Groves, also claimed to be God's
personal medium. In revivals at the newly organized Tabernacle Church,
he would "get under the power," jerk violently, and, he said, commune with
God.[87] He proclaimed a new revelation, a vision of the coming end times
that, according to rival George McCulloch, "sounded [more] like the wild
ravings of a heated imagination than the sensible statement of a minister of
Jesus Christ."[88] Despite critics, though, the sudden outbreak of the Holiness
movement shook the state and rattled regular Methodists.

Confronted with wayward doctrines, anxious Methodist and moderate
Holiness leaders reacted. McCulloch charged that faith healers and tongue-
speakers had fallen victim to fanaticism and condemned their "wild, unscrip-
tural doctrines."[89] The Methodist Northwest Texas Conference ordered its
ministers to wage war against the insurgent movement, and the denominational paper slammed Holiness as specious and heretical, as a "fungus formation" on Texas Methodism.[90] In 1885, a Methodist in East Waco compared the
Holiness followers to Shaw and his freethinking cohort. Things turned violent,
too. Masked men abducted Haynes on a frigid October night in 1879, threw
him into a waiting carriage, and took him to a nearby water tank to be dunked
violently until he agreed to exile himself.[91] When William B. Godbey preached
Holiness doctrines in the 1880s, critics "pelted [him] with rocks, dirt, and eggs."[92]
Holiness split the church. Believers broke away to form their own independent
congregations, but even within the Methodist family, theological and institutional division stunted unity. In 1890, alongside 1,076 bodies of the Methodist
Episcopal Church, South, and the 409 bodies of the black Methodists denominations, there were in Texas 402 Methodist bodies with various loyalties to
the Methodist Episcopal Church (the denomination's northern branch), the
congregation-centered Methodist Protestants, and Holiness sects that included
the Free Methodists and Congregational Methodists.[93]

Spiritual anarchy engulfed the state. The name of the denomination
hardly mattered: disorganizers and dissenters rejected mainstream churches.
By 1872, for instance, the Christian Church (the Disciples of Christ) had fractured in several cities owing to disagreements over mission work, denominational organization, biblical interpretation, and proper church practice. By
1886, the state denomination broke in two when the conservative churches,

branding themselves as the Churches of Christ, indicted organ playing and renounced all extra-congregational organizations as unbiblical.[94] The Texas split preceded the denomination's national division by two decades.

As the state's fragile denominations struggled to enforce theological orthodoxy and institutional loyalty, a vast world of freethought existed beyond the boundaries of the denominations. The feuding faithful shared a broader world with liberals, agnostics, freethinkers, and atheists. As organized religion reeled in the wake of war, Reconstruction, and disorganization, freethinkers continually contested Texans' spiritual loyalties and made substantial claims on public affections. Although the freethinkers are seldom integrated into religious histories, they too are part the history of southern religion. If denominational leaders demonstrated a newfound willingness to enforce theological conformity in their own organizations in the late nineteenth century, the very real public presence of skeptics and heretics exposed their still limited public authority. During the final decades of the nineteenth century, freethinking leaders and organizations attracted resources, notoriety, and numbers.

For some Texans, freethought came naturally. Even B. H. Carroll, later the state's leading Baptist preacher, described how easily doubt had filled his youth. Although his parents were Christians, and his teachers were Christians, he had wrestled with infidelity early in his life. "Before I knew what infidelity was, I was an infidel," he recalled. He questioned church doctrines, rejected Christ's divinity, and denied the Bible: "I doubted that it was God's book, an inspired revelation or His will to man." He pored through the writings of the great infidels: Hume, Paine, Rousseau, Voltaire, and others. At age seventeen he joined the Confederate Army. In the army camps he was not swept away by revivals or chaplains or a southern civil religion; instead, he gave himself to irreligion and cut his remaining ties to the church. The end of the war found Carroll edging back toward evangelical Christianity; but the ease with which he had given himself over to infidelity reveals the very real cultural power and appeal of nineteenth-century freethought.[95]

Lone Star irreligion had many sources. In contrast to much of the rest of the South, Texas imported many freethinkers directly from Europe. During the mid-nineteenth century, and especially in the wake of Germany's failed Revolution of 1848, many German intellectuals, liberals, and freethinkers settled in Central Texas and the Hill Country. Freethinkers populated cities, such as Sisterdale, Comfort, and Bettina; formed associations; held regular meetings; and blocked the inroads of religion.[96] Freethinkers kept churches out of Comfort, Texas, for instance, until 1892.[97] Although in lesser numbers and with diminished commitments, Czech immigrants also brought vestiges of European freethought with them to Texas. But these imported strands coexisted with native ones. Freethinking immigrant citadels persevered even as a powerful and parallel freethinking movement captured native-born Texans too. In the last decades of the nineteenth century, freethinkers tugged at Lone Star loyalties and increasingly commanded public attention.

Repudiated by the Methodist Church in 1882, J. D. Shaw quickly established a freethinking stronghold in Waco by forming the Religious and Benevolent Association the same year. Established as an unorthodox domain "for the worship of God, benevolent and religious works," the organization offered a forum for heterodox beliefs. Weekly lectures and discussions scolded organized religion and fostered freethinking. Its monthly magazine, the *Independent Pulpit*, offered a constructive voice for religious skepticism. It promised to "satisfy the growing demand of our most liberal and independent thinkers on the moral, intellectual, and social questions of the day" and found subscribers all over the world.[98] Leading citizens populated Shaw's freethinking organizations and subscribed to his journal. Doctors, lawyers, judges, and businessmen joined him in probing the boundaries of freethought. Shaw was not an outcast, an eccentric, or a lonely crank. A captain in the Pat Cleburne Camp of Confederate Veterans, he served on Waco's board of aldermen and was instrumental in transitioning municipal government toward a city commission.[99] In the freewheeling religious world of the nineteenth century, freethought could compete with organized religion for respectability.

The absence of skepticism has never stopped religious leaders from denouncing it anyway, but religious Texans were for a time confronted with the real thing. *Gatesville Advance* editor and budding Baptist leader J. B. Cranfill called Shaw's organization the "Hell and Damnation Society." Cranfill editorialized against the infidels by, as he put it, "castigating, blistering, caricaturing and satirizing Mr. Shaw and his contingents to the very best of my ability."[100] B. H. Carroll savaged Shaw, the Association, and its members in a particularly blistering sermon entitled, "The Agnostic."[101] Despite these complaints, the organization grew. In 1884, it built and began meeting in Liberal Hall, its own meeting space. The organization peaked in the late 1880s and was later reconstituted as the Liberal Society of Texas, continuing to draw healthy crowds to hear lectures on reason, truth, and other subjects.[102] And Shaw and his Waco constituents were not the only Texans championing freethought.

Farther north, the Dallas Freethinkers' Association met regularly throughout the 1880s and 1890s. Members gathered at Liberty Hall on South Ervay Street every Sunday night to discuss religion, science, and politics. Attendance ranged from as few as forty to as many as several hundred individuals, rivaling many of the city's largest Christian congregations. Members included physicians, publishers, and attorneys, and together they hacked away at Christian belief. Through lectures, debates, and discussions, they created their own world, untouched by religious authority.[103]

Although the freethinkers were certainly never a dominant faction in Dallas, their ideas still rippled across the public conscience. From the moment that "Give-a-Damn Jones" first sensationalized the young city with antireligious harangues in the early 1880s, Dallas freethinkers defied religious sensibilities. In one of Texas's fastest growing cities, prominent citizens gathered openly and prominently to denigrate God. Zion, this was not. The freethinkers distributed circulars defaming Christian faith. The *Dallas Morning News* covered each of their meetings. Readers could take in a skeptic's attack on the "uncorroborated ghost stories of a very contradictory and unreliable book" or the charge that "Hell and heaven are the inventions of human leaches called priests and preachers, who live upon the blood they suck from terrified ignorance."[104] When famed revivalists Dwight Moody and Ira Sankey visited the city in 1886, the freethinkers dedicated an entire meeting to revivalism. A physician diagnosed revivalists' "pathological symptoms"; a phrenologist linked religious fervor with the "torpid mind"; and an academic dismissed revivalism as the antiquated survival of a premodern superstition, designed only to satisfy an individual's primitive psychological needs.[105]

The Dallas freethinkers worshiped reason and venerated the skeptic's pantheon: they discussed Voltaire, Jefferson, Darwin, Spencer, Huxley, Carlyle, and others. A portrait of the Great Agnostic, Robert Ingersoll, adorned Liberty Hall.[106] Each year they celebrated Thomas Paine's birthday.[107] As in Waco, the meetings of the Freethinkers' Association focused on specific topics, including debunking miracles, championing evolution, and debating the constitution. During one typical meeting, Dr. David Mackay lectured on recent advances in neurology. The brain, he said, presented evidence against the immortal soul. "The bedrock, the zenith and nadir of all philosophy was to be found on the dissecting table," he said. "There alone can man know himself."[108] And yet, privileging free inquiry, they invited guest speakers from various faith traditions. "Jew, Mohammedan, Christian and infidel were equally welcome to have their say," the Association's president declared. They hosted debates with Protestant ministers and heard from spiritualists, theosophists, Adventists, and Mormons. In 1897, they invited Sahib Abdul Monon to lecture on "The Superiority of the Religion of the Prophet over That of Christ."[109] Populists, socialists, and women's activists spoke, too. The association debated Henry George's Single Tax plan, the Populist platform, and other proposed answers to the era's social crises.[110] Throughout it all, the freethinkers embraced spectacle and pageantry. They formed "a free-thought choir" and a secular Sunday School "to teach virtues and science."[111] The Dallas freethinkers created a rich and textured world. More importantly, they became a regular presence in the life of the city.

To critics and supporters both, the Dallas freethinkers were a living, breathing force. They occupied no less secure a station than many prominent evangelical leaders. In 1894, the prolific freethinking American publisher and lecturer Samuel Porter Putnam marveled at the men and women of influence then enrolled in Texas freethinking organizations and said "they are names which represent a great deal of influence in the community, and will do much, no doubt, to shape the destinies of this vast and splendid state towards the principles of republican liberty."[112] To nineteenth-century Texans embroiled in the era's dynamic religious world, there was little reason to doubt guest speaker John Leming when he prophesied, in 1897, that "the inevitable over-throw of orthodox creeds and teaching is at hand."[113] A leading Galveston real-estate agent, merchant, and businessman, George T. Bondies, prophesied "the time to be near at hand when the people of this country will not dare to trust the management of state to any but well proven Atheists, or persons who plan and execute exclusively for the life on this earth on the same prin-ciple as one goes to a shoemaker for shoes, to a lawyer for law, and to a priest or preacher for religion."[114] Nineteenth-century Texas lacked any discernible religious establishment, and in the age's cultural tumult, freethinkers chal-lenged the state's evangelical churches for cultural supremacy.

Among the state's critics of organized religion, no figure matched jour-nalist William Cowper Brann for caustic wit, influence, and an inexhaust-ible capacity for controversy. The son of a Presbyterian minister, Brann made a name for himself during the 1880s and 1890s by writing intelli-gent, opinionated, and venomous editorials for various newspapers. He worked for the St. Louis *Globe Democrat*, served as the editor of the *San Antonio Express*, and helmed the editorial desks of the *Houston Post* and *Waco Daily News*. In February 1895, he launched his own monthly paper, the *Iconoclast*.[115] Brann called it a "periodical of protest" and opened up against a host of targets. But he saved the worst for organized religion. Waco's Baptists and their Baylor University became his favorite targets. He decried Baylor as "that great storm-center of misinformation."[116] By 1897, the *Iconoclast*'s circulation spanned the globe and peaked at 100,000—five times more than that of the *Baptist Standard*.[117] In fact, in 1890, the state's regular Southern Baptists only claimed 130,000 members.[118] Brann added

FIGURE 1.1 William Cowper Brann in his *Iconoclast* office in Waco, Texas. Undated. Courtesy of the Texas Collection. Baylor University. Waco, Texas.

to the diversity of the nineteenth-century religious world by helping to pioneer the brand of acerbic journalism later perfected by H. L. Mencken in the 1920s. His unrelenting attacks against the Baptist establishment became legendary and unleashed a torrent of acrimony directed at him—acrimony that resulted in his death in 1898.[119]

"We know that frauds and fakes exist, that hypocrites and humbugs abound," Brann wrote in the *Iconoclast*. "Whether this be due to the pernicious activity of a horned monster or to evil inherent in the human heart, I will not assume to say." Brann was no detached critic. He was not a free agent or a nihilist in the nineteenth century's religious world. Brann championed a cohesive worldview, one that drove the bulk of the state's freethinking movement and that, in many respects, would challenge and check the emerging clerical movement under the guise of a secular anticlericalism. Brann never believed in a real-life devil, but, he said, "we may call that power the devil which is forever at war with truth, is the father of falsehood, whether it be an active personality or only a vicious principle." Brann declared war on that devil.[120]

Brann paired his cutting wit with rhetorical flourishes and launched it against the "hypocrites and humbugs," imagining himself soldiering for truth and reason. He championed abstract principles such as "honor, patriotism, [and] reverence."[121] Beneath his irony and his vitriol lurked a keen moral and intellectual conscience. "The world has need of iconoclasts as of builders," Brann wrote, and "can in nowise proceed without them." He enlisted his talents to topple the accumulated myths and superstitions of what he called an "unadulterated imbecility." "The unsafe building," he said, "must come down to make place for a better, the old falsehood must be eradicated ere the new truth can take root."[122]

Brann saw the Texas Baptists as a major pillar of that "unsafe building." He saw organized religion as a "rainbow-chaser . . . a fellow who mistakes shadows for substance and wanders off the plank turnpike into bogs and briar patches." He despaired that Christians failed to meet his standards. Brann sought to purify a world that "no longer produces heaven-inspired men but only some pitiful simulacra thereof." He disdained the "shallow self-seekers," who, he said, "aspire to ride the topmost wave, not of a tempestuous ocean which tries to the heart of oak and the hand of iron, but of some pitiful sectarian mud-puddle or political goose pond." The forces of organized religion, Brann said, blindly chased petty worldly concerns. They were, he said, "following the foolish rainbow of a fatuous utilitaria and getting even deeper into the bogs."[123] Brann's criticisms reverberated across the religious world. For truth seekers traveling along innovative and heretical paths, Brann offered an appealing countervision to religious orthodoxy.

But Brann was not the only idol of Texas freethinkers. Texans also knew and admired the nation's Great Agnostic. A friend to as diverse a cast of nineteenth-century Americans as Frederick Douglass, Walt Whitman, and Eugene Debs, Robert Ingersoll was a force in Republican Party politics and a popular national orator.[124] Ingersoll's ten-city Texas tour in 1896 drew frenzied followers from farms and towns, some coming from as far as a hundred miles away.[125] Ingersoll's manager mused that he needed a four-acre tent to accommodate the swelling crowds. Texan Anna M. Brooks traveled thirty miles on horseback to hear Ingersoll speak in Sherman and relayed her awe at the experience in an effusive letter she wrote to the *Truth Seeker*, the nation's leading journal of freethought.[126] A small community in northeast Texas even named their town Ingersoll.[127] The Dallas Freethinkers' Association praised the Great Agnostic's work, declaring that "every page shines and scintillates with wisdom and truth and beauty that glorify and exalt the reader, so each look at that picture will renew and strengthen our devotion of human thought, the immortal cause he so nobly champions."[128]

The culture of Texas freethought had many figures and many forums from which to draw. Shaw and his *Independent Pulpit*, the Dallas Freethinkers, Brann and his *Iconoclast*, even Robert Ingersoll: freethought was only one of many viable alternatives to religious orthodoxy in the Lone Star State.

Riven by divisions and rejections and ungoverned by orthodoxy or organization, religion in Texas registered minimal public authority and held even less hope for political influence. The churches were too poorly populated and outfitted to house a broader, more impactful movement, particularly while heretics, infidels, and iconoclasts besieged denominational upstarts. And yet, even as they slowly tamed their religious world, those few figures able to leverage religious power in pursuit of political authority would find themselves savaged by an anticlerical public wary of religious politics. Obstacles to the Bible Belt lay not only in the fractured disunity of the religious world but also in the fierce resistance of a reigning anticlerical culture.

2

Subduing the Saintly

THE ANTICLERICAL TRADITION

IN 1885, B. H. Carroll complained that whenever he said the word "prohibition," his opponents heard "Puritanism, Bigotry, Union of Church and State, [and] Fanaticism."[1] The first waves of prohibition elections were crashing upon the South and critics were targeting prohibitionist clergymen.[2] It was around this time that Senator Richard Coke told several thousand cheering Texans to "scourge" political preachers back to their pulpits.[3] Two decades after the birth and death of the Confederacy, it was possible for a sitting southern senator, in the heart of the state's Baptist establishment, in the shadow of what would become the nation's largest denominational college, to address the state's most prominent religious leaders and not only publicly flay clergymen but profit from doing so.[4] And he was not alone. Anticlericalism—opposition to the interference or influence of religion, churches, or clergy in public affairs—saturated Texas and much of the American South.

A generation later, in 1908, Henry Watterson, the Pulitzer Prize–winning editor of Kentucky's *Louisville Courier-Journal*, savaged a surging political Christianity: "Holding the ministry in reverence as spiritual advisers, rejecting them as emissaries of temporal power, I do not intend, if I can help it, to be compelled to accept a rule of modern clericalism, which, if it could have its bent and sway, would revive for us the priest ridden systems of the Middle Ages."[5] Similar words had echoed for years throughout the region as a clerical offensive forced partisans as well as opponents to grapple with religion, politics, and history. Anticlerics like Watterson expressed what had been the reigning worldview of the late nineteenth-century South. For most white southerners of those years, the language of the Bible Belt was as yet largely incomprehensible; they spoke instead the language of anticlericalism. They believed that American freedom was exceptional but fragile, too fragile to tolerate political preachers, and that liberty therefore needed to be zealously guarded against the still-scheming relics of a brutish and unenlightened Old World, against a past dominated by kings and priests.

Anticlericalism delegitimized a whole range of clerical activity. Public condemnation effectively blocked clerical transgressions into the public sphere, and, in the nineteenth century, much of that condemnation arose from within the denominations themselves. Anticlericalism was not synonymous with irreligion nor incompatible with religiosity. Although in part a practical concession to the restraints imposed on them by the freewheeling religious world, southern evangelicals embraced anticlericalism in their own churches. Prominent scholars have noted anticlericalism's foundational role in the rise and success of American evangelicalism, arguing that anticlerical attitudes fostered a flexible democratic faith unburdened by bureaucratic hierarchy or concentrated power.[6] And American evangelicals, at least in the white South, often preached an individualistic and otherworldly religion averse to contentious public issues, for the next world trumped the here and now.[7] Anticlericalism can be seen as the embodiment or enforcement of that otherworldly commitment, but anticlericalism was as much cultural as theological and, prior to the acceleration of the clerical crusade, anticlerical dogmas were typically taken for granted.

White Protestant Texans had largely committed themselves to saving souls, not the world. One of the state's earliest Methodist leaders, Homer Thrall, worked to stimulate, he said, the "the great work of diffusing through our entire population the savor of the knowledge of Christ." As a scholar, he wrote of providence and individual conversions, not politics and societies.[8] The problem of his generation was not in the public sphere or in schools or government, Thrall said, but in souls. When he found deserts in an otherwise lush religious landscape, when he tried to account for the scarcity of organized religion in the late nineteenth century, he didn't blame political radicals, liberal theologians, or immigrant saloons. He looked inward. "Oh," he lamented, "if every minister and layman had attained the full measure of personal piety, and exhibited the active zeal, of genuine missionaries, how many more precious souls might have been brought to Christ!"[9] Although the twentieth-century Baptist leader George Truett held an odd mixture of clerical and anticlerical beliefs, he nevertheless illuminated many strands of the apolitical faith that had reigned over much of the region. "The land-mark that most of all needs resetting in our American churches," he said in 1911, "is the predominant passion to save lost souls, and any church out of which has gone that passion is going on the rocks, and any church out of which has gone that passion is but a grinning, ghastly skeleton of a church; and any preacher out of whose preaching has gone that passion is no longer an evangelical preacher, preach whatever he may and however eloquently he will."[10]

A religious brand of anticlericalism forced early temperance reformers to renounce political ambitions. When the United Friends of Temperance traveled throughout the South after the war, they emphasized the personal, voluntary aspect of their creed, condemned political meddling, and renounced any potential prohibition legislation.[11] Well into the 1880s, even after the dawning of a robust clerical movement, many preachers still refused to support moral reform. Content to operate within traditional evangelical limits—emphasizing individual religious conversion and moral suasion rather than political campaigning or legal coercion—they saw prohibition and other issues as dangerous diversions and a serious impediment to their spiritual mission.

Amid the prohibition campaigns of the 1880s, the Lone Star evangelist Collin McKinley Wilmeth decried political religion. He warned that prohibition agitation "endangers spiritual life" and preached against the prohibition campaigns of 1885 and 1887 "with the hope that it may assist to check the tide which is now carrying so many preachers into politics and virtually out of the pulpit."[12] Likewise, John C. S. Baird, a veteran Methodist preacher, sensed a radical break with traditional southern Methodist practice. "For thirty-one years," he wrote, "unmixed devotion of heart and life have I lavished upon the M. E. Church South, and the consuming flame has been constantly fanned by the thought that non-interference in State politics is one of the primary laws of her being." For Baird, the lure of politics and other worldly cares loomed ominously. Citing scripture, he warned that "as members and ministers of the church of the Son of God, we are to remember that 'the weapons of our warfare are not carnal but mighty through God.' "[13]

J. B. Cranfill, editor of the *Baptist Standard*, fanned many anticlerical suspicions when he ran as the vice-presidential candidate of the national Prohibition Party in 1892. Many of his fellow ministers condemned him. "We are opposed to the preachers condescending to be politicians," wrote the editor of the *Mississippi Baptist Record*, "and have never seen one who ever did any good as a preacher, in any shape or form, who took such a step." The editor needled Cranfill and the *Standard's* readers: "The Texas brethren have our sympathy if it is true that one of their papers is to be run by such a man."[14] Cranfill fervently assured his subscribers that his political involvement in no way compromised his faith or his ability to edit a religious newspaper. Fears flowered. Some, Cranfill wrote, "have feared that we would run this paper as a partisan religio-political journal. On this point we desire to say, once for all, that the STANDARD is not a political paper. It does not expect to be. It is a Baptist paper and a religious paper. This is its aim and destiny, and our friends need have no fears that it will ever descend to the profession of politics."[15] Nonetheless, many did fear.

Anticlerical sentiment crippled early reform efforts. When some ministers became increasingly eager to flaunt cultural barriers and a clerical consensus began developing around at least a limited form of political engagement, critics ripped the movement. When B. H. Carroll's and other clerical leaders sallied forth to fight the prohibition battles of the 1880s, they did so without the strength or unity of the state's evangelicals. Internal weaknesses and religious anticlericalism prevented the formation of an effective clerical movement.

But if anticlericalism lingered within the churches, it reigned in public life. "We have retired the gods from politics," the American infidel Robert Ingersoll triumphantly declared on Independence Day, 1876.[16] Two years later, the Supreme Court tried to do just that when it ruled in *Reynolds v. United States* (1878) that Thomas Jefferson's depiction of the First Amendment as a "wall of separation" was "almost an authoritative declaration of the scope and effect of the [first] amendment."[17] Nationwide, religious activism seemed exhausted and suddenly absent from public life. Wartime disruption, the triumph of abolition, and the ordeal of Reconstruction sapped millennial energies in the North and bolstered anticlericalism in Texas and the South, where tradition continued to blunt the formation of the Bible Belt.

Anticlericalism could take particularly disruptive forms. Nineteenth-century Texans never licensed a political faith, and they hardly expressed an unqualified affection for preachers, either. Folklorist James Ward Lee later recognized a widespread hostility toward many ministers and believed that "the reasons for the lack of trust are almost too many to name." He said, "Clergymen have a long history of doing no physical labor but eating high on the hog ... Some have allowed themselves to become sanctimonious, some have meddled outside their proper spheres, and some have been caught out in flagrant misconduct."[18] In Texas, preachers were hardly unimpeachable. In the mid-nineteenth century, Methodist Homer Thrall recalled, Texas hooligans dunked ministers in rivers, brought squawking chickens to services, and smoked out church services by lighting smoke fires below church floorboards.[19] The extent of these actions and attitudes are easy to exaggerate, but to the extent that they existed they represented a broader culture of anticlericalism.

Culture, tradition, and history all impeded the formation of an asser-
tive Christianity in the Lone Star State, and so did law. Texas jurisprudence
subscribed to the *Reynold's* interpretation of a strict church-state separation.
Until a Reconstruction government rewrote its state constitution, Texas
joined most of the rest of the South in constitutionally barring ministers
from holding political office.[20] No idle clause, it resulted in elected ministers' removal from the state legislature.[21] "However unclerical it may be for
ministers to seek political preferment," Homer Thrall later complained, "it
is manifestly unjust to proscribe them like common felons."[22] But for many
years, Texans regarded political preachers as just that: illegitimate, corrupt,
and criminal.

Public life strangled clerical religion. In the schools, for instance, religion
had remarkably little direct influence. The state constitution of 1876 barred
public school funds from "the support of any sectarian school" and the State
Board of Education interpreted that clause broadly. Any teacher who led students in prayer or Bible reading, the Board ruled in 1881, forfeited their access
to state funds.[23] For the next twenty-seven years, the state of Texas blocked
school prayer.[24] Later, in 1926, H. L. Mencken's *American Mercury* would
report that "in the Bible Belt, school and church are one and inseparable,"[25]
but in the nineteenth century, both buckled under the weight of a popular
anticlericalism.

Many elected politicians embraced popular anticlerical attitudes. Texas
governor Oran Roberts championed the separation of church in office. In late
1881, as President Garfield lay dying from an assassin's bullet, Roberts refused
to declare a public day of prayer for his recovery. "It is all right to fast and
pray," he said. "I don't object, but I do not see the necessity for the governor of
a state directing its religious concerns."[26] Roberts denied even the influence of
religious principles on government and believed that faith should in no way
shape the state's government. According to him, religion had no legitimate
role—direct or indirect—in public life. [27]

Roberts was neither sensational nor exceptional. His attitudes and opinions sparked little uproar among Texans. Religious leaders never declared that
there was a "war on religion" or complained about political slights. Roberts'
anticlericalism matched the tenor of the late nineteenth century. "It has taken
a large and more arduous battle to divide the church from the state than it
did to achieve our national independence," he confidently declared. He and
many others feared undermining that separation. The "union of church and
state is all wrong," he said. Even to tiptoe across the church-state divide might
threaten American democracy.[28]

Although much has been made of the efforts of southern churches to push secession, bolster Confederate nationalism, and ameliorate postbellum anxiety, memories of the Civil War had infected political Christianity with images of fanatical abolitionists and religious zealots. Governor Roberts refused to issue thanksgiving declarations while in office because he reserved that kind of religious entanglement for northern fanatics. In the South's anticlerical memory, it was the North that had fanatically pursued its vision of a Christian republic, not the South. "The religious principle of New England and Ohio makes their politics," Roberts declared. "We have seen plenty of that in the war, and it is this unconscious, subtle union of the church and state in the public mind that shows to the front in days of thanksgiving and fasts of solemn prayer." [29] In the southern mind, northern political preachers had pushed antislavery agitation and sparked the war that killed several hundred thousand southerners.[30]

Meanwhile, freethinkers used their growing platform to blast religious politics as a relic of civilization's primitive past. The Dallas Freethinkers Association regularly attacked religious politicking. In 1894, the organization's president, Dr. Geno Scott Lincoln, said that religion "cannot properly enter into public affairs" and likely spoke for many when he declared "I will vote for any man no matter what his faith may be if he believes in keeping his religion out of public affairs."[31] Dallas freethinkers declared against tax exemptions for religious organizations, publicly funded chaplains, public support of religious schools and charities, oaths, the use of the Bible in public schools, and Sabbath laws. They demanded "that all laws looking to the enforcement of 'Christian' morality shall be abrogated." They promoted a political system "founded and administered on a purely secular basis" and committed themselves to "whatever changes shall prove necessary to this end."[32] Lincoln's successor as president of the association, Ormond Paget, similarly declared "that we object to the church in politics, and to the preacher who sues his pulpit for the spread of political tents that are subversive of our rights as citizens."[33]

In Waco, anticlerical fury raged across the pages of William Cowper Brann's *Iconoclast*. Brann leveled unrelenting attacks against the clerical movement and never missed an opportunity to denigrate the "fashionable politico-religiosity of Texas." He wrote, "There are ministers occupying prominent Texas pulpits who would not recognize the Incarnate Son of God if they met him in the road." Moral reformers, he said, made a mockery of thinking men everywhere. "He [the moral reformer] needs only to become a prohibitionist—not necessarily a teetotaler—cultivate a sanctified whine calculated to curdle milk, grab the crank of some pitiful little gospel mill and begin to grind." Brann's merciless attacks ultimately contributed to his demise, but for most of the nineteenth century, he captured the sentiments of a great number of anticlerical southerners.[34]

George T. Bondies, a prominent Galveston real estate agent, merchant, and businessman, put the matter plainly: "The issue between church and state is clean-cut and as irreconcilable as life and death. There is no use to mince matters. To the votaries of the church, the things appertaining to the eternal life are necessarily so overwhelmingly more important than the things solely appertaining to the present life, that they cannot hesitate for a moment in contemptuously subordinating the latter to the former." A nonbeliever, he freely embraced the "atheist" label and, in the 1890s, attacked moral legislation while calling for the dismantling of all existing Sunday laws. If the state could bar certain Sunday activities, could it mandate others? Could it require church attendance? "There is no stopping place for this sort of thing," he said. "Hence the separation of church and state must be stern and distinct, as otherwise it will inevitably lead to . . . a foul despotism."[35]

Together, religious and secular anticlericalism stifled the development of a potent clerical culture. Texas politicians acted swiftly to quell clerical incursions. When Dallas pastors petitioned the city council in 1895 to close saloons on Sundays, one alderman, Patrick O'Keefe, objected. "A scowl of disapproval drove every sunbeam from Mr. O'Keefe's countenance," the *Dallas Morning News* reported. "I am opposed to any crowd of preachers meddling in state matters," he said, "Churches have their duty to perform without monkeying with government." He urged the council to remain vigilant. "The time is coming, gentleman of the council, when this is going to be dangerous." Preachers demanded too much, he said. "After awhile it will get so we can't do anything without asking the preachers . . . it will get so after a while that a plumber can't fix a joint without asking a preacher." The Sunday closing petition was defeated, ten to two.[36]

Texans worked to blunt moral passions at the national level as well. In 1888 and 1889, New Hampshire senator Henry Blair proposed a national Sunday law outlawing all nonessential secular work on Sundays and a constitutional amendment mandating that public education cultivate "virtue, morality and the principles of the Christian religion."[37] Workers from the National Religious Liberty Association spoke in Dallas and warned citizens of the dangers lurking behind such legislation. The passage of such measures, they said, "is in fact trying to establish the christian [*sic*] religion in this country by embodying its principles in the fundamental law." Such legislation, if passed, "would have been nothing less than a union of church and state," they said.

"That we and our fellow citizens may enjoy the inestimable blessings of both religious and civil liberty," the two proclaimed, "we also believe it to be our duty to use every lawful and honorable means to prevent religious legislation by the civil government."[38] Nearly five hundred Dallas residents signed a petition against the amendment.[39]

Into this furnace stepped the state's nascent clerical movement. B. H. Carroll presided over the movement in its formative years. In the early 1870s, Carroll introduced to Waco's First Baptist Church several temperance resolutions that sparked "agitation and discussion" among church members. Carroll deftly steered the resolutions through church committees and won them unanimous approval during a general church meeting. The resolutions declared church members to be "alarmed for the cause of Christ, for ourselves, and for the rising generation." Citing scripture, members pledged themselves to "the cause of our blessed Redeemer" by personally abstaining from any and all "intoxicating liquors."[40] The resolutions reverberated among the state's Baptists. The heated prohibition campaigns of the following decade would later render these modest personal pledges innocuous, but they ruffled the feathers of conservative religious Texans when they were first introduced. As Carroll praised his congregation in the denominational press, critics inveighed against him. H. W. Stanton of Grapevine blasted Carroll. "How dare I, as a faithful watchman upon the 'tower of Zion,' seeing the 'sword of destruction coming,' keep my mouth shut and fail to 'give the people warning,'" he wrote. Stanton accused Carroll of straying from the church's holy mission and called his actions "anti-scriptural and detrimental to the cause of Christ." [41] Carroll was single-handedly shepherding his followers along a new and uncharted path. He would have to navigate the internal anticlericalism of the churches and the hostile anticlericalism of the secular world. But if any religious leader could confront such obstacles, it was B. H. Carroll.

By the 1880s, Carroll towered over the religious life of Texas. Baptist contemporaries widely regarded him as their state's greatest orator, scholar, bureaucrat, and theological policeman. Pastoring the state's flagship church, Waco's First Baptist, would already have wielded him enormous influence, but Carroll pursued all the avenues available to a popular preacher. He published numerous histories and theologies, threw himself into denominational work, bolstered the clerics' love of denomination building, and helped found Southwestern Baptist Theological Seminary. His weekly sermons outclassed those of his colleagues. The state's dueling denominational papers outbid one another for the rights to republish them. To hear a Carroll sermon was, by all reports, an unforgettable experience, but commentators always began with

Carroll's physical description. At six feet, four inches tall and weighing over 260 pounds, with a long, flowing white beard, Carroll cut the image of an Old Testament prophet. His spellbinding oratory and magnetic personality enthralled audiences. In 1878, the Southern Baptist Convention bestowed on him a high honor: Carroll delivered the official convention sermon. It was a hit. The awe-struck convention appointed him to speak at every subsequent convention, provided he attended.[42]

In 1883, the Southern Baptist Convention held its annual meeting at Carroll's First Baptist Church. Carroll had become, as his brother James

FIGURE 2.1 Baptist leader Benajah Harvey Carroll. Undated. Courtesy of the Texas Collection. Baylor University. Waco, Texas.

would later gush, "the Colossus of Baptist History."[43] Armed with enormous influence, Carroll began leveraging some of his power in the public sphere. Bristling against long-standing anticlerical constraints, he urged religious leaders to extend their reach beyond the pulpit. In his preaching, he evinced a desire for worldly involvement that later generations of activists would return to for inspiration. Meanwhile, as a longtime temperance advocate, Carroll emerged as the leading light of the state's growing prohibition movement.[44]

"It was in 1885 that the opening gun for prohibition in Texas was fired," James Carroll later recalled.[45] That year B. H. Carroll and other McLennan County prohibitionists organized a local option election: a countywide referendum on the manufacture and sale of alcohol. It had been decades since temperance had been introduced in the churches of Texas, but the prohibition movement was new and anticlericalism was entrenched. Carroll's cause was destined to fail. The vicious McLennan County campaign of 1885 revealed the full power of the anticlerical tradition.[46]

Carroll and the McLennan County prohibitionists tried to highlight the moral urgency of the liquor question. In a pattern that would become commonplace, antiprohibitionists, or "wets," turned the election into a referendum on the proper role of clergy in secular affairs. Although the prohibition movement is generally included under the umbrella of late-nineteenth- and early-twentieth-century reform movements, prohibition always evinced an overwhelmingly religious nature. As one opponent put it, "it is plainly obvious that the Christian element, inspired by the preachers, furnish the fanaticism of the movement."[47] Many budding clerics proudly played their part. In August of 1885, J. B. Cranfill traveled to Crawford to debate the merits of prohibition with representative Roger Q. Mills. Cranfill reveled in the experience. "The house was packed to suffocation," he later recalled, and "there was no standing room anywhere." The Baptist challenger gleefully imagined himself as David to Mills's Goliath, "with right and God on his side." According to Cranfill's account, like the Hebrew king he slew the giant. In his telling, he caught the congressman in glaring inconsistencies and won the crowd. Thirty years later, he still called it "the greatest single achievement of its kind in my entire career." Cranfill taught school, edited several newspapers (including the prominent *Texas Baptist Standard*), superintended Baptist mission work, ran as vice president for the national Prohibition Party, published several books, and served on the boards of numerous universities—but debating, and perhaps defeating, the popular antiprohibitionist congressman trumped them all. Cranfill believed he had won and loved that he had won.

But his small triumph mattered little in the larger scheme: overt activism only intensified anticlerical resistance.

Anticlericalism crushed the prohibitionists in the 1880s.[48] United States senator Richard Coke, the former Redeemer-governor of Texas, entered the fray, joining with other prominent Texans in attacking the preachers. He famously attacked the ministry in a speech that the *Waco Daily Examiner* said would "make ecclesiastical fur fly."[49] Coke exhorted his followers to take measures into their own hands to restrain a runaway faith and urged his listeners to "scourge back" the preachers.[50] Other accounts of the speech had Coke urging the crowd to "scourge the preachers back and stop their rations."[51]

FIGURE 2.2 Senator Richard Coke, ca.1870–1880.

Source: Prints and Photographs Division. Library of Congress. LC-DIG-cwpbh-03844.

When preachers mobilized in later years, they would replay Coke's harsh words to great effect, but at the time, Coke's attacks devastated the clerics.

"Senator Coke is by no means original in cherishing or uttering such sentiments," the *Waco Daily-Examiner* reported.[52] The popular press slammed the prohibitionist movement. "The News maintains that political preachers are a nuisance," read the *Galveston News*.[53] Freethinkers naturally blasted the campaign. From Waco, the freethinking liberal and fallen Methodist preacher J. D. Shaw castigated the political preachers in the *Independent Pulpit*. "The church is a dangerous factor in politics," Shaw wrote in one of his lengthy editorials. Others focused on Carroll. By highlighting his role as an activist minister, rather than the merits of local prohibition, opponents stifled the prohibition campaign. John Elgin, a surveyor and lawyer, charged that Carroll "had desecrated the Sabbath, set apart by God and the laws of Texas as a day of devotion, by using it to make a stump speech and fire the partisan heart," and that "he had betrayed the traditions of a church that made it its boast that it had always fought the union of church and state." Religious activists faced a cruel paradox: the harder they worked, the more devastating the anticlerical reaction. Religious leaders struggled for a solution and found none.

Carroll and his religious allies were constantly on the defensive, forced to concede that "to the question, is it proper for a minister of the gospel to engage publicly in political discussions, I answer no." Carroll pled only that his opponents be "moderate, dispassionate, and fair."[54] They would not be. "As is usual when the Lord and his people take part in political campaigns," Shaw wrote, noting the rancor and dissension sowed by the campaign, "the contest has been a bitter one."[55] Carroll noted that "union of Church and State float like specters through his [the antiprohibitionists'] mind's horizon." He recognized that the weight of history indicted clerical politicking. He realized that anticlericalism was no fleeting political fancy but a deeply rooted cultural vision.

If anticlericalism manifested itself most immediately in politics, it nevertheless depended on a broader vision that had shaped the way generations of critics regarded religion and their world. That vision implicated politicized religion in many of history's darkest chapters and saw government as a welcome safeguard against clerical machinations. It invoked historical images, from medieval inquisitors and Salem witch-hunters to Mohammaden savagery and primitive tyranny. In so doing, it defined the limited dimensions of an appropriate regional faith. Anticlericalism amalgamated history, government, and religion into a comprehensive, compelling, and animating vision. Texans imbibed deeply of it.

"The spirit of '76 still lives in the hearts of the people of Texas," one hopeful anticlerical attorney, Otis Bowyer, would write years later, in 1911. A fiercely fought prohibition election dominated headlines that year, as others had done in the years before and would do again after. But Bowyer's invocation of national lore had nothing to do with alcohol or the vast political questions swirling around it. According to Bowyer, the nation's founding "spirit" survived because Texans and other Americans "are deeply attached to the doctrine of religious liberty," and "they are just as determined in their opposition to ecclesiastical aggression." For Bowyer, as for legions of antiprohibitionists, the most hallowed moment in American history inspired but one legacy: the muzzling of aggressive religion.[56]

For many, the prohibition question was not about liquor, saloons, or drunkenness; rather, it was about the security of sacred freedoms. Opposing reform became a fight-to-the-death battle to preserve rights and liberties. The antiprohibitionists ("antis") appealed to a historical memory that framed the conflict in easy terms, conferred gravity on their position, and offered clear villains. The antis, proclaimed one supporter, battled against "centuries of prejudice and all the power of the church."[57] Anticlerical Texans drew from this preconception to suppress all but a spiritual Christian ministry. Grounded in such ideas, fear came easily and resistance naturally.

In 1887, in a typical speech opposing the first substantial push for statewide prohibition in Texas, State Senator Jonathan O. Terrell evoked the specter of theocracy. Referring to church and state, Terrell claimed that "each has its appropriate sphere of action, and when either invades the province of the other we are taught by its consequences, in the light of history, that a step toward tyranny has been taken."[58] This oft-recycled rhetoric spanned generations. Nearly thirty years later, against still-striving prohibitionist preachers, the "anti" line had changed little. "It is one of the ironies of fate that a preacher may become a scandal as well as a glory to civilization," Peter Radford and William D. Lewis, leaders of the antiprohibitionist Farmers' Union, proclaimed in one typical speech.[59] They denounced "the embezzlement of power on the part of the ministry in the present age" and warned, in the light of history, liberty-loving Texans to guard the line between church and state.[60] The hyperbole and the allusions to fate and the "the light of history" exposed the stakes: in a parochial political battle, the world hung in the balance.

Anticlerical imaginations ran wild. Bowyer believed that religious fanatics sought the enchainment of humanity. "Those engaged in forging these fetters had better pause and reflect," he wrote, for "the final result is not hard to foresee and foretell."[61] He was right: apocalyptic fears came easily to anxious

Texans. One anticleric's 1886 indictment of what he called "churchism" was typical: "always and everywhere it appeals to the supernatural to keep mankind in bondage, and it creates a ruling caste to govern their consciences, lives, and fortunes."[62] Shared nightmares united anticlerics in sustained resistance.

Such fears, expressed so virulently against an issue that can appear so benign, revealed Texans' deep-seated anticlericalism. Many could never consider the issue of prohibition on its merits, for the unmistakable presence of politicking preachers and other religious Texans aroused an automatic resistance. Anticlerics could never reconcile their vision of enlightened civilization with the reality of a modern clerical crusade. To these men and women, the seemingly anachronistic political ambitions of religious leaders simply should not have existed in the modern world. "The United States is probably the only civilized country of the globe where the question of Prohibition is being agitated at the present day," Shaw speculated in the *Independent Pulpit*.[63] To resolve this paradox, the anticlerics looked backward. Prohibitionists must be historical orphans, they assumed, the weakened but still dangerous spawn of a previous historical era. One supporter of the anticlerical governor Oscar Colquitt attached to his correspondence a sketch of a diminutive minister fighting the hands of a clock. The religious reformer, he wrote, "tries to reverse the time—back to the middle ages [and to] when the blue laws were enforced in New England."[64] The steady articulation of such a memory and its continued resonance nourished generations of anticlerical resistance.

"Let history speak," wrote a reader of the *Independent Pulpit*. "The world has known no tyranny like it, no tyrants like church tyrants."[65] According to such beliefs, the pages of history teemed with religious crimes. "Ecclesiastical intimidation," a doctor from Thornton wrote, "has been repeating itself in all ages of the world's history." Bowyer agreed: "Religious fanaticism has been the curse of every age and clime, and, like a simoom [desert storm], it blasts and withers all it touches."[66] To such men, the burden of history rested upon their shoulders. Civilization demanded their vigilance. This was the anticlerical vision: politicized preachers fighting for a benighted past versus anticlerics fighting for an enlightened future.

Suspicions and fears emerged whenever a clergyman commented on political issues in a local newspaper, a minister ran for local office, or a preacher gave a public speech against saloons. When such formerly isolated events became commonplace, as they did in the heat of a prohibition election, anticlerical history lessons became unavoidable. In a typical speech, one prominent San Antonio anti, B. P. Hintze, recalled the unparalleled power and enlightened splendor of ancient Greece and Rome and then spoke of their quick and subsequent decay. "What was the cause?" he asked. Certainly, his audience knew before he even answered, for J. D. Shaw and his *Independent Pulpit* published those lessons weekly: "It was the union of politics and religion that destroyed the civilization of the Greeks and Romans, and brought on the Dark Ages," Shaw wrote. "There followed an age so dark, so insane, so cruel, so bloody, that the world will not wash out its stains for ten thousand years to come," Hintze lectured. "Down through those long, dark centuries the prince and the priest came hand in hand like two giant robbers and murderers."[67]

The message to Texans was clear: religious fanaticism had polluted an entire era of Western history. "For thousands of years the human family had been governed and mis-governed, oppressed, plundered, and destroyed," Congressman Mills said during the 1887 campaign.[68] "Civilization stood still, the arts and sciences dragged along like snails, knowledge was kept concealed in her hiding places." Hintze, the antiprohibitionist, charged that "for a thousand years this world was so insane about the next world that no man of the age was brave and sane enough to write the history of the period."[69] Shaw blamed religious tyranny for "the numerous massacres and wards that blackened the history of European civilization from the time of Constantine to the present."[70]

Recurring allusions to "priests" and "Romanism" were no accident. Anti-Catholicism infected the national culture. Progressive Era Americans consumed mountains of anti-Catholic literature.[71] If an oppressive national mood was not enough, Texas's unique history and geography fortified those sentiments. Memories of Mexico and its jealous church laws colored Texas's origins story, and contemporaries breathed the revolutionary anti-Catholicism then emanating from across the border.[72] Racial and ethnic prejudice—Texas's sizable Catholic population was overwhelmingly Hispanic and German—only fueled anti-Catholic sentiment. For anticlerical Texans, then, Catholicism stood for the slavish, premodern hierarchies of king and priest and slotted easily into their rhetoric.

References to the Middle East, Muslims, and the prophet Mohammed appeared in anticlerical rhetoric with reliable frequency. "The real sure enough prohibitionist is the Mohammedan," Governor Colquitt argued in 1911. "They spread their church over a good part of Asia, and all of Egypt and Palestine, and threatened Europe, but they did it under the principle of prohibition—by force, with fire and sword."[73] To many Texans, religious fanaticism adequately explained the supposed decay of Middle Eastern civilizations. "The Turks were once a powerful and progressive people," but, said

J. O. Terrell, "after centuries of total abstinence, look at their physical and moral decay." Or look farther east, he suggested, and "cast your eyes on the Brahmins, of India, where you find the very paradise of prohibition, for they neither drink wine nor eat meat; behold a race physically, morally and intellectually degenerate—the murderers of girl children and the burners of widows."[74] Hyperbole, certainly, but such rhetoric nakedly exposed the virulent reactions of anticlerical Texans.

Texans looked closer to home for history lessons, as well. Portraying the South as a den of Puritanism would later become a common trope among critics of the Bible Belt. In "the Methodist prairies of the Middle West" and the "Baptist backwaters of the South," H. L. Mencken wrote in the 1920s, "Puritanism survives, not merely as a system of theology, but also as a way of life. It colors every human activity."[75] "The triumph of the evangelical sects also naturally involved the establishment of the Puritan ideal," W. J. Cash later wrote in his seminal *The Mind of the South* (1941).[76] But if the Puritan label meant something specific in Cash's time, it meant something entirely different in the late nineteenth century. Texans saw in Puritan New England the real possibility of an American theocracy. They recalled Cotton Mather, "blue laws," and scarlet letters with fear and trepidation.

Instinctively suspicious of aggressive Christianity, Terrell could only assume that "this doctrine of prohibition had its birth in the same inhospitable clime where witches were burned."[77] In 1914, Radford and Lewis, the current and former presidents of the Texas Farmers' Union, attacked prohibitionist preachers as the most recent manifestation of an intractable religious intolerance. "Our pilgrim fathers met it," they wrote, "when, through the influence of the clergy, a witch court was established at Salem, Mass., in 1692 that precipitated a legal holocaust, threatening to reduce the population to ashes." Now, as then, these threats could be "extinguished by the laymen uniting and forcing their preachers back to the pulpit."[78]

Insurgent clerics bemoaned the Puritans' malevolent hold over the South's historical memory. From the outset of McLennan County's disastrous local option campaign in 1885, B. H. Carroll knew that if he politicked for moral issues his anticlerical opponents would unleash an onslaught. "All over the field, as if from all the frogs of Egypt, and in every note, from the shrillest octave to the hoarsest bass," he said, "will come the croaking: Blue light, blue light, Mayflower, Mayflower, crank, crank, fanatic, fanatic!"[79] The backlash, he knew, would come. The anticlerics, he seemed to be saying, needed no learned discourses or complicated arguments. They could speak in easy epithets, as if by rote, for such words expressed generations of fears and suspicions, a whole idiom buried deep within the minds of Texans. Reaction, not reflection, trampled the first great clerical offensives in Texas history. The triumph of clericalism therefore required a new history with a set of new, usable images that could be easily deployed by legions of crusading clergymen and their allies. Longstanding anticlerical conceptions of history, however, also bled into conceptions of good government. The need to redefine the proper mission of the United States, in the past and in the present, posed yet another obstacle to the triumph of the clerical vision.

Looking back over a history of inquisitions and witch burnings, anticlerical Texans regarded the young American nation as a bright exception to a long historical darkness. Future senator Roger Q. Mills claimed, "Our government was created to secure personal, civil, political and religious liberty," that "these were new principles," and that "they had been denied by Kings and Priests through the whole history of the human family." "The makers of the Constitution," Governor Colquitt later lectured, "well knew the difficulties of allowing church and state to intermingle in the exercise of civil and religious authority."[80] The establishment of such principles was the American legacy, they believed, bequeathed unto the present day by Washington and Jefferson and the other founders It had survived owing only to the diligence of the their successors. And it was not their battle alone but the struggle of all American heroes throughout all of American history.

This intermingling of history, government, and religion crystallized during prohibition elections. In those campaigns, the anticlerical vision was expressed, its supporters united, and its leaders rewarded. Anticlerical Texans could believe that by voting against prohibition they were upholding the ideals of the founding fathers, that as antiprohibitionists they were defending progress and personally helping to bolster liberty and conscience against religious tyranny and superstition. And so, in the 1880s, Carroll and his allies stood prone, exposed to a repressive cultural tradition and a long historical memory. Carroll vainly tried to mute "the hue and cry about Church and State" with appeals to a broad and noble Baptist history ranging "from Christ until now," but this defense failed to assuage anticlerical fears.[81] Articulating a new brand of history would prove a much larger task.

In a sermon delivered on the eve of the 1885 McLennan County election, Carroll decried the scorn and reproach being leveled against the clergy. He and his allies had entered into battle against sin and immorality and all the corrupting influences of the saloon. And yet they, not the saloon owners or the brewers, were the ones eviscerated by public opinion. In an open letter, Carroll expounded on Isaiah 5:20: "Woe unto them that call evil good, and good evil; that put darkness for light, and light for darkness; that put bitter for sweet, and sweet for bitter." Carroll declared himself "a watchman on the tower, now nineteen years," and said that "fidelity to a sacred trust has made it my duty, as a watchman, to sound the trumpet and warn the people." And yet *he* was reproached. Carroll maintained that he expected to be denounced. "I knew well what speech would cost," he said, and "knew that it would make me a target for the archers." But, he explained, the burden of the clerical impulse weighed too heavily upon him. "Shall I be silent?" he asked, "Or shall I lift up the voice, cry aloud and spare not?" He decided he would not be silent, and, as a result, he "has been on the firing line since." Carroll and his brethren, as he claimed to foresee, were indeed the target of the archers. McLennan County remained wet.[82]

Despite their crushing McLennan County defeat, the prohibitionist clergy and their allies pushed forward. They successfully lobbied the state legislature and won approval to submit a prohibition amendment to the Texas electorate in August 1887. The Texas constitution, because it so strictly defines the duties of state government, requires frequent amendments. If statewide prohibition was to come, it would have to be through a statewide referendum. And whether or not the state legislators had been deaf to the uproar in Waco, few seemed to expect the fury that followed. J. B. Cranfill, the Baptist editor who spoke in the amendment's defense, recalled that the initial "fight was neither a long one nor a hard one."[83] Once the amendment was submitted, however, the entire state erupted.

The 1887 campaign became, in Cranfill's words, "the hottest and most eventful political campaign ever up to that time fought in Texas."[84] The secular press agreed. "The people of Texas have never been so stirred up by a political contest," the *Dallas Morning News* reported, and "the preachers and churches have never been so active and excited." The *News* found "preachers and politicians howling and singing, swearing and preaching until the whole State has become a bedlam."[85] The campaign locked religious activists and anticlerical opponents into brutal conflict. But anticlericalism again stifled the clerical partisans and exposed the limits of political religion in the nineteenth-century South.[86]

The vanguard of Texas clericalism had again mobilized to support the amendment. The Prohibition Amendment State Convention opened the campaign in Waco in March. Cranfill stood in awe of the assembled leaders. "There were giants in those days," he recalled. The titanic B. H. Carroll was then, Cranfill wrote, "in the zenith of his power" and he lent his denominational clout to the campaign.[87] But Carroll, wounded by the Waco debacle, had learned the consequences of naked religious activism. "Let the preacher in his duty & privilege as a citizen . . . attempt to make a speech in favor of prohibition," he wrote in his personal notebook, "and he is called a 'political parson,' 'fanatic' 'long-haired' and the cry is raised – 'Scourge him back' "[88] When delegates chose Carroll to chair the campaign committee, the clerical champion proposed a new, secular strategy.

Attempting to compensate for the McLennan County debacle, reformers constructed a secular facade to conceal their religious roots. The political preacher was still too poisonous a figure and they feared a backlash. Carroll told the convention that "the preachers will take a back seat" during the campaign and that "men of standing and ability who are members of the secular professions" would assume leadership instead.[89] Anticlerical fears, however, were so deeply embedded in the regional culture that even the prohibitionists' secular strategy could not pacify an already aroused anticlericalism.

The religious leaders, of course, did not simply withdraw, and several threw themselves into the campaign. Owing to his perceived success in 1885, Cranfill debated several prominent antiprohibitionists in crowded meeting halls.[90] Carroll, meanwhile, despite his disclaimers, spoke often in defense of the amendment. Religious publications, such as the *Texas Christian Advocate* and *Texas Baptist and Herald*, inveighed against the liquor traffic weekly. Many pulpits thundered against the evils of alcohol, and the churches remained, as they always would, the strongest base of anti-liquor sentiment. Nevertheless, the campaign reflected less of its religious roots than any effort in the state before or since. Religious leaders spoke defensively and denied their political aspirations. They did everything possible to downplay the appearance of partisanship. But it was not enough.

Even the reformers' muted campaign succumbed to the popular anticlericalism, and the scandal of political religion engulfed the state. The anticlerical multitudes charged ministers with political and spiritual heresy. State Senator J. O. Terrell said the "wave of excitement . . . comes to us impelled by the efforts of ministers of the Gospel and temperance lecturers." Prefacing his argument with declarations of admiration for "the truly pious minister," Terrell dismissed the clerics. "I bow before them as spiritual guides," he said, "but can not accept their guidance in temporal matters."[91] Waco's freethinkers said much the same. Conceding that preachers had rights as citizens, Shaw wrote that "the thing we object to is the obvious desire and intention of many preachers to subordinate our political institutions to the domination of the church."[92] He scorned the politicking preachers as "zealous, noisy, and acrimonious" and called them short-sighted, cloistered in sanctimony, and out of

touch with the anticlerical tenor of the times. "While many people are willing to tolerate their pretentions to divine sanctity, attend and endure their
sermons, now and then, and bear the expenses of the gospel," Shaw wrote,
"they are by no means ready to entrust them with the political destinies of this
country.[93] These sentiments were not confined to a freethinking minority.

As a congressman, Roger Q. Mills again fought against prohibition and
again accused Caroll and his followers of apostasy: prohibition, he charged,
was "brought in the bosoms of a Protestant political priesthood."[94] He quoted
Jefferson, railed against religious intolerance, and told the preachers to climb
back into their pulpits. He called the whole campaign a fraud: "It is wrapped
in the liberty of Heaven, but it comes to serve the devil . . . It comes to tear
down liberty and build up fanaticism, hypocrisy and intolerance."[95] In one
notable incident, Mills condemned Carroll's meddling and said, "hell was
so full of such preachers that their legs were sticking out of the windows."[96]
Congressman John Hancock likewise decried a "meddlesome and intolerant priesthood."[97] In San Antonio, crowds interrupted a prohibition rally
by pelting Methodist Rev. A. H. Sutherland with eggs.[98] The city's mayor
reportedly slapped a prohibitionist clergyman across the face.[99] Even the
aging Confederate leader Jefferson Davis came out against the amendment,
declaring that the "world had long suffered from the oppressions of government under the pretext of ruling by divine right." Denouncing "fanaticism"
and "political parsons," Davis asked, "If we begin the march of retrogression,
where will it stop?" Anticlerical southerners already knew the answer. "In
this," Davis said, "I see the forbidden union of Church and State. My grief is
real and relates to both."[100]

In addition to berating preachers in public, the antiprohibitionists organized. In May, a group calling themselves "True Blues" gathered in Dallas
to coordinate efforts against the amendment. *The Dallas Morning News*
reported that large crowds, which included the "leading minds of Texas,"
had turned out, overflowing the Dallas opera house. Whites and blacks com-
ingled and listened to speech-makers pontificate on liberty and fanaticism.
Congressman Mills "touched off the big gun," the *News* reported. In his two-
and-a-half-hour speech, he discussed liberty and self-government, blasted
prohibition, and slammed political preaching. Some in the audience said he
went too far; others, not far enough.

"The Legislature has submitted to us a proposition not in keeping with our
history or compatible with freedom," Mills said, "but dictated by the priesthood of this State." Noting that it was the centennial of the US Constitution,
he asked the convention if they wanted to give away the American experiment,

"to go back to the worn-out policy that dominated the governments of old, under which the people were governed and the human family was oppressed." Texans could vote, he said, and decide "whether we shall cross our hands as spaniels and slaves under the dictation of these men." Few Texans then trafficked in historical notions of a "Christian nation." Mills channeled instead the dominant anticlerical conception of American history. "Our fathers suffered and bled for liberty," he said, but he only asked that the convention vote against prohibition and political religion.[101]

Anticlerical attacks and the prohibitionists' own crippling self-consciousness led to a political fiasco.[102] On August 4, 1887, Texas voters turned out in record numbers to spare the saloon and rebuke the preachers.[103] When the final returns were tallied, prohibition received fewer than 130,000 of the nearly 350,000 votes cast.[104] Shaw's *Independent Pulpit* gloated. The paper judged the result a great rebuke against "the fanatical religio-political element" and credited the devastating defeat to the anticlerical reaction against an overreaching religious fanaticism. "These experiments," Shaw wrote, "amounted to nothing beyond exciting popular indignation and disgust at such anti-Southern, not to say anti-American, conduct." Underneath the hyperbole, Shaw, the freethinker, captured the sentiments of the state better than any leading clergymen. Despite the prohibitionists' best efforts,

FIGURE 2.3 "Pros must go." Anti-prohibitionist rally in Jacksonville, Texas, 1887.
Source: Cherokee County Historical Society.

clerical maneuvering overshadowed the merits of the liquor question and doomed the campaign.[105]

Despite successfully scourging the clerics from the public stage, many Texans pondered the future. "When the election is over and the result is known," the *Dallas Morning News* had asked before the voting, "what effect will it have upon the country?"[106] Some wondered if the clerics could be permanently suppressed. "A taste for conflict has been imparted, and those who in religious orders and in professional politics have developed this appetite will be expected to furnish the necessary pabulum," the *News* concluded. Religious leaders "have started a new political warfare and it must have its course."[107]

Although he gleefully celebrated the clerical debacles, the freethinker J. D. Shaw surveyed the future with foreboding. He interpreted the outbreak of clericalism as an omen. When Democrat Grover Cleveland recaptured the presidency in 1888, Shaw, like others, noted with disappointment that the national political parties had split mostly over tired sectional loyalties, not substantive policy differences. But this would not last, he said, for the older generations were passing and new dividing lines were being drawn. Doubting the ability of a bubbling progressivism to reorient politics toward the question of trusts and concentrated economic power, he predicted instead a new divisive politics of morality. "The election is now over and the excitement incident thereto has passed away," Shaw wrote, "therefore we deem it a proper time to point out some indications of a coming conflict that will put a heavier strain upon our constitution and the government than any that has ever existed in the past." He told his readers to look to the previous prohibition campaign for evidence of the looming struggle: "The conflict—inevitable, we believe—between Church and State, or between clerical authority and civil liberty." Shaw predicted a clerical insurgency. "The orthodox churches," he wrote, "led by their priests and preachers, will be on one side, and the true American citizens, led by the lovers of freedom and equal rights, will be on the other." The well-worn divisions of national political life life would be redrawn and invigorated. The stakes would be raised. Religious warfare would consume the nation.[108]

For the moment, however, once confident clerical warriors put down their weapons and retired. The "prohibition wave had spent its force," J. B. Cranfill later lamented. Its once loud advocates were, he said, "now pensively silent." Subscribers to the prohibitionist newspaper the *Advance* dropped from several thousand to a few hundred.[109] Some ministers, such as the Methodist Reverend Elijah Shettles, would in shame later disown the entire 1887 campaign.[110] Humiliated and chastised, the movement stood on the precipice of defeat. But a core of clerical activists stood ready to lead the beleaguered movement into the future.

Reflecting on their defeat, some activists felt that self-censorship, their reluctance to agitate openly—their capitulation to anticlerical expectations—had been their greatest liability.[111] According to this interpretation, too few religious leaders recognized that they truly were, in fact, political preachers. Afraid to confront that reality, weak-kneed reformers had lacked conviction, settled for washed-out rhetoric, tolerated internal dissension, and stumbled their way to defeat. Activists vowed not to repeat those mistakes. They hoped to build a broader and deeper movement, one buoyed by a distinct and powerfully animating worldview. Over the coming decades, the apostles of clericalism spread their vision throughout the state's religious establishment. They taught their colleagues to see the world as they did, to traffic in a noble religious history, and to share in the convictions of a fighting faith. Over the coming decades, they convinced their peers to agitate and organize, demand a stake in public life, and bend politics to their whim. Thus began the first chapter in the making of the Bible Belt.

3

Of Tremor and Transition

CRISIS AND THE ORIGINS OF SOUTHERN CLERICALISM

WHATEVER THE IMMEDIATE political fate of prohibition, the late nineteenth century also inaugurated a golden age of religious growth. The age's churches, along with its railroads, meatpacking plants, and steel mills, boomed. Church membership soared, denominations expanded, and imposing new church buildings pierced the skies. The professionalization of religious work gave part-time Baptist preachers full-time jobs and allowed itinerant Methodist circuit riders to stable their horses. Salaries, visibility, and prestige all bolstered a new professional caste presiding over growing congregations in magnificent new churches. Religious leaders would have been forgiven for throwing confetti and reveling in their ever-expanding spiritual conquests. But that was not to be. Religious leaders built and filled large stone churches yet complained of infidelity; they drew large salaries yet felt slighted; newspapers carried their sermons yet they felt ignored; they were big, but they felt small.

Contrary to changing realities, evangelical Texans comprehended and universally lamented a religious landscape of empty churches, disrespected preachers, indolent congregants, and a hostile public. They saw an irresponsible secular press, an amoral public school system, and a godless government. Each and every pillar of the modern world, they thought, absented God, and, perhaps worse, absented themselves. Adrift in an infant New South—the much-touted if only partially realized new world of industry and commerce—their large churches and expanding congregations afforded them no anchor against the perceived weightlessness of their world. Anxiety shook the common foundations of their religious domain. For a generation of emerging religious domain, crisis defined their outlook.

Perceptions of crisis are endemic to nearly all social movements and cries of spiritual calamity are as old as American religion. To understand the origins of the Bible Belt, then, it is necessary not only to understand clerics' specific new spiritual anxieties, but also to appreciate how, in their writing and preaching, religious leaders illuminated perceptions of misfortune, disseminated their desperate vision, and exploited the resulting widespread sense of crisis to build institutions, rewrite history, enter politics, and conquer public life.

Desperate visions drove reformers into the world, but a shared sense of crisis was not inevitable, nor was it accidental. Clerics taught one another to see the world through their own anxious prisms, to interpret the world through crisis, and to speak the language of embattlement. Notions of crisis drove the clerical crusades, but, in large part the clerics themselves were accomplices to its creation: clerics, in effect, created the engine of their own efforts. All their later actions against government and society and public morality depended on the assumed reality of a widespread spiritual, moral, and political crisis. A sense of embattlement not only united clerics and imparted a collective identity that minimized internal differences, it compelled religious Texans to act in the public world. Crisis conferred gravity and meaning to the seemingly meaningless lives of religious leaders and devoted believers. The push for prohibition legislation would offer Texans an outlet, a battle to be waged and won, and it drove Texas religion irreversibly into the world. Clerics planted the seeds of action in the rich soil of a spiritual crisis and harvested the Bible Belt. That story begins in the anxieties of the turn-of-the-century world.

As a century closed and another opened, Americans everywhere grappled with modernity. By the early twentieth century, industrialization had touched every town and hamlet. The great cities pulled their populations from American farms and foreign lands, and orderly managers bureaucratized American business. Poverty, meanwhile, accompanied progress, as ravenous markets devoured artisans and anachronized romantic notions of American yeomen. The presumed anchors of American culture suddenly seemed weightless. Amid all of the era's glorious material benefits—technological improvements, increasing standards of living—and all their debauching social side-effects—low wages, entrenched poverty—a plague of worry infected turn-of-the-century Americans. "Anxiety," the renowned historian Robert Wiebe wrote, "like the common cold, was a most egalitarian malady."[1]

The pandemic wrought fervent soul-searching and a brooding aimlessness. No region escaped its crippling effects and no social class was immune. Even as they braced themselves for the new industrialized world, Americans doubted the surety of their footing.[2]

South of the Mason-Dixon Line, boosters proclaimed a New South unbound by the barbarism of slavery and born of industrial progress. Blind to the debasing and pervasive poverty endemic to cotton farming and silent on the region's countless racial cruelties, they preached only a creed that prophesied the transformative Midas touch of business. But crippling insecurities flourished alongside New South hopes.[3] "The New South was an anxious place," historian Edward Ayers wrote.[4] Men and women in all walks of life found themselves thrust into a new world in which unrestrained commerce and unholy amusements seemed to menace regional stability. "There was a certain highly charged quality about everyday life in the nineteenth-century and early twentieth-century South," wrote historian Ted Ownby.[5] Texans, like men and women throughout the industrializing world, worried about the new and strange commercial colossus astride them. Looking upon a landscape of cities and railroads and shifting demographics, they worried.

If anxiety struck many, it hit religious leaders especially hard. They were the supposed arbiters of the rock of ages, yet perhaps no single group proved as vulnerable. Although many clergy embraced the New South creed and employed modern business strategies within their denominations, indeed as many of them did so, religious leaders nevertheless feared the corrosive effects of commercialism and an encroaching worldliness and wondered whether faith could survive the frenetic pace of modern life. The churches were in trouble, they said, and anxiety echoed across the region.

Reality, of course, contradicted common assumptions about religious decline. "Complaints frequently appear in both secular and religious papers concerning the decay of interest in religious affairs among the people of the United States," the *Dallas Morning News* wrote in 1900, "but they are not justified by the statistics."[6] After the tumult of the Civil War—which, perhaps surprisingly, rarely entered into clerical laments—Texas churches had prospered. All available data show remarkable growth in communicants, seating capacity, buildings, and property value. From 1870 to 1890, the formative years of the crisis culture, the population of Texas nearly tripled, growing by 273 percent. Meanwhile, there were almost nine times as many churches that together could seat almost eight times as many people. Between 1890 and 1906 (the years of two detailed national religious censuses), the population of Texas increased 58 percent; church membership jumped 89 percent. The value of church property and the salaries of clergymen increased as well.[7] Nearly every denomination shared in the harvest. Contemporary demographer Henry King Carroll, evaluating the 1890 census returns, noted that Texas "had an unusual growth in the period under consideration," even for the South, where "it will be found that in every State, save North Carolina alone, the net increase in communicants was large, considerably larger than the net increase of population, showing that the Churches in that section of the country, whatever may be said of other sections, enjoyed a high measure of prosperity."[8] Even the Methodists' Northwest Texas Conference saw fifteen solid years of growth—its membership tripled—despite declaring crisis in 1898. These were boom years for religion, so why didn't growth mollify clerical concern?

It is clear, as historians have noted, that religious leaders gave themselves to anxious worry at the precise moment their churches were booming. The evidence raises the obvious question, how could evangelical Christians believe themselves fragile and besieged while they achieved such triumphs?[9] But this is the wrong question. Church leaders often misdiagnosed the problem as one of raw numbers, but churches weren't emptying, they were filling. And yet, perhaps in their broader outlines, their cries were not irrational or manipulative but perceptive. While all the objective measures observable in census reports and church records corroborated a narrative of explosive growth, they veil the limits of religion in the turn-of-the-century world. Religious leaders carried the cause of Christ to new heights but their conquests were narrowly limited to memberships and fundraising and advances in denomination building, and, while significant, these were not the currency of the emerging clerical economy.

Although many individuals and associations joyfully publicized their rapid gains in membership and church growth, a disquieting unease nevertheless gripped the white evangelical mainstream. "Optimism is a very stupid and hurtful sort of thing if it fails to face the facts," George Truett said in 1911, after the clerics' perception of crisis had matured and a decade before he assumed the presidency of the Southern Baptist Convention. Omens loomed everywhere, he said. "That man who will put his ear down and listen with a little care shall hear the rumblings of subterranean forces that hiss under the thin crust of our civilization."[10] By that time, a full-blown spiritual crisis had infected the minds of evangelical Texans, and religious leaders spoke easily in apocalyptic terms. Anxieties had festered for decades. Throughout the late nineteenth century and into the twentieth, religious leaders spread a gospel of impending moral and spiritual catastrophe.

The published opinions of the Northwest Texas Conference of the Methodist Episcopal Church, South, epitomized the sudden development of the crisis mindset. Each year a "state of the church" committee reported to the annual meeting, and as late as the mid-1880s, these reports were unabashedly optimistic. Overseeing magnificent growth, the committee annually celebrated "a great ingathering of souls" and reported that "from almost every station and circuit and mission in the Conference the glad tidings come that the work of revival has gone gloriously on."[11] As the years passed, though, even as their organizations prospered, their outlook began to sour. They acknowledged that the church was working "in the face of brazen unbeliefs, amid the exultant shout of boastful infidelity and the trembling of the fearful," yet tried to maintain a positive outlook.[12] They admitted that the 1887 prohibition campaign exposed clergy to an unprecedented barrage of criticism, writing that "the election contest swept the State over on waves of extravagant bitterness, piling up the extremes of deformity; whirling and surging and seething angularity and prejudice and venom in the storm-wrought commotion. Of this the preachers shared, as victims beyond the lot of any other class."[13] The trauma of the campaign had catalyzed within the clergy the first nebulous feelings of embattlement. Still, the committee members steeled themselves against despair: Preachers "have said 'be it so; if we suffer with Christ we shall also reign with Him.'" They recognized that they had adversaries yet remained hopeful and proclaimed "an ever-brightening day."[14] But that positive sentiment withered over the coming decade. By the following year, 1888, the committee members "note[d] with pleasure some degree of improvements in the spirituality of the membership throughout our bounds. And yet, the tide of spiritual life in the church is far below what the grace, power and promise of God would warrant."[15] The Northwest Conference lagged behind other conferences in adopting the language of crisis, but it inhabited the same anxious world and finally succumbed to its dictates.

The committee's reports continued to darken until they admitted little hope. By 1898, the committee reported that "we have reached in the order of Divine Providence a crisis that is recognized by the most thoughtful minds of Christendom" and that "never before have such problems been presented." They lamented an "unusual and wide-spread spiritual dearth" and "a distressing apathy and hesitation upon the part of the Lord's hosts." They catalogued all the standard complaints of their times. "The spirit of the age is intensely secular and materialistic," they said, "and its blighting influence has affected the church." Moreover, the preachers were weak and the people wayward. There was "a seeming lack of unction and spiritual power in the pulpit," and "as pastors we find a want of deep Spirituality in our membership." Church members neglected their spiritual duties, the committee reported, and few prayed, kept the Sabbath, or maintained deep religious conviction. Given over to worldliness, they had lost their "deep anguish of spirit" and "vital piety." The crisis had set in.[16]

By the turn of the twentieth century, the spiritual crisis transcended the pulpit and infected much of the laity. Expressions of crisis could be heard everywhere. Morris Sheppard had joined the Methodist Church as a young law student at the University of Texas and became active in the Epworth League, the church's burgeoning youth organization. Deploying the same mix of personal magnetism and moral fervor that would later win him a United States Senate seat, Sheppard rallied support for the league by speaking to the times. Addressing league members in San Antonio in 1896, the twenty-one-year-old captured the anxious clerical worldview. He could not have been clearer. "The present is distinctly a period of tremor and transition," he said, "an era of bewildering incertitude in every phase of life and form of thought." Sheppard, though himself no clergyman, nevertheless spoke its language fluently. He saw what the clerics saw. Like his contemporaries, he did not see a promising New South rising around him, but, instead, a world in moral and spiritual peril. "Problems of almost inconceivable magnitude and of unexampled complexity are forming," he said and, sparing no hyperbole, warned that "the first sun of the twentieth century may illuminate a scene of universal war" and "revolutions may come in cataclysms and as swollen waters through a broken dike." Sheppard revealed how contagious the crisis could be for men and women of his generation.[17] People everywhere believed religion was in trouble.[18]

A perception that God, ministers, and the churches were devalued and powerless[19] had pierced the entire South and much of the nation at large.[20] The Virginia *Religious Herald* had asked as early as 1880, "Is the Pulpit Losing Its Power?" The Tennessee *Southern Methodist Review* had reported that "the preacher once received all reverence" but now, it seemed, the daily paper and a thousand other secular influences shaped morals and social habits and the pulpit had faded into irrelevance.[21] The nation devoured the Midwestern social gospeler Josiah Strong's *Our Country: Its Possible Future and Present Crisis* and its "proofs of our national peril."[22] Meanwhile, the great German sociologist Max Weber predicted religion's imminent death. It would be rationalized away, he said, murdered by modernity. Religious leaders feared that he might be right. Everywhere, and especially in the South, crisis gripped the clerical mind. When the George Truett said that "in our great country irreverence grins in the face of God," he could have been speaking from any part of what would soon become known as the Bible Belt.[23] Pessimistic spiritual forecasts and indictments of worldly society dominated religious thinking. In Texas, as elsewhere, the gloomy thoughts of clergymen and laity settled on common and specific themes: the invasion of "worldliness," the decline of churchgoing, and, perhaps most importantly, the decaying reputation of religious leaders. Each would prove vital in fostering the development of clerical culture. Texans emphasizes them all.

Of course, the barriers critics had constructed between churches and society were not impenetrable. Even as they criticized the inroads of the New South, evangelical activists never wholly rejected them. Clergymen embraced their new status as professionals, their denominations bureaucratized just as any modern business organization would, and higher education assumed a greater importance in their denominational careers. Their reform efforts evinced the full employment of modern methods in fundraising, organization, and publicity. When religion suddenly seemed imperiled and in need of defenders, clerics armed themselves with their vast denominational structures and their presses and their books. In fact, according to their salaries and education levels, leading parishioners and reformers were actually *more* intimately a part of the New South world than many of their opponents. However antimodern their rhetoric, most welcomed economic development and believed in visions of "progress."[24] Still, while many religious traditionalists would denounce reformers' obsession with worldly reform and retreat into their own fortress religions, clerical champions would drag the mainstream of Texas evangelicalism into full combat with "the world."

Although it was often ill-defined, an indictment of the modern world penetrated the clerical ranks. Explosive urban growth drew much of that condemnation. Many imagined that the cities, widely regarded as the front lines of the coming New South, were spiritual vacuums. City dwellers, it was believed, rarely went to church. The *Texas Christian Advocate* wrote, "Some go once a Sunday; some go only when it is convenient; some, we are told, do not go at all." Even members of urban churches seemed uninterested in attendance. "The great majority of our city members," the *Advocate* said, "are more or less indifferent."[25] But the unease transcended concerns about religion in towns and cities. Modernity's tentacles had spread throughout the entire country and penetrated every isolated community. One rural Methodist preacher wrote that even the people in his small community "are in such close touch with the world, that they are no longer the ''ignorant country folk' of a decade back. I found there, and I find everywhere I go, men ... know what the world is doing. They know what everything is doing except the Church."[26] Most clergy, however, refrained from issuing narrow indictments only of commercialism. They spoke instead to a broader and more abstract menace: "worldliness." Whatever that meant—and it meant different things to different people—it led to two deep-seated assumptions: that churchgoing was declining and that respect for religious leaders was fading.

Despite the considerable evidence to the contrary, this belief that church attendance was plummeting anchored the spiritual crisis. Texans believed fewer and fewer of their brethren honored the Sabbath by going to church. In 1886, *The Texas Christian Advocate* published a lengthy editorial titled, "The Decay of Church-Going." "Our people," it argued, "are unfaithful to the duty of church-going. God's house, with many of them does not stand first, but second."[27] The *San Antonio Evening Light* reported that "not more than one-half the pews [in the city] are regularly occupied on Sunday, and in many houses of worship, built and maintained at a great expense, the proportion is less."[28] The Northwest Texas Conference's prototypical lament noted only that "attendance upon preaching is not as general as it should be."[29] In 1904, an ecumenical council of churchwomen in Palestine, Texas, attempted a census of the city's church members to shame the city and stimulate attendance.[30] In Hearne, concerned citizens lamented the "neglect of religion" and claimed that "the people of this age, unlike their ancestors of a generation or several generations back, have so many interests a large proportion of them do not appear to be able to spare the time for church attendance and spiritual devotion."[31] So many different groups complained about a decay of churchgoing in so many different places that it became conventional wisdom. "It is generally admitted," the *Dallas Morning News* editorialized in 1907, "that there is a notable decline in church-going." Whatever the reasons—and clergy always eagerly discussed the reasons—most conceded that declining attendance "is a matter often discussed with grave concern by pastors and others who take an active part in religious work."

As southern clergymen imagined their religious world crumbling around them, they felt belittled. Mired in their imagined crisis, they complained of diminished authority and believed themselves assaulted upon all sides. The neurasthenic Baptist editor J. B. Cranfill, who so proudly debated antiprohibitionists in the 1880s, best captured the embattled clerical mindset. In his 1908 book, *Courage and Comfort*, he wrote: "There are those who hate the preachers. They curse the churches, they are opposed to Sunday-schools, they execrate the Bible, but every man who so lives and does is as rotten at the heart as Ahab. One of the finest tests of a man's heart character is the esteem in which he holds God's preachers, God's churches, and all holy things. A man is as much judged by the company he does not keep as by the company he keeps. He is as much judged by the things he hates as the things he loves. Every evil man on earth, who persists in evil and whose heart is set toward hell, hates preachers, opposes churches, and rails out against all God's enginery of good."[32] Looking back on his early career in the late nineteenth century, the prominent Texas Methodist George Rankin recalled that "churches were not generally respected and a preacher was no more than any other man. His cloth amounted to nothing."[33] Outside the churches, antireligious critics goaded the preachers. In the pages of the *Independent Pulpit*, J. D. Shaw interpreted the decline as "a merited rebuke to the arrogance of clerical egotism and a sign that the sanctuary is losing its hold upon the people."[34] He said New South advances were "too much for ecclesiasticism" and that "their [the preachers'] calling has survived its usefulness."[35] Clergymen resolved to forestall that reality. Rankin and Cranfill, in fact, perhaps best articulated the perceived assault upon their profession and carried with them forever an obsessive need to magnify their office and their personal standing. But they had not yet discovered the means.

As the decades passed and the perception of crisis spread, more and more religious southerners became concerned for the future of religion and attempted to diagnose the cause of supposedly empty churches and libeled preachers. Anxious Texans blamed some combination of hyper-commercialism, worldly diversions, secular education, poor parenting, and, alternately, too much politicking or too little politicking. Nevertheless, whatever *it* was, it was external. The *News* conceded that, maybe, "the 'getting along without religion,' to whatever extent it exists, may be due much less to any substantial change in the spiritual state and attitude of men than to the great change which has taken place in the social structure of civilization and the means of gratifying the social instinct."[36] In a world of saloons and theaters and social clubs, what appeal could the church make? From these instinctual resentments emerged an enemy for clergymen and lay leaders to combat. Far removed from their pulpits and pews, the threat lay somewhere "out there," in the world, somewhere beyond the traditional borders of evangelicals' Christ-centered world. If it could be defeated, conquered, and subdued, perhaps the churches would be liberated from its stranglehold and society cleansed of its moral pollution. These clerics dreamed wonderful dreams. They read a hopeful future into a nostalgic past. They imagined an Edenic paradise unsullied by the sin and corruption of worldliness. Nostalgia increasingly anchored Texans' indictment of the present.

Religious leaders produced depictions of the past that were as sunny and wonderful as their depictions of the present were dark and sinful. J. B. Cranfill often waxed sentimental. His nostalgia aggregated public respect, clerical humility, and good Christian homes. "The preacher in those good days was never thought of as a 'dead-beat,' but he was reverenced as a messenger of God, and his fervid talks, pathetic prayers, and soulful exhortations made an impress on the unpretentious home that has worked lasting good in the lives of the little ones that grew up in that Christly atmosphere."[37] Turn-of-the-century Texas author E. B. Fleming remembered only a universal godliness in his youth. He could "not remember of hearing of a skeptic or infidel in the whole county as far back as forty-five years ago. Everybody who could get religion was a member of some church, and those who could not get it rarely ceased to try, and never seemed to doubt the reality of heaven and hell, the existence of God and the inspiration of the Bible." The spiritual story of Texas, as Fleming and others told it, was a tragic "rise and fall" account. If their contemporaries disrespected the clergy, derided the church, and profaned the Sabbath, their forebears had worshipped openly, honestly, and unequivocally. Their memories overflowed with visions of respect and prestige. "Religion was far more universally respected than now," Fleming said.[38] In the nostalgic mind, irreligious and anticlerical villains usurped religious authority. Such declension narratives grounded the clerics' turn-of-the-century worldview, fueled their modern-day jeremiads, and eventually led to their great worldly crusades.

Beset by a disquieting sense of crisis yet drawn to the idea of a retrievable golden age, many religious leaders looked inward to their churches and called for a return to "that old-time religion." Revivalists sought to rekindle old evangelical fires and so light in men and women a faith bright enough to draw in strangers from the New South wilderness. "I know if the spirit of evangelization died out of our churches that our churches must die," said James B. Gambrell, a leading Baptist publisher and denominational leader.[39] Many religious leaders urged a spiritual renewal, a turn back to the simple evangelical message of a saving faith. "There is to some extent," the *Dallas Morning News* reported, "a feeling that Christianity as it exists today is imperfect because of compromises with the world—that a return to the pure teachings of the gospels would bring about a new and much better order."[40] As Gambrell put it, "you can not fiddle people into church."[41] Many religious leaders therefore called on their colleagues to work within the denominational structures and along traditional lines to redeem the fallen society. They channeled the logic of much early southern evangelical theology—that society was nothing but an aggregation of individual souls and that the winning of those souls would win the world. Clerical activists would later complain that their fellow clergymen had failed to realize that such narrow evangelism could never assuage their assumptions of a spiritual crisis. The problems of their age were external, they would argue, and the solution to their crisis therefore lay in extra-denominational work rather than the narrow church worlds they were accustomed to.

The sad career of William Carey Crane illustrates the tragic realization of those limits. As ministers toiled away saving souls, many questioned the value of their work. They worked hard but saw few results and felt less satisfaction. Many tried whatever they could to rescue themselves from despondency. Crane, a Virginia-born Baptist who settled in Texas, typified many proto-clerics' anxious and undirected groping for meaningful religious work. At once eager and aimless, Crane traveled westward seeking whatever distinction the Baptist Church could offer. He settled first in Mississippi and set about working within the Baptists' denominational world.

Armed with ambition, a bookish intelligence, and two degrees from Columbian College (now George Washington University), Crane spent the 1840s and 1850s climbing Mississippi's denominational ladder. Capable and determined, he received prestigious appointments to pulpits and university presidencies. By the time, he was forty, Crane, in addition to regular preaching, presided over a denominational college, coedited the *Mississippi Baptist*, had co-founded and served as vice president of the Mississippi Historical Society, and served as secretary of the Southern Baptist Convention.[42] But none of this satisfied him. His insatiable ambitions pushed him ever onward.

After a brief and apparently contentious stay in Louisiana, Crane accepted a pastorate at Houston's First Baptist Church.[43] He arrived in the city in July of 1863 and before assuming the pulpit met with the trustees of Baylor University at Independence, Texas. Impressed, they offered Crane the presidency of the institution, and Crane, attracted by the promises of a prominent station and a substantial paycheck, happily accepted. It was the wrong decision. The appointment—and the paycheck—would prove anything but lucrative. At Independence, Crane's life-long pattern of ascension faltered and stopped. Historian Daniel Stowell has written of southern religious leaders' successes in "rebuilding Zion" after the war, but that success was never easy and certainly never uniform.[44] For over two decades, Crane languished in material ruin, intellectual frustration, and psychological distress.

Crane taught most of the curriculum at Baylor, oversaw fundraising and administrative duties, pursued his scholarly interests, and served as the full-time pastor of the Independence Baptist Church. For over two decades he toiled, and for over two decades he exhausted his physical and financial resources. From the beginning, the school's perilous finances drained Crane of spirit and wealth. University trustees had promised him a $3000 salary and a comfortable home. Neither came to pass.[45] Crane depleted what resources he had to keep the university afloat. "Thousands promised me have never been paid, promises from people & organizations able to pay," Crane wrote in his diary. "I have spent nearly all my father left me to keep the educational enterprises of Independence in existence."[46] Worse for the scholar (Crane would go on to publish a well-read biography of Sam Houston), "My literary enterprises all hang fire, because of the difficulties, I encounter, in meeting monetary obligations, with repudiated endowment, repair pledges and delinquent tuition payers."[47] But if financial difficulties sapped Crane's enthusiasm, his shrinking social status devastated him.

Even before Crane had embarked on his Independence work, he wrestled with what to him were the cruel memories of wasted years. Early in his tenure he reminded himself that "[w]hat little I have done for my Maker is all worth remembering."[48] Crane dedicated himself to exiling those memories by throwing himself into his work. "What remains of life," he wrote, "must be vigorously occupied."[49] But his new work at Independence brought no reprieve. His labor at the university, at his pulpit, and at his writing desk could not satisfy him. "Alas!" he lamented, "my life is passing away with little utility to myself, with less to the world."[50] He described himself as "dispirited" and "ever ill at ease."[51] Each passing year stung him deeper. "Today I am sixty years old," Crane wrote on March 17, 1876. "The thought is a terrible one, for with it comes busy memories of failures, shortcomings, misimprovement, and evil. I have aimed high and tried to do good, but difficulties, dangers, and troubles of every sort have entangled my steps."[52] No matter how determined or dedicated to the Baptists' religious mission, Crane never felt the warm satisfaction of a fight well fought. His name appeared in few newspapers. No politicians asked for his endorsement. Outside of the state's insular religious world, few people took notice of him. In January of 1885, only weeks before his death, Crane complained that, "faced by difficulties, misunderstood and misrepresented, my lot has been a hard one."[53]

In a hostile world, Crane, above all, had to justify his life's work. He needed some evidence of his utility. He wanted only to be useful, for someone to notice and approve of his efforts. To win even limited approval. This was in Crane and in so many others of the coming generation. Striving amid the postbellum spiritual crisis, they needed an outlet. The hints, perhaps, were there. Crane noticed the energy attending his temperance sermons, and he lobbied congressmen and organized petitions for several educational schemes. But like most southern evangelicals of the nineteenth century, he directed blame inward ("I can but suppose that is my sinful nature, which has caused me the troubles of my life," he mused[54]). A new generation of clerical activists would turn that frustration outward, direct it against a culture, and build for themselves a movement. A new generation wouldn't suffer anxieties without comment. They would ask why, and clerics would provide an answer. But, given all of their wonderful gains, how could southern evangelicals despair in the first place?

Whatever their swelling membership rolls, rising church spires, and sky-rocketing budgets said, religion *felt* diminished. Spiritual power seemed diluted and weakened. Religious leaders, tasked with maintaining a crumbling moral universe, flailed before the ferment of the age. In the minds of evangelical Texans, religion was imperiled. Christianity hung in the balance. Whether specific numbers of men and women gave themselves to Christ ultimately proved incidental; the triumph of clericalism turned not on the winning of souls, the building of churches, or the heights of denominationalism, but on the respect and deference accorded to religion by the public and the standing and influence of religious leaders in the social arena. Here was the site of battle, the place where religious leaders staked their claim to leadership and where they felt most threatened. While institutional religion thrived, evangelical Protestants nevertheless felt their authority challenged and diminished. Distinction must be drawn, therefore, between the rising incidence of religious adherence and the larger influence of religious institutions.[55]

As historian Ted Ownby so vividly demonstrated, the all-entangling reality of modernity exposed local church fiefdoms to the corruptions of the world. New forms of cultural authority wrenched authority from homes and pulpits and put it in boardrooms, factory floors, and saloon halls. Religion suddenly occupied only one distinct sphere among many. Even as its churches boomed, the capacity for evangelical Protestantism to regulate the lives of ordinary men and women diminished. And if religious authority seemed diminished, so did the public standing of a new crop of professional clergymen.

Because preachers embodied religion's position in the broader culture, the question of religious authority increasingly involved the social status of religious leaders, who learned to fight back. Religion has occupied different positions of influence at different places in different times. Religious authority, as any authority, rises and falls in conflict and competition. Always contingent, it rests on the willingness of its partisans to fight. As the Texas case proves, the fate of religious authority waxed and waned as a result of public conflicts between two forces, between the clerical champions who would see religion enthroned and the anticlerical critics who would see it repressed. In this manner, the spiritual and the secular locked themselves in combat and forced Texans to choose sides. When the grasp of evangelical leaders over institutions and culture slipped, or seemed to, partisans jockeyed to maintain their standing, to bolster their organizational resources, and to reclaim their old status—which, in historical terms, was really a newly sought-after standing and a new role with new hopes for wide-ranging power and influence. The pangs of crisis awakened many to the capriciousness of religion and of religious authority. Like the scholars who now study them, the clerics realized that authority can ebb and flow.[56] If they could be diminished, they said, so too could they be empowered.

The accumulating burdens of the spiritual crisis pushed evangelical Texans to the brink, but, in the face of crisis, few clergymen retreated into their pulpits, resigned themselves to decay, and idly awaited an inevitable obsolescence. Instead, threats sparked the instinct for self-preservation. Clerics strove to endure. "Men from all walks of life," Robert Wiebe wrote, "already shaken by an incomprehensible world, responded to any new upheaval as an immediate threat." Threatened, "they had no alternative, they felt, but to select an enemy and fight."[57]

As the century closed, clerical champions promised a way out. "A crisis in the history of our country is certainly upon us," B. H. Carroll declared, but he also asked, "How shall we meet it? The opportunity of a lifetime is before us. How shall we use it?"[58] Men such as Carroll, the pioneers of the clerical culture, did not reject the premise of widespread spiritual decay. In fact, they rooted their arguments in the assumptions of crisis. Throughout the making of the Bible Belt, Carroll and his clerical allies would draw their commission from their unease. Pilgrims need the wilderness. Crisis opened despairing Christians to the possibilities of an activist faith. It created opportunities for a new generation of activists eager to engage the public sphere. If it was the world that diminished them, then it would be the world that would empower them.

George Truett, the Baptist leader, later showed how the crisis could spur action. "In our great country," he said in 1911, "the social world is filled with frivolities and vanities, and the business world crowded with dishonesties, and the political world bathed with graft, and the religious world mocked by formalism that is never to bring Christ's people to their knees." By 1911 his recitation of the spiritual crisis would have shocked no one. His words, well worn by that point, still roused his contemporaries to action. "Oh," he said, "this is no time, my brothers for that negative complacent soft-going optimism which says soothingly, 'All is well.' But what have I said this for? To chant a dirge? No, no. To sound out a jeremiad? No. But to beat a charge."[59] Clerics learned to use the assumptions of crisis to stimulate a publicly active and politically engaged religion. To do so they would discover the potency of moral reform—particularly that most alluring of crusades, prohibition—but their engagement, and the working out of a specific clerical culture, depended on and grew out of the spiritual crisis.

Speaking before a crowd at the Young Men's Christian Association in Waco, in 1893, J. B. Cranfill proposed an escape from the age's spiritual torpor. "It isn't always wise to carry our burdens on our hearts," Cranfill said, "It isn't wise to haunt the darkened corners and court the lowering clouds and listen for the mutterings of the storm." However deep the age's moral and spiritual pallor, the self-proclaimed neurasthenic chastised his audience for surrendering to anxiety and retreating so willingly into helplessness. "It is far better," he said, "to look up for the silvery light of the stars and listen and catch the paeans of joy and praise, to cast away the mold of sadness and sorrow on our heart that there may rest on it the song of the nightingale and the music of birds." Cranfill urged his listeners to rise anew. "Brother," he said, "if you are living in a graveyard, come out."[60]

Religious citizens, Cranfill said, had the power to exile the psychological tyranny of the spiritual crisis. Instead of languishing, they could act. "The men of this world, whose tread have caused the earth to vibrate, the men of this world," he said, "have made chances for themselves." Cranfill believed religious Texans had two choices: they could turn backward or they could look forward. Backward meant turning away from society, retreating into the sanctuary of nostalgia, and lamenting the cruel developments that conspired to denigrate religion. According to Cranfill, that choice only would breed a chain of sorrow. The present generation would look backward their entire lives and ultimately regret that it had done nothing. Cranfill recalled Edward Bellamy's sensational 1888 novel *Looking Backward*, in which a time-traveling American visits a utopic year 2000 and, "looking backward," finally perceives the barbaric cruelties of his own age. If the righteous consign themselves to inaction, Cranfill said, their grandchildren "will discuss the brutality of an age when license was the pathway to hell." Cranfill enjoined his listeners. "Will you look forward with me to a time when those children's children of ours will say, 'How could it be that my fathers, . . . in the meridian splendor of their glory, licensed in that wonderful country . . . 240,000 barrooms, the only business of which was to invite young men . . . unto death and unto hell?'"[61]

FIGURE 3.1 Baptist leader J. B. Cranfill, ca. 1916.
Source: Dr. J. B. Cranfill's Chronicle (New York: Fleming H. Revell Company, 1916), ii.

Instead of conceding the field, ministers and church members could fight. They could challenge the wickedness of the world and reap the reward of righteousness. And what a reward it would be. They could finally find the soul-comforting satisfaction that had eluded a generation. At the end of the battle, Cranfill said, "You shall look across the border into the other land and grasp the hand of a Redeemer." The apostles of clericalism promised that any who took the crusade would find harmony with God. More immediately, they promised salvation from the miseries of crisis. The noxious haze of anxiety would lift, and a flood of comfort and relief would wash over the land. "Looking forward to a time when all that here has been lost shall then be gained," Cranfill said, "oh, will you look forward tonight to a redeemed nation, to a millennial splendor." Such an intoxicating notion thrust religious Texans passionately and unapologetically into the world.[62]

Although the young Morris Sheppard seemed to be inviting his young audience to despair in 1896, the future "Father of National Prohibition" knew how to harness the crisis for positive action. The clerical movement depended on it. For every dread warning that "disaster frowns upon the brow of the future," Sheppard would add his logical addendum: the times therefore demanded action. He recognized, for instance, "the supreme necessity for some influence that would give moral force and efficacy to the impulses and ambitions of youth."[63] Young Americans could be spared, he said, but only if church leaders would "implant in his soul a purity of purpose and a morality of principal that enables him to stand out against the corruption of his time like a great white column against the blackness of an approaching storm."[64] But they had to have a worldly cause. Sheppard would find his in prohibition.

The anti-liquor crusade would become for Sheppard and the broader clerical movement, according to his metaphor, their great white column. As a United States congressman and later a United States senator, Sheppard devoted himself to the fight against liquor. And throughout his long career in defense of prohibition and progressive Christian nationalism, Sheppard spoke the language of spiritual crisis and clerical redemption fluently. "The field for His labor is wide and fallow," Sheppard had said, and "it offers the most brilliant and illiminable possibilities." If problems loomed, they were "problems which must be met and mastered by the young men and women of this generation."[65]

Methodist apostate J. D. Shaw meanwhile depicted the clergy as reeling in desperation. He said the religious establishment foresaw its fate "but just what to do about it is a problem they know not how to solve."[66] In the coming years he would echo common cries that moral reform was a political crutch for a fading faith, a way to enforce publicly what it no longer could privately. Perhaps he was right. In prohibition and other reforms, clerics exulted in their pursuit of righteousness. Fighting against liquor and a hostile world allowed clerics the means to play martyrs without paying the martyr's price. By forever battling against rapacious maladies, crusaders redefined themselves as heroes and saviors, and not impotent, decaying, or anachronistic relics of some bygone age. They found a cause and a language that opened up a world with stakes, that was direct, and visceral. The trick would be to convince the bulk of religious Texans that prohibition was the appropriate antidote for crisis.

Clerics sought multiple targets, but attacking public immorality—a monumental shift that, the following chapters will argue, was achieved through great internal strife and controversy—promised ministers the public status and self-identity they craved. By engaging the saloons and the theaters and the dance halls, Methodist George Rankin believed a pastor's "work counted for something as an asset in the community." Without sinking into the depths of crisis, he could never have felt the void in the first place. And without venturing into worldly reform, he could have never filled it. He would have languished within the church, building up congregations, winning donations, and achieving ever-more prestigious appointments but, like William Carey Crane, finding only soul-crushing feelings of futility. Instead, moral reform added consequence to a suddenly inconsequential-seeming life. Evangelical Texans felt adrift in the world and wanted some anchoring force to ground them and provide a stake in a moral future. William Crane felt beleaguered, always on the verge of success but never successful. He felt the crisis and had the ambition to challenge it, but he never found the means to conquer it, to channel it constructively. Rankin and others did. As Rankin put it, by pursuing reform the preacher found "His influence and personal presence stood for something, even outside his own congregation. He was a dominant factor in the forces that enter into the moral, the civic, and the religious life of the people."[67] In the battle against sin, desperate clergymen transcended the limits of their pulpits and redefined themselves as society's saviors. They found an enemy as vulgar and corrupt as they were pure and righteous. "In fighting the liquor traffic," Cranfill wrote in 1916, "I have learned what it means to combat the most gigantic and soul-less corrupting agency this land has ever known."[68] The future of southern religion, indeed American religion, depended on such men craving that titanic struggle and finding the means to wage it. As they did, their perceptions of weakness lead to the realities of strength.

Although evangelical Texans protested the onslaughts of modern life, and declared in a great chorus voice their weakness and vulnerability, their confrontations with the modern world only bolstered their political and cultural power.[69] Threats didn't weaken the churches, they invigorated them. In the face of hostility, real and imagined, evangelical Texans closed ranks. Their identity as religious persons suddenly carried new imperatives. They no longer went to church, volunteered, and donated to support mere institutions: they participated in church life to bolster God's beleaguered kingdom. If there had been no crisis or threat to religion, congregations would have risked routine and complacency. Instead, Texans innovated.

Between the time that prohibition suffered defeats in the 1880s and the time that it triumphed in the 1910s, the major strands of white evangelical religion in Texas and the broader South shifted their orientation and their methods and their scope. Private and personal became public and political. Suddenly, the religious world believed that public respect could not be shared. Clerical leaders made new claims to public respectability, influence, and relevance. As historian Beth Barton Schweiger has hinted, claims to lost respect and influence were in many ways "really just a matter of asking a different question."[70] Suddenly religious leaders clamored for roles they had never before played. Southern clergymen did not lose some mythical centrality to public life—they never had it in the first place. Their distance from the world had been a mark of distinction, a point of pride. But now, seemingly menaced on all sides, religious leaders could no longer retire into isolation. Instead, they demanded the world. And not only to be a part of it, but to conquer it.

In the tears of neurasthenic bodies, the complaints of anxious clergymen, and the fearful reports of denominational bodies, a sense of crisis spoke to a population wrenched by change and desperate for deliverance. A new corps of evangelical Texans offered them action. Senator Morris Sheppard and the state's religious establishment committed themselves to such issues as prohibition, they said, so that "man will rise . . . again to be crowned with the confidence and approbation of Almighty God."[71] But if they had never fallen, they could never have arisen. Their dissatisfaction drew them toward reform and compelled them to reclaim the world. The rising tide of clericalism attracted all those religious Texans resentful of the churches' seeming devaluation. A broader cultural vision still needed to be preached and built and disseminated, but the spiritual crisis had planted the seeds of that great harvest. With religious wishes and dreams institutionalized in a vast and powerful bureaucracy, all their longing could be mobilized into a great crusade. By the 1920s, the cause of Christ had made such great strides in the South that, in the words of Edward Ayers, southern churches "established a presence in private and public life they had never known before."[72] The crisis helped account for that transformation. It proved but one step on that long road from what historians have called "dissent to dominance"[73] or "alienation to influence,"[74] but that first step led southerners headlong into the Bible Belt.

4

The Road to the Bible Belt

MOBILIZING THE GODLY

IN THE SPRING of 1885, a Baptist preacher named Sumner Callaway read a sermon before a ministers' conference in Belton, Texas. "The hold which Satan has upon the world," he said, "is so thorough and all-pervasive, so enters into the ramifications of the life of society, that whatever would break his grasp must be well nigh omnipotent, must indeed be all-powerful." Callaway not only cataloged the accumulated fears and anxieties that preyed upon southern religious leaders, he identified southern churches as potential saviors. Callaway realized that pulpits contained enormous influence and that it was up to preachers to wield it. "She [the church] is rendered the more powerful or is enfeebled according to the use made of her," he said. The church, he argued, could be a static and stale institution or a dynamic base for world-saving activism. It was up to the religious leaders to decide.

Callaway knew that religious leaders had a role to play in society, but his vision of activism lacked the clerical innovations soon to transform southern religion. When he told the gathering, "The church of Christ is the grand instrumentality through which the world is to be freed from the domination of Satan," Callaway could only propose the soul-saving evangelicalism of past generations. Whereas clerics would later speak of religious leaders as shock troops in a moral war, Callaway still thought of them as "towers and buttresses." He identified religion's primary strength in conversion, in born-again members becoming "the light of the world," and in preachers proclaiming the Gospel. His social vision centered around individuals, he said, "for the character of the body will be fixed by that of the individuals composing it."[1]

Callaway wanted to solve a new generation's crisis with the old generation's solutions. His sermon embodied the anxieties of the age and illuminated a growing awareness that the churches had it within themselves to conquer the age's evils, but the meager returns of old-time methods and the enduring obscurity of their champions testified to their growing inadequacy. Callaway was no leader, and he proposed no practical program for the churches' salvation. It would fall instead on a cohort of activists to realize that clerical fortunes could be improved through the construction of new and powerful denominational bureaucracies, the pursuit of moral reform, and an assault on anticlerical assumptions. Activists would learn, for instance, that if they could reclaim historical memory and forever abolish hostile associations with witch trials and inquisitions, they could convince more and more Texans that government could—and should—be run along religious lines. Moral reform was only the most public manifestation of a brewing clerical movement composed of various enterprises that mobilized religious Texans and enabled the construction of the Bible Belt.

Although the towering Baptist leader B. H. Carroll won overwhelming public rebuke in his two forays into prohibition politics, he had nevertheless captured the imagination of anxious religious Texans. As they grew disaffected with old-time methods, they increasingly turned to Carroll's brand of fighting faith. More than any other figure, Carroll taught a generation of religious Texans to empower themselves by moving beyond traditional evangelistic concerns. He taught them to fight, and he led by example. From his pulpit at the First Baptist Church of Waco, Carroll fashioned the elements of the clerical crusade. As early as the 1870s, before the turbulent decades of prohibition politics, Carroll was engaged in moral warfare.

Reflecting the larger religious evolution from temperance to prohibition, Carroll began with his own congregation. He passed a series of temperance resolutions at First Baptist. The results encouraged his turn to moral reform. His church found itself united in moral purpose. The *Texas Baptist and Herald* reported, "The church in Waco is much stronger in its own self-respect, and has a much larger share of respect from the community, than before." These were the essential ingredients for the coming clerical crusade. And the congregation loved him for supplying them. "No pastor in the State, probably," the *Herald* reported, "has a stronger and more universal hold on the respect and affections of his people than Bro. Carroll."[2] Carroll's congregational work establish a model for the political battles of the following decades. He would set moral boundaries, place himself and any willing supporters on what he deemed the right side, attack everything he imagined to be on the wrong side, and reap professional and reputational rewards.

Carroll slowly freed himself from traditional religious constraints. He wrote in his personal notebook, "I am a preacher, but I am none the less a citizen." And being a citizen carried with it responsibilities, responsibilities not at odds with the pulpit. "My being a preacher," he wrote, "does not seal my lips & paralyze my arm."[3] Although Carroll's efforts in 1885 and 1887 collapsed under the weight of a hostile public, they also invigorated many in the churches. Moral reform supplied the remedy for their spiritual crisis.

The embattled victims of the spiritual crisis longed for public respect and hungered for social significance. Newly professionalized preachers fought for prominent positions that satisfied these cravings. They wanted to matter. Methodist minister Samuel Blackwell, lobbying for a new appointment, wanted "a place of consequence" and pled with elders to know "something of the standing I was to be accorded in the new field."[4] The Baptist leader J. B. Cranfill's remembrances are full of concerns about his public standing. From the time his father installed new metal bearings on his family's wooden wagon to his brief tenure running a general store, Cranfill obsessed over "prestige" and his "standing in the community."[5] The respect accorded a preacher became the measure of godliness. Methodist George Rankin distinguished holy North Texas from pagan South Texas because, in the latter, preachers were "not generally respected."[6] Because increasing membership, the growing number of churches, and expanding denominations did little to undermine the clerical perceptions that Texas and the broader South were in the midst of an acute spiritual crisis, activists would have to find ways to magnify their public standing.

"Never in Waco before was a community so interested in a church matter," Carroll noted after first proposing his temperance resolutions in the 1870s. "The attendant congregation was very large."[7] Temperance, and later prohibition, could lure wayward Texans back to church. Those already there would find a spiritual confidence that had eluded them. When the resolutions passed, Carroll noted the unprecedented "manifestations of sublime Christianity." At once, Carroll and his congregation found themselves perfectly "in harmony with the principles of Christianity."[8] The satisfaction proved impossible to ignore. But the turn to a larger movement did not only represent a transformative shift in the religious history of the South; it wrenched American history along a new path.

Whether targeting a local saloon or promoting a constitutional amendment, the religious push for prohibition in the South represented a departure from historical patterns and signaled a new era in southern religion. For generations, southern evangelicals lived in their own moral fiefdoms.

Denominations disciplined their own members (always a minority of the population) for various improprieties but hardly felt obligated or entitled to address the lives of nonmembers, let alone through interventions in public life. They certainly never relied on governments or laws. As historian Ted Ownby put it, the southern church "kept itself pure and left the rest of the world to its hellish ways."[9] Prohibition and the broader turn to moral reform changed all that.

Although most of the energy expended in the postbellum moral crusades went into the fight for prohibition, southern evangelicals never limited themselves to liquor and saloons. At various times and with varying intensities, they targeted prostitution, gambling, the theater, the circus, Sabbath-breaking, lotteries, obscenity, tobacco, dancing, card games, animal fighting, boxing, baseball, and a host of other public amusements. Although their critics claimed otherwise, the alarms they raised against these and other alleged vices were never cynical or calculated, or even illogical. The years after Reconstruction had witnessed the rapid rise in popular amusements and popular culture. The expansion of cities, availability of mass transportation, and rise of mass media conspired to bring these secular distractions to the masses and challenged the evangelicals' carefully constructed world.[10] Some of the amusements were simply competition—churchgoers might forgo Sunday services and attend baseball games instead, for instance. But the campaigns against sin and recreation were always about something more than that. Theaters and saloons encouraged a leisurely ethic that was at odds with the culture of evangelical religion. Drinking and dancing were narrow-minded self-indulgences. Professional sports and other diversions appealed to the base instincts of aggression and competition. At a moment when religious southerners felt besieged, on came the saloon to embody all of the soul-destroying sins of the secular world. When young preachers arrived at their new charges eager to save souls, they were confronted with temples of sin and iniquity instead. The young Methodist C. N. Morton, newly arrived in the lumber town of Caro, Texas, complained that he had found a sluggish congregation and a booming skating rink. But if the moral crusades were a response to the proliferation of these secular forms of recreation and amusement, they originated in a shifting religious world of denominations and professionalization.

Evangelical denominations expanded in scope and scale in the years after the Civil War. Denominational committees, boards, publications, schools, and associations offered new routes along which to pursue clerical power and prestige. Ambitious, striving clergymen could advance themselves professionally by winning pulpits in ever-larger and ever-wealthier urban churches. The story's details changed from locale to locale, but in its broad outlines the Texas chapter shares the regional and national story: evangelical religion emerged from small and independent rural congregations with part-time pastors into an immense and ordered bureaucracy led by religious professionals in prominent urban pulpits and denominational offices.

Congregations had been at the center of southern religious life before the Civil War. Evangelicals jealously guarded their independence and spurned the rigid strictures of distant organizations. Many believed "churchianity" sapped spiritual vigor and had poisoned the stale old, stale churches that were supposedly decaying all along the eastern seaboard. Southern Baptists, for instance, explicitly sent "messengers," not delegates, to associational meetings and general conventions.[11] Over the course of the nineteenth century, however, lured by respectability and compelled by the age's mania for bureaucratic organization, denominational superstructures arose and reoriented church life away from local congregations.

At the end of the century, Baylor University's president Rufus Burleson reflected on his denomination's phenomenal expansion. "I have seen the little band of 1900 Baptists become a grand army of nearly 300,000," the aging shepherd proudly proclaimed. The other dominant Texas evangelical denomination, the Methodists, celebrated the same. One Methodist minister wrote, "[W]e are in the midst of an era of Church Building—the greatest ever known in our history."[12] The smaller Texas denominations, such as the Presbyterians and the holiness churches, reported similar trends.

Once afterthoughts, evangelical denominations became actors in the ongoing drama of American religion. Although religious Texans worried about the corruptions of the modern world, they willingly employed modern means to build denominational structures.[13] Religious bureaucracies often appeared little different from the corporate versions arising across the country. An eminent public relations expert reminded Dallas readers that "churches are business institutions" and preachers were professionals. He believed "every minister should be trained to business," should earn the position just "as the bookkeeper earns his right to keep books, as the doctor earns his right to practice, and as the salesman earns his right to represent his goods."[14] Religion was a business, and business was booming.

After the Civil War, the denomination offered an immediate path to prestige and power. Ambition, a key ingredient in the clerical culture, first manifested itself here, in the organizational world of evangelical religion. No sooner did denominational construction invigorate clerics than it plunged them into competition. New bureaucracies offered a multitude of roles and positions for religious strivers in which, far from the eye of those in the pews, would-be religious lords intrigued and maneuvered against one another.

The bitter contest for advancement played out most vividly among the Texas Methodists, who empowered their denominational bureaucracy to direct careers and decide appointments. Elijah Shettles, a reformed drunkard, dedicated bibliophile, and committed prohibitionist, served briefly as a presiding elder for a series of circuits—geographic clusters of Methodist churches ministered by itinerant clergy—in north-central Texas during the first years of the twentieth century. His brief tenure awoke him to the ugly reality of church appointments.

Ministers complained to Shettles about their appointments. C. E. Simpson languished several years on rural circuits before departing for another conference. "I loved the old Texas Conference as [I] can never love another," he told Shettles in 1907. "Fourteen years of my best life and blood was cheerfully given to her," he said. For his toil he had bounced from circuit to circuit, moving sideways in the church hierarchy. "If I had had any encouragement I never would [have] transferred," he explained, "but I can't help but feel that I was not appreciated." As his career stalled, his pride ate away at him. "The thing that hurt me most was to see others that were no better preacher than I, and had not done any more for the church than I had done, promoted and I was left to take what remained after the others had been provided for." Simpson complained of cliques and favoritism.[15] He was not alone.

"I am just about as much disgusted as I ever was in my life," wrote the pastor of Marlin's First Methodist Church, I. F. Betts, on hearing of a colleague's transfer in 1910. "It is the same old song: the bishop has fallen into the hands of the politicians."[16] Another Methodist minister had vented the same frustrations three years before. Samuel Blackwell had lobbied Shettles for a favorable appointment in his conference. "I have been in the itinerancy of grace," he wrote. "I have served hard circuits and have worked and toiled in season and out of season." He had slowly advanced in his home conference and now held "a good station," but cliques conspired against him. "This is my 9th year," he wrote, "and I have had no "friends at Court" to "boost" my case."[17] He hoped Shettles could transcend the profession's pettiness, but others accused Shettles of favoritism, too.

Sometime before 1905, G. E. Cameron completed his second year as station preacher in Henderson. He reported regular growth and took pride that "my people want me back." He expected to serve a third year in Henderson. He was reassigned, however, "to almost no appointment." He accused two elders, Shettles and C. R. Lamar, of conspiring to remove him from

Henderson to make room for an acquaintance of theirs. "I have felt just as I use to when a boy and a larger boy would impose on me just because he could and had the advantage," Cameron wrote. He called his elder a "political trickster" who "would kill anybody to care for himself and his cherished friend." When Shettles received Cameron's complaint, he deflected the criticism and hoped Cameron would take the "joy that comes from a consciousness of duty faithfully performed."[18] Few surrendered to such satisfactions. Many passed-over preachers lamented that politics had entered their profession. The need for constant professional striving disenchanted the losers and the languishers, who were left to decay on the margins of the denominations, while the most ambitious and politically shrewd held positions of authority. Professionalization burdened the religious leadership with perhaps unseemly vanities and infected every level of the hierarchy with resentments. And if local preachers gave themselves over to these feelings, so, too, did elders and bishops.

Annual and general meetings played out like political conventions. Amid the business of religion, attendees eager to win denominational offices sowed suspicions, traded favors, and glad-handed each other to win delegates. When Bishop Seth Ward died in 1909, speculation and rumor shot through the state's professional Methodists. The phrase "I hear" commonly prefaced some worried speculation that a faction or clique stood ready to overtake the proceedings and elect a particular slate of candidates. Referring to some unknown cabal, Isaac Z. T. Morris, one of Texas's pioneer preachers, decried an upcoming general conference in 1910. "I hear that they are combining delegates from Texas and they are going to stand united . . . [T]hey are going over there to take everything in sight."[19] C. A. Tower feared that the elderly Bishop Joseph Key would take advantage of the vacuum Ward's death had created to purge a clique of emerging clerics. "I have it on good authority," he wrote, "that he is going to reinstate the old regime in our Conference." He warned fellow presiding elder Elijah Shettles. "I hear," he wrote, "that Bishop Key intends to bring on a cyclone among the elders." He fretted. He, Shettles, and all the young striving blood in the conference could be finished. Luckily, they survived.[20]

During the first decade of the twentieth century, George Rankin established himself as the leading prohibitionist among the Texas Methodists and one of the denomination's most ambitious professional climbers. At the same convention, in 1910, Rankin made a power play for the open bishop's office. Word of his maneuvering spread. Many feared Rankin could wrangle enough delegates to dominate the convention. Rural pastor Jesse Lee said, "Rankin is mixed up with petty politicks; and [referring to Senator Joseph Bailey, the controversial political kingmaker of Texas] has played the game with a Joe Baily [*sic*] hand." Wary Methodists believed that if Rankin won enough support, he could succeed in becoming a bishop. "There could be no greater calmity [*sic*]," Lee and, revealing the jealousies and struggles that were rife in the conference, warned, "woe-betide some of us fellows that have not bowed at his shrine."[21] When Edwin Mouzon ascended to the office as a compromise candidate, a wave of relief swept over Rankin's opponents. Suddenly, the petty politics of men became divine planning. "God was in it all," Jesse Lee said. I. Z. T. Morris added, "I regard it as one of the greatest demonstrations of the hand of God in the management of the affairs of the church as I ever saw." It was a rare rebuff to a leading cleric. But for Rankin, such setbacks were few.

Although he failed in his quest to become bishop, George Rankin achieved plenty of other denominational successes. After several successful church-building and sin-fighting stints in Kansas City and Houston, Rankin won an appointment to one of the state's most prestigious pulpits: the First Methodist Church of Dallas. Rankin recalled the chilly reception he received when he was introduced to the members of the North Texas Conference. "Individually many of the members of the conference extended to me a cordial welcome to their fellowship, but generally speaking my reception was a trifle cool and formal. As a body they were not prepared to accept me with open arms." Rankin asked why and reported a fellow minister responding, "Why should I thus welcome you to our conference and to the first appointment in it, when you know as well as I do that I ought to be in that pulpit myself!" Rankin understood then the consequences of the hypercompetitive world of the striving clergymen. "Transfers for the leading appointments in the conference were not overwhelmingly popular in those days," he concluded simply.[22]

Amid the competitive frenzy, religious strivers utilized all possible means of self-promotion. While personal connections and denominational politicking greased the wheels of advancement, the engine remained church growth: increased members, upgraded buildings, and surging funds. The expansion of the denominations burdened ambitious religious leaders with expectations of constant growth. If ministers still claimed to preach "the old-time gospel," the most successful incorporated new-time methods of organization and management. In 1907, referring to a recent transfer, Methodist bishop Edwin D. Mouzon laid bare what the twentieth-century denomination valued most: "Johnson [the transfer] is a fine man, fine mixer, good preacher, good money-getter. Fact is it was his success as a money-getter that led to his transfer. He did so well at Coronal [Institute], raising about $33,000 last year that Southwestern wanted him."[23] Mouzon spoke more like an organization man than a spiritual shepherd because, in many ways, he was. The new religious order rewarded the church builder rather than the soul saver. And, in return, the church builder expected to steadily advance to increasingly prestigious (and well-paid) appointments. J. B. Cranfill heaped praise on a Baptist colleague, John Boyet, of Honey Grove. "He has had few equals in the Texas Baptist pulpit," Cranfill wrote, and yet he remained in an otherwise small and insignificant pulpit. "I have often wondered why Boyet did not bloom out in to a metropolitan pastorate."[24]

A striving preacher expected to travel the path from small and insignificant rural pastorates to large and influential urban "first churches," in the way that B. H. Carroll presided over Waco's First Baptist or George Rankin over Dallas's First Methodist. Such pulpits gave their preachers prestige. J. Frank Norris, for instance, would preside over Fort Worth's First Baptist (and be able to boast that it was the largest church in the United States—not the last time Texas would claim the distinction) and George Truett would pastor Dallas's First Baptist.[25] But the denomination opened other paths as well. Cranfill, Carroll's self-proclaimed protégé, was only intermittently a preacher; it was through the editorship of the *Baptist Standard* that he exercised his considerable influence. Meanwhile, at the denominational colleges, men such as Rufus Burleson held sway over an intellectual realm that was seeping ever more into the daily life of the denominations.

A maze of possibilities for denominational advancement elevated the ambitious and furnished them with the tools of influence. At the same time, internal denominational striving laid bare a new ethos of advancement, the do-whatever-it-takes-to-triumph creed of a new clerical generation. But if the denominations unleashed bitter infighting and strong egos, they also offered beleaguered religious leaders new opportunities to exert themselves. A preacher was no longer only a preacher, he was an organization man, an editor, a publisher, a striver, an organizer. He was a well-oiled machine of advancement. And he would take the churches with him.

The ambition that thrust many into the denominations often thrust them into the world as well: clerical labor flowed across cloistered denominational worlds into the broader regional culture. As the case of George Rankin demonstrates, success in the public arena could mean success in the denomination. His efforts in both worlds were linked, and his denominational status rose in concert with his work as a moral reformer. Throughout the coming decades, the most aggressive political activists were typically the most ambitious denominational workers. Religious editors were often the most vocal in politics. Men like Rankin and Carroll, holding some of their denomination's best appointments, were protoypical in, travelling along the twinned paths of worldly activism and denominational success. Crusading helped them professionally: moral reform sparked excitement and built up congregations, sometimes superseding the need for more sordid denominational maneuvering. They could build up churches—and their reputations—by rallying around public issues.

Religious education offered one early example of how denominational work could intersect with public concerns. As early as the 1880s, denominational leaders in Texas discovered the power of religious education. A sporadic prelude to larger political battles, educational concerns nevertheless proved an early and recurrent site of struggle and self-assertion for religious leaders.[26] A commitment to education united religious Texans without the rancor and controversy of politics. Throughout late nineteenth and early twentieth centuries, religious Texans never abandoned their faith in religious education. They lauded the schools as sites of religious evangelism that could pay future dividends. The denominational secondary school, said Bishop Mouzon, in 1913, "creates its own patronage in a large measure. It brings Christian education with its lofty ideals to boys and girls who, without it would never have come under their power."[27] J. M. Carroll agreed, "Whoever awakens, develops & directs the ambition gets the child."[28] Leaders praised Christian education for creating believers and inculcating Christian values. It was no surprise, then, that the simultaneous expansion of secular public schools and the establishment of a secular public university in Texas unsettled many.

In 1881, Methodists from the East Texas Conference joined their evangelical brethren in condemning new rules imposed by the State Board of Education that cut funding for public schools with opening or closing prayers or scripture reading. The Methodists said the board "pandered to the infidel, the atheist, the dregs of society." One schoolmaster urged that "Texas, with all the wealth of her present and the promise of her future, be not bound to the destroying wheels of infidelity and sin."[29] The new rules wound their way through the courts and formed a part of the brewing clerical crusade. But no issue inflamed the churches more than the establishment of the University of Texas in 1883. It was too much for some religious Texans. Formerly humble church leaders lashed out against public education.

J. M. Carroll declared "all education incomplete, onesided & hurtful without Christian education."[30] Echoing a common refrain, Burleson, as president of the denominational Waco University,[31] decried the state's embrace of public schools. He claimed the system was "being manipulated by Infidels & Godless men for the ruin of our Children & Texas." In many parts of Texas, he said, educators were disregarding the Bible and schools were disallowing prayer. Christian taxpayers, Burleson wrote, supported a system that was "prayerless, Christless, and Godless." He called it "mournful & appalling" and pled for all good Christians "to rescue our Grand system of public education from Infidels & wicked & narrow-minded men."[32] William Carey Crane, Burleson's counterpart at Baylor University in Independence, particularly resented the establishment of the University of Texas. He called the inevitable institutionalization of "rationalism" as "a blow at faith" that "aims to undermine all religion and the Christian religion especially."[33]

Both Crane and Burleson, sought to rescue "youth just emerging from its swaddling cloths and stretching out its free arms."[34] Education bridged the gap between the anticlerical church leaders of the nineteenth century and the clerical champions of the twentieth.[35] It was no accident, for instance, that B. H. Carroll said "the school room is the battle-field."[36] Public education would linger long after prohibition as an issue in American religious politics, and although it never conjured the same vivid fears as saloons and liquor dealers, it nevertheless galvanized many southern evangelicals. Concerns over public schooling fueled the expansion of Sunday schools and the building of denominational colleges, institutions that incubated a growing clerical caste and disseminated Christian values to a broader population.

The late nineteenth century and early twentieth centuries became the era of the denominational college. When the struggling Baylor University merged with Waco University, it was on its way to becoming the largest Baptist university in the world. The Methodists founded Southern Methodist University in Dallas, in 1911, fulfilling Rev. Nathan Powell's dream of launching "something big."[37] The Christian Church took control of Add-Ran College in 1889, slowly expanded it, and by 1911, had relocated to a new Fort Worth campus, rechristened the school Texas Christian University, and established a sizable endowment.[38] A host of smaller denominational schools supplemented these flagship schools with campuses across the state. Meanwhile, new theological schools produced new professional clergymen. The Austin Presbyterian Theological Seminary opened in 1902. Southern Methodist University established its own seminary, the official theological school for all Southern Methodist Conferences west of the Mississippi.[39] In a shrewd bureaucratic maneuver, the ubiquitous B. H. Carroll founded Southwestern Baptist Theological Seminary in 1908, which went on to become one of the largest seminaries in the world.[40] Each of these schools endowed the leaders of the clerical crusade. From lofty perches, ensconced in respectability, and freed from the petty minutiae of congregational life, academic churchmen found an institutional base for the culture of clericalism. J. M. Carroll declared denominational schools vital to "the greater awakening of our people & the further upbuilding of our cause."[41] Schools opened religious Texans to the possibilities of their denominations and to the value of concerted and organized efforts in pursuit of religious empowerment. Christian education boomed.

The triumph of clericalism, however, was as much a victory of ideas as it was of politics or offices or organizations. The college builders recognized that. And so, before they ever won political battles, the clerics waged and won wars over conceptions of history, government, and theology. Religious publications—denominational newspapers and periodicals, religious histories, clerical autobiographies, and printed sermons—fueled the clerical insurgency. J. B. Cranfill recalled an illustrative example from his own family. His cousin Sam "by all human environments and training, should have been a Baptist." Cranfill's whole family was Baptist. Even their acquaintances were Baptists. "Cousin Sam" *should* have been Baptist. But he was a Methodist. Sam's father (Cranfill's uncle) once met the famed Methodist preacher Lorenzo Dow and, impressed, subscribed to a paper Dow edited. Sam read the various editions scattered around the house as a boy and was converted. "The paper made him a Methodist," Cranfill said. "The only Methodist Cranfill I have ever known," he argued, served as an "object lesson" in the power of the denominational press. It made Cranfill "a persistent friend of Baptist and Christian literature." He put it plainly: "The man who writes the books and edits the papers of a people is the influential man."[42]

In the early years of prohibition agitation in Texas, Cranfill edited the *Advance,* first in Gatesville and then in Waco. The paper supplied a growing subscription base with weekly articles and editorials decrying the evils of liquor. Following its success, Cranfill purchased the fledgling *Western Baptist,* rechristened it the *Texas Baptist Standard,* and rescued it from near-bankruptcy. Through shrewd maneuvering, Cranfill crushed Samuel Hayden's rival *Texas Baptist and Herald*. By 1894, the *Standard* claimed eighteen thousand subscribers. A decade later, in 1904, it had thirty thousand. The paper was valued at more than $25,000.[43] It had an unquantifiable quality, as well: it wielded influence.

For sheer impact, no endeavor in Cranfill's life matched having editorial control of the *Standard*. As far as "the production of work of enduring value," Cranfill said, no other positions "carry with me a feather's weight." He called it "the happiest and most useful of my life's work."[44] In 1904, he cashed out, pocketing $10,000, a small fortune. Although he never lamented his new-found wealth, he forever regretted relinquishing "the greatest throne of power and service with which my life has ever been blessed."[45] Cranfill wasn't wrong. His experience at the *Standard*, and the experience of his counterparts at the other state papers, illustrated the power of the denominational newspaper in shaping the culture of religious Texans.

Newspapers glued scattered denominational worlds together. By the turn of the century, all major state denominations had joined their various news outlets into single statewide publications. All across Texas, religious readers consumed the same news, the same editorials, and the same emerging vision of the world. No other forum united Texas churches so effectively. Annual meetings and interpersonal correspondence offered only fleeting bonds—the newspaper bound the state denominations together every week.

The men behind these papers became giants. Cranfill, his successor James Bruton Gambrell, and their Methodist counterpart, the wrangling, rambunctious George Rankin, achieved unprecedented influence. If the heads of denominational colleges shaped the minds of their students, religious editors reached entire denominations. Many articles even appeared in the secular press, too. No other religious office reached into more homes: by 1911, the *Baptist Standard*, for instance, claimed a circulation of 75,000.[46] Never before had a handful of religious Texans spoken with such amplified voices. From their lofty perches, they broadcast the clerical culture across the state. They became Texas's most influential religious figures. And to a man—they were always men—they encouraged the coming crusade.

The denominations also produced a bumper crop of biographies, histories, and theologies. Professional clergymen, now reared in theological schools and freed from having second jobs, devoted themselves to reading and writing. A growing audience harvested the memories of the old timers, the opinions of the firebrands, and the myths of the hagiographers. Nostalgic denominational histories and biographies (and, as testament to the clerics' self-importance, autobiographies) steeped anxious religious Texans in a raw but noble tradition of perseverance, righteousness, and activism.[47] Thriving publishing houses, such as the Methodists' branch of Smith and Lamar in Dallas, flooded the market with religious literature. Suddenly readers everywhere could consume the tales of pioneering preachers or the invigorating Sunday sermons delivered by clerical champions. Some, such as Edwin Mouzon, published dozens of books in their lifetimes.

Contradicting Menckenesque stereotypes of clergymen as rural hicks or irrational mystics, religious scholars swelled the ranks of the early clerical movement. Methodist Claude Carr Cody, dean of the College of Liberal Arts at Southwestern University, in Georgetown, worked on a grand history of the state's Methodists and believed, as he told a clerical ally in 1911, that "the sooner it is done the better it will be for Texas Methodism."[48] As went history, he realized, so went the denomination.

To win the political war over prohibition, religious leaders had to fight larger battles over history, government, and religion. Christian activists, looking for a path into the public sphere, could not merely navigate around the anticlerical culture, they had to conquer it and create their own alternative. Only by crafting a clerical countervision potent enough to challenge and overcome the crippling anticlericalism could they emerge victorious. Over several decades, they did so. Most Texans still clung to their well-worn anticlerical beliefs, bolstered by deep-seated visions of witch burnings and longings for secular government. But by the late nineteenth century, a community of religious activists had nurtured and then spread their own innovative vision. Anxious to shepherd prohibition through the political system, they also wanted more. They wanted a larger stake in the public life of Texas, the American South, and, ultimately, the entire nation. To that end, and to legitimate their ambitions, the clerical champions created their own usable past, redefined the scope of proper government, and justified their religious beliefs.

In 1872, Homer Thrall published *History of Methodism in Texas*, still perhaps the most authoritative account of the Methodist Church in early Texas. Thrall called his work "an unpretending volume" that "hardly aspires to the dignity of a history" and, time and again, humbly stressed its insularity. He limited his story the struggles of his denomination and rejected any claim that he was writing Texas history. Thrall wrote of personal piety and of bringing souls to Christ, not of wars or politics. The book was an account of conferences, camp meetings, church foundings, and Bible societies. For Thrall and other traditional church leaders, religion was a cloistered world disconnected from its secular surroundings.[49] That Thrall published his history at all, of course, and that it was read widely, sounded the coming of the clerical vision. But Thrall's characteristic humility contrasted with the boastfulness of later religious scholarship.

Zacharius. N. Morrell published his autobiography the same year that Thrall's denominational history appeared. If Thrall's humility aligned him with tradition, Morrell's self-importance foreshadowed the mainstreaming of the clerical vision. Morrell, a pioneering Baptist preacher, rejected Thrall's timidity. He confronted history, Christianized it, and gloried in his triumph. In his account, and in others that would follow, the distance between the spiritual and the temporal narrowed. "My personal history in Texas," Morrell wrote, "is interwoven with the state of society and the rise and progress of civilization and religion." The history of Texas was incomplete without such men as he. "My purpose," he wrote, "has simply been to lay the foundation for the historian."[50] Religious Texans devoured Morrell's unified history of settlement, Texas independence, Indian wars, and other thrilling scenes—all presided over by Morrell. The book went through three printings. The first, of a thousand copies, reportedly sold out in weeks.[51] Baylor University president William Carey Crane, struggling to sustain his infant institution, drew inspiration from the "thrilling scenes depicted by Z. N. Morrell" and urged others to do the same.[52]

In the second half of the nineteenth century, religious activists confronted the past as if, as their elementary pronouncements suggested, for the first time. "Events give character to time," lectured Crane. "Without events years would pass away without lessons; without epochs; dark, black and chaotic." The success or failure of the clerical movement hinged on the ownership of events. During the disastrous political campaigns in the 1880s, men such as B. H. Carroll witnessed firsthand the damage wrought by an anticlerical conception of history. And so, before religious leaders reformed society's morals, they had to revise its past. A new history, they believed, could legitimate their mission, fortify their standing, and lead them to victory. "Hence," Crane said, "we look about us for memorials of passing time and monuments of illustrious deeds."[53]

Religious activists sensed that religion's centrality in the coming order of things depended upon a usable past, and they set about furnishing one.[54] Like Morrell and Thrall, they laid the foundation with the publication of denominational histories, historical journals, biographies of the great evangelists, and their own autobiographies. In 1909, for instance, Methodists formed the Texas Methodist Historical Association with the explicit goal of reemphasizing their denomination's role in Texas history. "In writing the history of a State, it is too often the case that a superficial view is taken of the factors that contributed to its development," wrote Reverend John H. McLean, the association's inaugural president. "The soldier and statesman are sure—but seldom is mention made of the education and formative influences of the pulpit, the religious press, Christian education, and the Christian home."[55] Such works served up an idealized version of the past filled with righteous warriors and pioneering preachers, heroes sufficient to refute and replace anticlerical memories of tyrannical priests and runaway Puritanism. Religious reformers would no longer be historically orphaned, some anachronistic sickness to be

quarantined. Rather, they would be the culmination of history, the fulfill-
ment of a holy lineage. As Senator Sheppard later said, before a group of Texas
Methodists in Texarkana, "the song that ripples on the lips of Clio, muse of
history, is a song that sounds our eternal charge."[56]

As prohibition and other moral reform movements matured, their champions increasingly challenged the anticlerical version of history. "The next fellow who stands on a Texas platform and introduces that ghost of Washington's
day to scare the people away," a prominent prohibitionist, H. A. Ivy, wrote,
"ought to dress himself in knee breeches with buckles, a powdered wig and
other habiliments of colonial times, to enhance the humor of the farce."[57]
Men like Ivy rejected a tainted history of religious corruption, excess, and
oppression. Instead, newly motivated clerics began to articulate their own
ideas. They imagined themselves as participants in a transhistorical movement. They Christianized secular heroes, and they recast the proper boundaries separating church and government.

If the creation of a Christian vision sounds conspiratorial, it was not. New
religious histories were not being crafted in memory factories by conniving
clerics. Rather, they emerged naturally from the anxieties and concerns of
turn-of-the-century religious leaders. The promotion of the Christian vision
inevitably imparted meaning upon the lives of its champions. Angst-ridden
parsons found solace in a simple idea: that they were not worthless, that they
had a role in the world, and that the burdens of their faith dictated action. The
first clerics, in Texas just as in the South and much of the rest of the nation,
rooted themselves in a nascent Christian vision and found comfort there.
Over time, as they acted to effect their clerical dreams, they developed and
expanded their vision to include clearly articulated ideas about history, politics, and faith. These refined ideas were not cynical or duplicitous; instead,
they were the authentic expressions of a new generation of religious leaders.
As they sallied forth into the public realm in pursuit of prohibition and other
moral reforms, it was this clerical vision that sustained them, that provided
solace in defeat and jubilation in victory. It was the indispensable element of
the clerical crusade. And as moral reform advanced, the vision matured.

To the Texas clerics articulating their new vision, the whole of history
vindicated their struggle. They looked into the past and felt compelled to
act in the present, as if beholden to a holy commission, something "behind
the superficial changes in forms of government, the coalition of tribes and
nations, [and] the rise and decline of empires," as Morris Sheppard explained
in 1912, months before he was elevated to the Senate.[58] Christianity, the new
editor of the *Baptist Standard,* J. B. Gambrell, explained in 1914, "does not

turn its course at the command of kings, governors or presidents."[59] Religious leaders believed themselves the inheritors of a righteous tradition and therefore the bearers of transcendent responsibility. "We should proceed now, as always," Gambrell wrote, "under the compelling conviction that we hold the truth in trust for the world."[60] Holding the truth in trust for the world: clerics embraced that idea, and the burden of action that followed.

As heirs to a commission, activist religious leaders lashed out. "It is the business of Christianity," Gambrell wrote, "to hurt what is morally wrong, and promote what is socially right. Paul went after Peter when he was wrong. Christianity is a corrective, not a mere coddler." Reformers had no need of a strictly otherworldly brand of evangelicalism and therefore moved beyond a traditional emphasis on personal conversion and an individual's relationship with Jesus Christ. They increasingly believed in a fighting faith whose "normal condition," Gambrell said, "is that of the most powerful militant factor in civilization."[61] Christians in Texas, the South, and throughout the nation, such men believed, had to be roused to action. "What we must do, my friends," Sheppard said to his audience in Texarkana, "is to labor for the placement of God and religion at the head of all human activity." So doing, Sheppard believed, "we shall deserve to hear on mortal shores as well as shores immortal a great Amen, suggestive of approval on the party of deity of our efforts for mankind."[62] But to win political support, they first enlisted the aid of history and its heroes.

As clerics crafted their histories, they had to grapple with their anti-Catholic prejudice. Many viewed Catholics with disdain.[63] J. B. Cranfill, for example, had introduced a resolution at the Southern Baptist Convention of 1894 with such declarations as, "We view with grave concern the aggressions of the papal power and its manifest design to dominate this country" and "We believe it our duty as Baptists to resist the encroachment of Romanism in all of its forms."[64] But the clerical crusade—and the sizable strength of the state's Catholic voters—at times eroded elements of that prejudice. Prohibitionists published tracts by Catholic writers and arranged speaking engagements for priests, some of whom breathed deeply of the clerical vision and could neatly enunciate the historical, political, and religious sensibilities so ardently championed by their Protestant contemporaries.

In 1906 Reverend Father James M. Hayes of Dallas celebrated the 130th anniversary of the signing of the Declaration of Independence with a special service at the Cathedral of the Sacred Heart. Speaking on "American patriotism," Hayes reckoned "worthy indeed is such a subject of the pulpit of the Church of God!" Although he declared himself to be against a "union" of church and state, Hayes went to absurd lengths to finesse the issue. "Because I believe in the Church, and because I believe in the State," he said, "I believe that Church and State should work in harmonious relationship for the glory of God and for the emancipation and elevation of men." Hayes, a Catholic, was among the mass of Christian activists reconceiving the relationship between Christian churches and the American government. The state had nothing to fear, these believers argued. As Hayes said, "There is no conflict between the American flag and the cross of Christ."[65]

Hayes's assertions "our American nation is the greatest on earth" and "it has been raised up by Divine Providence" were, in the long history of American Christian pronouncements, fairly pedestrian. Reading God's will into American history was hardly novel. But Hayes and the articulators of the Christian vision went beyond a providential view of American history and found, in a new vision, historical sanction for their new aims. The past justified more than their faith: it licensed and compelled their actions in pursuit of the Christian vision. They began quoting the founders favorably (perhaps none more than George Washington, who in his farewell address invoked "religion and morality" as "indispensable supports" for the nation's political endurance). "The Republic must draw its life from the religion and morality of its citizens," Hayes said, echoing such sentiments. Christianity, the rock of ages, was now the rock of the nation, the foundation for history's greatest success. Because, Hayes said, "in God we trust. It has been so from the beginning, it is so now, and may it be so until the end. With trust in God and with confidence in the people America shall endure." Although Hayes's Catholicism set him apart from many of his clerical contemporaries—Catholicism and the largely Protestant prohibition movement coexisted in tension—his ideas put him squarely in the mainstream of the emerging Christian vision.[66]

At every opportunity, religious leaders gathered to dictate a new shared Christian history. They produced an insular tradition of righteous church leaders, but an effective Christian vision required something more. Its communicators needed popular ideals and popular figures to work for them. Rescuing the founders and inscribing Christianity in the the story of the nation's founding was an obvious first step, but Texans and their peculiar attachment to their own mythology demanded another. As typical episodes involving the titans of Texas history reveal, they set about sacralizing Texas's secular heroes.

In 1893, Baylor University president Rufus C. Burleson spoke in the House of Representatives to honor the 100th anniversary of Sam Houston's birth. He delivered a speech intended to fully Christianize the Texas hero. Combining

equal parts sermon and history lecture, Burleson illuminated the three formative influences in Houston's life. First, he listed the maternal gifts and abiding
faith of Houston's mother. Next came his teacher, a Dr. Anderson, a mind-
opening influence who taught Houston to learn from himself, from books,
"and above all, with God, the father of light." Books were the last influence on
the Texas hero, and none more so than the Bible, Burleson said. But that worthy trinity, of course, only facilitated the one greater, overshadowing influence. "The crowning glory and power of all the formative influences was his
firm and ever abiding faith in God as an all-wise and ever present Heavenly
Father. This was his anchor of hope on the dark and stormy ocean," Burleson
said. "This was his Gibraltar when assailed by a thousand adversities."[67]

It may have been a stretch to imagine he could transform the rambunctious, rambling, part-time Cherokee into an exemplar of the Christian religion, but Burleson spoke from some firsthand knowledge. In the twilight of
his life, Houston, in part to appease his pious wife, decided to publicly join
the Baptist Church. In 1854, as a young preacher in Independence, Burleson
had had the honor of baptizing the old war hero. "Well, General," a friend
is supposed to have said later, "I hear your sins are washed away," to which
Houston replied, "If they were all washed away, the Lord help the fish down
below."[68] But if Burleson had whitewashed one Texas hero, another minister
completely reinvented another.

In 1910, in a bizarre ritual involving the "Father of Texas," patriotic Texans
exhumed Stephen F. Austin's remains from a Brazoria County cemetery,
paraded them through the state by railroad, and reinterred them in the State
Cemetery in Austin some days later. At the reburial, the eulogizing minister,
Dr. Richard J. Briggs of the First Congregational Church of Austin, lauded
Austin as a "God-chosen and God-inspired man." Using Austin's invented
religious deeds, Briggs implored the state's youth to act, "This heritage is now
descending to you from the hands of those who have so faithfully guarded
it through the generations now passing from the stage of action. Will you
be faithful to it?" For Briggs the Congregationalist, as for Burleson the
Baptist, as for the whole clerical crusade, history was an exhortation. It was
the engine of an active church and an empowering legacy for contemporary
religion. "Renew the fires of your enthusiasm," Briggs urged, "baptize the
coming generations in the glorious traditions of your history."[69] Christian
activists already were. And out of those traditions would emerge a new vision
for the present.

Activists now linked themselves to tradition. As the well-known Baptist
leader George Truett declared in 1911, beleaguered crusaders "will remember

their fathers and by such memory they will be inspired to bravest and unfainting endeavor."[70] Referring to prohibition campaigns, Senator Sheppard wrote: "These contests will mark a distinct epoch in the struggle for righteousness in human government. It is a struggle as old as human history. From the primeval fall man has been warring with the power that led him first to disobey his God. Through centuries of murder, tyranny, drunkenness, lust and all other crimes and vices that comprise the heritage of a fallen race, the yearning for righteousness in government and in conduct has never left the human heart."[71] Religious leaders proudly, and without humility, deigned to restore man, once fallen, to grace. Out of this connection between past and present emerged a new conception of government.

Activists rejected the anticlerical notion that government was a shield against any overstepping religion. They turned that idea on its head. Government, many came to believe, could and should be a holy weapon in the hands of the righteous. The separation of church and state was a fiction, they believed, and the dictates of their faith demanded that idea's abolishment. Methodist minister Robert Shuler, who later won fame in Los Angeles as the fundamentalist "Fighting Bob" Shuler, came of age in the Texas prohibition crusades. To Shuler, there never was, and never could be, church and state separation. "There has never been a great national reformation or governmental revolution that was not to some extent touched by the influence of the church," he wrote. "Christianity has ever pointed to the right in morals, society, and government."[72] Only the corrupt and sinful, Shuler insisted, feared and resisted the power of an active church. "It is the wicked that tremble and well they may tremble," he wrote, for "righteous men have no fears and need have none."[73] In turn-of-the-century Texas, clerics were indeed learning to be fearless.

In the 1870s, the inward-looking works of religious literature had proudly boasted of their limited ambitions. Men such as Homer Thrall claimed to include in their denominational histories "no glorification of Methodism" and "no fulsome adulation even of those deceased."[74] How very different from what religious Texans were reading so shortly thereafter. Thrall's own Methodists, from their denominational presses, were now producing works in droves boasting of their gloried history and their coming triumphs. "Over our moving columns a cloud of glory has hovered by day and night, and this evening we look back over a history that is little less than a continued miracle," read one bishop's collected sermons and addresses.[75] When this conceit won widespread adoption, a religious politics would be unstoppable. In the early twentieth century, the obsession with prohibition testified to that triumph.

As the decades passed, the most ardent activists drifted closer and closer to a pure version of the clerical vision. As uncompromising as their most extreme opponents, radical clerics embraced their sacred history and supported an unfettered religion and a righteous government. Sheppard, the committed Methodist, embodied this commitment. As senator, Sheppard worked harder and more successfully than any other national legislator to pass a constitutional prohibition amendment. He acted, he said, so that "man will rise . . . again to be crowned with the confidence and approbation of Almighty God."[76] Sheppard was among the most prominent and powerful advocates of the Christian vision. He pushed early for a prohibition amendment and, breathing deeply of Christian reform, framed it as a life-and-death struggle between the forces of good and evil. "The issue is plain," he said. It would determine the fate of the nation and align the American soul, irreversibly, toward God or Satan. "It will determine whether this is a Christian Nation."[77] The great hope of the clerical vision, the idea of "a Christian nation" inspired the clerical conquest and marked a turning point in the history of southern religion. Grounded in such potent images, clerics had to act. Religious leaders translated their larger cultural vision into a practical political program aimed at liquor, saloons, and drunkenness. Within the churches, as prohibition became gospel, alcohol came to embody evil and all the ills of the modern world. To prohibitionists, no claim could be too drastic, no indictment too extreme. The abolition of strong drink would signal society's redemption and remove the major impediment to the realization a Christian nation.

With such unyielding zeal, the clerics embarked upon the path to victory. Their numbers swelled, their organizations matured, and battles began to turn. In the course of their campaigns, prohibitionists would deftly exploit a thousand new political advantages: denominations contained a built-in bureaucracy complete with experienced speakers; the national resurgence of the Anti-Saloon League organized ministers as speakers and lobbyists; segregation and electoral reforms strengthened the voting power of middle-class whites; and the national mania for reform legitimated the antiliquor crusade. But the reformers' true strength lay elsewhere. Like the anticlerics, the prohibitionists now believed they had history and good government on their side. They had harnessed myth and memory. They had the belief that they battled for God. This was the ultimate power of the Christian vision. Rooted in history and government and religion, the crusaders' holy commission sustained their efforts. As the years passed, the evidence of their eventual success mounted. Even as they suffered several narrow statewide defeats, local victories began sweeping across the state.[78] "It is coming," said Baylor president

Samuel Brooks. "It is as sure as the roll of time," the logic of "the whole trend of social growth through the ages."[79] The Christian vision had prepared them for nothing less, for as Senator Sheppard proclaimed, "civilization sweeps toward God."[80]

Clerics and denominations constructed efficient educational and literary noisemaking machines that rewarded ambitious strivers and amplified religious voices above the din of anticlericalism. Denominations had created the means to reach beyond their narrow church worlds and from this new base religious champions foisted their distinct visions of religion, politics, and history on the whole culture. The Christian vision advanced in fits and starts, but over time, its effects were undeniable. It convinced liberty-loving Texans that good government could tolerate, and indeed needed, the influence of religious activists. Clerics implanted their unique ideas of history, government, and religion deep into the region's cultural memory, united religious southerners around notions of civic righteousness, and maneuvered politically to defeat anticlerical opponents. The triumph of the clerical vision enabled it all.

In 1924, H. L. Mencken stumbled upon what he called "the Bible Belt." In typical fashion, he scorned the rising intensity of religion in the region. But he made an astute observation. He noted that evangelical Christians were itching for a fight. "What they long for," Mencken wrote, "is a bomb." Little did he know, they had been building one for years.[81]

5

Triumph in the Churches

THE CLERICAL INSURGENCY

DECADES OF DENOMINATIONAL construction and consolidation had transformed Texas religion. Churches grew, ambition flourished, money flowed, and religious colleges and newspapers abounded. Denominational leaders had assembled the raw materials of the Bible Belt, and, at the turn of the twentieth century, now labored to awaken within their congregations and their clergy the spirit of political activism. The postwar spiritual crisis continued to plague anxious evangelicals, but clerical leaders complained that too many clergymen and too many congregations were refusing to act. Christians who did not yet subscribe to the clerical vision had to be roused from idleness and despair and convinced that they should fight for righteousness. Flush with visions of clerical empowerment and preaching the power of a new prohibition gospel, a clerical insurgency set out to conquer pulpits, congregations, and communities across Texas.

Clerical activists incited their brethren to act, but clergy and congregations needed convincing. "We do not stand in need so much of men and influence and money as we do of conviction that our enterprises are of God," the *Baptist Standard* declared in 1892.[1] Talented clergy filled the pulpits, money flowed into the denominations, and educational and journalistic endeavors boomed. But to what ends? Clerics believed that their church members stood still and, in a fragile spiritual world, were convinced that idleness wrought disaster. "You need to do something to stir the people out of their inaction," Methodist bishop Edwin Mouzon urged Elijah Shettles, one of his presiding elders, early in 1912. "Anything is better than stagnation."[2]

In 1909, Methodist pastor Thomas M. Brownlee arrived in Kosse, Texas, to find his new congregation immobilized and indolent. "I don't think I ever saw a people more satisfied at doing nothing than the people here," he wrote. "They have tried to do nothing [for] so long [that] they actually believe that they can't do any thing and do not desire to do any thing." Void of ambition or aspiration, "they think they are too weak to even exist," Brownlee said. If, according to clerical clerical activists, action defined religious health, the Kosse Methodist Church appeared ill. Brownlee prescribed all the regular clerical remedies to rouse the congregation. "Since studying the conditions and getting an insight into the real needs and demands within the bounds of this Charge," he wrote, "I felt like I ought to write a book, edit a paper, build a Church, repair another, organize a League, preach on Infant Baptism, make about five hundred visits, and a thousand other things which I will not now mention, in order to awaken interest and arrouse [*sic*] the Church to doing something." No word of preaching the old-time religion, no word on "Christ and Him crucified." The modern preacher now drew on a hundred practical, proactive plans in the clerical handbook: publishing, church building, and organizing. The modern age demanded constant agitation. Stillness meant death. "We have simply got to do something," Brownlee said, "or we are gone." He had learned the lessons of the spiritual crisis. He had imbibed the culture of clericalism.[3]

The clerical gospel not only invigorated the denominations, it roused and empowered ambitious evangelical leaders. The crisis-ridden neurasthenic of the nineteenth century yielded to the proud warrior of the twentieth. Freed from secondary work and flush with large audiences and great resources, the minister's great potential for public influence captivated many. A pioneer in advertising, Nathaniel C. Fowler Jr., marveled at the preacher's many advantages. He believed the clergy were uniquely positioned, and uniquely burdened, to conquer the secular sphere. The preacher, he wrote in 1906, not only headed powerful new organizations, he bore "the responsibilities of eternal consequence." Fowler joined in the clerical chorus. To shy from the times and abdicate one's duty, he wrote, "is the greatest menace to society." "The church today," he claimed, "needs the aggressive Christian, the man with physical and mental power, the man who can strike a physical as well as a mental blow for good."[4]

Ministers could claim a dignity and worth nearly unmatched in the secular world, but, in the hostile culture outside the churches, they said, their position had to be aggressively defended. Once a controversial pioneer of the clerical culture, B. H. Carroll had become a lion, a man followed, loved, and emulated. At the 1898 meeting of the Baptist General Convention of Texas, his long, flowing beard noticeably whiter but his towering figure and booming voice as captivating ever, Carroll inspired an audience now eager to follow his lead. In a sermon entitled "An Office Magnified,"[5] he called for the preachers' explicit empowerment. "The office of a minister must be magnified," he said, "glorified always, everywhere, and by all incumbents." Doctors healed the sick, teachers taught the youth, and police maintained the public order, yet no position in society matched the ministers' holy charge: the clergyman's "trust is sacred and God himself confers it." Building from that simple premise, Carroll urged his listeners to realize the power of their office "by giving yourself wholly to it." Then, in the soon-to-become ubiquitous martial language, Carroll roused his audience to action: "Let every watchman blow his trumpet at the coming of the sword. Let every sentinel cry out on his post: 'To arms! They come! The foe—the foe!' "[6] The preacher held the keys to heaven, but now his work was the world.

Clerical encouragements reverberated across Texas. The call to arms sounded from nearly every pulpit and religious press in the state. At Baylor, President Brooks, preparing a lecture on "real religion," urged his fellow Christians into the arena. "Religion is not a system of beliefs," he wrote, "it is a life." In similar lecture on Christian "social duties," Brooks assured his listeners that "Christian life is not a debating society; it is a working force."[7] The ubiquity of such calls testified to a revolution in the southern religious worldview.

Nuance eroded. Clerics created a world without neutrality, without disinterest. At a Dallas revival meeting in 1896, the evangelist Henry Marvin Wharton said, "There are only two sides, the Lord's side and the devil's side. Every one of us here to-night is on the one or the other, and friends, there is no halfway ground."[8] In 1900, in *History of Texas Baptists*, Benjamin Franklin Fuller depicted a divided world "of the righteous and the wicked," and drew "the radical and essential difference" between them.[9] Religious Texans awakened to this stark and irreconcilable division. "I am seeing more and more of the wichedness [*sic*] and sin of men every day," wrote the Methodist I. Z. T. Morris in 1907. "Oh!" he said, "how we do need a great revival in the church."[10]

The clerical worldview abolished all possibility of neutrality or disinterest. At the 1896 Dallas revival, Rev. Wharton told the story of a physician he knew. Wharton had preached that "anyone who is not serving the Lord is serving the devil." The physician objected, and said, "I am not serving the Lord, but I want you to understand I am not serving the devil." The preacher declared neutrality a service to Satan. He explained it this way: duck hunters use decoys. They set wooden ducks in the water, the wooden ducks attract real ducks, and the real ducks become prey for the hunter. The apathetic man was the devil's decoy, Wharton explained, because his apathy lured others away, stealing men, women, and children away from the churches. Wharton concluded, "There never was a time when Jesus Christ's people were more called upon to show their colors and to come out upon God's side."[11]

Cleric's persistent martial metaphors depicted a world at war, and they indoctrinated in their followers a fighting creed. It was the duty of religious Texans, the crusaders said, to engage with evil and never turn back. In December 1900, Presbyterian minister J. Gilmore Smith preached what the *Fort Worth Morning Register* described as "something out of the ordinary run of Sabbath talks." Smith tried, the paper said, to define a Christian. According to Smith, "a Christian is God's man." He is God's man at all times, he said, "in the darkness or in the light; when the sun is high or when the sun is low; when the tibe ebbs or when the tide flows . . . A Christian is a Christ in the world. . . . Whatever is for the uplift of the world, the Christian should interest himself in that. . . . The office of an angel is not higher." The true Christian must therefore use his voice, Smith argued, "never keeping silent when he ought to speak [and] bearing testimony against wrong, injustice and falsehood," and act in the world. "There is no sight so soul-inspiring," he said, "as to see a Christian throw himself into the thick of the battle."

Smith had to ask so fundamental a question—what is a Christian?—because he was providing a new and novel definition. In the tumultuous upheaval of the spiritual crisis and the dramatic launching of the clerical crusades, religion itself was changing, and changing rapidly. But men like Smith made sure to lay the issue bare. They were clear in their declarations: "The one thing for you to find out if you are a Christian," Smith said, "is not a new Christ . . . but a new view of Christ. Get the right conception of Christ. Get the true idea of Christ's mission among men." Audiences were hearing similar sermons across the state. From Smith, Carroll, Cranfill, and all the gathering armies of the new clerical movement: the true Christian was a fighter.[12] Religious Texans were engaging the world, and that engagement increasingly defined them as religious.

And it increasingly identified the region. Religious southerners prayed for action and looked to clericalism for salvation.[13] "Standing on the summit of this unparalleled century and casting our glance forward into the next, pregnant with untold possibilities," Methodist bishops in 1898 pledged that "this General Conference is confronted with extraordinary opportunities, and therefore with momentous responsibilities. God help us to be equal to the times in which we live."[14] In 1903, the Southern Presbyterian General

Assembly complained that churches "have been moulded by, rather than helpfully moulded, the spirit of the age."[15] Just as the weight of the spiritual crisis threatened to wear down southern religion, clerical insurgents arrived with their inspirational exhortations. They promised release. They promised action. And they declared war on all of the constraints muzzling their new, aggressive religion.

In May 1898, Smith reissued his call to arms. He expressed frustration with lingering anticlerical impediments. "It has been said to me of late your business is to preach the gospel, you are supposed to be dead to all civil life," he said. But Smith called the withdrawal of the church from public life "the greatest evil of the times." He complained that "the church has failed to do her duty." He recognized instead the great, untapped potential of an activist clergy freed from inflexible constraints. "The church of the living God holds the balance of power and if both men and women would unite and exert the power at their command they could raise a blast of public sentiment along those lines that would make the politicians bend before them." He prodded his followers. "Your duty and my duty and the duty of every man and woman calling themselves Christians is to go into politics," he said.[16] Over the following decades, they would—but first they needed a rallying point, a symbol that fortified their convictions, allowed for self-reinforcing ritual, and offered a way into politics. They found it, slowly, in prohibition and other moral reforms.

Popular moral evils, once on the periphery of religious concerns, moved increasingly to the foreground. As the clerical groundswell flooded communities across the state, pastors targeted local saloons and theaters and dance halls. Caro, for instance, was a small East Texas town that had experienced a boom when the lumber industry and the railroads arrived at the turn of the century.[17] Overseen by a family of local lumber barons, the Whitemans, the town carved from a denuded wilderness a post office, schools, drugstores, general stores, grocers, and a Methodist church. Rev. C. N. Morton arrived in 1907 with orders from his presiding elder to tend souls, "not to meddle with local affairs." But in Caro, the pilgrim Morton found spiritual laziness and worldly abandon. The Whitemans ran everything, including church life. "Mrs. W. dictates the policy of the church," Morton complained, "but she is not religious and has drawn around her some of the upper tens of the town who are not only irreligious but frivolous and irreverent in church." Worse, they bankrolled sinful amusements. Noninterference was a fool's errand. "When local affairs take the form of a 'skating rink' with billiard and pool room attached and I am called upon not only to refrain from saying anything

FIGURE 5.1 "Vote as you pray." Prohibition rally in Nacogdoches, Texas, ca. 1900–1904.
Source: Prints and Photographs Collection, di_06790. Dolph Briscoe Center for American
History. University of Texas at Austin.

against it but to indorse [*sic*] it with my presence," Morton fumed, "I feel
like the limit has been reached." Morton announced that would launch a crusade.[18] Others were doing the same in other small towns and cities throughout the South.

Local option elections—countywide referendums on liquor—erupted
everywhere and convulsed local communities. A freethinking agent of the
liquor dealers, Ormond Paget, for instance, reported that a 1907 election in
Milam County "was bitter and personal" and estimated that partisans spent
$10,000. Paget described the antis there as "fighters . . . men who spared no
effort to win—who were sleepless and tireless.[19] These were not casual elections. They were life-and-death struggles for the soul of the South.

Precisely because they were not casual or passionless, local antivice crusades inflamed religious excitement. Local actors were consistently awed
by the wonderful side-effects of their crusades. The rural Methodist minister Jesse Lee began assaulting sin in Franklin, Texas, in 1907. "O Ile [*sic*] tell
you," he wrote, "I was after the dancers and card players with a hot spike." For
months, he preached against dancing, drinking, and gambling. "I have run

into them with all the force of the Gospil [*sic*]," he wrote. He predicted that "God is going to bless my coming meeting as He has not heretofore blessed this town." He wasn't wrong. The results, as he reported them, were nothing short of phenomenal: attendance at his Franklin church was up, attendance at the ballroom and barroom was down. "My ministry has been attended with wonderful power in the last weeks," he said, accompanied by "a greate [*sic*] gain Spiritually." "I don't see how I can turn loose here now," he said.[20]

Moral reform inevitably bound religious communities together and defied the languor engendered by the spiritual crisis. It is a sociological truism that group identity derives from shared characteristics as well as from shared difference.[21] Self-identity stems not only from the things individuals believes but from those they does not. Moral reform captured this. It was a kind of social glue that united pastors and congregants into a distinct and meaningful moral community. In Caro, Morton marveled at the effects of his anti-skating rink campaign. "We have had and are having the severest test we have ever experienced and it has brought us closer to God and made us to feel as never before the need of His help," he wrote. The church's previous pastor had survived by acquiescing to the town's leading family and keeping quiet about the local skating rink. But the congregation languished. Now Morton found that uniting against the "skating rink craze" invigorated his congregation. "I believe," Morton predicted, "there is going to be a reaction which will be for the glory of God and the good of his cause."[22]

Activism invigorated the clergy. They found the answer to all their aggressive exhortations, a platform from which to exert their own moral authority, and an evil sufficiently menacing to magnify their station. "Friends," Rev. Wharton said at the 1896 Dallas revival, "there is something in the thought that we are on the right side."[23] Fighting vice, and all of the organizational minutiae that accompanied it, made vivid the clerics' self-declared war against immorality. Before assuming control of the *Baptist Standard*, J. B. Cranfill had edited the *Waco Advance,* served on a Baptist missionary board, and lectured against vice. But he described his religious work in grander terms: after a brief respite, he said, "I hastened back to Waco to plunge again into the thick of the battle I was waging for the conquest of Texas for Christ and His cause."[24] The neurasthenic preacher, prone to restless nights and panic attacks, had found his place in the world. He mattered for something. And if he mattered, then all of religion mattered. If the clerics succeeded, then religion could be redeemed, the crisis eradicated, and a wayward culture restored to God. Baptist luminary George Truett, at the height of the clerical crusade in 1911, likened one Baptist gathering to "a great council of war where God's men have surveyed the battle-field and have taken cognizance of their forces," before concluding simply that "the issue is the conquest of the world for the savior."[25]

With so much at stake, the clerics threw themselves into battle. George Rankin recalled his first assaults on the barrooms, saying, "As for the saloons, I opened up on them. It was time for somebody to come to the front and challenge them to mortal combat." All over Texas—and all over the country—preachers and other religious leaders were declaring war. "I threw down the gauntlet," Rankin said, "and turned loose a fusillade upon them."[26] He delivered sermons, raised funds, coordinated local option campaigns, and spoke out in the press. All the competing impulses of the clerical culture collided in Rankin's career. An ambitious and aggressive advocate for an expanded church, Rankin longed to see religion enthroned and its champions recognized. He found in moral reform a mechanism for personal advancement. By attacking saloons, gambling halls, prostitution, and other easily identifiable evils, ministers won fame and advanced their careers. Rankin's anti-vice crusades in Houston garnered headlines and, he recalled, "brought me and my Church work into prominence, not only in the city, but throughout that portion of the State."

The logic of moral warfare invigorated religious life. Anxiety-wracked Christians could see past the spiritual crisis. They could finally touch righteousness. They escaped what they saw as the sinking wreckage of an unfashionable old-time gospel and exiled the spiritual fears of the preceding generation. The clerics recognized the great power that was theirs. Many won fame and professional advancement. Rankin himself, after helping pass a local ordinance that closed saloons on Sunday, marveled at what "can always be done when the moral element stand by a courageous leader."[27] The power of that recognition stirred religious Texans. For the next decade—and for the next century—it inspired the wall-destroying fervor of Christian activists. The logic of Christian politics impelled its champions out into the world, against the strongholds of anticlericalism, and into the lifeblood of the public culture. "If we as individual Christians set down and fold our hands," Presbyterian Rev. M. W. Robison said in 1902, "we turn our government over to the mob, and must expect corruption and lawlessness."[28] But if they acted, the clerics promised, they could expect wonderful rewards. They would win the esteem and respect of their peers. They would see their churches grow, their careers furthered, and the spiritual crisis evaporated. A floundering religion would be saved. But barriers still remained. Anticlerics still lurked within the churches.

The accelerating clerical culture provoked a reckoning among the denominations as anticlerical traditionalists and clerical activists clashed and struggled. The battle was brutal, and the bloodletting severe. From the beginning, many had resisted the denomination-building fervor of the late nineteenth century. Cranfill had been reared by Primitive ("Hardshell") Baptists, for instance, stubbornly biblical Christians opposed to mission work and worldly entanglements.[29] Such critics of excessive bureaucratization—"disorganizers"—still lurked in evangelical churches.

Tasked with putting a program together for a Methodist district meeting in 1908, Rev. J. B. Turrentine bristled at the task. He hated the meetings. He called the hyper-organized denominational structures "weights instead of wings." He lamented the soulless and undemocratic hierarchy of the denominational bureaucracy. "We are fast building up an oligarchy. . . . The tendency is too much towards centralization." The rapid period of denomination building had decayed lay power. Fewer laymen attended denominational meetings, and fewer felt empowered within the church. "The Methodist church," Turrentine wrote, "belongs to the membership of the church, not connectional boards nor conference boards nor our Bishops nor even our preachers." The culture of clericalism privileged the authority of religious leaders, and clergymen therefore seized religious life. "It is a fact," Turrentine wrote, "that we preachers have gradually absorbed or acquired in some way about all the authority the church has."[30]

Turrentine wasn't alone. The "disorganizer" ethos that had fractured denominations a generation earlier persevered into the next. As religious organizations exploded all across the country, alienated churchgoers criticized strict creeds, high clerical salaries, and rampant commercialism. Fort Worth readers could sympathize with the rants of Baptist preacher Arthur Gee, in Ohio, when he complained that "churchianity is taking the place of Christianity."[31] The spiritual crisis provoked soul-searching among anxious evangelicals. Self-proclaimed redeemers offered several diagnoses. In an editorial, in 1907, on the assumed decline of churchgoing, the *Dallas Morning News* identified two possibilities: "One insists that the ministry has lost its influence in the higher line by going into politics too deeply, while another contends that the trouble comes of the ministry's failure to go far enough into politics and other practical lines." The *News* identified the latter explanation with clerics who believed that "Christ has been presented as a servant instead of a king, . . . because some have tried to distinguish between the secular and the religious and thus isolated religion from God's great world."[32] Others weren't so sure.

Anticlerical resistance persisted within the churches. Several denominations had fractured over issues of denominationalism, missions, education, and politics in the nineteenth century, and the internal strife survived into the twentieth. Some disaffected Christians retreated to rival denominations. James William Lowber and the Christian Church (the Disciples of Christ), for instance, welcomed anticlerical Christians into their expanding denomination.[33] By mirroring much of the theology of southern evangelicalism while still privileging congregational autonomy, the Disciples harvested much anticlerical discontent.

Around the turn-of-the-century, Lowber had invigorated several Texas Christian Churches with exclusively spiritual calls. In just five years, Lowber reportedly grew the First Christian Church of Fort Worth from around two hundred members to around eight hundred and oversaw the construction of an imposing $30,000 stone church. From Fort Worth, he took charge of the American Christian Missionary Society's mission in Galveston and turned a membership of a few dozen into 125 and moved them into a new $8,000 church. Finally, in 1896, he took his talents to the Central Christian Church of Austin and, as he had done so many times before, oversaw construction of an imposing new building that his contemporary, the Texas historian Eugene Barker, called "one of the handsomest and most commodious stone church buildings in the city, and even in the state." As skilled at subscribing funds and organizing congregations as he was delivering sermons, Lowber won acclaim. Texas's elder statesman John H. Reagan praised him widely. Lowber became Chancellor of Add-Ran University (later Texas Christian University) and lectured regularly. He published several acclaimed books. Learned and well-spoken, in his preaching Lowber always, in Barker's words, retained "a good degree of evangelical pungency and fervor."[34] The church expansion Lowber oversaw was typical of the era, but he steered it toward spirituality, not politics. He walked only half of the clerical path.

As an apostle of the Christian Church, Lowber shared his denomination's historical disgust for squabbling and strife. In a 1902 article, Lowber justified the Disciples precisely because they abhorred worldliness: "The gospel is God's power for the salvation of both Jews and Gentiles," he wrote, and "the Holy Spirit in conversion operates through the gospel. The word of God is the sword of the Spirit; and for this reason the apostles were sent in every direction to conquer the world for Christ. They conquered with the sword of the Spirit, and not *with* the literal sword as did Mohammed and his disciples. The fact that Christianity conquered the world by love and not by force, is one great reason why it has impressed itself upon the very face of civilization."[35]

Barker, the secular historian, praised Lowber for his restraint: "He is never warped by prejudice, nor made narrow by partisanism. If, when treating of great social evils, some righteous indignation burns through his terse and compact sentences against the moral apathy of society, in the presence of such inexcusable wrongs, they are never degraded by any tone or color of moral malignity."[36] Increasingly marginalized within mainstream evangelical churches, disaffected religious Texans flooded into the pastoral care of such shepherds. Others, however, remained in the old churches. They fought from within.

In 1897, S. O. Mitchell preached a sermon at Dallas's First Baptist Church urging the congregation to focus on spiritual concerns. He preached from Colossians 2:10: "Ye are complete in him." He told the congregation to get out of the world and out of politics and come back to Christ. "He wished," the *Dallas Morning News* reported, "that the great Baptist brotherhood of Texas would . . . have done with this external wrangling and war that is now tearing homes and churches and peoples asunder." He promoted an old-time gospel of personal redemption. Only though Christ, he said, could believers find salvation. Mitchell closed the sermon with a vignette. He told of a prominent businessman, an old and profane man who had sinned and gambled his years on earth away. But then he visited his eleven-year-old granddaughter, who read scripture to him. The words converted him, Mitchell said. He came to Christ, and the church received him. There were no anti-vice crusades, Mitchell said, no politicians elected, and no campaigns waged. Only the pure gospel.[37]

Even some who dabbled in reform confessed their doubts. In his country church, Jesse Lee longed for a widespread religious resurgence, but after reading English evangelist J. Stuart Holden's *The Price of Power*, reconsidered his political commitment. Holden—and Lee—feared for religious spirituality. "No man who does not renounce all forms of leadership other than the spiritual can ever know the endowment of a personal Pentecost," Holden wrote.[38] Lee agreed and urged his colleagues to heed Holden's words. Lee urged a program of revivals, but "let it be understood it is to be of the strictest Evangelical type," he said.[39]

When a persistent anticlericalism had dogged the infant clerical movement at the end of the nineteenth century, official denominational policies and pronouncements had lagged behind the brewing clerical insurgency. In 1888, the Southern Baptist Convention rejected several prohibition resolutions. President James P. Boyce declared them counter to the convention's stated aims of "eliciting, combining and directing the energies of the whole denomination in one sacred effort for the propagation of the gospel."[40] The other denominational behemoth, the Methodist Episcopal Church, South, agreed. "Our church is strictly a religious and in no wise a political body," the organization proclaimed in 1894. "The more closely we keep ourselves to the one work of testifying to all men repentance toward God and faith toward our Lord Jesus Christ, the better shall we promote the highest good of our country and race."[41]

As a young pastor in 1899, George Truett had pleaded with the Southern Baptist Convention to preserve the Baptist's spiritual mission. At that point in his career, the young upstart championed evangelical spirituality. In a speech before the convention, Truett urged humility in the pulpit. He preached a simple gospel: "Christ and Christ only." It was pure, he said, and biblical. But worldly reformers undermined it with their worldly obsessions. For them, the redeeming gospel of the spirit was not enough. "Does someone say," he asked, "that this theme is 'too narrow?' " No, he countered, it is everything, "it is an infinite ocean." Anything else was superfluous, unbiblical, and heretical.[42]

Truett turned to the Apostle Paul, who, he said, "might have taken to the lecture platform to be what they now call a "moral reformer." He might have spent his days declaring against the popular sins . . . or against the abuses and corruptions of government." Instead, Paul "steadfastly clung to one sufficient theme, 'Christ and Him crucified.' " To anticlerical Christians like Truett, a true faith clung to Christ, Paul, John the Baptist, and the apostles. The insurgent reformers, on the other hand, innovated unbiblical traps and falsehoods. "There is now a great itch abroad in the land demanding 'reform,' " Truett warned. "The air is filled with screaming voices which propose to adjust the discordant elements of both church and state." Truett urged vigilance.[43]

So, too, did Robert Lewis Dabney, a learned Presbyterian transplant from Virginia. "The appropriate mission of the minister is to preach the gospel for the salvation of souls," he wrote. What did a law or a politician matter when dealing with eternal souls? A true Christian, Dabney claimed, would never deviate from pure evangelism if he believed in the redeeming power of Christ. He would see the fleeting emptiness of worldly care. Dabney even concluded that "one great source, therefore, of political preaching may always be found in the practical unbelief of [the preacher] himself." Clerics neglected the work of God. "What is this," he asked, "but treason?"[44]

Dabney was an aging spiritual voice but an influential one. He had trained a generation of Presbyterian ministers, first at the Union Theological Seminary at Hampden-Sydney College, in Virginia, and, after 1883, at the

Austin School of Theology in Austin, Texas.[45] Even while capturing popular
attention for his militant Lost Cause mythology, he indoctrinated his students in the rigorous otherworldly demands of the evangelical ministry, or
what his denomination called the "doctrine of spirituality." He published a
collection of lectures, *Sacred Rhetoric*, as a "guide to the evangelical Protestant
preacher." He said that proper preachers, relying only upon the "plain truths"
of the Bible, need only be the messengers of a simple saving faith: "Christ
and him crucified." That was it. That was a minister's only mission. The pulpit itself, Dabney said, was sacred. God "has appointed one place into which
nothing shall enter, except the things of eternity, and has ordained an order
of officers, whose sole charge is to remind their fellow-men of their duty to
God." A minister may play his part as a citizen, but "[i]n the pulpit he is only
the ambassador of Christ."[46]

If any particular heresy tempted the good gospel minister, Dabney said,
it was politics. "The scriptural doctrine of the preacher's mission and warrant also decides at once against an abuse of the pulpit, to which the clergy
have always been prone. It may be named with sufficient accuracy by the popular phrase, 'political preaching.'" Politics seduced both Catholics and the
Protestants, he warned, and "its tendency has always been to embitter party
spirit, to provoke bloodshed, and to corrupt the hearts of the hearers. . . .
Clergymen are accustomed to deference and unused to contradiction. . . .
They become accustomed to sanctifying their creeds in their own eyes, and
regarding their quarrel as God's. Thus their very animosities become holy in
their view." Political preaching, Dabney concluded, rested only on the wayward minister's "self-love and vanity."[47]

Many churches held out against the clerical onslaught. Austin's University
Methodist Church boasted of its minister's noninterference in politics.
Despite criticism from leading reformers, Rev. D. Emory Hawk, according
to reports, "remained firm in his determination never to discuss politics
from the pulpit in spite of the charges."[48] The anticlerical tradition remained
rooted in the evangelical churches. As activists maneuvered to capture key
denominational offices, strongholds of resistance plagued the clerical insurgency. Some, such as Dabney, penned eloquent theological appeals; others,
such as an anonymous Dallas church member, dropped beer receipts into the
collection plate. Whatever their methods, the anticlerics defied the clerical
insurgency. But they wouldn't resist for long.[49]

By the early twentieth century, clerical arguments inundated southern
churches. Denominational leaders penned pleas for activism. The *Baptist
Standard* inveighed against the humble preacher: "Our little pen-knife

preachers are not worth much. They are in the Kingdom what minnows are along the edges of the mighty ocean." Although not yet ready to embrace the "political preacher" label and quick to disclaim violations of church and state separation, church organizations nevertheless advanced the clerical agenda. "Civil government must be run on principles of righteousness," they declared.[50]

Whereas in 1887 the impudent politics of Carroll and Cranfill and other prohibitionists had scandalized the religious establishment, divided church-going Texans, and undercut reformers' efforts, when the new generation of church leaders eagerly embraced the clerical insurgency, their critics carried increasingly little currency. The denominational organizers of the previous decades had won their battles and the political preachers of the current decade would now win theirs.

Anticlerical Baptist and Methodist ministers faded into irrelevance. Sympathetic to reformers, Methodist preacher A. Y. Old nevertheless refused to preach prohibition and closed his pulpit to reformers. Although church members and denominational officials complained, Old stuck to his principles. Anticlericalism "never failed to bring censure upon me," he said. "I have felt that standing so true to my conscience in this issue, I have been set back into more or less obscurity as a Methodist preacher."[51] His career dead-ended on an out-of-the-way circuit in Central Texas. The new denominational world rewarded church builders and political organizers. Traditionalists fell by the wayside. Others were pushed.

The urgency of the clerical activists overwhelmed their opponents. In Cameron, Texas, reform fever riled Rev. J. T. Smith's Methodist Church. A lost local option election had provoked an uproar among the membership. The church turned against itself. "My people are very sore some of them," Smith wrote his presiding elder, "and doing now it seems to me some very imprudent things." The church's Sunday school leader opposed prohibition. The congregation knew it when they put him in, but the rising pitch of the prohibition battle unbalanced everything and the members turned their frustrations against him. Though he otherwise engaged actively in the entire spiritual life of the church, and many of his prohibitionist opponents missed prayer meetings and ran businesses on Sundays and skipped services, the clerical culture held prohibition as a defining issue, and the Sunday school leader was on the wrong side. A bloc of members set an ultimatum: either the teacher resigned, or they would. For preachers and churches untutored in or unaligned with the clerical crusade, the insurgency unsettled everything. "O," Smith wrote, "I tell you I am in it."[52]

Purges were not uncommon. Thomas D. Cobbs, an attorney from San Antonio, mourned his expulsion from his Baptist church. A self-proclaimed "devoted and earnest Christian," Cobbs nevertheless resisted the prohibition frenzy. For that alone he lost his church. "On account of my prohibition views," he wrote, "I was driven storm-tossed from the church I loved." He inveighed against his pastor, "whose narrowness and fanaticism led him along lines of injustice and injury," but he refused to repudiate the church. "I do not attack Christianity because it is not responsible for it. Men are often misguided and take up wrong views." He decried the "fanaticism" of the zealots. Though the church had turned him out, Cobbs said he still clung to the true spiritual church. The clerics were imposters, he said. But the clerics were winning. There were Cobbs in churches all across the country, heretics exiled for political foot-dragging.[53]

Clarence Ousley, a Fort Worth newspaper editor, cringed. He conceded the liquor traffic's debauching malevolence, but he abhorred the purges. "Within my acquaintance," he said, "I happen to know several men of Christian profession or sympathy who have been alienated from the church or from active participation in its affairs or from generous support of its work by the cruel speeches and writings of Christian ministers."[54]

In 1911, amid that year's contentious political contests, a prohibitionist preacher asked to speak at the Houston Young Men's Christian Association. Eager to avoid controversy, the local branch agreed but only if the speaker promised not to talk about prohibition. The stpiulation outraged the *Baptist Standard*. The paper editorialized that the association "should strike out the name Christian" from its title. "For an organization to pretend to be Christian, and refuse to side against the devil's chief agency on earth, is a clear misuse of a sacred name and an abuse of Christian confidence. Let it [the YMCA] be the Y. M. A.," the paper declared.[55] In the crusade against liquor, there was no middle ground. "The things of Christ," editor Gambrell avowed in 1910, "are things about which there can be no division among God's people. Every saloon is a menace to Christian work. Every one of us should be ready all the time to fight the saloon. I am ready to part with every friend of mine who wants to stand between the saloon and the enraged anti-saloon people of this State."[56] Such declarations only reinforced religious leaders' willingness to purge dissenters from positions of influence.

University Methodist Church in Austin clung tenuously to its apolitical Methodism. The incumbent minister, D. E. Hawk, spoke against political preaching. In 1912, the church's board of stewards requested that their next minister continue the tradition. They asked that Hawk's successor "take no dish in politics, but confine himself entirely to the Gospel." The *Temple Daily Telegram* reported the subsequent developments read "more like a political novel than a story dealing with the assignment of clergymen according to the rules and regulations of the Methodist church." Bishop James Atkins answered the steward's request by appointing Robert Shuler to the office in a clear affront to the board of stewards. Shuler certainly lived up to his future nickname, "Fighting Bob." He was a fighter. His strident rhetoric put him in the vanguard of aggressive religion.[57] The stewards complained and requested a replacement but to no avail. The Methodist hierarchy refused to replace one of its own.

By the early years of the twentieth century, the clerical insurgency had maneuvered its supporters into the best appointments, built the largest churches, and captured the highest church offices. Denominational presses churned out clerical material, denominational schools churned out politicized students, and empowered congregations exalted reform-minded laypersons. Evangelical religion had been revolutionized. To influence the broader culture, to earn for the South the "Bible Belt" moniker, the clerics had waged larger battles. They disseminated, for instance, a veritable ideology with views of history and government and God. And while the secular world awaited, churches were falling into line. Away from the mainstream anticlerical culture, churches were now massing for rebellion. Inside the denominations, militant new ideologies prospered. Fervor and zeal trampled hesitance. The world lacked for religion and morals; clerics would supply them. The battle that had riven the churches now spilled public life.

Religious voices pushing for broader political engagement grew ever louder. Everywhere they looked in the churches, anticlerical resistance seemed broken. At a 1905 meeting of the Baptist Pastors' Conference in Dallas, church leaders proudly and openly preached politics. Rev. E. E. King of McKinney discussed "The Pastor's Relations to Current Questions." "When the wicked rule, the people mourn," he said. Preachers should not be complicit. "It is to be feared that the pastor has in some instances, by his timid if not cowardly silence as to politics, contributed to the groans and tears of his people." To abstain was, in effect, to license. He asked, "Is he not set as a watchman on the walls of a city, who seeing an evil coming on the land should speak to the glory of God and the saving of a people?"[58]

At a meeting of the ecumenical Dallas Pastors' Association, in 1907, Rev. J. W. Hill of the Dallas First Methodist Church delivered a paper on "civic righteousness" that spoke to the minister's role in public life. Should he "advocate or oppose any suggested legislation, or should by word or pen espouse any cause that has its final settlement at the ballot box—this is a question that has elicited much discussion." He decided that ministers should. Legislators and electorates, he said, would never find morality or ethics by themselves. Ministers had to act as teachers and guides, "to fit and adjust the shifting sands of civil enactment until they shall conform to the granite configuration of the eternal principles of righteousness." Religious leaders must not only exemplify morality, he said, they must actively fight for it. He laid the issue bare: "The issues are joined. The conflict is between what he [the preacher] believes to be right and what he thinks to be wrong. Neutrality is out of the question. Trimming or fence riding is morally impossible. Jesus said, 'he that is not for me, is against me,' and it will hardly be denied that every principle embodied in civil enactment, which has a moral bearing, either furthers the cause or retards the progress of our Lord's gospel among men."[59]

Such sentiments sounded across the state as the cry for politics swept through the churches. J. Frank Norris declared that preachers had "political as well as pulpit rights."[60] Methodist minister and editor George Rankin began winning headlines with forceful political harangues.[61] "I hold that it is the duty of every Christian to go into politics and stay in," J. B. Gambrell wrote in 1908.[62] Preachers prodded their congregations to vote their religion. In 1910, Rev. Edwin C. Boynton of the North Dallas Christian Church delivered a typical sermon. "There are those who tell us that religion has no rights in politics," Boynton preached, "that for it to seek any is to create a union of Church and State." But Boynton rejected the spiritual version of his faith. Anticlericalism was as a relic that "arises out of the old conception that religion is a question of theology," when, he said, religion actually "is a question of life, and in whatever way or sphere a man lives, if he is a Christian, he must live as God wills." His message was clear: a Christian must vote as he prays. In the coming prohibition election, he urged his congregation to vote "as only an enlightened Christian can, for the chance to destroy the liquor traffic as a stepping stone to the final solution of the liquor question."[63]

Increasingly, the clerical rhetoric spread beyond the pulpit. In a 1909 meeting of the Dallas Baptist Pastors' and Laymen's Conference, future state governor and Baylor University president Pat M. Neff, then the county attorney for McLennan County, said about the "Christian citizen," "Crowned with the glories of war and decked with the flowers of peace, robed in the mantle of religious freedom, holding in one hand the constitution of his country and in the other the Bible of his God," the Christian citizen "stands today before the world the biggest, and the best, the noblest and the divinest gift this earth holds up to its maker." He urged all Christians to engage in public life: "Every

Christian ought to be a politician to the extent of taking an active interest in every public or political question that touches the morals or the material prosperity of the people." Tumultuous times demanded righteous engagement. "It was criminal," he thought, "to be silent when your country needs your voice."[64]

Other prominent laymen supported the clerical movement. In 1909, attorney Silas C. Padelford defended the preachers' political push for prohibition. He began with old claims: preachers "demand merely the right and privilege of free men" to "the right to an untrammeled vote." But few now relied on such a narrow argument, and Padelford embraced new ones as well. He, like the clerics, divided the world in two. He said two forces pulled at the souls of man. "Most every person," he wrote, "turns either to the spirit of his God or the spirit of the devil—the liquid dispensed at the saloon." If liquor blocked religious progress, and if religion should be unhindered, then any obstacle to religion therefore became a proper political target. "Anything that destroys the human soul, anything that destroys reputation, anything that injures the home, anything that impairs the course of pure religion anything that destroys the benevolent influence of the church is fit and proper to be denounced from the pulpit." He said, "It is the burden duty of the ministers to oppose by all honorable means and to destroy if possible this traffic."[65]

The chorus of clericalism sang. No gathering better captured the energy of the movement than the Baptist General Convention of Texas. The atmosphere of its annual meeting in the fall of 1908 was electric. Convention president Robert C. Buckner struggled in vain to tame the crowd. He used a large songbook as a gavel and spoke against "all of this applause and rejoicing." "Let's not indulge in this, please," he pleaded, "This is not customary." But this was not a typical Baptist meeting; it was a celebration: it proceeded, newspapers reported, "in the nature of a big prohibition rally." The convention rejoiced in a "banner year." Never before had more churches been built or more people baptized. The Baptist body reveled in its accomplishments. Religious workers, the state missions board reported, delivered more than forty thousand sermons, distributed a million pages of religious literature, signed up nearly twenty thousand new members, and organized over two hundred new churches. The meeting stood in stark relief to the self-pitying meetings two decades earlier, during the depths of the crisis years. The mood even washed over President Buckner. During one speaker's personal account of the rising power of religion, passion boiled over and the convention spontaneously sang "Blessed be the name of the Lord." Buckner broke down and admitted "that to sit in this convention was almost like being with God in Heaven."[66]

Moral reform dominated the Baptist meeting that year. Dr. J. L. Gross of Houston's First Baptist read a report on the Sabbath. "Whatever tends to destroy reverence for the Lord's Day," he said, "will also impair the influence of the Lord on the hearts and lives of the people, and thus strike a death blow to the heart of our churches." The fate of the nation depended upon the fate of the churches. "Non-observance," he said, "will in the end shake the very foundation of our republic." He called for battle: "We fight to the death with Christian weapons, the sentiments, institutions, or practices . . . that in any-wise diminishes our Christian Sabbath." Stores, mail, fairs, shows, saloons, sporting events: they all desecrated the Sabbath. "This," he said, "is the rotten-ness at the very heart of our religion." But instead of surrendering to despair, as had a previous generation, the gathered Baptists embraced their opportunity for reform. Clerics had to confront Sabbath breakers. "In love and patience, we must convert them to our way of thinking, or else we may lose our coun-try and our religion in its highest and noblest form." The body adopted the report on Saturday and appointed two preachers to the board of directors of the Sunday League of America. The body moved to petition the state legis-lature. They moved that legislation be passed protecting the Sabbath. They urged that "no fair, performance, or game can occur on Sunday" and that a heavy fine be levied in support.[67]

But if the Baptists and other leading denominations pushed for an expan-sive moral reform agenda, prohibition dominated all. No issue could compete with the anti-liquor crusade's visceral appeal. B. H. Carroll, now the elder statesman of the clerical movement, reminded reformers, prohibition "con-cerns every single vital interest of the people individually and collectively, socially and intellectually, civilly and politically, financially, morally and reli-giously." In light of this, "how can I remain silent?" he asked.[68]

The clergy's wholesale embrace of prohibition propelled that issue into the public arena.[69] Prohibition became *the* political issue of the day. One politician wrote as early as 1905 that "the position of public men upon this question has invited or repelled their following more than their view upon all other questions combined: when the issue becomes acute it dominates every other issue."[70] It had become acute, and for a time it dominated every other issue. And, just as in the 1880s, on came an avalanche of anticlerical criticism from outside of the churches. In rushed the resistance. Critics urged their sup-porters to "lock their shields in a stern and unbroken front."[71] They hardly needed to be reminded.

Traces of anticlericalism remained within the churches, but only traces. If the Baptists and Methodists were mostly drained of criticism, some

FIGURE 5.2 "Vote for God." Prohibition rally in Lufkin, Texas, ca. 1911. Courtesy of the History Center, Diboll, Texas.

within mainline denominations could still cling prominently to the old ways. In 1911, for instance, Bishop James Steptoe Johnston of the Episcopal Diocese of Western Texas rehashed the old religious anticlericalism. He conceded the destructiveness of liquor and castigated the saloons, but he warned his fellow Christians to stay out of politics. "Moral suasion," he said, should be the domain of the church, not government. He blasted the "unthinking masses," the "sheep," who blindly voted as their ministers preached. He reiterated his hate for the liquor dealers and their corruption of politics. But, he said, "Paternalism in the past has been, and we may well believe in the future will continue to be, detrimental to the highest development of individual character."[72] But the battle for control of most major Texas churches had long since passed. The clerics had won. Once dominant, Johnston's anticlerical sentiment now set him apart from the majority of religious Texans. Johnston, an elder in a mainline denomination with few Texas members, demonstrated how marginalized anticlericalism had become. Rev. W. Irving Carroll, pastor of Dallas's First Congregational Church, registered a similar complaint to Johnston's: "I believe in the entire separation of Church and State." A minister may interfere in spiritual matters, he said, but "has no authority for dictatorial interference in the affairs of society in general."[73]

While these men demonstrated the continuing anticlerical commitments in some churches, most of the evangelical denominations had converted or purged their anticlerical members and embraced prohibition. Johnston and Carroll had been passed by. The Episcopalian Johnston spoke of tradition amid a world of innovation. He could only praise his own denomination for its repudiation of dogmatic prohibitionist creeds. "This is the freest church in the land," he said. "No other . . . allows such latitude of opinion to its ministers and members, on all subjects, when held loyally within the limits of the great fundamental facts of Christianity." He slammed his rival denominations, Catholic and Protestant both, saying "Protestantism is not without its self-constituted popes." But Johnston was now mostly alone and no longer expected the clerical crusade to be stopped by clergy. Instead, he predicted, "The evils resulting from the course now being pursued to enlist the churches, as such, in the present crusade may, in the near future, act like a boomerang, and in the end do untold injury to the cause of Christianity."[74] He rightly anticipated the fury of anticlerical resistance but spoke then from a minority position. The times had passed him by. The new century belonged to the evangelicals and to the culture of clericalism. But if they had conquered the churches, a wary public remained.

Anticlericalism, defeated within the denominations, still dominated public life when moral warfare erupted across Texas during the first decades of the twentieth century. Conflict engulfed politics and culture at all levels as moral reform became the pressing struggle of the age. The character and the consequences of that struggle are the subjects of following chapters, but even as clericalism graduated from insurgent church culture to dominant ideology, as it moved from the denominations into the public arena still some strands of resistance lurked among religious Texans. Repressed, marginalized, and weakened, unhappy dissidents felt resentment. The desperate remnants of anticlerical Christianity testified to clericalism's persistent divisiveness. One episode among the Methodists is illustrative.

Over the course of his career, Edwin Mouzon had ranged across religious divides. For much of his tenure as a Methodist bishop, he led the forces of clericalism. He mobilized troops in political contests and won headlines for maligning politicians. In 1911, he infamously confronted the state's sitting governor. And yet he wore the clerical mantle uncomfortably. The church's unending political crusades still troubled him. He had won the bishop's seat as an alternative to the fighting editor-cleric George Rankin. At the height of the prohibition crusade, while his peers stoked political agitation, the bishop urged restraint. He urged his cohorts to remember their spiritual mission.

Mouzon sensationalized his clerical brethren with a 1912 Christmas Day sermon he delivered in San Antonio. His message was simple: the church's political adventures must be reined in and its spiritual mission must be reemphasized. He shared his contemporaries' political commitments but feared they had become obsessions. It was time, he said, for the church to return to Christ. "I am pleading, I say, for a more spiritual ministry—for a ministry which draws men to Christ, even as Christ drew men to himself," he said.[75] It had been years since a high-ranking official in a major evangelical church had delivered such an appeal. "Here in Texas," Mouzon confided afterward, "many of our preachers have had more zeal than knowledge. A word was needed from someone in authority, which would go out to those on the outside," he said.[76]

The speech rippled over the region. Mississppi Methodist James D. Barbee Jr. read about the speech in the New Orleans *Time-Democrat*. He loved it. Barbee adhered to an old brand of evangelical Christianity. "I am profoundly convinced that the extent to which our ministers have participated in unwise political discussion largely accounts for the dearth of spirituality among us at this time," he wrote. As the speech worked its way through church circles, Rankin, Mouzon's old rival, denounced it in the *Texas Christian Advocate*. Barbee was ecstatic. He hoped the controversy could rekindle the clerical-anticlerical debate and push back against the clerical insurgents. It "affords a capital opportunity," he said, a chance to deliver "a clarion call for a more spiritual ministry."[77] The controversy did spread. Rankin begrudgingly reprinted the speech in the *Advocate*, where its anticlerical frustrations appealed to anticlerical exiles.[78]

Frank E. Thomas, a Methodist presiding elder, agreed with Mouzon. "It has rejoiced me that you have sounded this warning note to the ministry to be careful lest in their zeal for outward reforms they neglect their plain duty as under-shepherds of Jesus Christ." Thomas subscribed to the old-time religion and he rejected clerical claims to the true faith. "It is very easy for a minister when stirred by the sight of evil all about him to honestly assume the role of reformer but the plain teaching of the New Testament and the verdict of history is against him," he said. "Sooner or later he [the reformer] wakes up to the fact that his sheep are scattered, his real leaders missing, and his power to reach the lost sheep absolutely gone." The wayward church would win the scorn of the world, Thomas said. He praised Mouzon for leaving a written record testifying that not all Methodists had stood idly by.[79]

Far from heralding an anticlerical resurgence, though, the grousing of anticlerics only testified to their insignificance. Many of Mouzon's correspondents were aging leaders marginalized by the clerical uprising. Some repeated their well-worn refrains and hoped for change. "Too many of our young men (and some older ones) go too far in moral reform and seem to forget that God has called them to save the world through Jesus Christ instead of reform the world through their efforts," wrote Allen Tooke, a Methodist preacher in Fairfield.[80] Others complained but conceded the field anyway. I. Z. T. Morris, now sixty-one-years old and having served Texas Methodists for forty-one years, believed the battle had been lost long ago. The young clerics had accomplished their coup. "The impressions throughout the Church (it may be they are among men of my age only) is, that the spirituality of the Conference is lost," he wrote.[81] Some, of course, still yearned for redemption. James Kilgore, a presiding elder in Houston, wrote to Mouzon to say, "We need to be delivered from an influence which has injured the church too long, and you alone can do it."[82] Mouzon was all they had, and Mouzon was hardly a prototypical anticleric.

Nothing much came of Mouzon's plea, and even he would later lose himself in political campaigns. Anticlerical opposition faded in the churches. In 1910, the Texas Christian Missionary Society invited prohibitionist gubernatorial candidate Cone Johnson to speak before its convention and adopted a resolution supporting that year's prohibition campaign. Appalled that a politician should address a religious meeting, a small number of dissenters offered an addendum that stated: "We are unalterably opposed to this convention, of our brotherhood as a body, participating in any way in personal or in partisan politics." It also indicted the convention for allowing Johnson to speak before it: "We deprecate the entanglements and agitation that have arisen on account of the action of the temperance committee placing on the program a man who is asking for a political office." When the addendum went to a vote, six men supported it; over one hundred opposed it.[83]

By the second decade of the twentieth century, the clerics had triumphed in the churches. Activists claimed nearly every position of importance in the major white evangelical denominations. Having purged or silenced dissenters, they moved on to the next battles. Confident in victory, they turned to the public culture and targeted politicians and cultural critics. They were mobilized; religious anticlerics were marginalized. The exiles who wrote to Mouzon were artifacts of a bygone era. Diminished in number and inconsequential in impact, they retreated to the sidelines of the ongoing cultural struggle for the heart and soul of their society. Meanwhile, clericalism burst at the seams.

The clerical advance across the late nineteenth and early twentieth centuries was a broad pattern, not a clear-cut moment or a specific event. Nevertheless, the accumulating evidence of a suddenly regnant clerical culture hinted at a tipping point. Seen in a certain light, a moment appears, sometime around the turn of the century, when the anticlerical brand of southern evangelicalism collapsed and tensions within the denominations relaxed. The guns went silent. The churches were won. If no one could quite identify a precise moment when anticlerical resistance evaporated, early-twentieth-century clerics nonetheless seemed to sense that they had won. They were unshackled and eager to avenge their long imprisonment.

One extreme episode illustrated the newly combustible combination of denominational institutions, religious grievances, and unchecked aggression. In Waco, in late 1897, Baylor University students adopted a resolution condemning the state's great iconoclast, William Cowper Brann. Several armed students abducted him from his office, took him to campus, bound him, and, at gunpoint, amid a great crowd of students and faculty, forced him to recant his slanderous statements against Baptists and Baylor and swear to leave the city within twenty-four hours. But Brann stayed, and, six months later, in April, 1898, a fed-up Baptist shot and killed him on the city's streets.[84] It was an exceptional incident, but it nevertheless captured how aggrieved, angry, and uninhibited religious Texans had become.

A new era was dawning. All across the state, religious activists buzzed with energy. Preachers excited their congregations, denominational papers incensed their readers, and politicians were embracing a new brand of Christian politics. George Truett embodied those stunning changes. Once, he had shied from the public sphere. Now he engaged it. No longer were there narrow calls for regenerate sinners and redeemed souls. Gone were anticlerical disclaimers. The clerics had a nation to win. In 1911, Truett traveled to Boston to evangelize the new clerical theology. "What," he asked, "is the task of America? The task of America is that she herself become thoroughly and truly Christian." He explained: "America is to be Christian in her commerce and in her politics, in her art and in her education, in her literature and in every phase and fibre of her social order."[85] Truett and his brethren longed for something previously thought unattainable: a Christian nation.

Although clerics had conquered their denominational worlds, in the public sphere they would still have to struggle against longstanding fears and suspicions. How could they hope to win enough cultural capital outside of their cloistered worlds to compel the public realm to submit to their politics? Their effort to achieve prohibition would depend on the popular appeal of the clerical culture, the political power of new denominational offices, and the long ideological battles fought over government and history and proper religious practice that preceded the Bible Belt. But because clerics confronted the entirety of southern culture, part of the answer lies also in the ways in which clerical leaders would increasingly harness southern norms in service of their moral crusade.

6

Marking Morality

GENDER, RACE, AND RIGHTEOUSNESS

IF TEXANS HAD learned to acquire their moral identity through a new fighting faith, they practiced it through their politics: the pursuit of prohibition reinforced moral boundaries and sustained moral communities. But if the allure of righteousness pulled religion out of the pulpits and pews and propelled it into the world, what exactly did the clerics' moral community look like? In the land of Jim Crow and in the shadow of a nascent southern woman's movement, how did the religious pursuit of prohibition overlap with the region's many prevailing social and cultural divisions?

This chapter explores how activists both harnessed and subverted two dominant regional discourses—those surrounding race and gender—to clothe themselves in the garb of righteousness. Prohibition did not merely reflect or reproduce regional norms, but neither did it occur in isolation from them. The creation of the clerics' moral community depended on an ever-changing amalgamation of race, gender, class, religion, and politics. Prohibitionists at times minimized the salience of race and gender by drowning those distinctions in a sea of seemingly race- and gender-neutral moral criteria. But at other times, and even at the same time, their efforts overlaid these divisions with transcendent, intractable importance—the dominant moral politics of the period not only divided voters, it exiled entire populations from the clerics' moral imagination. Who would, and who wouldn't, be exiled?

Decades before Morris Sheppard introduced the Eighteenth Amendment outlawing the production, sale, and transportation of alcohol in the United States Senate, he urged Methodist youth in Texas to find "a purity of purpose and a morality of principal that enables him [youth] to stand out against the corruption of his time like a great white column against the blackness of an approaching storm."[1] Sheppard's metaphor hinted at the relationship between race and moral reform. The turn-of-the-twentieth-century South witnessed both the dramatic rise of political religion and the tragic descent into Jim Crow segregation. Confronted with the ugly virulence of many reformers' racial rhetoric, particularly the black-male-as-rapist trope deployed so often by Deep South prohibitionists, the southern prohibition movement can seem rooted in an easy-to-digest program of racial prejudice and social control.[2] One recent account of southern prohibition judged the movement's capitulation to regional racial thought "essential to the movement's ultimate success in the region."[3] But while race inevitably played a role in the creation of the reformers' moral community, the connection between race and religion, at least for white southern evangelicals, was neither simple nor direct.[4] Race was an integral part of the moral crusade—but only a part.

As reformers increasingly imagined themselves on the righteous side of a cut-and-dried division between saints and sinners, politics increasingly provided the measure of morality. Two impulses therefore tugged at reformers: through the articulation of a class-based, color-blind "best sort" and "worst sort" conception of society, reformers challenged regional racial norms by innovating a merit-based moral community. At the same time, however, the demographic realities of regional voting patterns—black Texans voted consistently against prohibition—threatened to condemn black Texans and make race just another marker of morality in the eyes of white activists.

Although African Americans in Texas accounted for a smaller percentage of the population—17.7 percent in 1910, down from 30 percent before the Civil War—than in any of the other eleven former Confederate states,[5] and an ever-growing Mexican American population increasingly complicated black-white dynamics,[6] geographic bonds, family ties, Confederate mythology, the cotton economy, self-identity, and history nevertheless marked Texas as a full-fledged member of the South.[7] And although the state produced few overtly virulent race baiters, it nevertheless evinced all of the barbaric worst of southern racism.[8] Throughout it all, however, white religious leaders in Texas spurned racial virulence for a peculiar kind of racial and moral paternalism.

Few prominent religious leaders in Texas indicted African Americans as inherently savage or dangerous, and most of them rejected hard-edged racial hatred and resisted stoking racial fears. Instead, captive to the legacies of pro-slavery Christianity, clerics embraced a racial worldview that judged blacks a childlike race of helpless dependents desperate for white guidance and leadership. Although the black exodus from white churches after emancipation had unsettled many whites, the burdens of racial paternalism allowed clerical leaders to resist the allure of a whites-only Christianity.

Throughout the late nineteenth and early twentieth centuries, white evangelicals maintained African Americans as objects of spiritual concern. Whatever their earthly relations, one 1872 article in the *Texas Baptist and Herald* argued, whites and blacks shared an eternal destiny. "The negro will be represented in the great congregation of the blood-washed at God's right hand. . . . He ["the negro"] is a legitimate object of our prayers, charity, and instruction."[9] Two decades later, the *Baptist Standard* reiterated, "If God has made of one blood all the races of men—and the Bible so teaches—the negroes are as much the subjects of gospel address as we are, and it is as much our duty to evangelize them as to send the gospel to our own people."[10]

Texas clerics generally refused to denigrate blacks as beasts or brutes. They condemned popular racist tracts: in 1902, the Baptist General Convention of Texas denounced Charles Carroll's *The Negro a Beast*; in 1903, J. B. Cranfill condemned Thomas Dixon's *The Leopard's Spots*.[11] In 1893, the Texas *Baptist Standard* published a plea for black evangelization with the following caveat, "Perchance some one who holds exalted opinions of this bloated anglo-saxon braggadocio atmosphere we Southern negro-haters have will say I am crazy over this subject."[12] Although they were assuredly believers in white supremacy, white clerics spurned the kinds of incendiary rhetoric that riled so many to violence around the turn of the century. And they never abandoned African Americans to racial violence.

White religious leaders in Texas decried lynching. "If we wantonly destroy the negro, we destroy our own souls," wrote Baptist preacher William T. Tardy.[13] Baptist minister A. J. Kincaid called "every one of these lawless lynchings . . . a murder [that] may be added to the total of the other murders."[14] After hearing about a Georgia lynching, J. B. Gambrell wrote, "the men in Georgia who burned that hapless negro at the stake burned the constitution and all the laws of Georgia, burned down the whole superstructure of civilization, and stripped every human life, under the influence of the maddening spirit, of all protection."[15] The *Baptist Standard* declared itself categorically opposed to racial violence: "We believe that any man and every man who participates in any kind of a mob or lynching becomes a murderer. The nature of the crime committed has no bearing whatever on the case."[16]

White religious leaders in Texas renounced the passionate hatred and violence that nourished lynching.[17] In fact, they blamed lynching on the same prevailing irreligion that had led them into public life in the first place. J. B. Gambrell hoped evangelical religion could soften racial tensions and ameliorate racial strife: he rooted mob violence and race hate in the absence of "civilization" and civic education. He believed that "every preacher in this land ought to fulminate against mobs and against the spirit that panders to the low and vicious in politics, until there is a change of atmosphere."[18]

Several historians, however, have explored religious pursuit of moral reform in the South and discovered rabid race-baiting.[19] Some have attributed the success of the clerical movement to the exploitation of racial fears and the weaponization of racist rhetoric. In areas of the Deep South where the most virulent strains of racism ruled, this was perhaps the case. But in Texas, reformers resisted the urge to indulge such tactics. Lone Star reformers sometimes wielded race as a weapon, but no less frequently or intensely than did their opponents. In fact, Lone Star clerics were just as often on the receiving end of racial attacks. "The preacher of applied Christianity here has been the object of withering contempt," reflected Baptist preacher William T. Tardy. " 'Negro lover' has been the epithet flipped from the tongue of the low-born and the vicious."[20]

"The remarkable success of the [prohibition] movement in the South was often attributed to the presence of the Negro," C. Vann Woodward wrote in his seminal *Origins of the New South*. But Woodward agreed with those who argued "the saloon has been abolished and retained in the communities of the South without apparent reference to the presence of the negro." The only correlation, he said, was "a high percentage of native-born, rural, Protestant elements in the population."[21] Prohibition and the triumph of clericalism depended on an activist brand of evangelical faith funneled through notions of morality and righteousness, not the crude exploitation of southern fears by race-baiters. In Texas, of course, the gravity of race weighed on all. If the reformers were forced to contend directly and overtly with fraught race relations, as they were in many parts of the Deep South, they would. The movement could thrive with racial exploitation, just as it could without it. The proper study of southern prohibition therefore asks not only how prohibitionists exploited or accommodated white racial fears, but how the pursuit of prohibition—and the rising tide of clericalism—reshaped the South's existing racial norms.

Clerical activists approached race with both inherited regional prejudices and innovative clerical conceptions of righteousness. Whether or not they imagined blacks to be debauched brutes, they still regarded African Americans as potential allies, as redeemable souls capable of moral action and with claims to respectability and worthy of a home in the clerics' righteous community. Prohibitionists assumed educated African Americans could live justly, vote morally, and join in their growing reform movement. White reformers could therefore reject or manipulate any overpowering, mystical division between black and white. They could, at times, side with black allies over white opponents. Such was the power, however limited, of the reformers' moral universe. Broader dynamics than race alone moved southerners to construct the Bible Belt.

Both reformers and their opponents lived in a racialized society, but the emerging prohibition movement constructed something more than race.[22] Race was a part of the clerics' morality—but only a part. They innovated something more alluring than a simple rehashing of southern racial divisions. Race become just one of several possible markers of morality. Clerics mixed ideas about race with notions of citizenship and respectability and all the cultural weight of white southern Protestantism. They offered morality, godliness, righteousness. Morality became their obsession, not race—or at least not race alone. The steady spread of moral politics testified to the clerics' appeal and heralded the arrival of the Bible Belt. Notions of righteousness undergirded it all. Whether morality was channeled through racism or racialized rhetoric, it reworked public antagonisms into new group identities and glued together a vast new subculture committed to religious activism. Morality cleaved the South in two.

White religious leaders imagined a divide between a "better sort" and a "worse sort" that transcended the rigidities of the American color line.[23] It became the central explanation for why some supported their crusades and others opposed them. An aging Methodist, William S. Herndon, lectured across Texas in favor of statewide prohibition in 1887. Herndon was, according to his contemporary Francis W. Johnson, "on the moral side of all social questions" and "was the central figure upon the stump in favor of the banishment of the saloon." But it was Johnson's descriptions of Herndon's supporters that revealed the reformers' social imagination. Johnson said "Texas's best citizens gathered to hear him tell of the evil of intemperance."[24] Among blacks and whites both, such reformers said, there were those who traded in irreligion, vice, and immorality. These fallen citizens—of both races—rejected God and religion and forfeited membership in the clerics' moral community. But there was another group, the so-called better sort, that welcomed religion, embraced the moral mission of the reformers, and trafficked in righteousness. Such a divide, reformers said, split across race. Whites and blacks both had their own better and worse elements.

"There are two very distinct classes of Negroes, the good and the bad," declared B. F. Riley in 1909. "This led to a grave disadvantage to the race, for when a crime was committed it was attributed to the Negro race, not to the criminal alone who committed it." Riley, who resigned his pulpit at Houston's First Baptist Church in 1907 to head the Texas chapter of the Anti-Saloon League, called it an unfair judgment "in the face of the fact that so many are struggling to raise their race to higher planes."[25] Clerics sought to rescue this better class of blacks. "The disposition to recount only the misdeeds of the unworthy Negroes," Riley wrote, "has built up a partition between the two races." According to such understandings, regional salvation lay not in a whites-only movement but in a bests-only one. "Nothing short of a general popular movement which would bring into exercise the best of both races will relieve the situation in the South," Riley concluded. Despite the region's venomous racism, he proclaimed "He ['the Negro'] is not without thousands of friends among the better people of the South."[26]

Riley demonstrated a remarkable commitment to racial uplift, but even rigid white supremacists embraced the idea of a morally hierarchical black population. Writing in the *Baptist Standard* in 1899, J. B. Gambrell affirmed the existence of "two races, widely different in every respect." He said, "They are, indeed, at the extremes—one the foremost race in the world, the other the rearmost race in the world." But amid his racial boundary-setting he ceded the existence of a better sort of black citizen. "That a respectable minority of them have attained to an intelligent conception of the situation, and are worthy and good citizens, I cheerfully bear witness," he wrote.[27]

Clerics' commitment to black spiritual life, opposition to lynching, and embrace of a black "best sort" testified to a racial worldview that imagined moral reform as a program of racial uplift. Most Texas clerics ascribed the tragedy of African American life not to innate racial shortcomings, but to history and environment. The *Baptist Standard* combined traditional white racial judgments with an understanding of black obstacles and recognized some measure of black progress. It said southern blacks "are struggling against fearful odds. They have the deep prejudices of the narrow-minded, the effect of centuries of slavery, and, worst of all, their own ignorance and passions to contend with." The paper lauded African American development and said, "He ['the negro'] has made as great progress during the twenty-eight years of his freedom as any people with like enslavement and similar subsequent environments ever made."[28] Riley published *The White Man's Burden* in 1910, with, he said, "special reference to the responsibility of the white race to the Negro problem." While exhibiting all the paternalistic racism of his upbringing, he prescribed a role for blacks in the making of American history, urged blacks to take pride in their race, and rejected notions of racial inferiority by blaming environmental disadvantages. He denounced southern racists for their ignorance and blasted the quiet critics of racism for their silence.[29]

Prohibition fit neatly into this worldview. Clerics attacked liquor as a drain on black life. "The negro," the *Baptist Standard* read, "is, when uncorrupted by the defects of the saloon and other agencies of the devil, run by white men and licensed by political parties that are dominated by white men, more easily influenced by the gospel of Jesus than his brother in white."[30] Such judgments only confirmed the utility of moral reform as a central plank of racial uplift. A few prominent white religious leaders, including Joseph Martin Dawson and Riley, committed themselves to working with African Americans. Riley went beyond encouraging rhetoric by demonstrating a profound willingness to organize and work with southern blacks and he helped establish the Southern Negro Anti-Saloon Federation in 1909.[31]

When clerical leaders incorporated racial uplift into their moral programs, it fit well. Clerics believed moral politics would not only affirm the role of religion in public life, it would free the black race from misery. Defeat the saloon, they said, and the black population would finally flourish. "The basis of the Negro problem, so-called, is the liquor problem," Riley proclaimed in 1909. "Ignorance, poverty, vagrancy, demoralization, debauchery, divorcement, lawlessness, and criminality, so far as these relate to the Negro, are, in the largest measure, due to the saloon."[32] He was not alone. "The white man's liquor and the white man's blood make a hellish combination in a black man," wrote Baptist preacher William T. Tardy.[33] Many therefore saw prohibition as the central plank in a platform for black uplift. For instance, one contemporary called prohibition in Tyler "a great blessing to the race." He said it "has enabled the Negro to spend money for a home in town, buy a farm and make himself and his family independent and happy."[34] Prohibition worked like magic, they said, and progress followed.

Prohibitionists did, of course, deploy regional racial rhetoric. While they denounced lynching, for instance, the *Baptist Standard* also editorialized that "saloons brutalize and profligate blacks and white women suffer from their outrages."[35] Such ugly rhetoric exposed many clerics' paternal racism. Like children, white prohibitionists said, blacks must be spared from bad influences lest they become corrupt and criminal. White Texans didn't advocate prohibition because blacks were beasts that needed to be controlled, they advocated it because, in their minds, liquor *made* them beasts. Reformers applied the same argument, without the region's black-male-as-rapist trope, to all other races: prohibition saved everyone. In the moral universe of the prohibitionists, saloons fostered juvenile delinquency, domestic abuse, and broken homes. It bankrupted farmers and trapped workers in poverty. It made men insane. Clerics therefore believed prohibition would antiquate asylums, empty jails, and liberate men's weak constitutions from liquor's blighting menace. While in the South these arguments often became racialized, racialization was never essential. And in Texas, a broad moral identity, not a narrowly racial one, increasingly tied reformers together—sometimes across racial lines.

If liquor oppressed the African American community, white religious leaders reasoned, then black leaders could be enlisted as allies. Riley claimed that "the better class among the colored people were engaged in stoutly opposing strong drink, and in inculcating the principles of sobriety as far as they might." He lauded "their preachers, teachers, land owners, and thrifty men of business" and declared them willing "to cooperate with the better element of whites in driving out the saloon."[36] It was a common claim of white clerics that the better sort of black leaders stood with them. But did they?

After emancipation, religious African Americans embarked on a path of spiritual independence. Blacks fled white churches and formed their own congregations in their own churches under their own pastors. "With or without our concurrence," lamented one white Methodist, "the colored people were slipping out from under our control."[37] Blacks demanded freedom, whites demanded obedience, and racial fracture followed. The era of white religious rule ended, and with it, biracial worship.[38]

Black Texans nurtured several renowned evangelists. John L. "Sin Killer" Griffin, the "Rapid-Firing Gun Evangelist" sometimes called, after the popular white southern evangelist, the "Sam Jones of the Black Folks," captivated black audiences with rousing oratory.[39] The "black Billy Sunday," J. Gordon McPherson, crisscrossed the state proclaiming gospel truths and racial uplift. Black southerners quickly entrusted their religious leaders with social authority. Many viewed a preacher's political and religious roles synonymously. Just as their white brethren were learning to do, black ministers often proclaimed the right to "preach politics." And like white clerics, black preachers too spread the gospel of morality and they too tied their estimation of the world to the world's estimation of themselves. At the turn of the twentieth century, when the moral impulse tugged the hardest, "Sin Killer" Griffin perhaps best embodied the black cleric. He flayed the world's moral lassitude and incorporated the redemption of morality into the redemption of the black race. In the summer of 1903, for instance, Griffin held a weeks-long revival meeting at Dallas's Mount Zion Colored Baptist Church. When it ended, Griffin took the meeting to a pool along the Trinity River where the crowd sang of "old time religion" and "washing in the Beautiful Stream." Griffin, tall and in white robes, delivered one of his typically cadenced sermons. "The negro problem will never be solved," he said, "until you learn to serve God and tend to your own business." He told the crowd that sin filled the jails with African Americans and kept the race down. But there was a solution, he said. You could be saved. You could receive the "B.A.," the Born Again, "the first degree of the king's college." He sang as he immersed several in the river: "Oh come, sinner, come, no longer in wickedness roam."[40]

In addition to fighting sin with sermons, many black preachers embarked on the clerics' great moral crusades. Black political activism did not die with Reconstruction; nineteenth-century Texas offers examples of black political participation and biracial political cooperation.[41] Edward Ayers's masterful *Promise of the New South* captured the importance of prohibition to the era's racial politics. "Indeed," Ayers wrote, "blacks enjoyed their greatest political activity and visibility of the entire New South era in the prohibition movement." He quoted an 1881 North Carolina newspaper lamenting that "the colored man comes off the field full of smiles" because "he has lived to see the day when his former owner takes him by the hand as a man and brother, and joyfully labors with him as an equal citizen either for or against prohibition." Ayers concluded, rightfully, that "although based in separate organizations, black and white opponents of liquor associated publicly, spoke from the same platform, celebrated together, and warmly talked of each other in their newspapers."[42] The Texas experience supports such observations.

White religious activists welcomed African American support. "I have learned with great satisfaction that you have undertaken to organize the Negroes of the South in opposition to the Saloon," B. H. Carroll wrote to Riley. "This unfortunate people, in their poverty and ignorance have no greater foe than the saloon. If, by any means, they can be led to see that their highest step towards the elevation of their race is to put themselves against this, their deadliest enemy, then such means ought to be employed."[43] Such means were.

During the 1887 campaign, thousands of prohibitionists rallied on a summer day in Fort Worth. Black and white ministers addressed multiracial audiences. White observers commended several of the African American speakers. Rev. A. A. Grant won particular praise from the *Fort Worth Weekly Gazette*. "His speech ranked high," the paper read, "and was a pleasing and pleasant surprise to the vast crowd who stood around him and encouraged and interrupted him alternatively by vociferous applause." A black preacher named Samuels, from Texarkana, also spoke. The *Gazette* commended his

"speech of considerable length and great force" and touted his "apt illustra-
tions and irresistible witticisms." It reported that Samuels "appealed to his
colored friends in eloquent pathos to cast one vote for that freedom which
would follow from suppression of the whisky traffic and which would be but
little less than that which they obtained when the death of slavery was pronounced in America."[44]

Grant and Samuels were not alone. Several African Americans assumed
prominent roles in that year's campaign. Some, such as black leader Mack
M. Rodgers, worked in blacks-only organizations, but others worked within
white organizations. If their churches were segregated, their moral efforts
could, at times, become integrated.[45]

A white Methodist preacher from Sulphur Springs, Joshua Hicks, dis-
regarded any possibilities of social equality. In social life, he said, the color
line was safe. But as for politics, Hicks believed and hoped biracial political
cooperation could sink the saloon. Northern reformers, he said, saw "no good
reason why the two races should stand arrayed against each other at the ballot-
box." He agreed. "That such is the case here in the South, no one can deny."[46]
Hicks perhaps lived on the margins of the religious and political establishment. In a few short years, he would join the Populist movement, abandon
his Methodist creed, and embrace a host of unpopular religious positions.
But his sentiments reflected the variety of opinions, and occasional embrace
of biracial politics, that defined much of the prohibition movement.[47]

Much about black churches after Reconstruction paralleled developments
in white churches, and many of the same impulses that moved whites also
moved African Americans. Black leaders indicted the age's moral decay and
its pervasive irreligion. They linked immorality with the plight of black society. They linked their cause with the fate of their race. When a bishop from
the African Methodist Episcopal Church, Evans Tyree, a black Tennessean,
visited the Northeast Conference of his denomination in Bryan, Texas, in
1906, he said blacks had all the tools for racial uplift and that religious leaders
had only to wield them. "It is our duty to teach our people righteous living,"
he said, and to

> teach them to be honorable and upright in the sight of God and man.
> . . . The negro must build character. We must live and practice moral-
> ity in this country or we can not hope to amount to anything. We are
> character-builders. You must build up character, and when you do
> this you will find that we have many friends. Complaints and wailings
> never yet raised a people. Stopping to quarrel with the stick that trips

you up does not help you on your journey. Races are lifted up like kites by the adverse current, and often the greatest blessings are brought to us by the heaviest storms."[48]

Tyree believed that African Americans' public support for moral reform would advertise the merits of their race. "If a man calls me a monkey I know he is mistaken, because I have two legs, and I may not be able to convince him by argument, but my work will tell." Tyree urged the better sort of his race to assume moral leadership over the worst. He told the assembled leaders to "reach out to that class of negroes who are taking us to destruction."[49] Across Texas, black religious leaders preached a gospel of morality and right living that conformed to the expectations of white reformers. And yet, despite the rhetoric of the better sort of black religious leaders, the reality of black support never matched the dreams of prohibitionists.

As with any community, black Texans exhibited their own social and cultural divisions. Successful black southerners struggled to navigate the South's tragic descent into barbarism in the decades after the Civil War. In Paris, Texas, for instance, the site of a particularly infamous lynching in 1893, middle-class black leaders carved out a measure of prominence and prosperity. Two African Americans served on the city council and another on the school board. Long-standing black community leaders looked warily on the influx into the city of working-class blacks unmoored to the city's black community. Henry Smith was one of those.[50] Economic growth shifted populations, enlarged cities, and unsettled old things. Strange new populations troubled whites just as they troubled blacks. White newspapers peppered their pages with editorials blasting the behavior of recently arrived black migrants and black youth while praising the old, deeply rooted "better sort" of blacks. Obituaries of deceased African Americans, for instance, lauded the "old time negroes." But the new generation, these paternalistic whites said, had forgotten their place, turned their backs on righteousness, and descended into barbarism.[51] Some blacks, believing that the "better class" might be spared, hoped that the gates to citizenship and respectability might still be open before them.[52] Prohibition might offer them passage.

If opposition to moral reform threatened to confirm white suspicions of black immorality, then black southerners could contradict white expectations by embracing moral legislation and cement their status as a "better class." If they failed, however, they would conform to white prejudice and give credence to white suspicions. While moral crusades offered opportunities to bridge racial divisions, the imperatives of those crusades inevitably shaped how Texans made sense of race. To fall on the wrong side of the prohibition issue left African Americans vulnerable to a pernicious form of moral exile. White evangelical activists could compound racial thought with transcendent moral judgments. And they did.

Although many African American leaders supported the moral crusades, and many black preachers spoke loudly against the saloon, the vast majority of black Texans never followed suit. Removed from the culture of white Protestant moralism and hostile to restrictive legislation, most voted against prohibition. The work of the righteous few would never overcome this undeniable fact. Many leading black figures joined the majority of black voters and opposed prohibition. Rev. Melvin Wade, a prominent black leader in Reconstruction Era Texas, favored the antis. Erstwhile Populist leader John B. Rayner received brewers' funds and stumped across the state against prohibition.[53] Even Sin Killer Griffin courted the brewers for cash by organizing black voters against prohibition.

Many of the same sentiments that motivated white anticlerics induced black opposition. Disdain for pie-in-the-sky creedalism—as well as the allure of financial compensation—moved Rayner to oppose prohibition as the movement picked up steam in the twentieth century.[54] The preachers and their moral zealotry, he said, stunted black progress with their emotion and superstition. "You cannot reason with intolerant bigotry," he wrote privately, "nor discuss with religious fanaticism."[55] He likewise slammed the pretensions of the black "best sort." He decried the "hotel flunkies, barbers, dude school teachers, ignorant preachers, [and] saloon waiters"—the state's black establishment—for blocking practical, here-and-now programs for uplift.[56]

Many African American churches, meanwhile, maintained their resistance to moral reform. Although black preachers endeavored to sustain a vibrant tradition of black political engagement, many religious African American southerners reflected the same anticlerical sentiments as white southerners. Conservatives in the Colored Methodist Episcopal Church, for instance, played to white anxieties about black activism by railing against political entanglements. When the organization formed in 1870, it borrowed the Discipline of the Methodist Episcopal Church, South but amended it to explicitly disassociate itself from worldly work. The body decreed church buildings "shall in no wise be used for political purposes or assemblages." "As ministers of the Gospel," Bishop Lucious H. Holsey explained, "we make no stump speeches and fight no battles of the politicians." He pointed to the white churches as a model. "There was no Politics in the establishment of their Church by their white brethren in the South," he said. "They are only to follow Jesus Christ and his Religion." The sentiment was not Holsey's alone. One black Georgian complained "there was a General hue and cry to cast Politics out from the Church and he himself had been threatened with expulsion from his own Church for asserting his civil and legal rights."[57] Prohibition campaigns crystallized such rhetoric, as when a black preacher in 1887 accused his prohibitionist counterparts of "converting the Sunday school rooms into political halls."[58] Similar antiprohibitionist sentiments would undo much of the good will "better sort" black prohibitionists had earned with white clerics.

Despite the work of activists, black prohibitionists could never disassociate the majority of African Americans from the stigma of the antiprohibition countercrusade. Everywhere, black voices rose up against prohibition, and everywhere, whites were listening. When sixty black delegates joined a "true blue" antiprohibition rally in Dallas in 1887, observers noted the natural alliance of black Texans and white antiprohibitionists. "Mixed up with the Texas people," a friendly reporter waxed, "they feel like the old times had come again and the long, long estrangement was over." Such hopes—and historical judgments—were fanciful, of course, but the delegates played a substantive part in the convention. They worked in committees and successfully amended several resolutions. Wade addressed white congressmen and judges and other prominent leaders. "I think differently from any who have spoken to-day," he said. "I have reason to be uneasy. I hear you gray-headed old white men, rocked all your lives in the cradle of liberty. Now if you are fearful of your liberty," he said to applause, "what do you suppose I must feel?" Wade and other black Texans knew the sting of restrictive legislation. He pledged his support to the "true blues."[59]

No matter how vocal the support of some black leaders—support that white prohibitionists courted and praised—white prohibitionists could never shake the conviction that the "worst sort" of black voters dominated the African American electorate. Conventional wisdom aligned with voting patterns: black Texans opposed prohibition. Time and again, black votes blocked prohibition.[60] Close contests only crystallized the importance of a near-solid black voting bloc. When B. H. Carroll reflected on the earliest statewide prohibition defeat, he said, "In the great campaign of '87 it was the almost solid Negro vote that defeated State Prohibition." To religious whites increasingly anxious to secure their stake in public life, the "better class" of blacks seemed increasingly imaginary, and the "inferior class" of blacks had to be silenced. [61]

Voting restrictions arose in this context. The strength of antiprohibition sentiment among black Texans doomed black political life. Clerics increasingly imagined most black Texans as nothing but obstacles on the road to a moral rebirth, rather than as part of a bipartite community variously composed of allies and enemies. To avoid further defeat, prohibitionists purged voting rolls. Moral leaders linked elements of the black population with moral and electoral corruption. Prohibition and disfranchisement flowed together. While still touting the existence of a black "better sort," prohibition elections allowed whites to magnify and demonize the "worse sort." Reformers tagged their electoral enemies as opponents of moral progress and obstacles to a godly commonwealth. And so, they had to be removed.

In the early twentieth century, Texans disfranchised broad swaths of the population. Through a combination of poll taxes, white primaries, violence, intimidation, and fraud, Texas substantially suppressed political participation.[62] By purging voter rolls with race-blind poll taxes, reformers hoped to purify the electorate and empower the respectable best sort of citizen. If grass-roots fraud and intimidation overwhelmingly targeted black Texans, some legislation, such as the poll tax, crossed racial and ethnic lines to target the entire "worst sort." The opinions of the state's architect of disfranchisement reflected his neat belief in a cross-racial, best-and-the-rest conception of society.

Alexander Watkins Terrell spearheaded voting restrictions in the state legislature. The son of slaveholders, he detested black political participation. He called the Fifteenth Amendment "the political blunder of the century." But he hardly esteemed poor whites, either: he detested their suffrage just the same. "Whether universal manhood suffrage is good for the country," Terrell wrote in 1906, "depends entirely on the sort of men who vote." Although early in life an antiprohibitionist and religious skeptic, Watkins later joined the prohibition movement and aligned himself with the state's progressive politics. His arguments flowed across the color line and reflected the clerics' best-and-worst rhetoric. He targeted what he called "the thriftless, idle and semi-vagrant elements of both races" for disfranchisement.[63] Others echoed his sentiments and supported his efforts.

Moral reformers paved the path for disfranchisement. State representative Pat Neff steered voting restrictions through the state legislature and introduced poll tax legislation in 1899 and 1901.[64] Later in life he would claim the restrictions "had nothing to do with the Negroes. . . . We drys put that in there to keep the wets from stealing elections from us."[65] Neff, a committed Baptist, later defended prohibition as governor, in the 1920s, and then served fifteen years as president of Baylor University. His thoughts perfectly capture the nexus of religious conviction, political reform, and disfranchisement. He believed the worst elements of the African American population, as well as those of Hispanics and Germans, joined with poor whites and impeded the flowering of godly politics.[66] Disfranchisement followed.

Agrarians, workers, African Americans, and Republicans organized against voting restrictions, but in vain. The "Terrell Election Law" passed the state legislature in 1903.[67] Another set of restrictions passed two years later. Political participation plummeted. The white vote was cut in half and black political participation practically disappeared.[68] With black voters' political stake diminished, cooperation with the black "better sort" faded from the prohibitionists' view. Drained of their electoral strength, African Americans became irrelevant to the reformers' political calculus. Submerged now by the "worst sort," blacks became obstacles to reform. Notions of black agency faded and efforts at racial cooperation dissolved.

In June 1911, two to three hundred black Texans attended an antiprohibition rally and barbecue in Fort Worth's Douglas Park. Beer and barbecue flowed and an all-black band interspersed speeches delivered by a "colored contingent." The mayor had planned to address the crowd but canceled at the last moment. Turnout was low, and little was said or done of interest.[69] A few days later, however, at the opening of the 1911 prohibition campaign in Dallas, the prohibitionist Cone Johnson denounced the meeting. Johnson said the keynote speaker promised an inevitable hike in the price of alcohol if prohibition was enacted. "No dodging the issue there," the prohibitionist Johnson said, "no attempt by this unsophisticated negro to becloud the main issue; he toed the mark and announced the gospel."[70] Black Texans, he said, were slaves to the bottle. In such cases, class distinctions disappeared as the best class was dissolved into the worst class and forgotten.

Reformers increasingly turned their back on black voters and revoked elite black membership in the "better sort." In 1914, the *Baptist Standard* called prohibition "a struggle for a higher Anglo-Saxon civilization against the slum civilization of the great cities."[71] In lily-white primary elections, a limited racial politics pushed both sides toward race-baiting. In 1912, prohibitionist candidates Cone Johnson and Morris Sheppard accused antiprohibitionist Jacob Wolters of intending to use African American voters in South Texas. Wolters denied it. He lauded his "record in the fight for the supremacy of the white man" and supplied telegrams from South Texas county officials testifying that "negroes never vote in the Democratic primaries in our section of the State." The letter said, "Jake Wolters was one of the men conspicuous in the fight for a white man's government and the elimination of the negro from local politics."[72] Prohibition could devolve into vulgar racial politics.

Prohibitionists increasingly lumped all blacks into the antiprohibitionist camp. Despite the best effort of reformers to foster the black "best sort," overwhelming opposition to liquor reform instead marked most blacks as irredeemable members of the "worst sort." Indicted in the public mind, some black leaders still sought redemption in the prohibition movement. If blacks could be seen supporting the dry cause, they reasoned, they would scrub clean the patina of racial corruption. They would inject themselves firmly into the "better" camp.[73] But they were too few in number and reformers' efforts at disfranchisement, targeted at the "worse sort," drove most of the remaining black prohibitionists back to the antis.

While most white prohibitionists in Texas had refused to raise the dreaded specter of racial equality in their efforts, some succumbed. After a local option defeat in Bell County, the *Belton Reporter* attributed African American opposition to prohibition as evidence of the leveling effects of alcohol. "The negroes," it read, "say they vote for whisky because at the polls and in the saloons are the only places where they can be equal with the white folks."[74] The article hinted at a growing truth. One brewer put it best when he praised black antiprohibitionists who, "without pay, took the platform in defense of liberty of conscience and citizenship qualification."[75] Antiprohibitionists recognized and exploited black yearnings for citizenship. Brewers believed "If they ["the negro"] can be brought to realize that the holding of a poll tax receipt is the best asset they can possess to gain standing in the community in which they live, it ought to be a convincing argument to stimulate them to qualify as voters."[76] African Americans advanced this argument themselves. M. H. Broyles, a professor at Prairie View College, organized a session of the Texas Negro Convention in 1911. "Special stress," he wrote, "will be put upon the question of the payment of poll taxes as a necessary part of the duties incident to good citizenship, it being our aim to especially stimulate an interest on the part of our people in their qualifying themselves in every way to become worthy citizens."[77] For despite increasingly severe obstacles and restrictions, Texas's emphasis on the best and the rest meant that large numbers of black men could still vote in nonprimary elections, particularly in statewide constitutional referenda and local option elections. Even in diminished numbers, they remained a crucial voting bloc that could sway contests.

Local contests continued to see prohibitionists and antiprohibitionists compete for black votes. "The election in Caldwell County was very close," one anti reported in 1911, "in fact, the negro vote, to a certain extent, controlled the situation."[78] Another, in Navarro County, recognized that "the colored vote was the balance of power."[79] Black votes were still crucial. Antis courted them and many prohibitionists still hesitated to forsake black voters. "We ought to be doing missionary work among the colored brethren without delay, as the enemy is hot after them at this moment," one of the brewers' political agents wrote during a campaign.[80] The black leader and organizer J. B. Rayner reminded his brewer-benefactors that his speeches and organizing kept black Texans "from making campaign thunder for the intolerant and fanatical prohibitionists."[81] But prohibitionists could never capture the black vote. White reformers retreated. And when they did, their appeal to the "better sort" collapsed and exhortations to the best class of black Texans evaporated. Rather than diminish racial divisions, the clerics' vision of a shared, cross-racial morality increasingly magnified them.

Prohibitionists made the Bible Belt by marking morality, by drawing lines between the "best" and the "rest." In the end, they succeeded because they could both incorporate and transcend southern racism. They could unite a mostly white community—and largely exile a black one—using religious and political questions, not explicitly racial ones. If they intended to race bait, they no longer needed to be explicit. White clerics founded the Bible Belt on something more powerful and ultimately more palatable than crass racial appeals. They built it on a sense of righteousness. This is what lingered. This was the belief that later transplanted itself outside the region, where, just as in the South, religious activists could learn to lump hostile blacks and whites together into something both less and more than race. They would target secular opponents, liberals, the poor, "elites." They would have enmity for opponents of all stripes. Under the various markers of morality, moral reformers would be the best class. They would be the righteous ones.

Just as race entwined itself with the clerics' new moral identity, conceptions of gender and righteousness fused together within the clerical crusade. By exploiting the labor of churchwomen but confining their efforts safely within their male-dominated organizations, white male prohibitionists freely drew on the tropes of gender to reinforce their stake in public life. Clerical activists leveraged their self-proclaimed defense of women, children, and "the home" to further justify their new public roles even as public-minded women were forced to look elsewhere to realize their own political ambitions.[82]

The oft-told tale of prohibition and southern women's efforts goes something like this: women carved out spheres of influence within the safety of the evangelical churches, built a unique women's culture around such concerns as mission work and moral reform, and moved beyond the boundaries of the churches to engage public life through institutions such as the Women's Christian Temperance Union (WCTU) and political reform movements such as prohibition. Then, confronted by the meager returns of moral suasion and encouraged by a movement culture promoting rapidly expanding public ambitions, women pushed deeper into public life to embrace secular reforms and ultimately work for suffrage. The archetype of this evolution might be a middle-class Methodist woman involved in mission work who, swept up by Frances Willard's southern tours in the 1880s, joins the WCTU, embraces temperance, pushes for prohibition, and agitates for suffrage.[83] Little in Texas, however, recommends this familiar narrative.

Women, of course, did find outlets within the churches and in temperance work. Women carved independent spaces within the several evangelical denominations.[84] "In no sphere does woman shine so radiantly as in religious service," wrote Dawson, the state's leading proponent of social Christianity, in 1914.[85] In missionary societies, educational endeavors, and benevolent work, women worked behind the male face of denominational leadership. As Annie Armstrong, leader of the Women's Missionary Union, said in Dallas in 1894, "Women's work is, much of it, hidden work, as are the springs that feed the water courses in the mighty river."[86] Over the course of the late nineteenth and early twentieth centuries, women expanded their denominational work. "The church, which has always regarded her as its willing handmaiden," an anonymous contributor to the *Dallas Morning News* wrote, "is realizing the fact that she is not the passive slave she has been in the past."[87] A new generation of reformers began to look to women as instruments in the coming redemption of the region.

By advocating prohibition, women inarguably became agents in the making of the Bible Belt. In 1907, the temperance committee of the Northwest Texas Conference of the Southern Methodists praised the "Ballotless Legion" and the "hearty co-operators of our Christian womanhood."[88] With or without the vote, women worked for moral reform. In a 1903 local option election in Longview, women marched from the churches in the morning and worked on voters all day. Church bells rang every hour and, when a majority decided against the saloon, women crowded into the county courthouse to sing "Praise God, From Whom All Blessings Flow."[89] Similar scenes repeated themselves across the state. On a cold and wet November election day in 1907, women and children paraded through San Angelo with banners that read "Save Our Homes and Our Boys."[90] In a 1904 local option election in Sherman, the president of the state's WCTU pled for prohibition while, according to the organization's official organ, "children threw over her head the snow-white banner of prohibition, with its ribbons floating in the breeze, and she urged the people to vote 'for God and home and native land.'"[91]

Prohibitionists welcomed women's work. The state's chapter of the Anti-Saloon League, for instance, praised women's missionary organizations and called for the united co-operation and influence of Texas womanhood."[92] But perhaps no organization looms larger in the scholarly imagination of gender and prohibition than the WCTU. As one recent account of southern prohibition put it, "The primary agency through which women participated actively in the prohibition movement was the Women's Christian Temperance Union."[93] The WCTU's hold on historians can hardly be exaggerated. Besides being a vehicle for women's self-assertion, the organization has variously been portrayed as a kind of intersectional glue that reunited North and South behind the banner of a godly whiteness and as an international agent of moral imperialism.[94] Southern historians champion the WCTU, in the words of one historiographical observer, as "an agency of heroic feminism that allowed women to break free from the shackles of domesticity."[95] That narrative arc continues through much of southern women's history and the history of southern prohibition. It usually begins with Frances Willard's southern tours.

Willard, an Illinoisan, became president of the young WCTU in 1879. She invigorated the organization with her energetic "do everything" reform program and set about planting unions all across the country. But in Texas she faltered. When Willard barnstormed across the Lone Star State in 1881 and 1882, she garnered headlines, raised funds, collected signatures, and organized a network of unions and auxiliaries.[96] But she failed to establish a firm foothold in the state. Despite hearty welcomes, packed churches, crowded speaking halls, and several glowing reviews in the press, Willard received a decidedly mixed response from religious Texans. The *Texas Baptist* ignored her visit and, a week after her departure, attacked female activism: "Place her [a woman] before the public as a politician or an advocate from the rostrum, even of social reform or religion, and you rob her of her God-given retiring modesty and weaken her influence over man."[97] Although she spoke to overflowing crowds and won much praise, Willard suffered from her associations with unpalatable northern women's movements. In Paris, for instance, no clergymen would allow Willard to speak in their churches.[98] Meanwhile the injunctions against political preaching worked doubly against women. A peculiar form of gendered anticlericalism stymied Willard's tours: the *Galveston Weekly News*, for instance, highlighted female activists to warn against a new "politico-theological organization." In the face of such resistance, Willard despaired. "Never in my life—not even in Europe—have I felt so cut off from my own kindred."[99] She left, and her efforts evaporated.

Texas women were slow to promote temperance and prohibition, let alone embrace the seemingly radical agenda of the WCTU. Historian Judith McArthur deftly captured the struggles of the state's WCTU in her account of Texas clubwomen, *Creating the New Woman*. As she quoted one anonymous San Antonio woman who wrote in 1886, "The women of the South may be slow to undertake this work because of a false idea, born of their conservatism, that it is unwomanly."[100] By 1888, the Texas WCTU claimed only 1,500 members, and nearly two-thirds fled later that year when the national organization formally endorsed women's suffrage. A Denison, Texas newspaper editor blasted the union's work as outside "the peculiar empire of woman." When Willard toured the state, he said Willard "had stepped out of the sphere in which her Creator placed her and taken upon herself the duties belonging solely to a man."[101] In 1892, there were only 769 members in the state. "It is hard to get our women to do public work," one official complained. "They are afraid of public criticism and afraid that if they join the W.C.T.U. they will be ushered into politics or made to speak in public."[102] In Tyler, a Baptist minister had to helm the local union. At the height of the state's prohibition frenzy, the organization still claimed fewer than 2,500 members. Membership stagnated. Chapters floundered. In 1913, Houston had only two temperance unions and a grand total of fifty-two members. After thirty years of existence, the Dallas union had only forty-six.[103] In Galveston a series of unstable unions came and went.[104] Throughout it all, the state organization had neither the resources nor the initiative to construct a state headquarters.[105]

The Texas WCTU languished. It lacked organizational muscle, financial resources, and cultural acceptance. Texas churchwomen found few native reform traditions from which to safely draw. And while prohibition is often depicted as broadening women's roles, as a kind of midway point between domestic life and suffrage politics, in Texas and other parts of the region that judgment must be tempered. Within a few short years, Willard was forgotten. Repelled by her toxic association with woman's suffrage and other seemingly radical measures, reformers retreated.[106] Prohibitionists did not really reject the union; there was no major union presence to reject. An alliance with a woman's reform group simply lay outside the realm of cultural possibility.

But what about work within formal denominational structures? Despite women's expanding work for missions, education, and benevolence, the evangelical denominations were slow to support women's public work. Women worked as auxiliaries, as subordinates of male-dominated denominational structures.[107] Baptists, for instance, abrogated any active role in pushing women's rights. As Texas church historian Leon McBeth wrote, "every significant step in the emerging role of Southern Baptist women was preceded by comparable developments in society."[108] The denomination constrained women's work. "A great responsibility rests upon our women concerning the temperance question," a 1902 *Baptist Standard* editorial wrote, but that responsibility was indirect, personal, and confined to the home.[109] "When you encourage [a woman] to become a politician," the paper declared a decade later, "you have inflicted a serious wrong on her."[110]

In his many prohibition campaigns, B. H. Carroll's consciously veiled female activists. Of the innumerable rallies held before the 1885 McLennan County local option election, only one featured a female speaker. "The W.C.T.U. might have been a great power in this struggle," president of the Texas union, Jenny Bland Beauchamp, wrote after the prohibitionists humiliating defeat in 1887. Instead, she said, prohibitionists capitulated to antiprohibitionist cries of "Short-haired women!" Men like Carroll believed, according to Beauchamp, that "We must not let the women in; it is too unpopular."[111]

The weakness of women in the clerical movement meant that, when suffrage came, it emerged from movements and traditions incubated outside of the churches.[112] When searching for the origins of female reform movements in Texas, historians have pointed away from the evangelical churches and the prohibition campaigns and organizations such as the WCTU. They point instead to the secular women's club movement burgeoning among elites in the state's growing cities. In other words, suffrage emerged from clubwomen, not churchwomen. Women's clubs crafted an alternative female space in which middle- and upper-class women—"new women"—celebrated literature and learning, pushed the new science of home economics, championed women's colleges, lobbied for sanitation laws, advocated pure food legislation, and supported public education. Clubs, first organized around reading and culture and later around public issues, developed in isolation from the WCTU and the state's evangelical churches. While the WCTU embraced a host of controversial political questions, women's clubs abstained. And they profited. By 1901, the Texas Federation of Women's Clubs had twice as many members as the state's WCTU; by 1910, four times as many.[113] By invoking their maternal prerogative and "domestic expertise," clubwomen bridged public and private life without offending southern gender norms. Clubwomen packaged suffrage in the safe language of women's domestic qualifications. According to Judith McArthur, they "reconceptualized and de-radicalized" suffrage by divorcing it from the perceived radicalism of the WCTU.[114] By eschewing controversial issues—an option foreclosed to the Texas chapters of the WCTU—they crafted a successful women's movement and eased the road to suffrage. But the Texas suffrage movement not only emerged from different organizations, it emerged from entirely different populations of women.

In 1897 a regent of the state's Daughters of the American Revolution urged women into battle. "Whether it be with tongue or pen," he said, "she will find truths that call for her advocacy." Clark imagined a firewall of patriotic women protecting the nation. "Daughters," he said, "be vigilant. You may avert the ruin of your country, and preserve to future generations the right which your ancestors bought with blood, and made sacred by many sacrifices!"[115] But who would do the work? One anonymous female dissenter wrote in the *Dallas Morning News* that "men usurped the right to build a wall around woman and call the inclosure 'her sphere.'" She called upon "educated, broad-minded women" to enlist for women's rights. And that's precisely who worked for suffrage.[116] Divorced from the constraining culture of the state's evangelical churches, elite white women constructed a parallel, autonomous women's culture organized around elite-based clubs and benevolent societies, not mission work or religious education or prohibition.[117]

Clubwomen were more likely to be affiliated with the upper-class Episcopalian or Presbyterian churches than the more popular Baptist or Methodist churches, and they were unlikely to be particularly active in their denominations, anyway. McArthur called clubwomen "church-going women but not churchwomen."[118] Elizabeth Hayes Turner's detailed investigation of Galveston women concluded "that elitism more than evangelicalism drove the southern women's reform movement."[119] When Turner broke down the religious affiliations of the leaders of the Galveston Equal Suffrage Association, she found that the majority were Episcopalian or Presbyterian (she found as many Methodists and Baptists as Jews and Swedenborgians).[120] Noting these women's "relative inactivity in church prayer groups and women's societies," Turner suggested that "civic-mindedness, a sense of status, and notions of the unfairness of women's political inequality were at heart more important motivators than faith."[121]

Two of the state's most prominent suffragists testify to the centrality of secular upper-class women in the state suffrage movement. Jane Y. McCallum was influential and prototypical. The wife of a school superintendent and mother to small children, McCallum nevertheless engaged in women's clubs and civic work. She participated in Shakespeare clubs, joined the Texas Colonial Dames, and eventually found her way to suffrage work. In 1914, she joined the Austin Woman Suffrage Association and the following year became its president. She wrote a suffrage column for the Austin papers. A half-hearted Presbyterian, the well-heeled McCallum leveraged her exalted

FIGURE 6.1 Travis County women registering to vote, 1918.
Source: W. D. Hornaday Collection, Prints and Photographs Collection, Archives and Information Services Division, Texas State Library and Archives Commission. #1975/70-5449.

social station to exert herself in secular life.[122] The state's leading suffragist, Minnie Fisher Cunningham, repeated the pattern.[123] The first female graduate of the University of Texas Medical Department in 1901, she married a prominent lawyer and businessman, worked in Galveston for public health efforts with the Women's Health Protective Association, joined the Galveston Equal Suffrage Association when it formed in 1912, and became president in 1914. An observant Methodist but a tireless advocate for the vote, her activism bypassed the church; she castigated a foot-dragging religious conservatism for slowing the movement.[124]

Reformers stymied prominent prohibition work by women. The most publicized efforts came from outsiders. Carry Nation won national fame in Kansas, but it was during her ten years in Texas that she first felt called to God's service. While there, she lived through the brutal anti-liquor campaigns of the 1880s and saw the withering blows leveled at preachers and prohibitionists. But her activism went nowhere in the Lone Star State; only in Kansas could she enter the lists for prohibition.[125] She returned to Texas years later as a national celebrity. In early 1908 she visited—or "raided," as the papers reported—San Antonio. After registering at the old Bexar Hotel as "Mrs. Carry Nation. Your Loving Home Defender. Medicine Bow, Kansas," she stopped at city hall to see the mayor (he wasn't in), toured several saloons (peacefully, to the disappointment of several waiting reporters), grunted at the Texans' beloved "Alameda," spoke at Calvary Baptist Church, lectured at Market Hall, and peddled as many souvenir hatchets as she could before riding to Houston the next day.[126] A flash of lightning, she came and went and nothing much changed.

Although historians have perhaps oversold the opportunities for women afforded by evangelical churches and the prohibition crusade, the broader tropes of gender nevertheless infused the clerical crusade. If prohibition in Texas remained under the domain of male religious leaders, how did gender shape the tactics and assumptions of male prohibitionists? The concept of honor has served southern historians well.[127] If scholars have overstated the possibilities for women in the region's temperance movement, they have nevertheless rightly approached the role of gender among male prohibitionists through the motif of southern honor.[128] Although often posited as a foil for southern evangelicalism earlier in the nineteenth century, clerics harnessed the idea of honor in their campaigns. Male prohibitionists spoke often of upright manhood, pure womanhood, and that treasured sanctuary of the Victorian imagination, the home. And so, in a southern world of male chivalry and female purity—of cavaliers and their ladies fair—men were compelled to act and protect the fairer sex. Women were pure but fragile vessels of goodness, passive bystanders beset by a corrupted manhood. Honor demanded their defense. Southern religious leaders led the way.

"The home" saturated reformers' rhetoric. George Truett had called the home "the very base of civilization," but in 1911 he warned that "the home by a thousand reasons is beleaguered and imperiled, and when the home goes down everything holy in our civilization is tottering to its doom."[129] When Morris Sheppard aligned himself with the victims of organized sin, he spoke the language of the home: "As the blood of the first victim of human violence cried out from the ground, so today the widowed and the orphaned, the tenants of desolated homes, the drunken and the crazed, the ghosts of blighted ambitions and broken lives, the victims of hunger, poverty, and disease cry out."[130] The domain of women, the site of childhood, a refuge of warmth and love, the building blocks of civilization, shelter from the besieging cruelties of the world: the stakes were too high for reformers' to stand idly by. The home needed defenders. It needed prohibition.[131]

"Inspired with a love of God and the safety of our Southern homes," J. B. Cranfill said, he and other prohibitionists "have essayed to bare our breasts in defense of principle and risk our all on this issue."[132] Liquor and the saloons widowed wives, orphaned children, fueled domestic abuse, and plunged families into poverty. The Statewide Prohibition Amendment Headquarters distributed a printed sermon delivered by Methodist Rev. W. F. Packard on Mother's Day in 1911.[133] Packard pointed to the state's six hundred thousand homes and said "each of these homes has a mother who is its guardian angel. Whatever is an enemy to the home is her enemy, and threatens her peace and her power for good in molding the future citizenship of the state." The brewers and saloonkeepers conspired against the home, he said. They had "been granted licensed by law to slay 10,000 mothers' sons annually." Packard asked "How can I, on Mothers' Day, fail to denounce a business that is the greatest enemy to mother's influence? She has no voice at the polls. I will speak in her behalf, today!"

Religious activists appealed to long-standing notions of southern honor by championing themselves as masculine protectors. Preachers couched their appeal in the language of manhood and masculinity. "To raise the whole denominational level," J. B. Gambrell said, "we must raise the level of Christian manhood."[134] While prohibitionists offered roles to women and were sometimes denounced for associating with suffragists and "short-haired women," activists quite easily armored themselves in the language of masculine duty and feminine vulnerability. Cranfill explained to a Waco audience that prohibition and religion could revitalize both manhood and womanhood: "I like to look forward to the time when we will have a brighter boyhood, a sturdier manhood, a more forceful and brighter womanhood, if that be possible, which I doubt."[135]

Texas senator Morris Sheppard, as with so much else, neatly captured the confluence of the clerics' many gendered concerns. "O gentlemen," he said, "before you take your stand on the side of these infernos, may you think of the mothers that are praying for a liquorless Republic, of the women this traffic has widowed, the children it has made fatherless, the manhood it has wrecked, the virtue it has damned—of the maniacs it has produced, of the misery of men once strong and proud."[136]

Honor demanded male action on behalf of women. But it wasn't only honor that constrained female activism, or that evangelicals had to concede and adapt to it to be effective: it was the natural outgrowth of the logic of clericalism, a logic that said preachers and other male religious leaders were supreme leaders, moral caretakers, and that they should hold sway. Clerics didn't capitulate to southern honor; honor and clericalism flowed naturally together. Out of their marriage emerged a clerical movement couched in righteousness and primed to sweep away the vestiges of southern anticlericalism.

The history of southern prohibition can too often become a history of concessions and capitulations. Prohibition, the narrative goes, surrendered to patriarchy and accommodated the region's reigning racism. Prohibition becomes, in such accounts, just another way for southerners to communicate their bigotries and perform their prejudices. The clerical crusade seems epiphenomenal, noteworthy only for mirroring southern culture, and not an innovator of norms or a mover of culture. But the proper tale, as the case of Texas clerics suggest, is instead one of agency and action in which clerics outmaneuvered their opponents not by surrendering to the whims of their regional culture, but by harnessing that culture, exploiting it, and transforming its many components into the essential markers of a new moral identity.

7

Unto the Breach

THE POLITICS OF CLERICALISM

WITH THE OLD anticlerical self-consciousness washing away, a new and aggressive tide of clerical activism crested. Clerical leaders rebuilt their movement after the humiliating defeats of the 1880s. Professionalized leaders conquered the denominations, expanded publishing houses, and occupied major urban pulpits. Membership grew and money poured into religious coffers. Denominational colleges were well funded and well attended. Religious periodicals had vast circulations. Denominational boards and private religious ventures blossomed. And in this expanding religious world, clerics crafted and deployed a usable history and pioneered new and alluring visions of church and state. They captured the cultural high ground. They harnessed race and gender in the service of righteousness. They wrought morality into a usable identity and created a best-and-the-rest social division that both incorporated and transcended traditional southern cultural norms. Their electoral reforms purged much of their political resistance. At the beginning of the twentieth century, everything was in place for a religious conquest of public life. The foundations for the Bible Belt had been laid.

As the new century began, the aggressive clerical mood penetrated the deepest ranks of religious leadership and convinced evangelical Texans to overcome their doubts and refuse to yield any longer to the culture of anticlericalism. All over the state—and all over the region—activists undertook the prohibition crusade. Moral reforms attracted massive numbers, mobilized communities, created new organizations and institutions, and ultimately transformed the very nature of religion in Texas. Politics and Christianity became increasingly intertwined, grafted together so seamlessly that the two seemed indistinguishable. Religious leaders preached the prohibition gospel and, working through local churches and organizations such as the Texas Local Option Association and the state's chapter of the Anti-Saloon League, saturated Texas with literature and organizers and lecturers. Fighting county by county in local option elections, over the course of several decades they dried up great swaths of the state. They were winning. Counties were going dry. A smarter and more committed movement was growing.

When the conditions for the clerical emergence had been met, reformers forsook the local option system and set their sights on the state, provoking the greatest clash between religious activism and anticlerical hostility Texas had ever seen.[1] Clerics could not march unimpeded into public life. If they had conquered internal dissent, they still had to confront a secular world's age-old anticlericalism. Winning the churches had been easy. It took clerics relatively little effort to convince Texans with a stake in spiritual life that religion was besieged and the righteous should organize. But the conquest of public life would be different: at the turbulent intersection of religion, politics, and public life, religious reformers and anxious anticlerics crashed headlong into combat.

Vicious waves of public anticlericalism had long unleashed scorn on "political preachers." Outside the churches, venom and vitriol were a cleric's reward. But now, with religious leaders mobilized, anticlerics fretted. Surveying rising clerical sentiment in 1907, one Corsicana attorney feared that the "union of church and state is the hope of every preacher in Texas."[2] Worried Texans braced for battle. Critics called the prohibition movement an "ecclesiastical invasion" and urged anticlerical opponents to "scourge them back." But for well over a decade, the question of prohibition—and political Christianity—dominated public debate in Texas and across much of the South. Religious activists pushed other reforms, of course. Sabbath laws, antiprostitution crusades, antigambling movements, and religious education all drew followers. But none so riled the world as prohibition.

The rancorous statewide contests for prohibition revealed a desperate battle between the proponents of an aggressive, politicized religion and the defenders of a traditional, inward-looking evangelicalism, between those who believed religion should reign in public life and those who believed it should not. Through the politics of prohibition, clerics and anticlerics vied for legitimacy. Clerics declared their political rights and boldly wrestled their way into the political debate. And for the first time in Texas history, anticlerics struggled to stifle the insurgency.

Throughout the South, the prohibition movement and its evangelical champions were marching to victory.[3] In 1907, Georgia became the first southern state to go dry. Alabama, Mississippi, North Carolina, and Tennessee soon followed. By 1915, nine southern states prohibited the manufacture and sale of alcohol. Texas was not yet among them.[4] Unlike most other states, Texas, owing to the particularities of its constitution, had to pass prohibition through a constitutional amendment submitted by the legislature and decided by popular vote. And as the years passed and the contests piled up, Texas neither decisively defeated nor passed prohibition. Instead, the two sides stalemated, keeping the battle between clericalism and anticlericalism lodged firmly in the forefront of the public consciousness.

For well over a decade, liquor politics dominated public life in Texas. Congressional contests fell along wet-dry lines. Four consecutive gubernatorial contests (1910, 1912, 1914, and 1916) divided over little more than prohibition. Voters debated the submission of a statewide constitutional prohibition amendment on four occasions (1908, 1910, 1914, and 1917). Throughout it all, the whole state erupted into discussions on the proper public role of preachers.

The southern marriage of region and religion was a process. Anticlericalism, to borrow a line about Rome, would not die naturally; it would have to be assassinated.[5] The Bible Belt was not a natural or logical culmination of impersonal and unavoidable trends. It was deliberate. And the statewide struggle for prohibition marked the most important piece of that process. The clerics' final battle for the Bible Belt would come through old-fashioned politics.

In 1901, Georgetown Baptist D. L. Hamilton condemned an anticlerical editorial in the *Houston Daily Post*. He knew critics of religious politicking awaited in the public sphere, and he knew they would resist the coming statewide campaigns. "Whenever the devil is disturbed, whether in society or politics, his emissaries are certain to rebel." He called anticlericalism an "old and threadbare" doctrine, a "relic of the past," but he anticipated the fury that awaited the clerics. "No preacher expects anything else but antagonism," he wrote. Hamilton and other activists steeled themselves against an inevitable backlash: "The preacher who avoids misrepresentation and persecution is one who never combats evil." The clerics were eager for a fight.[6]

Secular hostility did indeed loom. As the Methodist J. W. Hill noted, "Men who never darken the door of a church, and some of whom are confessed and outspoken infidels, are suddenly seized with an agonizing shiver, and quake and tremble for the safety and security of the Christian religion whenever a minister enters the lists in the interest of moral reform and undertakes to apply the principles of the gospel to the civic conditions of the times."[7] Most, though, would eschew pretenses of saving religion.

With clericalism and anticlericalism once again enjoined in political battle, the twentieth century saw new generations fighting old fights. In 1909,
Rev. Arthur W. Jones, chairman of the state's Anti-Saloon League, hoped
to recapture the sensation of the 1887 debate between the Texas senator
Roger Q. Mills and B. H. Carroll by challenging Mills' son, political aspirant Charles H. Mills, to a debate. Mills declined, saying, "My ideas of the
duties of ministers in matters both spiritual and temporal are so widely at
variance with the views on like matters entertained by men like Mr. Jones as
to make a mutual accommodation between us impossible." He blasted the
clerics. "It is my belief that when the Savior said 'My kingdom is not of this
world,' and laid down the doctrine that there is a dominion of Cesar and a
dominion of the Church, Cesar having nothing to do with the Church nor
the Church anything to do with Cesar, that he drew the line clear and distinct between Church and State." Mills set forth all the coming anticlerical
arguments. "I do not now seek, and have never sought, to meddle in matters
spiritual. They belong to the Church, and are the business of its ministers.
Correlatively, I think that ministers, as such, should not meddle in matters
political."[8]

Despite the rhetoric of such critics, the clerical insurgency caught its opponents off guard. By 1908, prohibition stalked the corridors of the state capital.
Drys lobbied and pled with state legislators to put a prohibition amendment
to the state constitution on the ballot. Anticlerics recoiled. Stunned, an
eclectic mix of hostile Texans immediately formed permanent antiprohibition organizations. The largest, formed in Houston that October, just prior
to the Baptists' jubilant annual statewide meeting, laid the issue bare: they
distrusted religious ambitions, feared for the separation in church and state,
and longed to preserve a public sphere unsullied by the churches. Meeting in
Houston's Turner Hall, and greeted personally by Houston mayor Baldwin
Rice, the assembly resolved, first, that prohibition challenged individual liberty, and, second, that "it stands for a standard of citizenship, morals and
religion which inevitably leads to a union of church and state."[9] State representative Temple Harris McGregor told the assembly, "We have learned to tell
the difference between the preacher that carries a glad hand and a warm heart
and the peripatetic, political preacher that would sow the State with strife."
The rhetoric delighted the crowd. It was, the *Dallas Morning News* said, "like
touching a match to prairie grass." Louis Wortham, another state legislator,
warned against "the extremes of fanaticism" and, to great applause, closed his
speech by declaring, "These fanatics shall not crucify free Americans upon
this cross of intolerance."[10] Others piled on. "I am one of those who believe

that the Christian religion is wholly one of moral suasion and ought not to be backed up by the sword," another speaker declared to cheers.[11]

Anticlerical Texans sought the means to stifle clerics, to "defeat this pernicious heresy."[12] When the state legislature reconvened some months later, in 1909, state senator Edward Kellie introduced a bill to make it illegal "for any person whomsoever . . . in any church house . . . to speak, lecture or talk upon political subjects, conditions, or matters." He proposed criminalizing political preaching. His bill would make it a misdemeanor punishable by up to a $50 fine and ten days in a county jail.[13] It was a farce, of course, and his bill was tabled, but its sentiments spoke to many and foretold the rash of anticlerical anger soon to be unleashed in the coming prohibition campaigns.

Political races in Texas became little more than referendums on prohibition.[14] And when elections became referendums on prohibition, they invariably became referendums on religion as well, proxy wars fought over evangelicals' aggressive public forays. Traditional boundaries between pulpits and politics seemed to collapse. In the prohibition movement, anti-liquor rallies often mirrored church services. One such meeting in 1908 was fairly typical. Gathering at a county courthouse on a Friday night, the crowd began by singing "Stand Up for Jesus," and a minister followed with an invocation. Religious hymns interspersed various speakers bemoaning the ills of liquor and touting statewide prohibition. The gathering concluded as the assembly sang "When Christians Shall Vote as They Pray," and a second minister offered the benediction.[15] Anticlerics were sure to recoil.

In 1910, the struggle for the Bible Belt in Texas exploded. By that year clerics propelled prohibition into the forefront of state politics. Decades of organizing and agitating now spilled out of the churches. The churches exclaimed their wholehearted commitment to the prohibition crusade. The official position of the North Texas Conference of the Methodist Church in 1909 was typical. "The saloon is the direst enemy of sober manhood, of pure womanhood, and of prattling childhood," it declared. "It is the arch-enemy of the home, the foe of the university and school, the iconoclast of the age. God grant that the ascending prayers of our Christian men and women may speedily be answered in the destruction and overthrow of the rum traffic in Texas!"[16] A joint letter signed by Methodist and Presbyterian ministers in 1910 predicted that "two great forces will be arrayed against each other. On one side will be found the home, the school and church, and all who labor for morality and the good of our State. On the other side will be found 4,000 saloon-keepers and every evil force associated with the saloon and the brewery."[17] J. B. Gambrell agreed. "The vastest evil, the deadliest evil, the one greatest overshadowing upas tree [a tall, tropical, poisonous tree] of the whole world," he wrote in the *Standard*, "is the organized liquor traffic." Gambrell eagerly attacked the liquor traffic week after week. "It is an obstruction to the kingdom," he wrote, "it is a blight on the souls of men; it is the enemy of all good; it blasphemes Almighty God; profanes everything holy, scourges the human race and damns untold millions of souls."[18] The Texas Christian Missionary Society officially proclaimed the saloon a "seductive instrument of the evil one" and "the most blighting curse that blocks the way of Christian progress and defies the armies of the living God." Intoxicating liquor proved "the greatest tragedy of mankind," and the liquor traffic was "the most destructive institution that hampers and hinders our Christian civilization."[19]

In 1911, Houston attorney Jonathan Lane would write, "These disclaimers [the prohibitionists], as a rule, think the English language insufficient to enable them to express their bitterness, hatred and ill feelings toward those of us who do not agree with them on this subject."[20] But such stark rhetoric pointed to the determined ferocity of crusading clergymen. "The preachers will not take a back seat," the *Baptist Standard* declared. "We expect them to continue to preach prohibition, talk prohibition and work for prohibition."[21] Clergymen of all denominations "locked shields for the purpose of destroying the liquor business," said the *Dallas Morning News*.[22] "We favor precinct prohibition, county prohibition, and statewide prohibition, the utter annihilation of the saloons," declared the Methodist's North Texas Conference. "The Church is the eternal foe of the saloon and the licensed liquor traffic and will never be satisfied until the legalized sale of liquor shall cease in Texas."[23] J. B. Cranfill expressed overwhelming pride in his dedication to prohibition. "My attitude on the temperance and prohibition question," he wrote in 1916, "has been that I was a friend to every movement, and every man that looked to the annihilation of the drink traffic. I have fought for prohibition in precinct, county, state and nation, and am still fighting for it."[24]

As such rhetoric suggests, by 1910 renouncing prohibition was tantamount to renouncing Christianity. While political rallies often resembled religious services, so too the reverse. Religious revivals could focus on the liquor question. Preachers frequently employed the gospel of prohibition in their services. Prohibition became the message. One heavily attended revival in Fort Worth on the eve of the 1910 primary election vilified the liquor traffic and appealed for "prohibition and purity." Replacing traditional hymns with "Take the Stars and Stripes from the Saloon," the revival claimed a number of converts, not from preaching Christ crucified but the saloon prohibited.[25] The boundaries between religion and prohibition faded. "If I find a Christian preacher, I find an anti-saloon man," Dr. Joel Halbert Gambrell, brother of the influential editor of the *Baptist Standard*, remarked. "I never saw otherwise. I hear there are a few. I don't care to meet them or to cultivate acquaintances."[26] Prohibitionists had conquered tradition and could no longer tolerate an introverted, cautious brand of Christianity. Through a determined program of zealous commitment and constant agitation, they would reforge the role of religion in society.

With uncompromising fortitude, legions of clergymen and laypeople undertook the prohibition crusade. Although time has rendered their battle against liquor quaint, foresight alone should not diminish the apocalyptic urgency of moral reformers. When the clerical culture matured, an army of evangelical Protestants stood primed to overthrow the old political order. In 1910, clerics finally overwhelmed the traditional wall separating the clergy and the churches from politics. Decades of organization and agitation culminated in that year's political elections. Suddenly, clergy were everywhere in public life. Their rhetoric, their concerns, and, most of all, their single dominant issue, prohibition, washed over the state.

The 1910 gubernatorial election was the first statewide election that prohibition fully dominated, and, therefore, the first in which religious activism became the consuming political issue. Voters decided the prohibition issue that year in two ways: first, by voting for gubernatorial candidates that divided mostly on prohibition; and, second, by deciding whether to submit a state constitutional prohibition amendment to a statewide vote. If the "submission" measure passed, the amendment would be decided by a statewide referendum the following year, in 1911.

Prohibition therefore dominated state politics in 1910. It confined all competing issues to the periphery. In the months before that year's Democratic primaries—the de facto general election across most of the South—the *Dallas Morning News* conceded, "There is no use disguising the fact that prohibition is the paramount issue and will decide the election."[27] Surveying the 1910 gubernatorial election, a member of the State Board of Medical Examiners, Radford O. Braswell, observed, "All issues are eliminated from the race at present except statewide prohibition." He lamented that the issue had even entered the race but realized, "It has and will be the deciding principle. The people are lining up on these issues and ignoring all other issues."[28]

Political candidates lined up on both sides of prohibition. Religious leaders managed to run Cone Johnson, a lawyer, politician, and sometime Methodist lay preacher, for governor. Described as "a zealous and devout Christian," Johnson was a powerful candidate in a race that many clergy declared was "the spirit of God manifest in the conduct of men and the church of Jesus Christ in action against the liquor traffic."[29] His program was clear; his targeted constituency obvious. "The foremost question in the minds of all the world today," he asserted, was "what are we going to do with the manufacture and sale of whisky?"[30] As the champion of religious reformers, Johnson became instantly relevant. As an adversary of political Christianity, so too did his opponent, Oscar Colquitt. "If I cannot choose the weapons with which I must fight," Colquitt argued, "I will have to accept those tendered me."[31] A longtime politician and former State Railroad Commissioner, Colquitt confronted the prohibition issue head on with blistering indictments of prohibition and "political preachers." Johnson had the insurgents; Colquitt had tradition.[32]

Colquitt masterfully exploited anticlerical anger. A middling politician with few political convictions, Colquitt was nevertheless a veteran of numerous prohibition elections and boasted a long and contentious history with leading religious leaders. When prohibitionists stormed into state politics in 1910, the fully credentialed anticleric stood primed to lead the resistance. That year prohibition had become, as one supporter pointed out, "the supreme, paramount issue before the whole people."[33] Without qualification, Colquitt called for the support of all those opposed to prohibition and politicized religion. By exploiting anticlericalism and portraying his candidacy as the last defense against a rising tide of religious fanaticism, Colquitt's campaign gained traction.

Colquitt coalesced anticlerical support early in the campaign. He had won accolades in late 1909 for a very public and very contentious dialogue with George Rankin. The exchanges became a sensation. Colquitt printed them and used them as campaign material. He mailed them to supporters. He exploited Rankin's attacks because Rankin embodied the fears of anticlerical Texans. When Rankin took to the state newspapers to belittle a political candidate as a pawn of the liquor interests, a defender of immorality, and a fallen Christian, many recoiled. Rankin charged that Colquitt "would rather be Governor than go to heaven."[34] Few Texans were used to preachers waging open political warfare in the public sphere. Moreover, Rankin was no obscure, low-level preacher. He stood at the heart of Texas Methodism. As editor of the *Advocate*, Rankin was highly influential in shaping Methodist opinion in Texas. Many expected he would be elected bishop. But Rankin was not alone. His actions were sanctioned by his church and by the mirrored actions of a multitude of clerical activists. The Methodist North Texas Conference, of which Rankin was a part, wholeheartedly endorsed not only his crusade

FIGURE 7.1 Governor Oscar Colquitt, 1910.
Source: Prints and Photographs Division, Library of Congress, LC-DIG-ggbain-03690.

against liquor, but also his assaults on Colquitt. "We commend and approve," read the Conference's official minutes, "the bold and courageous stand taken in favor of prohibition by Dr. Geo. C. Rankin in the Texas Advocate."[35] All of this aggravated an already anxious public, and Colquitt swooped in to exploit it.[36]

As prohibition and its ministerial champions dominated public discussion, anticlerical politicians such as Colquitt became rallying points for disaffected Texans. One Methodist voter wrote to the Colquitt campaign and divulged that he had graduated from Southwestern University, knew George Rankin personally, opposed the saloons, and subscribed to both the Methodist's *Texas Christian Advocate* and the Anti-Saloon League's *Home and State*. He seemed to be the prototypical prohibitionist, but attacks from Rankin and others moved him to support Colquitt in the primary. "While I am a Methodist in belief," wrote another, "I hold in supreme contempt a political preacher, be he Methodist or anything else." Ministers such as Rankin and "fanatical preachers like him" were slowly fueling a backlash among Texans wary of clerical ambition. "I believe," wrote another Colquitt supporter, "that many of them have grown so fanatic over the question that they are loosing [*sic*] sight of true religion and their God, and are following shadows and delusions."[37] Clerical leaders had successfully overcome most denominational resistance but a larger secular culture still eyed the clerical insurgency warily. In the early twentieth century, anticlerical thought still pervaded Texas culture and Texas politics.

Colquitt, sensing widespread anticlerical anxiety, struck back. The candidate rallied his supporters with refrains of "the place of a preacher is in the pulpit and not in politics."[38] Audiences carried signs reading "The Old-Time Religion is Good Enough for Me."[39] Colquitt attacked Rankin and the prohibitionist preachers, and the people, at least a bloc of them, loved him for it. A Dallas businessman wrote Colquitt that "a preacher turned politician is always dangerous. So don't be too easy on him on account of 'The Cloth,' he is dragging it in the mire."[40] One supporter wrote that he had "just read your 'romp' on the political preacher" and, "it makes me feel like I just wanted to take you by the hand and give it a *hearty shake*. In my opinion, you have him up a tree. Just keep him there."[41] Another wrote that he "enjoyed the tilt you had with Rankin and am proud of you—go after them and stay with them."[42] Colquitt did. Attacking Christian clergy was winning him an election. "A little Methodist preacher," one Colquitt organizer wrote, "is making more noise against us than all the balance combined, and I think in the end it will be to our advantage."[43] A newspaper editor from Eagle Pass, after reviewing the Rankin exchange, conceded that "Colquitt is all right." He said simply, "I love him for the enemies he has made."[44]

Prohibitionists, active, organized, and carrying all the momentum, still stumbled before widespread anticlerical anxieties. One man published "A Texan's Soliloquy," an essay bemoaning that a political campaign "so interests my Sainted minister, the guardian of my soul, that he forsake his watchtower and join the rabble, leaving even my soul naked to mine enemies."[45] Every public attack on Colquitt seemed to backfire on the religious leaders. An insurance agent wrote, "Unscrupulous Preachers are bringing a well deserved reproach upon many churches."[46] At a stop in Groveton in June, a supporter presented Colquitt with an anticlerical poem he had written. Among its many verses, it read, "They [the prohibitionists] profess to be followers of the Christ / And in his loving faith abide, / But if He acted like they do / Well– He ought to have been crucified."[47]

The 1910 election produced no clear mandate. When the returns came in, Colquitt stood triumphant—but barely. And so, too, did the submission measure for a statewide prohibition amendment. The divided result— Colquitt nominated but submission passed—satisfied no one. Although Colquitt profited from anticlericalism, the state still teetered between clerical insurgency and anticlerical tradition.

The defining characteristic of the 1910 campaign had been the infusion of religion into politics. Prohibition organizations did not simply utilize or work in concert with the religious establishment: they *were* the religious establishment. Viewing prohibition organizations as anything other than interdenominational interest groups is an error. The Texas branch of the much-touted Anti-Saloon League (motto: "the church in action against the saloon") was nothing more than an alliance of church leaders. Both the president and vice president were church leaders and of its fourteen official male prohibition field organizers, thirteen were ordained ministers.[48] The league regularly corresponded with statewide religious figures. J. H. Gambrell was for a time the superintendent of the League's Texas chapter. In 1909, he urged Rev. Elijah Shettles to write to his state senator and representative to endorse submission in that year's session.[49] He begged other ministers to preach prohibition and organize voters in their counties. To Gambrell, the clergy and their evangelical denominations were "the strongest and most powerful religious and moral forces in the State."[50] Another prohibitionist, Thomas Blanton, surveyed the roster of an earlier Anti-Saloon League meeting and noted approvingly that "with a few exceptions the above are preachers and are the strongest pastors of their respective churches in this State, and you cannot get together a finer body of representative Christian gentlemen than the above named men."[51] Local organizations also blended leaders from the evangelical denominations. The leaders of the Statewide Prohibitionist Organization of Dallas County, for instance, included preachers from the city's Baptist, Methodist, and Presbyterian churches.[52] From top to bottom, religious leaders blended prohibition, faith, and politics.

Despite these mixed results, a clear shift was evident in 1910. In the 1880s, anticlerical Texans humiliated clerical activists. Not only had prohibition been defeated by enormous margins, but the preachers themselves suffered ridicule. Anticlericalism had seemed unassailable. And for a time, it was. But the tight 1910 elections testified to a new order of things. "A change has taken place," wrote one antiprohibitionist in 1910. "Preachers go about making political speeches. . . . Many preachers are on the stump and in many instances have full management and control of political gatherings at which candidates speak. . . . How does this comport with that Democracy which advocated 'separation of Church and State for the good of each!'"[53] Anticlericalism proved effective in the near term, but would it last? Was it now only a desperate, rearguard action?

J. H. Gambrell reviewed the election a week afterward and, though the results were mixed, saw only promise. The preachers had mounted the most aggressive campaign in the history of Texas religion, and instead of being "scourged back to the pulpit," as they had been in the 1880s, they had held strong. Whatever the immediate results of the election, evidence mounted that they could not now "be driven back into the pulpit and have their mouths closed." Gambrell said, "The man who has any notion that such a program will work does not know Texas preachers." And if they lost the governor's seat, the submission of a prohibition amendment to a statewide vote would still proceed. In a year, the prohibition issue would reign once more. Gambrell predicted that religious efforts would intensify, not retreat. "Practically the entire ministry of Texas will meet this challenge with the Spartan courage that belongs to every true minister of Jesus Christ."[54] Despite Colquitt's effective deployment of anticlerical anger, clerics now believed that anticlericalism would decay. To Gambrell and many others, the elections, though by no means a victory, showed that the clerics could persevere. An emboldened clergy now stood ready to engage unapologetically in the political process, to shake off whatever minimal fetters still tied them to tradition. Their recent forays had only intensified their resolve, bolstered their conviction, and accelerated their sense of urgency. "Without delay and with no crimination or recrimination, we must get together," wrote the *Standard*. "We have just begun to get ready to fight."[55]

The passions enflamed in 1910 flared in 1911. As expected, the state split into warring camps. The referendum that year witnessed religious leaders' willingness to challenge anticlerical resistance and all the drama of the previous year returned. Texas once more plunged into religious politics.

"Now," a Fort Worth Methodist wrote in 1911, "I am exceedingly anxious that every minister will feel that the time for aggressive and united action is at hand."[56] He had little reason to worry. On June 8, 1911, Texas prohibitionists formally opened the statewide campaign. A series of rallies convened at the

Fair Park Coliseum in Dallas. As many as two thousand men and women attended the initial session. State congressman and prominent prohibitionists attended. Speakers included Thomas Ball, a Methodist, chairman of the statewide prohibition organization, and future gubernatorial aspirant; Father Patrick J. Murphy, the oft-deployed prohibitionist Catholic priest; and Cone Johnson, the Methodist lay preacher and recently defeated gubernatorial candidate. They rebuffed a previously held meeting of the "anti-State-widers" and demonstrated their willingness to challenge anticlerical taboos. "They [the antiprohibitionists] say they are opposed to the union of Church and State," Cullen Thomas of Dallas said, "So are we, but I would rather see the State the bride of the Church than to see it the consort of the saloon." [57]

Methodist minister Hillen A. Bourland delivered the invocation and the male chorus of the Central Christian Church then sang "Satan's Want Ad," a hymn that told of dying drunkards and gamblers and the young sons doomed to follow them. The assembly called for an encore, and the chorus happily obliged. Thomas Ball then assured the crowd that they were fighting for a just cause, that corrupt brewers and businessmen propped up the opposition, and that the antiprohibitionists' criticisms were misguided. He attacked the antis for "denouncing the minister for participating in the prohibition campaign" by promising that prohibitionists were not fanatics. They were, he said, only concerned citizens. They adhered to proper legal procedure. But, disclaimers aside, he promised the audience that they fought for righteousness, for morality, and for all the good things men and women should fight for. He assured his listeners that as chairman of the prohibition committee, he would rally all Texans "who refuse to bow the knee to Baal in the struggle now on for the redemption of Texas." Ball called prohibition a proven "benediction to the people wherever it has been tried."[58]

After rebutting the antis at great length, Ball repeated the rote facts and statistics of sympathetic doctors and economists so commonly proffered by prohibitionists. Ball then lectured Governor Colquitt on the Methodist discipline, the denomination's statements of doctrine and belief. Colquitt was traveling the state claiming that many in the pulpits knew too much about politics and not enough about religion, and that, as a Methodist, he should not be slandered for opposing prohibition. Ball happily lectured Colquitt on the Methodist discipline. He asked Colquitt to look around at the many Christian preachers and laymen in attendance and to see where the Methodist church stood.[59]

Cone Johnson, the prohibitionists' defeated gubernatorial candidate, called for renewed action. He decried "the doctrine of fatalism," calling it a "doctrine unworthy of a man living in this enlightened age. It will not stand at the bar of enlightened citizenship and will crumble away at the bar of God."[60] Others worked on the crowd. Father Murphy called for the assembly to help the Christian churches—Catholic and Protestant—oppose wickedness by embracing "the clearly written laws of God Almighty." Meanwhile, organizers enlisted activists. J. B. Gambrell organized the distribution of subscription cards for donations.[61] Activists departed the convention with renewed commitment—the churches had launched their offensive.

The state's two largest Protestant publications, the *Baptist Standard* and the *Texas Christian Advocate*, became veritable prohibition papers. They redoubled their efforts and barraged their readers with anti-liquor arguments. Their editors called for Texas churches to temporarily release their pastors to work for prohibition. "Every pulpit in Texas," the *Baptist Standard* wrote, "should blaze with moral indignation against the unholy and shameful union of saloon and state."[62] With renewed fervor, religious leaders carried the rhetoric and tactics of the previous campaign into this new prohibition fight. Ministers traveled the state preaching prohibition and delivered Sunday sermons against the liquor interests.

Tensions mounted. A bodyguard of detectives accompanied Governor Colquitt as he campaigned against the amendment. The *New York Times* reported, "The authorities believe that there are cranks on either side who would not hesitate to take human life in the name of the cause they advocate."[63]

The activism of religious leaders, expressed not in anonymous death threats but in unrestrained public agitation, evinced a clear renunciation of historical barriers. Campaigning clergy had transcended all lingering restraints. On July 15, 1911, the press reported that Edwin Mouzon "practically read the Governor out of the Methodist Church in an address last night."[64] "The Governor of Texas so closely identified himself with the liquor interests, while at the same time professing and proclaiming himself to be a consistent member of the Methodist Church," Bishop Mouzon later recalled, "that I felt it my duty publicly to make known the inconsistency of his position."[65] Colquitt countered by claiming "I certainly shall not concede that my pastor or members of the Methodist Church have any right to control my conviction on political questions." He said, "I deny the right of preachers to take the Methodist Church into politics."[66] But it was too late. They already were. The question became, could they any longer be scourged back?

On June 5, 1911, the antis launched a counteroffensive at a convention in Fort Worth. Delegates swamped the city and jammed the railroads for the opening. The organizers and the railroad companies estimated that there were eighteen thousand visitors. The different rail lines added extra coaches to the existing trains and ran thirteen "special" trains of ten to fifteen extra coaches each to handle the traffic.[67] When they arrived, the antis overtook the city. County delegations paraded through city streets. Bands played. Vendors catered to the affair: a clothing store advertised "Anti Hot" suits of mohair to combat the summer heat, while Overland featured its "Anti Car"—anti-noise, anti-skid, and anti-trouble. Fort Worth became an antiprohibitionist's town. On Monday morning, according to reports, as many as ten thousand delegates filled the Fort Worth Coliseum to capacity for the meeting's opening session. Many had to be turned away while, inside, speakers excoriated the prohibitionists.[68]

Fred S. Dudley of Paris, a prominent attorney and businessman, denounced religious intolerance. He condemned the "political demagogue and the fanatical bigot." He admitted his reservations about the role of brewers in politics, but he added, "I am also opposed to church domination." He declared himself "opposed to the church being brought into politics by a class of men who take more interest in a political question than they do in a church question." He deployed all the usual anticlerical lines. "The church's kingdom is not of this earth," he said, and the "rights of the citizen must not be sacrificed upon the altar of bigotry." Dudley breathed the anticlerical culture. He spoke its language. He recalled all of the once-potent images that swept the preachers from public life in decades past. "If we glance through the pages of the world's history," he reminded the audience, "we find that some of the greatest atrocities ever conceived by mortal man was born of and encouraged to execution by those claiming to act in God's name."[69] Others joined in the attacks.

"Would the prohibitionists," Jonathan Lane asked, "nullify and destroy the works of the God they pretend to worship?" It was a rhetorical question, of course: "They do so in the position they take, whether they are aware of it or not." The attorney upbraided the "wild fanatics" and "enthusiastic zealots who demand prohibition." He urged the convention to fight back. "Force the designing little fellows and bad men out of your pulpits," he urged, "and make your churches what they ought to be, i.e., God's home on earth, where love, peace, tolerance and Christianity and nothing inconsistent therewith are taught." Business magnate Hiram M. Garwood blasted "a union between church and state, which is thoroughly repugnant to the ideas of this people." He labeled prohibition an affront to personal liberty, fairness, and property rights, and rebuked it for attempting to "drag the very name of religion and its ministers into the mire of partisan politics."[70]

"No governmental question has ever been settled right when complicated by religious sentiments," the convention officially resolved. Preachers, it said, had no authority outside of the pulpit. "The proper domain for the determination of questions affecting the spiritual welfare of mankind is within the church, and the proper sphere of the solution of temporal affairs is outside the church." Lane, who chastised religious leaders as "political preachers," "itinerant loafers," and "fanatical people," asked the assembly if anyone "has the right to convert the pulpits into political rostrums, or the church buildings into political meeting places on Sundays?"[71]

While vendors busied themselves catering to visitors, city churches fought back. "Christian people should not lend their presence," suggested Rev. Joseph W. Caldwell of the Taylor Street Presbyterian Church, "and ought to pray that God will bring their councils to naught." Rev. J. H. Stewart, pastor of Mulkey Memorial Methodist Church, preached from the text, "And he pitched his tent toward Sodom." The Fort Worth Methodist Pastors' Association met the following day and condemned the governor for supporting the antiprohibitionists.[72] But such interventions further provoked anticlerical resistance.

The antiprohibition campaign focused the energy of the state's anticlericalism. "The preacher who talks prohibition from the pulpit," an antiprohibition pamphlet read, "talks politics in the pulpit."[73] One anti, Otis Bowyer, chastised prohibition for exciting "so much bitterness." He rejected the old clerical boilerplate: every political question was a moral question, he said. Prohibition was not unique. The issue was liberty, not morality. Texans would reject prohibition, he said, because they still valued individual and religious liberty and were "determined in their opposition to ecclesiastical aggression."[74]

During the campaign, Governor Colquitt, as clerics had warned, brought the power of his new office to bear against the proposed amendment and campaigned aggressively against the clerical movement, or what he derided as a "frenzied fanaticism."[75] In Cuero, for instance, large crowds braved the July heat to hear him excoriate the proposed amendment and its clerical supporters. According to the *Dallas Morning News*, "He scored the preacher in politics, and hoped for the time when such preachers would return to preaching true religion and desist from determined efforts to join Church and State."[76] The speech, red meat for anticlerical Texans, was a hit. Newspapers and politicians across the state begged for copies.

This type of aggressive action brought Colquitt and the state's Methodist establishment into open conflict. Bishop Mouzon was not the only church official to rebuke the governor for his insufficient Methodist commitments.

In May, Colquitt's local Methodist church formally requested that the governor resign from membership. Mouzon, meanwhile, redoubled his attacks. A week before the election, Mouzon again repudiated the governor's Methodism, asserting that Colquitt was "professing it with his mouth while denying it with his deeds."[77] Mouzon's controversial attacks stirred tensions in an already tense race. More than five thousand people were reported to have waited outside Beethoven Hall in San Antonio, where Colquitt was scheduled to speak the following day, to hear his response. Representative Fitzhugh F. Hill of Denton County defended Colquitt by addressing Mouzon and the Methodist Church, declaring that he "had always been under the impression it was a church of Christianity" and that "those who desired to read him [Colquitt] out of the church desired the State to have more religion than the church."[78]

Anticlerical Texans were long wary of the churches' propensity for exiling antiprohibitionists. Mouzon and the Methodists' movement against Colquitt rekindled old fears. During the 1910 campaign, one Colquitt supporter wrote to the candidate to tell him about his expulsion from the ministry. The author, Baptist S. R. Carruth of Memphis, Texas, described how "more than twelve years ago, I quit my law practice and went to preaching, continuing this work until less than two years ago, the church of which I was pastor desiring that our pulpit be partly devoted to the cause of prohibition asked me to resign." He began a small religious paper to maintain his preaching, but the paper never took off.[79] In the 1911 campaign, critics frequently cited such purges as evidence of the clerics' fanaticism. Attorney and businessman Fred Dudley, for instance, said, "If an opponent of statewide prohibition does not belong to the church he is classed as a saloonist, as a vile enemy to society and the homes. If he happens to belong to the church, and speaks out against the prohibition idea in many instances he is thrown out of the church and his hat thrown after him. Prohibition in the eyes of the fanatic makes a man holy, qualifies him for office and guarantees future salvation." He recalled one particular instance when "An aged minister of the gospel who dared to voice his honest opposition to the principle of prohibition was silenced from preaching and expelled from the church. I can almost see him now," he recalled, "stripped of his right to preach the word of the lowly Jesus, crippled, decrepit, cast beyond the pale of the church, defenseless and alone. A victim of bigotry." Jonathan Lane told of a Baptist church in Burleson County that expelled a Mr. Murray, "not because he was a drunkard, not because he was not a Christian, but because he is chairman of the organization which is endeavoring to the defeat the adoption of the proposed amendment: that they demanded of him that he either get out of the church or cease to exercise his God-given right to vote and act as he pleases in a political matter, and when he declined to surrender his personal convictions he was expelled from the church."[80]

Throughout the 1911 campaign, antiprohibitionists raised the cry of "extremism" to sink their rivals. A real estate agent from Nacogdoches, for instance, foretold of "danger in the future growing out of the intolerance of the leaders on the prohibition side."[81] On the eve of the election, dozens of prominent Texans, including leading businessmen George Littlefield and John Kirby, published an open letter lamenting the best-and-the-rest distinctions peddled by the prohibitionists. "The proscription of the sale of intoxicants is but an incidental part of their purpose in the contest," which, they wrote, "has passed beyond the mere prohibition question."[82] Churches wielded a "weapon of religious terrorism, ostracism and outlawry . . . The ban of the religious outcast has been put on humble and devoted citizens who dare to own an honest conviction." A vote against prohibition, they said, was a vote against oppression and fanaticism. Voters must therefore "decide whether a tyranny of opinion shall be established in this State."[83] By the time the July 22 election arrived, the election had become as much a referendum on the proper role of the clergy as it had on liquor.

And, as in 1910, the antiprohibitionists rallied just enough frightened Texans to their cause to defeat the moral reformers. When the 1911 returns arrived, statewide prohibition had been defeated for a second time but, again, by the narrowest of margins.[84] Prohibitionists, now trained to judge their opponents as illegitimate, cried corruption. They charged the antis with financial impropriety and blamed voter fraud and the manipulation of African American and Hispanic voters. They vowed to press on.

In January 1912, Mouzon knew that "the call to an aggressive campaign is now ringing through the church" and exhorted his readers to take up the crusade once more: "Let the battle be pressed all along the line!"[85] That year saw new campaigns. Prohibitionists broke with state Democratic tradition and challenged Colquitt for reelection by nominating a Texas Supreme Court Justice, William Ramsey, to run in the Democratic primary. Prohibition was the only issue separating the two candidates. Although Ramsey mounted a serious challenge, the power of incumbency proved insurmountable.[86] Prohibitionists had launched another campaign and failed to unseat Colquitt. They again collapsed before their opponents' anticlerical onslaughts. But throughout the election prohibitionists continued to target Colquitt's positions within the Methodist church. Governor Colquitt had been a member of Austin's First Methodist Church and had the support of its pastor,

Dr. William D. Bradfield. There, Colquitt had weathered Mouzon's onslaught and maintained membership in the Methodist Church. But the heated 1912 campaign forced the issue, and one Sunday Bradfield formally broke with the governor and forced him to resign from First Methodist. The church's board of trustees granted his release and reissued his letter of membership for him to take elsewhere. The governor was now churchless. Many speculated about his next move. Some thought he would transfer to University Methodist, but he would find no refuge there. The Methodist hierarchy had purged its apolitical pastor, D. E. Hawk, and the new minister, "Fighting Bob" Shuler, carried the torch of militant clericalism.[87] Colquitt searched in vain for an apolitical church. By 1912, it might have seemed as though there were none.

In a 1914 editorial in the *Baptist Standard*, J. B. Gambrell spoke for all of Texas's prominent religious leaders when he declared that "a preacher who doesn't stand in his personality, in his thinking, and in his activities for humanity against all the debasing and corrupting influence of barrooms, with allied evils—gambling dens, redlight districts, and such like—is a faded out, anemic, and worthless sort of preacher."[88] Again and again prohibitionists struggled to capture state politics, and again and again they were narrowly defeated. But their relentless crusades continued. The anticlerics continued to score their victories, but their resistance now lacked the sustained stopping power of previous generations. Battered but intact, the crusade continued. The clerics kept coming.

By 1914, prohibition had swept across much of the country and had become dogma among most evangelical Texans, yet the embrace of moral reform and the shift to an active, politicized religion continued to stall in the anticlerical tumult of Texas politics. In 1914, reformers once again took to politics and once again saw anticlerical attacks savage their efforts. As the state descended further into a decade of religious controversy, the sting of anticlericalism still struck. Colquitt led resistance for years before ceding the field in 1914 to his successor, the colorful James "Farmer Jim" Ferguson. Ferguson showed just how far-reaching anticlerical sentiment could be. Whereas Colquitt and his allies attacked political religion on a conservative platform of limited government, Ferguson assumed the anticlerical mantle under the guise of a resurrected Populism.

Speaking "exclusively to that coterie of political clergymen who prostitute their high calling," W. D. Lewis, the president of the Texas Farmers Union in 1914, had one request: "return to the pulpit."[89] By that year the clerical quest for a moral kingdom verged on triumph: the great wave of moral reform had crested and, though battered, increasingly seemed unstoppable. In 1955, historian Richard Hofstadter famously derided the whole lot—prohibition, Sunday laws, and other moral crusades—as a "rural-evangelical virus."[90] Rural support for prohibition is still taken for granted. While rural areas absolutely voted for prohibition in higher percentages than cities, the voice of the Texas Farmers Union, the alluring rhetoric of politicians such as Farmer Jim Ferguson, and the anonymous laments of countless others all testify as well to a rural, insurgent brand of anticlericalism, and to a repudiation of the moral community that religious reformers fought so hard to construct. Many adhered to an agrarian identity and an agrarian politics unencumbered by the demands of religious reform. Confronted daily by the harsh reality of rural life—poverty, tenancy, uncertainty—many Texas refused to surrender their world and their concerns to crusading masses of clergymen. In their resistance they embraced an agrarian community yoked to agrarian concerns. The final stage of anticlerical resistance rested on that number of rural Texans who would not tie themselves, or be tied, to the budding world of religious reform.

The general trend of religious growth in the New South veiled the diverging fortunes of rural and urban religion and the roots of much rural resistance to moral reform. As the case of Texas suggests, and as a whole genre of historical and social scientific research is busy revealing, religion, at least in the United States, has survived, and even thrived, in the shadow of modernity. The growth of industry, urbanization, and bureaucratic life, perhaps to the surprise of both defenders and critics, did not lay waste to American religion, wither the churches, or secularize the nation. In fact, the transformations of the twentieth century proceeded apace with faith and at times facilitated religious expansion.[91] The American South was no different. Despite the crisis-stricken complaints of clergy, religion blossomed.[92] Church membership outpaced population gains in nearly every state, including Texas, in the decades after Reconstruction.[93] And the era's religious growth transcended mere numbers. On the backs of a new class of ministerial leadership, religious authority expanded into areas of public life it had never known.

But if religion flourished in the New South, it did not do so evenly. Urban areas claimed a disproportionate share of church construction and membership growth. Whatever the boasts of rural religiosity or the lamentations of urban apathy, New South cities bred religious vitality.[94] Newly popular denominational newspapers published there, newly expanding denominational colleges educated there, and grand new churches, larger and richer than any before, arose there. Texas typified these trends. Baylor University, the world's largest denominational college, trained Baptist youth in the emerging city of Waco. Both the *Baptist Standard* and the Methodist *Texas Christian*

Standard published out of Dallas. J. Frank Norris's First Baptist Church in Fort Worth grew to become one of the largest congregations in the United States. Such powerful urban pulpits bestowed new authority on a rising caste of professional religious leaders.

The preachers in the city "first churches," men like Norris and B. H. Carroll in Waco, found their sermons widely disseminated and their political opinions widely quoted. Under "the allure of respectability," and in line with the professionalizing tenor of the times, ambitious southern ministers won coveted new appointments in wealthy urban congregations. City preachers often earned twenty times more than their rural brethren, the difference between a sharecroppers' earnings and the salary of a high-earning professional.[95] They traveled no circuits, practiced no other trade, and suffered few financial hardships. Instead, they lived in large parsonages, ministered in imposing churches, and isolated themselves ever farther from the burdens of rural life.

Rural pastors did not stand blindly by. Far from the New South's booming cities, country preachers struggled with inadequate salaries, ambivalent congregants, and limited political influence. They felt alienated from the university-educated professionals preaching in ostentatious city churches.[96] The urban boom bred rural resentment. While some rural religious leaders strove to emulate the power and respectability of city churches, many did not. Some retreated into a self-conscious spirituality, freed from the affectations of urban wealth and social sway. Specific sects, such as the Primitive Baptists, rejected the worldly incursions of their more influential cousins. Most, however, simply retained their focus on a personal faith and clung to some form of democratic organization that deemphasized distant denominational leadership.[97] The distance from upwardly mobile, politicized moral reformers prevented the development of strong ties between rural congregants and urban clerics and portended a break between moral and agrarian reformers.[98]

In some aspects, agrarian faith challenged outright the religious vision of moral reformers. Nineteenth-century Populist leaders were ambivalent about prohibition and the religious establishment. Some openly declared for prohibition. Populist leader Ebenezer Dohoney embraced an unorthodox faith but incorporated prohibition into his stable of reforms.[99] Among the more mainstream champions of the Populist movement, popular lecturer James "Cyclone" Davis most prominently aligned his Populist support with prohibition and mainstream Protestant principles, believing that a "people's faith" could fuse morality and agrarian politics into a sensible political platform.[100] But many of the agrarian rebels rejected the brewing clerical consensus. They resented that evangelical denominations so often aligned with Bourbons (conservative Democrats) after Reconstruction. As historian Walter Buenger discovered, in northeast Texas areas of opposition to prohibition in 1887 overlapped with bastions of Populist support.[101] Many agrarians rebelled against the dominant churches. More often, though, rural faith waged no open war against the clerical vision, opting instead for what might simply be described as a kind of sluggish resistance.[102] But passivity was enough: ambivalence isolated many agrarian Texans from the moral crusaders.

Turn-of-the-century rural faith struggled to survive. In the shadow of the growing cities, rural religion—and rural clericalism—languished. At the close of the twentieth century, as net church membership was growing overall, less than 30 percent of rural Texans belonged to an organized church. One minister complained that it would take an ascending balloon to get rural Texans to look upward to heaven.[103] And so, while urban churches thrived, rural church buildings decayed and rural pulpits remained unfilled. Many rural churches had not yet discovered the clerics' ability to thrive on their own anxieties and insecurities. As sociologist of religion Dean M. Kelley wrote in the 1970s, "What costs nothing accomplishes nothing." They had not yet learned to be embattled and draw strength from that embattlement.[104]

Some religious Texans recognized their rural problem. While Texas Methodists were sending missionaries around the world, one country preacher suggested that religious leaders must face the question: "Have we a Country Problem?"[105] Few, however, followed up his suggestion with action.

The new denominational giants, the professionalized leaders ensconced in prominent pulpits and universities and newspapers, often lived up to critics' charges of detachment. Aloof from agrarian life, they reveled in bland pronouncements and romanticized rhetoric. The farm was pure, they argued, it was a fortress of intense religiosity and impenetrable virtue. One Texas Baptist praised rural churches as "nurseries of pure religion" and as a shield against the "vanity, liquor, gambling, Socialism, Sabbath desecration, infidelity and cesspools of shame of the cities."[106] "A boy on the farm," Baylor University president Samuel Brooks said, "has God for a partner in some respects seemingly more vital than the boy in the city."[107] "People have not got the circus out there," J. B. Gambrell wrote. He called it a "blessed thing they have not the theater there and they have not the circus there, and they have not the bar-room there and the gambling hall; they have not a hundred things that they have in the city. They are immune out there." Gambrell and his ilk loved the *idea* of rural life. They wanted to immunize the world by remaking it in their imagined image of the country.[108] But such idealizations by university-educated clergymen and longtime city dwellers too easily exposed their distance from the realities of rural life. At the very time independent farming was collapsing, Brooks celebrated what he saw as Texans' universal affluence: he boasted that "there is almost no abject poverty in the whole commonwealth."[109] Unfortunately, the spiritual and economic oasis gleefully imagined in many pulpits proved illusory. Equipped with blind assertions, religious denominations ignored a mounting agrarian crisis. While a rural world died, clerics tilted at whiskey bottles. They were unaware, sometimes willfully and callously, to the tragic circumstances of rural life.

The agrarian crisis had begun decades earlier but accelerated in the early twentieth century. The rural decline that provoked the Populist insurgency in the nineteenth century had not died with the Farmers' Alliance or the People's Party; it festered. Farmers still constituted the vast majority of the population; and trapped by the cotton economy's ever-deepening cycles of poverty and debt, more descended into tenancy every year. In 1910, half of Texas farmers, about two hundred thousand people, owned no land. Many more teetered on the brink, one poor crop away from crippling debt and the dismal cycle of poverty and economic hopelessness.[110] Channeling long-standing yet steadily increasing insecurities and harnessing the lingering power of Populism's diffused energy, the Texas Farmers' Educational and Cooperative Union (the Farmers Union) was founded in 1902 to organize cotton cooperatives and gain political clout for beleaguered farmers. By 1908, the Union claimed more than 100,000 Texans and a quarter-of-a-million southerners as members.[111] Moral reformers were caught off guard when these same members spearheaded a fiery agrarian resurgence that would threaten prohibition's hold over Texas politics.

In 1914, at the height of the prohibition agitation, the Farmers Union mobilized to cripple the mania for moral reform. W. D. Lewis and his predecessor, Peter Radford, barnstormed the state to make their case against prohibition. "The introduction of a liquor bill invariably has swept the calendar of all other measures, however meritorious, and has thrown the legislature into a seething mass of dissension," they said. And no matter the results, "when the battle for supremacy is over, the price of cotton will not be increased 1 cent, the rate of interest on our debts will not be reduced a penny and it will be no easier for a farmer to buy clothes for his family, to educate his children or to obtain a home."[112]

Prohibition confined competing issues to the periphery. In 1910, Oscar Colquitt had successfully appealed not only to anticlerical Democrats but to all the various groups whose interests had been marginalized by the liquor issue. All of the prohibition agitation, a critic wrote, "strikes right and left upon the heads of those who do not think prohibition the supreme, paramount issue, before the whole people, to the dire neglect of every other issues [*sic*] in the campaign." He denied that prohibition "is a paramount issue in any political contest; it is a moral question and a personal one at that."[113] Supporters denounced prohibition as a distraction, as an obstruction blocking more pertinent concerns from legislative consideration. A lawyer from Fort Worth, for instance, felt that continued prohibition agitation "should have no place in our developing state."[114] "A whole hemisphere of wind is being wasted," one critic declared. The debate amounted to nothing more than "a great deal of loud talking and absurd disputes in politics.[115] "I don't believe," Colquitt said on the eve of his election, "that the people of Texas ought to be torn asunder, neighbors and friends divided against each other and sections of the State estranged over a question like this."[116]

In 1910, during that year's campaign, J. D. Payne, a rural Texan from Hall County, lamented having to choose between Colquitt and the Christian ministry and condemned both for not addressing the plight of poor farmers. Until the churches would agitate against the problems of rural poverty and farm tenancy, he argued, they lacked credibility. "If you can't help him otherwise than saying God bless you, then don't put your physical body on his burdened back and holler 'Down with the saloon! Down with whisky!'" To Payne, the choice before him was a no-win situation: "One would be just as reasonable as the other."[117] Most, however, expected the political fascination with prohibition to end swiftly. Unfortunately for Payne and others, a string of ambiguous results left both sides aching for further conflict. The prohibition issue remained, a towering blight overshadowing the rural crisis.

In 1914, with prohibition and the clerical crusade having dominated public life for several years, the leaders of the Farmers Union, Lewis and Radford, pled with political leaders to go "back to the soil with legislation." Frustrated that unceasing prohibition agitation precluded an agrarian political agenda, they urged voters to shun the moral crusaders and vote instead for those politicians "who are in genuine sympathy with their needs and understand their problems." Moral reform was an impediment, they argued, and it had to be suppressed. And so Radford and Lewis, in pursuit of a political program of "an improved market system, cheap money, rural credits, organization, cooperation and proper facilities for preparing, storing and transporting products to the market," set about undermining moral reformers—clergy above all.

Radford and Lewis savaged political preachers. They praised "that large body of consecrated ministers who refuse to be lured from the pulpit," but laid into the crusaders: "It is well for the friends of religion to pause and con-sider the distance we have traveled toward a union of church and state." The anti-liquor crusades, they said, deviated from a long and noble anticlerical tra-dition that ran from Christ's outburst at the temple to the Texas Revolution and the state constitutions that forbade preachers from political office. But "the difficulty of keeping the preacher in the pulpit is as old as religion," they said.[118] They tagged the Salem witch trials and the Spanish Inquisition as logical outgrowths of politicized religion. "When in control of government," they said, "the pulpit politicians invariably undertake to perform legislative miracles such as casting out witches with the flame of a torch, suborning con-science with shackles and enforcing opinions with the guillotine."[119] They cautioned their audience that "we are hurrying toward a crisis."

Bolstered by funds from Texas brewers, Farmers Union leaders spent 1914 attacking prohibition and its clerical boosters. They reminded the public that prohibition had already dominated state elections in 1910 and 1912, led to a statewide referendum in 1911, and that "the past three or four sessions of the Legislature have done little else but wrangle over the liquor question."[120] To move beyond the confines of moral politics, they proposed a simple solu-tion: "political preachers should be regulated." Their suggestion, perhaps less tongue-in-cheek than they would have admitted, called for legal limits on political preaching. "We think a ministerial clause should be written in the present Constitution . . . and legislation should also be enacted preserving the sanctity of the pulpit from political vandalism."[121]

Although such legal proscriptions never materialized, the Farmers Union's larger strategy worked. Throughout the state, distressed agrarians distilled all the politicking and maneuvering of the period, at least for a short time, into a clear battle between two types of reform: moral and agrarian. Moral reform-ers never understood the economic desperation behind the resurgence of agrarian politics. "The fact cries to heaven," Samuel Brooks said in 1916, "that too often rural people beg the government to rid their cattle of ticks, their horses of charbon [anthrax], and their hogs of cholera. They appear ignorant or blind to that fact that in our cities hot-beds of vice win the credible and passionate county boys. City booze joints are worse for country boys than ticks for country cattle."[122] With such myopic insistence on the primacy of prohibition and moral reform, and the continued rejection of agrarian con-cerns, rural disaffection seemed inevitable.

Horace Bishop, a Methodist presiding elder stationed in 1914 among rural pulpits midway between Waco and Fort Worth, sensed his faith's declining appeal in the countryside. He knew that the ongoing professionalization of the churches and their monomaniacal obsession with city saloons—an obsession he partly shared—offered nothing tangible for struggling tenant farmers. "Our preachers and churches are entirely out of touch with the renters of land," he said.[123]

Some clerics tried to brandish their country bonafides. "Now, there are not many of us but what have been common folks at one time or another," J. B. Cranfill told a crowd at the Waco YMCA. "Now, I was myself," he said to some laughter. "You know, we are town folks now, aren't we, but we needn't be stuck up about it. We are just country people moved to town, that is all we are."[124] In a state only just embarking on a long path toward urbanization, he was partly right. And yet, while posing as representatives of the people, the clerics clung to their role as the "better sort." Whatever their proclamations, professionalized preachers hungered for cultural authority, middle-class respectability, and elevated social status. Most of the movement's leaders emerged from universities and seminaries and were often neutral, if not antagonistic, to rural political concerns.

James Ferguson harnessed this alienation by channeling decades of anger and despair into his 1914 gubernatorial conquest. He captivated the state with schemes to shield rural Texans from their financial predators. He attacked the greed of large corporations, corporate lawyers, and wealthy landholders. He advocated rent caps, rural credit, storage facilities, public warehouses, increased funds for rural schools, marketing systems, and a public commissioner to publicize up-to-date pricing. "Let government assist those who plead for opportunity," he said.[125] Throughout the campaign, Ferguson articulated the concerns of anxious farmers and desperate renters. It worked. In a matter of months, he emerged from relative obscurity to challenge and defeat prohibitionist Thomas Ball. Ball not only chaired the prohibitionists' 1911 campaign, he was a corporate lawyer. He was the perfect foil for Ferguson's farmer-friendly appeal.[126] After the election, Horace Bishop remarked that "Mr. Ferguson's campaign was well organized and walking delegates were seeing the renters in shacks and making them believe that F. [Ferguson] was working for them."[127] Accusations of corruption and demagoguery clung to Ferguson, but his supporters felt, as one said, that he "must pay this penalty for proposing a measure of relief to the great body of men who produce the wealth of the country."[128]

Ferguson's campaign was a throwback to the agrarian politics of the 1880s and 1890s. He captured the latent energy of a demobilized Populism and, as the New York Times aptly noted after the election, "polled practically the entire vote of the counties which were strongholds of Populism."[129] Prohibitionists

FIGURE 7.2 Governor James E. Ferguson, 1914.
Source: Prints and Photographs Division, Library of Congress, LC-DIG-ggbain-16894.

had worried during the campaign that farmers were "taking to Ferguson's land proposal like a hungry cat to a piece of fresh beef liver."[130] And why not? He was the first Texas governor in decades to appeal so openly to rural voters. As one supporter put it in 1918, "Jim Ferguson is the only Governor Texas ever had that ever attempted to do anything for the masses who earn their bread by the swet [*sic*] of their brow."[131]

Ferguson cast his campaign for rural uplift against farmers' frustration with moral reform. The mania for morality, Ferguson claimed, concealed the debauching realities of farm tenancy and sharecropping. He swore to put an end to all prohibition agitation. Referring to any future liquor legislation, he promised "I will strike it where the chicken got the axe."[132] Ferguson said his campaign represented a "clear cut declaration to stop the prohibition agitation." Like Colquitt before him, Ferguson rejected the rights of preachers to dictate politics. Echoing Richard Coke's infamous plea for Texans to "scourge" preachers back to their pulpits, Ferguson said "Let us scourge from the Democratic ranks in Texas those who would destroy our grand old party by raising issues which have no place in a democratic home."[133] Ferguson and his allies, according to Elijah Shettles, constituted "a gang who spews on the ministry and the churches in this country the vilest of slanders, and who do not care a continental for anybody's church."[134] He may have been right.

Ferguson attacked his opponent, Thomas Ball, as a corporate shill exploiting misguided clerics. Ferguson depicted the campaign in simple terms: "on the one side are the farmers, laborers and business men engaged in a struggle against corporate interests and political preachers." He told one crowd that "some of these political preachers of today have got quite an idea of morality in this country, and quite an idea about both religion and politics."[135] Rather than run from the Farmers Union's caustic anticlerical rhetoric, Ferguson embraced it. He labeled Radford the "the farmer philosopher of Texas" and his campaign disseminated his and Lewis's printed pamphlets on the campaign trail.[136]

Ferguson's campaign and the Farmers Union's attacks resonated. One Atascosa County attorney complained to the prohibitionist politician Thomas B. Love that "the Radford-Lewis propaganda—preachers to their pulpits and the prohibition question to the background—has had its effect, in this county at least."[137] Ferguson rode his agrarian, anticlerical platform to victory. John Morris, a prosperous merchant, lamented that "the result shows that the farmers were made to believe it was a fight between corporations and the working class of people. The Farmers Union had poisoned speakers all over the country, firing them with indignation." The whole affair, he wrote, was a "shame to the state's religious and moral efforts."[138]

"We have 220,000 tenant farmers roaming from farm to farm," the Farmers Union leaders had lectured, and "this seething torrent of unrest must be reckoned with in the coming campaign."[139] It was. Weary of the unceasing political conflict against vice, and the inattention to farmers' issues, many rural Texans turned against moral reform. They maligned its clerical champions and united behind upstart politicians willing to challenge the imperatives of a politicized religion. "For eight years," the newly elected lieutenant governor, William P. Hobby, said after the election, Texas "has been torn politically by the question of statewide prohibition. We took the ground that there were other questions worthy of consideration. We asked the people to drop the prohibition question and turn their attention to the material interests of the State."[140] By attacking prohibition and its clerical champions, Ferguson and others were able to hand the drys yet another defeat. Ferguson won a clear victory, and submission was defeated.

For a time, it seemed as though prohibition and the clerical offensive had stalled. Ferguson's two-pronged approach of agrarianism and anticlericalism had won the antiprohibitionists another dramatic victory. But still the reformers marched on. Despite several defeats, the prohibition issue, at the head of a great religious crusade, was too powerful and its supporters too organized and too determined to retreat. Fueled by their own momentum, sustained by their institutional strength, and soon furthered by the exigencies of a world war, the clerics continued their crusade.

8

Anything That Ought to Be Done

THE TRIUMPH OF CLERICALISM

IF THE CRUSADERS had limped into the second decade of the twentieth century, they would leave it triumphantly. The clerical advance had been slowed only temporarily. Soon anticlerical influence would flicker and fade and the clerics would reign victorious. Fleeting political defeats could not blunt the rising power of the state's evangelical subculture. The clerics' cloistered denominational worlds sustained their efforts through all the bitter partisan battles of the early twentieth century. Shielded from the stormy winds of politics and the public's anticlericalism, the clerical culture nourished new generations with the gospel of politics.

In 1914, George Truett held the Lewis Holland Lectureship at Southwestern Baptist Theological Seminary in Fort Worth. Although Truett was among the most vocal defenders of Baptist tradition and an avowed proponent of the strict separation of church and state, Truett nevertheless recognized the preacher's new mission. Each of his lectures on the power of the pulpit wove together the assumptions of the clerical movement. Truett urged his audience of preachers and soon-to-be preachers to reconsider the potential of their office. He urged them to take up the crusade. He urged them to finish constructing the Bible Belt.[1]

Truett attacked anticlerical restraints in his lectures at Southwestern. He even went so far as to reject the notion of a democratic church. "The preacher's throne is the pulpit," he said, "for there he must rule in royal fashion." Preachers should not be slaves to others' consciences, he argued, but agents of a new moral awakening. He urged his listeners to resist the confines of spiritual otherworldliness. Instead, he said, "See the preacher as the advocate and champion of every worthwhile reform, of all true progress everywhere." He reminded his listeners to never forget the importance of soul-saving and of the essential spiritual mission of evangelical religion, but he believed the power of the pulpit was too great to be so narrowly restricted.[2] "Within the pulpit is the place of the greatest forces in this world, the most strategical forces," he said. Unshackled, the preacher could make his mark upon civilization.

Indeed, the preacher already had. Truett, like other apostles of the clerical culture, inserted religious leaders into the forefront of American history. "What a debt our nation owes to preachers!" he declared. "What an interesting article that would be for some man to write on: 'The Debt of the Republic to its Pulpit.'"[3] American history, he said, depended upon the nation's preachers. Don't see them as meek and humble shepherds, Truett urged. "See them as patriots, for the true preacher is always the true patriot." Nourished by such rhetoric, by a potent and now-mature clerical vision, a new generation of activists graduated into the world and gleefully clashed against anticlericalism.

In the 1880s, religious activists lacked consensus, resources, and a common, motivating culture. By the late 1910s, they had them all. Anticlericalism had no institutional foundation; the clerics had their churches, denominations, papers, and colleges. The pulpits and pews and a vast denominational machinery supplied energy and momentum. Meanwhile, the culture of clericalism turned the logic of anticlericalism on its head. Every "scourging," every defeat, every public rebuke and anticlerical repudiation only intensified the clerics' sense of persecution and embattlement, the very lifeblood of their movement. Once the clerical coup overtook the churches and installed their leaders as the heads of the denominations, there was no turning back. There was no off switch. The logic of clericalism worked itself unceasingly.

The unending struggle for prohibition helped to normalize religious politicking. Early in the clerical crusade, many prohibitionists hesitated to admit to political meddling. In their minds, they could follow morality into the public sphere in pursuit of such moral issues as prohibition without becoming "political preachers." In 1910, for instance, even amid its boisterous pleas for politicized religion, the *Baptist Standard* sought publicly, time and again, to extricate itself from naked political maneuvering. Prohibition, it said, "did not originate with any organization whatever . . . The whole movement is non-partisan."[4] But such sentiments evaporated in the heat of unrelenting and unending statewide prohibition battles. The same year that the *Standard* sought a political middle ground, Rev. Edwin Boynton of the North Dallas Christian Church proffered a once-taboo notion of church and state: "In a just and moral government, religion and the State are inseparable." The sin condemned by churches and the crime condemned by the state shared common roots, he said. "The greatest question before any State . . . is the character of its citizens, and for morality every State must provide."[5] Doubts about politics fell. By 1914, the *Standard* refuted its last trace of self-consciousness and reminded its readers that the burdens of their faith demanded unrelenting and unapologetic activism.[6]

And so, against withering anticlerical attacks, the crusaders stood strong, redoubled their efforts, and recommitted themselves to the public sphere. By 1914, the state's white religious population took the burden of politics for granted. Baptist pastor A. B. Ingram wrote in the *Baptist Standard* that, according to his reading of scripture, preachers had always been "aggressive agitators." "It is the business of the preacher to fight sin," he said. "His commission demands a truceless warfare."[7] J. B. Gambrell agreed: "Preachers that will not lend themselves to the destruction of this masterpiece of the devil's work are not doing their duty; they have no right to the respect of their fellow citizens, and what is more, they won't have much of it."[8]

Narrow public defeats masked the distance that clericalism had traveled. While prohibitionist preachers had embraced a public role for several years, they now shed any lingering strands of self-conscious hesitation. "I have no apology to make for the service I have rendered as an advocate of temperance and prohibition," Cranfill wrote.[9] "If that makes me a political preacher," Ingram said, "then I gladly accept the title."[10] Swept up in the crusading spirit, the evangelical establishment of Texas, resolute and unwavering, refused to cower to anticlerical expectations.

In 1915, the Baptist General Convention of Texas formally recognized the denomination's social commitments by forming the Social Service Committee. The committee resolved that, "truly speaking, the secular side of life is inseparable from the moral and the religious." Claiming a wide mandate, the body declared it the duty of the righteous "to correct the wrongs of individuals and of all forms and conditions of society, whether they be in political, church, social, amusement, business relations, or whatever or wherever they be found."[11] The clerical movement, by the close of the second decade of the twentieth century, readied itself to sweep away the last stale vestiges of anticlericalism. "Our Church is rich; our people have vision; our preachers are loyal and heroic," Edwin Mouzon said of the Methodists in 1913. "Now," he said, "Let the Whole Line Move Forward." Mouzon saw the dawn of the Bible Belt. He recognized the power of religious leaders. He saw that their voice was loud, their power manifest. "We have come to the consciousness of our power," he wrote, "and we have just discovered what we can do: We can do anything that ought to be done."[12]

The clerics primed themselves for victory. Even amid temporary defeat, they expected nothing less than ultimate triumph. Fort Worth's fundamentalist prophet J. Frank Norris led many of the clerics' legislative efforts. Rebuffed in his efforts to secure a daylight saloon-closing bill in the spring of 1911, Norris demonstrated the clerics' newfound resolve: "God is on his throne and right is eternal," he said, "and whatever be the issues of this or any other election, the forces of evil will be dashed to pieces like the potter's vessel and righteousness cover the earth as the waters do the sea."[13] The twentieth-century crusaders would not be scourged back into their pulpits. Nor, even in the face of defeat, were they willing to confine their vision to the borders of the South or the Lone Star State.

"We make a mistake in confining our efforts to save a few individuals, here and there," Reverend Boynton preached at the North Dallas Christian Church in 1910, "when our aim should be a nation in a day. When Christian people can quit singing psalms long enough to get good rich blood in their veins and get out into the realities and struggles of life, Christianity will mean something in the world."[14] Clerical ambitions swelled. Cone Johnson beat the drum of a broad and unbounded prohibition movement. "Our fight is against the saloon: we seek its destruction and believe that the time has come and the public opinion is ripe, not only for its destruction, but for the outlawry of the business. This is no short-lived agitation: it is Nation-wide: it is world-wide."[15] But before they could embark upon a worldwide movement, they faced obstacles at home.

While anticlerical remnants still raged and tradition still lashed the preachers, the anticlerical world was dying and the clerics now knew that they could weather its death knell. Motivated by their potent cultural vision, rooted in righteousness, and sustained by a vast store of institutional resources, the clerics clung to the inevitability of their triumph. James Ferguson's 1916 reelection as governor would mark one of the last achievements of a decaying anticlericalism. The clerics' political impulses continued to orbit around prohibition, that holy crusade to exorcise a corrupt institution and purify a populace, and, despite multiple statewide defeats, the prohibition movement had matured into an efficient engine of reform. Statewide setbacks notwithstanding, prohibition leaders and their progressive allies were winning the ground war. Local elections fell to prohibitionists, who captured control of the state legislature and sent the nation's soon-to-be moral champion to the United States Senate, heralding the final stages of prohibition's ascent not only in Texas, but in the nation.

In January 1913, packed galleries in the Texas Capitol greeted thirty-seven-year-old Morris Sheppard as the state's newest United States senator. The committed Methodist and former Epworth League organizer, Sheppard had pushed for prohibition in previous elections, he said, so that "man will rise ... again to be crowned with the confidence and approbation of Almighty God."[16] At the state capitol, he delivered a speech outlining a broad progressive platform. The galleries applauded, but the loudest

FIGURE 8.1 Senator Morris Sheppard, 1914.

Source: Prints and Photographs Division, Library of Congress, LC-DIG-hec-03592.

ovation accompanied his indictment of alcohol and his promise to "oppose this scourge from hell until my arm can strike no longer and my tongue can speak no more."[17]

Senator Sheppard did not appeal to the clerical crusade as much as he was a part of it. Sheppard worked longer, harder, and more successfully than any other national legislator to pass a prohibition amendment to the United States Constitution. Mere months after entering the Senate, he greeted two thousand prohibitionists from the Anti-Saloon League and Women's Christian Temperance Union on the steps of the United States Capitol and led them in a rendition of "Onward Christian Soldiers."[18] That same year he introduced his first resolution calling for a constitutional amendment banning the manufacture, sale, and transport of alcoholic beverages. He became the legislative point man for the nation's mobilized moral crusaders and a tireless advocate of Christian nationalism. Sheppard had become the link between Texas's brewing Bible Belt culture and national politics.

Narratives of the postbellum Bible Belt too often emphasize only southerners' insularity. White southern denominations seem isolated, consumed with harboring their own sectional resentments. Religious historian Samuel Hill, for instance, wrote long ago that the "aftermath of the Civil War sealed the South's tendency toward introversion."[19] Little has changed. "In the South," one recent account argues, "Christian nationalism died with the Confederacy."[20] But religious southerners also turned outward, and moral reformers commingled their cause with that of the whole country. Sheppard came of age in a South consumed by moral crusades and eager to engage the nation. "We need not deceive ourselves," Sheppard declared in 1914, "A Christian nation cannot tolerate the liquor traffic. We must array ourselves for a higher civilization or a lower one." He called passage of a prohibition amendment "the most solemn duty that has confronted Congress since the death of slavery," and said, "It will determine whether the moral forces of the Nation are the dominant ones. It will determine whether this is a Christian Nation."[21] Such were the stakes.

But Sheppard was not the only new leader in the clerical movement. The combative logic of clericalism had bred a new kind of religious warrior, a no-holds-barred brawler infected with anarchic pugnacity. Their rhetoric more extreme, their attacks more personal, and their targets more expansive, they battled individual newspaper editors, Catholic priests, chiefs of police, Hollywood actors, labor leaders, jazz musicians, black leaders, and Protestant ministers of insufficiently militant politics or theologies. The educated reformers and denomination builders who had so recently taken control of longstanding institutional bases now realized they shared the stage with a number of pure, unadulterated fighters who forsook the old anchors of institutional power to fight from the grassroots and who built improvised moral empires out of the frustrations of common parishioners. But before capturing headlines as "fundamentalists" in the 1920s, this new breed of fighter worked from within the clerical insurgency, lashing out against liquor and anything other than 100 percent loyalty to the clerical cause. They were men such as Fighting Bob Shuler, who at pastorates in Austin, Temple, and Paris (Texas)

FIGURE 8.2 J. Frank Norris (*left*) with fellow fundamentalist and moral warrior John Roach Straton, 1928.

Source: Prints and Photographs Division, Library of Congress, LC-DIG-ggbain-34064.

scourged the "pussy-footers, soft-soapers, issue-dodgers and general trace-kickers," and said, "God and the world are dead tired of the spineless preacher. He is a parasite in and on any community." [22] Shuler's monthly *Free Lance* perfectly captured the new combative attitudes of the final phase of the clerical crusade. And he was not alone.

J. Frank Norris was the most successful of the new breed. Norris's gospel was pure combat. A savagely ambitious, controversy-starved, ever-belligerent publicity hound, Norris in the 1920s would become perhaps the nation's most powerful fundamentalist by waging war against Jews, communists, Sabbath-breakers, integrationists, Baylor University, the Southern Baptist Convention, Catholics, liberals, and everything in between.[23] But in the 1910s, he was still busy battling vice and building his Fort Worth Baptist church into what one historian called "a southwestern religious empire."[24] Reflecting later on his rise, Norris said, "I didn't use a pearl handle pen knife . . . I had a broad axe and laid it at the tap root of the trees of dancing, gambling, saloons, houses of ill fame, ungodly conduct, high and low, far and near. And you talk about a bonfire—the whole woods was set on fire."[25]

Shuler and Norris and the other fighting clerics worked alongside the denominational leaders and newly installed politicians and continued to bear down upon liquor and the last strands of anticlerical resistance. As war fervor burned slowly beneath American culture, the clerics readied themselves for their long-awaited victory. The time had come, Shuler wrote in 1917. "The Day has dawned for the making of history in Texas, for the saving of a State, for the redeeming of the Lone Star Empire. Patriots are needed. The call is for men, undaunted and unafraid, unpurchased and without a price. Any other kind will go down."[26]

The clerics had found their champions. The wave had crested and now readied to crash. And then the First World War came. Time and steady momentum alone might have won Texas, the South, and the whole nation for prohibition, but that would never be seen. Instead, the First World War wove a nationalistic "100 percent Americanism" so seamlessly into domestic moral reform that prohibition swept through Texas and submerged the American political system. It was, of course, a testament to the longtime efforts of the clerics to partition society into saints and sinners, capture their denominations, moralize race, harness the tropes of gender, and seize the pages of history that, when the war arrived, the ensuing rush of patriotic fervor came bearing the cross and worked its way naturally through the nation's churches and religious leaders, bringing religious reform to the forefront of the national consciousness and making prohibition a wartime imperative.

World War I rallied the nation against the supposed evils of Germany, and Texas reformers used the patriotic fervor engendered by the war to topple the state's teetering anticlerical resistance.[27] As public schools barred the teaching of German, cities changed German street names, and libraries took German books out of circulation, prohibitionists decried alcoholic beverages as an unaffordable wartime luxury, products of unpatriotic German peddlers, and a threat to soldiers' health.[28] On April 6, 1917, the day that America formally entered the Great War, Senator Sheppard wrote to President Wilson to plead the case that national efficiency would be "enormously enhanced, if the liquor traffic could be wiped out."[29]

Prohibitionists linked American brewers—Pabst, Schlitz, Anheuser, Busch—to Germany. "Do these," Shuler asked, "sound like the names of men who love America?" Contending that "these big brewers are America's greatest enemies at home at this moment," he suggested that "fighting Germany at home would be a pretty good battle cry at present."[30] The state's Anti-Saloon League declared that "to talk now about patriotism and about our supreme task's being to win the war and not to seek the immediate destruction of the German breweries and German-owned saloons is to belie one's every word."[31]

When the Baptist General Convention of Texas met for its annual convention in Dallas in November 1917, the Convention's Civic Righteousness Committee suggested that as soldiers fought abroad, moral citizens must do battle at home. "We believe that a day never came before when the call was as strong as now to the righteous citizen to put every ounce of his blood and strength into the fight to make the world what Christ intended to be—a safe place for a Christian democracy."[32] George Truett read a special statement declaring, "It is our profound conviction that in the reconstruction of the world, on a democratic basis, all the moral forces of society will be needed, acting in concert, for the exaltation and maintenance of proper standards of righteousness in civil government and everywhere else."[33] "This war is not all bad," wrote Shuler. "It takes a cross to make a Christ complete. It takes a fire-crowned bush to send a Moses on his way."[34]

Positioned as the defenders of both righteousness and Americanism, the preachers and their allies leveled their opponents. Former governor Oscar Colquitt, for instance, still believed he could ride anticlericalism and his antiprohibition record into office as he prepared to challenge the ailing Charles Culberson for a US Senate seat in 1916. But the European conflict unleashed withering new cultural forces within the United States. Culberson bluntly laid out his strategy: "Are the people of Texas going to stand by President Woodrow Wilson or the German Kaiser?"[35] Culberson and his allies were unrelenting, and Colquitt's support evaporated. As expected, Culberson routed the former antiprohibition governor.[36] "The overwhelming defeat of Colquitt is regarded as an American victory," the *New York Times* reported, and the voters of Texas "have shown their resolve to put America first."[37]

For the moment, Governor Ferguson remained a stubborn obstacle to the enactment of statewide anti-liquor measures, and he continued to veto all legislative paths to prohibition.[38] But the state's prohibitionists continued working locally through local option elections. After drying out nearly all of North, West, and East Texas, the prohibitionists finally purged some of the state's stubborn urban holdouts.[39] Dallas County fell on September 10, 1917. Cities of similar size had gone dry when their states adopted prohibition, but "as far as we are able to learn," wrote the chairman of the local dry campaign, M. H. Wolfe, "no city the size of Dallas has ever voted in favor of prohibition in a local option election."[40] The clergy, of course, had led the assault. Fighting Bob Shuler singled out Edwin Mouzon for special praise, saying that "[w]hen the local option election was on in full blast in Dallas County, he laid aside his robes of ecclesiastical authority, took the stump, and delivered some of the most telling blows ever delivered in Dallas or North Texas for civic righteousness and sobriety." The campaign, he said, "proved conclusively that a Bishop in the Methodist Church may get down on the ground floor and, forgetting the dignity of his office, fight the devil with a battle axe sharp and terrible."[41] And so, Shuler wrote, "Local option goes marching on."[42] McLennan County, where, in 1885, Richard Coke had urged voters in Waco to "scourge" the preachers back to their pulpits, went dry in October. "It has been suggested by many persons," the *Dallas Morning News* reported, "that, at the rate Texas is going dry by local option, the question of Statewide prohibition soon may be purely academic."[43]

Although state after state was falling to dry forces, Texas clerics had so far failed to complete their conquest. It was Governor Ferguson, they knew, who held their state back. By 1917, he increasingly seemed to stand alone as the last major political obstacle to statewide prohibition in Texas. But suddenly, he seemed vulnerable. A Populist after populism had long since ended and poll taxes had exiled the poor from political life, antiprohibitionist and antiprogressive when prohibitionist-progressives stood ready to conquer the state, Ferguson had roused nearly every powerful constituency in Texas— save the brewers—against him. The prohibitionists' uncompromising march toward total victory demanded immediate action. They could no longer wait for regular election cycles and the vagaries and corruption of Texas politics to accomplish their task for them. They just needed an opening. And when James Ferguson declared war on the University of Texas, he gave them one.

In a state crippled by rural poverty, Ferguson denounced the university as a "rich man's school," a cliquish world of fraternities and sororities built for and sustained by Texas elites. Ferguson had to fight to extract from the legislature a special $1,000,000 appropriation for rural schools; he objected to spending one-and-a-half times as much on a mere three thousand university students from the state's most privileged families.[44] More importantly for the power-hungry governor, it was out of his hands. In 1915, he had tried to itemize the university's budget and was rebuffed. He tried to have members of the faculty fired and was rebuffed. He tried to choose the university's president and was rebuffed. When, in 1916, the Board of Regents, without Ferguson's approval, named as president Robert Vinson, an ordained Presbyterian minister and head of Austin Presbyterian Theological Seminary, Ferguson had had enough.[45] In 1917, he vetoed nearly all of the system's appropriation. "If the University cannot be maintained as a democratic University," he said, "then we ought to have no University."[46]

The governor's enemies united against him. Ferguson's veto had enflamed passions among the state's genteel class and among his longtime political opponents, bringing together multiple constituencies in protest. Prohibitionists joined with the university-educated lawyers in the legislature and counterattacked. An anti-Ferguson coalition of wealthy university alumni and donors, prohibitionists, progressive Democrats, and a newly emboldened women's suffrage movement cohered.

As women emerged from political exile through the secular club movement and into the suffrage movement, long-standing clerical ambivalence to female political participation in Texas crumbled.[47] Suffragists and prohibitionists joined to oppose Ferguson. In one protest in front of the capitol building on Congress Avenue, demonstrators erected a small speaking platform decorated with orange and white bunting (the colors of the state university) and two orange, eight-foot banners that read "Women of Texas Protest." Leaders of the women's movement spoke throughout the day; near midnight, the protest moved to a nearby park where Fighting Bob Shuler preached a raucous condemnation of the governor.[48] The onslaught of progressive women added to an already potent clerical movement and together they helped to unseat the sitting governor.

Although constitutionally barred from doing so, on July 23, 1917, the prohibitionist Speaker of the Texas House of Representatives, Franklin O. Fuller, called a special session of the legislature to impeach the governor. The House dug up old accusations of financial improprieties and, after weeks of hearings, drew up twenty-one articles of impeachment relating to the university veto and Ferguson's personal finances. Most damning was evidence that in 1914 Ferguson had accepted a $156,500 loan from an unknown source, popularly believed—correctly—to be Texas brewers. Ferguson called the whole ordeal a "kangaroo court," but the Senate cleared the two-thirds threshold necessary to remove the governor.[49] On September 26, 1917, the state's newspapers announced Ferguson's impending removal, and, in a bid to avoid future political exile, Ferguson preemptively resigned.[50] The great political thorn in the side of Texas prohibitionists had been plucked out and tossed aside. "Texas stands redeemed," Shuler wrote. "God and right go marching on."[51]

Ferguson's agrarian strain of anticlericalism had depended on a volatile mix of personality and rural alienation. But, aside from the brewers, it had appealed most forcefully to those with the least political power. In an expanding industrial state with across-the-board voting restrictions, it rested upon an eroding rural foundation and one man's magnetism. This last exceptional strand of anticlericalism might have unraveled naturally with time, but before that could be seen the clerical conquest, wartime fervor, and Ferguson's ill-fated move against the university tipped the balance.

While Ferguson's enemies hatched plans for their coup at home, in Washington, D.C., Morris Sheppard spearheaded the congressional drive for national prohibition. In August 1917, the Senate approved the senator's resolution to submit to the states a constitutional amendment prohibiting the manufacture, sale, and transport of alcoholic beverages. It passed the House, and on December 18, 1917, Congress sent it to the states for ratification.[52]

Texas clerics, after deposing Ferguson and preparing to conquer the state, looked to take credit for such national victories. The Texas Anti-Saloon League distributed a statement signed by leading clergymen that read: "We congratulate the people of Texas upon the unparalleled progress in the recent past in our fight for a dry State and a dry Nation and upon the worthy part our Texas people have had in securing the many brilliant victories at Washington culminating in the passage of the resolution for national constitutional prohibition by both branches of Congress."[53] Senator Sheppard drew special praise. "He has challenged the open saloon, shaken his fist in its face and dared it to come out in the open and fight ever since he was a youth," said his fellow Methodist Robert Shuler. "When other so-called prohibitionists were politicking around trying to get the support of the antis and add that support to their pro following, Morris Sheppard was running for office straight out as a simon pure prohibitionist who would rather die than compromise a single inch of the issue."[54] William Jennings Bryan had addressed the Texas legislature that spring and said he "thanks God for a Senator Sheppard in the United States Senate."[55] And soon after passage, state legislatures were already preparing to ratify the amendment. The Texas legislature, called into special session, angled to be among the first.

With Ferguson removed and his executive veto gone, the legislative path to statewide prohibition finally lay open. Prohibitionists immediately bombarded the newly seated governor, William P. Hobby, with appeals to call a special session of the state legislature to ram through as much prohibition legislation as it could as quickly as it could.[56] In late 1917, the Baptist's Civic Righteousness Committee, exulting in Ferguson's removal, declared, "We definitely and specifically call upon Governor Hobby to convene the legislature in special session in January, 1918, and to submit to them such liquor legislation as will rid our state by statute of the saloons, till it can be done forever in 1919 by constitutional amendment."[57] "The time has come," wrote Bob Shuler. "If Mr. Hobby is ready we are ready."[58]

But Hobby waffled between his old political patrons and the new rising power of the Bible Belt. Clergy waited uneasily, willing to endorse Hobby should he call the special session, but also, having just toppled a sitting governor, promising Hobby's inevitable destruction if he delayed their now-inevitable triumph.[59] Prohibitionists leveraged the threat of political insurgency by dangling the potential candidacy in the upcoming regular gubernatorial election of prohibitionist Earle B. Mayfield, a state railroad commissioner and former state senator who would later, in 1922, win election to the United States Senate as a prohibitionist Klansman.

Mayfield laid bare the prohibitionists' intentions: "If Governor Hobby will convene the Legislature at once and make Texas dry as a bone, he will write his name deep in the affections of the people of Texas, and school children, unborn, will read in history of the man that drove liquor from our State; but he will work his own destruction if he thinks for a moment he can run with the hare and bark with the hounds on the prohibition question."[60] The whole weight of the prohibition crusade threatened to crash upon Hobby. "This State is clearly prohibition, and Mr. Hobby knows that fact," wrote Bob Shuler. "He cannot more surely commit political suicide than to begin to dilly-dally and flim-flam with this imperative question."[61] "Let the Governor prove his faith by his works," said Baptist preacher and state Anti-Saloon League leader Arthur J. Barton.[62] But as Hobby delayed, Mayfield wondered whether the governor "has sinned away his day of grace."[63]

FIGURE 8.3 Senators Morris Sheppard (*left*) and Earle B. Mayfield, veterans of the prohibition movement and products of the clerical crusade, 1925.

Source: Prints and Photographs Division, Library of Congress, LC-DIG-npcc-26678.

Prohibitionists pressured Hobby throughout the fall and winter. "I again beg our Governor to tell the people what he proposes to do in regard to outlawing the liquor traffic in Texas," Mayfield declared that October.[64] In November, the Denison YMCA sponsored Senator Sheppard, who spoke on "Christian Citizenship."[65] Two months later, on January 21, the Episcopal bishop William T. Capers delivered a graduation sermon in San Antonio on "The Patriotism of Christ." "We hear much of Christ as our savior," he told his young listeners, "let us today think of him as a citizen of his nation, a true patriot."[66] Hobby waffled as long as he could but, compelled by prohibitionists and wartime reformers, realizing that he could not stand in the way of prohibition and survive any longer in Texas politics, he finally relented. On February 2, 1918, he called a special session of the state legislature to finally pass statewide prohibition legislation.[67]

Before the legislature met, the state's Anti-Saloon League issued a public statement signed by representatives from each of the state's major Protestant denominations and denominational newspapers. "We are now in the final drive against the evil of strong drink both in our State and our Nation," it read. "Our task now is to complete the drive with all possible dispatch." The letter petitioned the legislature to pass rigorous prohibition laws and urged "that the pastors and churches and all other moral forces begin at once a steady stream of letters and telegrams to the Governor and to the members of the Legislature." As the petitioners made their case, they marveled at "the power of the preachers, the efficiency of the churches and the supremacy of the moral and spiritual forces of our country" amid the exigencies of war. "We rejoice in this new credential given the Christian religion as the chief factor and force in all that makes for the good of the Nation and of the world in this hour of their supreme need," it read.[68]

The special session convened on February 26 and legislators threw everything they had at the liquor question. They passed prohibition laws that restricted saloon licenses, bolstered anti-bootlegging laws, and passed a "ten-mile law" banning the sale of alcohol within ten miles of any army base or naval yard. Since military bases were housed in nearly every major Texas city—most notably in the "wet" holdouts of El Paso, Fort Worth, Galveston, Houston, and San Antonio—the law effectively shuttered over a thousand Texas saloons, decimating the number of legal establishments in the state. But the legislature didn't stop there. On March 4, it ratified the Eighteenth Amendment, making Texas the eighth state to do so. And then, knowing that it violated the state constitution and would likely be thrown out by the courts but thumbing its nose and passing it anyway, the legislature passed a statewide prohibition law shuttering all the remaining saloons, breweries, and distilleries in Texas.[69]

"Governor Hobby made history today," wrote the *Dallas Morning News*, after Hobby had signed the statewide prohibition bill into law on March 21, 1918. The bill was baldly unconstitutional: the state constitution reserved "local option" for Texas counties, judicial precincts, and municipalities. But it didn't matter. With Ferguson gone, the prohibitionists had made up for lost time and Hobby had saved his political career. State representative and prohibitionist Ice Reeves wired that "Hobby was elected Governor at 3 o'clock, when he signed the State-wide dry bill." The *Dallas Morning News* observed that "other pros were heard to make the same declaration."[70] Mayfield, "in view of the splendid achievements of the legislature," withdrew his candidacy for governor.[71]

The prohibition measures had passed overwhelmingly and with little controversy. So quick and great had the prohibitionist victory seemed that few paused any longer to wonder whether it was right and proper, whether the crusaders speaking in pulpits, writing to newspapers, or petitioning politicians should have been preaching and demanding the things that they were now preaching and demanding.

That spring, Ferguson mounted a feeble challenge to reclaim the Democratic gubernatorial nomination, peddling the same well-worn anticlerical rhetoric that had won him so much so recently. Chastising an ever-growing train of political opponents, he reserved special animosity for religious leaders. "Oh, you political preachers," he said, "don't ever think I'm afraid of you, because I am going to continue to skin you from hell to Haw River like I've always done."[72] He wouldn't get the chance. By 1918, his brand of anticlerical demagoguery had expired. The rhetoric finally fell flat. "Jim Ferguson's tirade against the 'political preachers' has become one loud scream," wrote Bob Shuler. But, he added, "we can not say that we blame him. If ever a man got rough treatment at the hands of Christian ministers, that man was Jim Ferguson."[73] Ferguson continued on about the "politicians, political preachers, office seekers and church hypocrites," but, as Shuler argued, it no longer mattered: "Let him foam and rant! He and his kind are forever done for in Texas."[74] One Texas paper articulated a new consensus: "It is generally a safe proposition to beware of the candidacy of the man who talks about 'political preachers.' . . . As a class they [preachers] are not going to line up on the wrong side."[75]

The prohibitionists continued to surge. Triumphant at the polls in 1918, they now angled to dominate the Democratic Party machinery at that fall's state party convention in Waco. "Instead of turning over to the enemy every position of trust and place of power within the party," urged Shuler, "let the men who have fought for righteousness take the reins." [76] And they did. Prohibitionists and progressive delegates captured the Party, rewrote the state Party platform, and declared loudly for prohibition and progress.[77] The chairman of the executive committee proclaimed that "all things have become new."[78] J. B. Cranfill returned to the Democratic Party after three decades in the Prohibition Party, and amid cries of "Cranfill, Cranfill," he "made a rousing speech" before the convention. According to the *Dallas Morning News*, "He declared, amid laughter, that he wanted the opportunity to preach the funeral service of John Barleycorn."[79]

The ground had shifted, and it had shifted suddenly. By the fall of 1918, when the renowned evangelist Billy Sunday spoke before a capacity crowd at the Fort Worth Coliseum—the same building anticlerics had filled to castigate political preachers in 1911—telling them, "The trouble is we have no God in American politics," religious leaders were the ones not only filling arenas with supporters, but winning elections and scourging their opponents.[80]

It was in large part World War I that crowned the clerical crusade. The war pushed the entire country into a wave of reform. "We must reckon with that fact that the war set Prohibition ahead from five to ten years," wrote the general superintendent of the Anti-Saloon League and Methodist minister Dr. P. A. Baker.[81] In 1918, the Disciples' *Christian Courier*, while noting "the general quickening of the moral conscience on the part of the people," praised the tireless efforts of moral reformers, but conceded that "war conditions are the mighty factor that is bringing things to a head."[82] The war accelerated the work of clericalism. It amalgamated God and country and politics. Never before had prohibition and its preachers been yoked so closely with patriotism and national destiny, and it was that combination that finally broke the back of anticlericalism.[83] "However much we may deprecate war," wrote Bob Shuler, "the law of compensation still obtains, and for all the sacrifices we as a people are making, we are reaping a wonderful harvest."[84]

And what a harvest it was. A governor deposed, another bullied into submission, and statutory statewide prohibition passed by a captured legislature. When the Civic Righteousness Committee of Baptist General Convention of Texas met in Dallas in December 1918, it resolved "that in our judgment more has resulted in the year just past for the betterment of mankind that [*sic*] in any single year since the Resurrection Year." Not only had the Allied Powers won the war, "the world enemy—strong drink—has been whipped and beaten around the globe."[85] And the victories kept coming.

On January 16, 1919, Nebraska became the thirty-sixth state to ratify the prohibition amendment, pushing it past the three-fourths threshold needed for adoption. The Eighteenth Amendment was ratified. National prohibition had been made constitutional. When news of Nebraska's ratification reached the Senate, senators broke decorum and loudly applauded Morris Sheppard, crowded him on the floor of the Senate chamber in congratulations, and paid him tributes in speech.[86] "The mothers and Christian citizenship of the Nation," said senator William Kenyon of Iowa, "are thanking God that there came to Congress a man with courage, persistency, devotion, and love of humanity that he has manifested in standing amidst all the storms of abuse not only in the Nation, but around this Capitol, and fighting the good fight to the end. It is my humble judgment, and I know that it is the judgment of millions of people in the United States that no greater service has ever been performed to humanity or righteousness and to the real best interest of this Nation, than has been by the Senator from Texas, Mr. Sheppard."[87]

In Texas, jubilation greeted the news of the amendment's ratification. Prohibitionist leaders celebrated the following evening at a banquet in Dallas's Southland Hotel. J. B. Cranfill, in his capacity as toastmaster, praised the generations of religious leaders and temperance activists who had embarked upon the clerical crusade, who "were prohibitionists when it was not safe to be, and fought for prohibition when it was almost suicide to do so." The assembly prepared a telegram for Senator Sheppard that read, "We salute you as the foremost man in America in connection with the triumph in the victory over the saloon."[88] Later that summer, J. Frank Norris traveled to Washington, D.C., to thank Sheppard personally by presenting him with an engraved set of silver on behalf of "the largest Sunday School in America."[89] The exchange, between the powerful leader of one of the nation's largest congregations and "the father of national prohibition," testified to Texas's new leadership in America's moral politics.

Texas had been voted dry, but the clerics wanted a final constitutional victory at home and they scrambled to beat the implementation of the national prohibition amendment with a statewide amendment of their own.[90] In October 1918, the Texas Court of Criminal Appeals ruled part of the statutory prohibition bill unconstitutional. Rev. Atticus Webb, the superintendent of the state's Anti-Saloon League, said, "The decision only emphasizes what we have contended all along, that the prohibition question is not settled and won't be until we write it in the Constitution."[91] The *Baptist Standard* argued, "We must not depend on the uncertainties of statutory prohibition, war-time Prohibition, or even the National Amendment."[92] The state legislature submitted an amendment to voters on May 24, 1919.[93] The prohibitionists would get one last shot at a statewide constitutional amendment. After so many years of bitter conflict, few now doubted the outcome. Victory finally loomed.

"Our cause has won," declared the chairman of the statewide prohibition committee before the election. "Not only do the men and women of the state believe in sobriety but the whole nation has come to that position."[94] "In a few days Texas will have redeemed her good name," Bob Shuler wrote. "Home, church and school will have won their long-prayed-for victory." He said, "Saturday the 24th settles it. We win. Sobriety reigns. Decency is enthroned."[95]

Although victory seemed assured, Rev. Webb urged vigilance, "Everywhere you turn, the pros, both pastors and laymen, are saying, 'Oh, we will win without effort,' to which every anti answers a hearty 'Amen!'" Webb warned of complacency. The Great War had ended, he said, but the war against alcohol continued. "We must simply become alive to the situation and go 'over the top' for a glorious victory. Pros of Texas, in God's name, arouse. Get busy and swat John Barleycorn all up and down the line. Rum must be destroyed."[96] The chairman of the statewide campaign committee, R. Harper Kirby, urged Texans "to vote in mass, to vote with all your strength, to work, to give your time and talent, to organize for victory, to stay all day at the polls and on the streets and otherwise, working legitimately and honorably for our success."[97] "May 24th is the eventful day," wrote Bob Shuler in an issue of *Free Lance* devoted to the election. "Let every patriot walk up to the Ballot Box on the 24th and vote for home and child, for school and church, for civilization and the rule of manhood. Then we will have redeemed the state of the lone star and forever repudiated that outfit of thieves and political crooks."[98]

Senator Sheppard returned to Texas to campaign for the amendment. "You ought to match the Constitution of grand old Texas with the Federal prohibition amendment," he told voters in Houston.[99] "God grant that a mighty crowning victory shall come to right on May 24th," wrote Kirby, explaining that "Texas voting dry on the 24th means much to prohibition in the nation and even in the world."[100] "Let us redeem our good name," Shuler added. "Let us bury the broken past and go forward to make a sober state by God's great help."[101]

And after so many decades of bruising, hard-fought political campaigns, on May 24, 1919, the Texas prohibitionists finally triumphed. The statewide prohibition amendment passed by a vote of 159,723 to 140,099.[102] "The adoption of the Prohibition amendment to the State Constitution marks the successful culmination of fifty years of ardent temperance propaganda in Texas," declared the state's self-appointed "historian of the Dry Movement," H. A. Ivy. "In the future annals of Texas," he wrote, "May 24, 1919, ought to stand out as the second greatest day in the history of the State—the day on which the people of Texas, at the ballot box, pronounced sentence of eternal banishment upon the old tyrant, King Alcohol."[103]

In 1920, after three frustrating months in Fort Worth, a letter to the *Star-Telegram* asked, "If there is a church in the city of Fort Worth where a man may go and hear the gospel preached, where the minister takes his text from the Bible?" The writer, a man named E. S. Brackton, said that he and his wife, both Baptists, had visited one of the city's renowned churches, "but were forced to listen to discussions of local questions, political and otherwise, in which we were not interested, but not one word of religion or the teaching of Jesus Christ did we hear." The next week they changed denominations. "The theme of the preacher was the qualifications of a certain man to be Governor of Texas," Brackton reported. "I have not been in Texas long enough to be familiar with or interested in its politics, but even if I had I would not expect to go to church for political information, but to hear the gospel of Christ." He feared he might need to sample every church in the city before he could find a church where he and his wife "could go to hear the gospel preached." He asked for advice. "Any church will do," he said, "just so religion is preached and not politics."[104]

The clerics had won their immediate aim by achieving constitutional prohibition, but however narrowly conceived, the politics of liquor masked a more fundamental transformation. As Fighting Bob Shuler put it after Governor Ferguson's 1918 defeat, "The preachers of Texas will not 'back to their pulpits' save with a message of truth and right on every question that presents itself. They have learned that they have a man's place in God's world and the right to speak out for right and justice in every issue that confronts them and their people. No cheap demagogue can intimidate them. No loathsome battle cry of viciousness can chase them to shelter. They are out in the open for truth and right and justice and God."[105]

With the triumph of prohibition, Texas, the South, and the nation recognized the coming reign of political religion. "We believe that the cause of Christ is being and will be carried forward as never before in the history of the world," resolved a Baptist committee in 1919.[106] As the Baptist preacher William Tardy put it in 1920, "We are the heirs of all the ages, we are the wearers of the crown, and the bearers of the scepter."[107] The culmination of history, the arbiters of righteousness, the lynchpin of a nation. The clerics had made the Bible Belt.

Prohibition would, of course, be repudiated in time, but it would not pull preachers back to their pulpits nor break up the new clerical consensus.

"We rejoice that State and National prohibition amendments are accomplished facts," declared a committee of Central Texas Methodists, "[but] the work of the Christian Church is not yet done."[108] Prohibition had demarcated the breaking point between an anticlerical past and a religious-political future. Armed with righteousness, the clerical movement broke a long history of public detachment. Prominent clergymen dared to challenge the dominant culture of anticlericalism—and they triumphed. Never again would their political ventures be so easily and reflexively challenged. And never again would their ambitions be so restrained.

Epilogue

STEELED BY DECADES of conflict and armed with a potent new political theology, the makers of the Bible Belt spread their fiery new gospel across the country. When white and black southerners poured out of the region during the remainder of the early twentieth century and settled especially in the Midwest and ever-rising West, they carried the clerical culture with them.[1] In *From Bible Belt to Sun Belt*, Darren Dochuk argued that the southernization of the vast American Sun Belt depended upon an inherited "Texas theology," a mix of uncompromising missionary work, Christian nationalism, and a "faith blended with politics."[2] Understanding the nature and origins of that Texas theology provides the key to understanding the politicization of southern religion and the roots of the American religious right.[3]

Texas supplied more than its fair share of migrant-clerics. Two in particular—Robert "Fighting Bob" Shuler and J. Frank Norris—nationalized clerical culture in the 1920s. Both nurtured the pugilistic faith forged by their elders in the prohibition battles of the early twentieth century. They trafficked easily and naturally in Christian nationalism, moral warfare, and political conflict. Applying the lessons he learned in the Texas prohibition crusades, Shuler electrified the city of Los Angeles in the 1920s with his fierce, uncompromising moralism. Soon he operated one of the largest and most influential churches in the West.[4] His compatriot, J. Frank Norris, operated one of the largest in the entire country.[5] Proclaiming a "give 'em hell" brand of Christianity, he spread his fundamentalist faith across the nation.[6] During the 1930s he started a second church in Detroit that quickly became a primary conduit for the Bible Belt's northern migration. By the 1940s, Norris preached to a larger congregational following than any American in history until that time.[7]

But even as evangelical Texans were spreading the gospel of religious politics, the impossibility legal enforcement and lingering anticlerical resentment doomed national prohibition. The clerics' groundbreaking achievement unraveled around them. Prohibitionists scrambled to defend the Eighteenth Amendment throughout the 1920s and early 1930s, but, in 1933, the Twenty-First Amendment repealed national prohibition and various state laws tore down statewide liquor laws. Scandal had consigned prohibition to a punch line in American historical memory, forever discrediting the crowning accomplishment of the clerical insurgency. But it hardly mattered. While clerics had ridden the liquor issue into power, by the time it deteriorated they were already secure in the Bible Belt. Prohibition would fail—though in some states dry counties still remain—but the clerics would persevere. "Civilization sweeps toward God," the aged Senator Sheppard told a Methodist congregation in 1934, and "the song that ripples on the lips of Clio, muse of history, is a song that sounds our eternal charge."[8]

As Texas clerics nourished the southernization of American religious life, they continued to tend their own regional Zion. On January 16, 1923, Pat Neff acknowledged the burden of his oath of office by "kissing the leaves of God's Book" and proclaiming his "deep consciousness of the responsibility that goes with it."[9] Governor Neff, a committed Baptist, veteran of the prohibition crusade, and later president of Baylor University, riding the crest of the clerical movement, delighted in the realization of the Bible Belt. "I greet you with the wish that the spirit of Christ may dwell in the hearts of our people," he said in his official 1922 Christmas message. He acknowledged the "Government founded under His guidance" and proclaimed Texas a thriving Christian state: "Church bells and school bells ring in symphony a glad acclaim to the splendor of our civilization."[10] Neff spoke the clerical idiom, and, as an insurgent, he had assisted in the making of the Bible Belt. Now, as governor, he marked its maturation.[11]

By 1926, Texas had more churches than any other state and from their pulpits clerical leaders wielded unprecedented influence. Although historical narratives have described a religious retreat from public life following the humiliations of the 1925 Scopes "Monkey" Trial, southern clerics hardly resisted effecting monumental political changes. In 1928, the Baptist fundamentalist J. Frank Norris and the more moderate Methodist bishop Edwin Mouzon, two Texas veterans of the clerical crusade, joined with regional allies to wrench parts of the one-party South away from the Democratic Party. For the first time since Reconstruction, in opposition to Democratic presidential candidate Al Smith, a Catholic antiprohibitionist, large numbers of southerners shattered a long political history and harkened the later coming of a seismic political reorientation by abandoning the Democrats and voting for the Republican Herbert Hoover that fall. But the effects of the Bible Belt extended beyond party politics.

Perhaps 150,000 Texans joined the rejuvenated "second" Ku Klux Klan in the 1920s. While many white Protestants opposed the extremes of the organization, legions of clerical Texans were primed to follow the hooded warriors and their public promotion of an illiberal moral redemption.[12] Much of the second Klan's motivation, at least in the Southwest, wrote one historian, "lay not so much in racism and nativism as in moral authoritarianism."[13] Progressive Democratic leader Thomas B. Love argued in 1922, for instance, that "the Ku Klux Klan in Texas is made up almost wholly of misled and misguided good people who are on the moral side of moral questions."[14] At a rally that same year against the Senate "Klandidate" and prohibitionist leader Earle Mayfield, a seventy-one-year-old Church of Christ preacher named Rev. W. H. Kittrell alleged, with some exaggeration, that "90 percent of the Protestant preachers are in the Klan"[15] While his anti-Klan sentiments drew on the region's once-powerful anticlerical culture—Kittrell simultaneously denounced "the man who wears the clerical robe and drags it into the mire of politics"—he also symbolized its obsolescence. His brand of anticlericalism had expired. Mayfield won his Senate seat with wide religious support and served in the Senate alongside the Christian nationalist Morris Sheppard.

As the clerics consolidated their political conquests, some turned back to refocus themselves on religious life. The birth of fundamentalism—a militant strain of Protestant Christianity rooted in the defense of biblical literalism—owed much to the clerical impulse. Many clerical activists turned their self-righteous hunger for purity inward by targeting moderate denominational rivals and insufficiently committed cultural warriors. Fundamentalism thrived in Texas. Norris's politicized fundamentalism helped him build a massive congregation.[16] Robert Shuler's aggressive fundamentalism had profited him in Texas before he moved West to grow his Southern California megachurch.[17] In Texas and elsewhere, resurrecting earlier traditions of denominational insurgencies, fundamentalists rocked the major denominations. The state's Baptist establishment was hit particularly hard. From Fort Worth, Norris denounced the denomination's flagship, Baylor University. Faculty from the Southwestern Baptist Theological Seminary contributed several articles to *The Fundamentals*, a series of religious booklets that gave fundamentalism its name. But Baptists weren't alone. Texas Methodists, Disciples, Presbyterians, and Episcopalians were all ripped apart by fundamentalist insurgencies.[18] From his base in Dallas, Congressionalist minister Cyrus Scofield spread fundamentalism across the world with his monumental best-seller *The Scofield Reference Bible*. Together with the newly formed Dallas Theological Seminary, Scofield helped to popularize dispensationalism, a peculiar form of fundamentalist eschatology that proclaimed God's particu-lar control over history and the coming end times.[19]

The rise of fundamentalism in Texas provoked many of the same con-troversies that famously erupted in the Scopes Trial in Tennessee. In 1923, two years before the famous Tennessee law banned the teaching of evolution in schools, in the Texas state legislature a Baptist minister joined with a lay-man to co-sponsor an anti-evolution bill. In 1925, the University of Texas blocked the employment of any "infidel, atheist, or agnostic."[20] Although nei-ther episode provoked a national media firestorm in any way comparable to Scopes, they nevertheless testified to the arrival of the Bible Belt. But while clerics continued their conquest of public and private life, pockets of anticler-ical resistance remained.

Critics still lurked within the confines of the new Bible Belt. Although purged from office, James Ferguson managed to hold together strands of anti-clerical resentment and populist discontent. By artfully exploiting rifts in the Democratic Party, he returned to the governor's mansion with the election of his wife, Miriam, in 1924. Neff, the departing governor, allegedly left an open Bible in the governor's office with an underlined verse urging the Fergusons to use their reclaimed office to illuminate God's path. Jim Ferguson closed the Bible and threw it into a corner. "Sunday School is dismissed," he is supposed to have said.[21] Although Ferguson's resurgence was short-lived, anticlerical-ism continued to reappear from time to time. In 1929, for instance, state rep-resentative J. Lewis Thompson of Houston said that political preachers have "reflected no credit to the State or church" and proposed a constitutional amendment barring preachers and priests from holding elected office.[22] By the late 1920s, however, such tactics were threadbare. Thompson's actions attracted little attention and the embattled Fergusons soon departed the political scene yet again, allowed the clerical culture to continue its work.

While the Klan's bigoted moralism faded from view after the 1920s, fun-damentalist churches and religious politics continued to dominate the state. W. Lee "Pappy" O'Daniel combined modern media, religious appeals, and anti-New Deal conservatism into a powerful movement during his tenures as Texas governor and United States senator in the 1930s and 1940s. Morris Sheppard championed a brand of Christian nationalism in the Senate until his death in 1941. Baptists J. Frank Norris and George Truett shepherded powerful megachurches in Fort Worth and Dallas, where they inspired new generations of fighting clerics into the 1930s and 1940s.[23] Norris's hard-edged protégé, W. A. Criswell, ascended to the prestigious pulpit at Dallas's First Baptist Church in 1944 and grew the already sprawling megachurch into the largest and arguably most influential church in the Southern Baptist Convention. A leader of postwar American fundamentalism, an anti-civil rights champion, a fierce anticommunist, and an architect of the Baptists' postwar conservative resurgence, Criswell laid much of the groundwork for the formation of the modern religious right.[24] Criswell's church also, incidentally, claimed postwar America's most popular evangelist, Billy Graham, as a member for over half a century. Graham's national crusades launched a national evangelical resurgence, and in Texas he found particularly fertile ground.[25] He capped one of his signature "crusades" with Explo '72, a large ecumenical gathering in Dallas in 1972 that Graham advertised as the "religious Woodstock." Eighty thousand youth filled the Cotton Bowl to hear Graham and other leaders urge evangelicals to bring Jesus Christ to every American.[26]

Amid this spiritual explosion anticlerical tradition flickered. Shreds of memory still tugged at Texans. It was no accident, for instance, that in 1960 John F. Kennedy chose an audience of Texas ministers to hear his famous defense of religious liberty and absolute separation of church and state. Meanwhile, some religious leaders resisted openly aligning themselves with resurgent religious conservatism. Despite its history of political activism, the Baptist General Convention of Texas rebuffed the fundamentalists and refused to fully embrace the religious right throughout much of the late-twentieth century.[27] But such holdouts represented little of the sea change reshaping southern religion. With divisions between politics and religion long since collapsed, activists could wed the Republican Party to conservative religion and enthrone the religious right as the heirs of the Bible Belt, the evolutionary culmination of a nearly century-old clerical triumph.[28]

The Methodists sing an old hymn, "A Charge to Keep I Have." George W. Bush adored it. He sang it at a private church service the day he became Texas governor in 1995 and later used it in the title of his autobiography. Two months after arriving in Austin, Bush hung a blue-toned oil painting in the governor's office depicting a weary Methodist circuit rider (bearing an uncanny resemblance to Bush) traveling a rugged mountain road. It was titled, "A Charge to Keep." Bush sent a memo to his staff: he wanted them to see and reflect upon the painting. He said the painting was based on the hymn, and he took the opportunity to cite his favorite verse, one urging listeners "to serve the present age" by "do[ing] my Master's will." The painting and the hymn and the accumulated victories of political religion inspired Bush to wed God and government. "This is our mission," he said. Referring to the horseman, he said, "This is us." The painting remained in the governor's office until, in 2001, it moved with Bush to the Oval Office. In interviews, the president continued to cite the painting as an inspiring emblem of America's religious heritage and as a personal reminder of his own sacred charge.[29]

Today, religion and politics collide and cast their shadow over American life. In recent years the Bible Belt has produced political prayer rallies, school-board battles, and faith-based presidencies. President Bush, the born-again Methodist, perfected the alliance of conservative politics and conservative religion. In the WallBuilders organization and in his many best-selling books, Texan David Barton, a Republican leader and evangelical minister, assails the "myth" of church and state separation as he leads the charge to Christianize America's history. In late 2011, Texas governor Rick Perry believed he could launch a successful bid for the Republican presidential nomination by appealing to a Christian America. He launched his campaign with a massive prayer rally in Houston's Reliant Stadium, decried a "war on Christianity," and topped the polls before a series of political stumbles doomed his campaign. Senator Ted Cruz tried to assemble the same coalition of Christian conservatives four years later. He opened his 2016 presidential campaign at Jerry Falwell's Liberty University, courted evangelical voters, and finished second in the a historically crowded Republican field. George W. Bush, David Barton, Rick Perry, Ted Cruz, Billy Graham: they are all the heirs of clericalism, the children of the Bible Belt, the sum of battles fought and won a century ago.

From a hostile culture in which anticlerical critics scourged political preachers, religious activists toppled a meek and otherworldly faith, conquered evangelical denominations, and sallied forth into public life to demolish the final lingering barriers to the construction of the Bible Belt. Clerical crusaders tamed a freewheeling religious world, taught their disciples to think in terms of a "Christian nation," conferred a distinct and privileged cultural station on their righteous followers, organized politically behind issues such as prohibition, and stifled anticlerical resistance. The clerics' unrelenting activism transformed the American South and soon thereafter the entire nation. Their efforts made the Bible Belt. And because they did, politics and public life would ever after be refracted through some sacred lens. The clerics not only created a place where, as H. L. Mencken phrased it, "Beelzebub is still as real as Babe Ruth," they constructed a world in which Christian heroes laid the foundations for a Christian republic and in which Christian activists would be compelled to entangle themselves inextricably with public life.[30] The Bible Belt drained political religion of controversy and convinced anxious Americans that faith should be a force in the secular world. Such is the legacy of the clerical triumph. And it lingers still.

Notes

INTRODUCTION

1. *Waco Daily Examiner*, August 29–30, 1885; *Galveston Daily News*, August 30, 1885; *Dallas Weekly Herald*, September 3, 1885. Coke's speech is cited in many accounts, including James D. Ivy, *No Saloon in the Valley: The Southern Strategy of Texas Prohibitionists in the 1880s* (Waco: Baylor University Press, 2003), 40; and Joe L. Coker, *Liquor in the Land of the Lost Cause: Southern White Evangelicals and the Prohibition Movement* (Lexington: University Press of Kentucky, 2007), 80.

2. Mitford M. Mathews cited Mencken's definition of the term in his 1951 *Dictionary of Americanisms*, vol. 1 (Chicago: University of Chicago Press, 1951), 110. Mathews, in putting together his *Dictionary*, explained, "He [Mencken] was delighted that there was a possibility of a dictionary of this kind and pledged his heartiest co-operation . . . In reply to a latter I wrote him about 'Bible belt,' he explained so neatly what he had meant by the term when he coined it and I made free use of his words in the definition which appears in the dictionary" (xii). Mathews's citation is also quoted in Stephen W. Tweedie, "Viewing the Bible Belt," *Journal of Popular Culture* 11 (Spring 1978): 865–876. See also Charles Reagan Wilson, "The Bible Belt," in *Encyclopedia of Religion in the South*, ed. Samuel S. Hill, et al. (Macon, Ga.: Mercer University Press, 2005), 117.

3. Mencken didn't coin the term in the glow of the 1925 Scopes "Monkey" Trial, and neither did he intend to only slam the region's devotion to biblical literacy and its corresponding suspicion of evolution. He had coined the phrase a year earlier and also derided the region's moral politics, what he called its "comstockery" after the famed moral legislator Anthony Comstock. H. L. Mencken, "Editorial," *American Mercury* (November 1924): 290–292; Mencken, "Comstockery," *Prejudices: Fifth Series* (New York: A. A. Knopf, 1926), 15–21. See Gaines Foster, "The End of Slavery and the Origin of the Bible Belt," in *Vale of Tears: New Essays on Religion*

and Reconstruction, ed. Edward J. Bloom and W. Scott Poole (Macon, Ga.: Mercer University Press, 2005), 147–148.

4. John B. Boles, *The Great Revival, 1787-1805: The Origins of the Bible Belt* (Lexington: University Press of Kentucky, 1996); Christine Leigh Heyrman, *Southern Cross: The Beginnings of the Bible Belt* (New York: A. A. Knopf, 1997). Gaines Foster has most prominently championed this revision of the Bible Belt's origins in his *Moral Reconstruction, Christian Lobbyists and the Federal Legislation of Morality, 1865-1920* (Chapel Hill: University of North Carolina Press, 2002).

5. "If religion in the Old South has become a mature field," Paul Harvey wrote in 2002, "scholarship on the era since the Civil War is still, relatively speaking, in its adolescence." Paul Harvey, "Religion," in *The South*, by Rebecca Mark and Robert Vaughn (Westport, Conn.: Greenwood Publishing Group, 2004), 408. Daniel Stowell reached similar conclusions in his study of the post–Civil War South: "The scholarship of the Civil War and Reconstruction eras is voluminous and especially rich, but too few scholars have examined the religious life of the postwar South." Daniel W. Stowell, *Rebuilding Zion: The Religious Reconstruction of the South, 1863-1877* (New York: Oxford University Press, 1998), 10. Over the past several decades, elements of a core narrative have been crafted by, among others, Paul Harvey, *Redeeming the South: Religious Cultures and Racial Identities among Southern Baptists, 1865-1925* (Chapel Hill: University of North Carolina Press, 1997); Ted Ownby, *Subduing Satan: Religion, Recreation, and Manhood in the Rural South, 1865 1920* (Chapel Hill: University of North Carolina Press, 1990); Stowell, *Rebuilding Zion*; and Beth Barton Schweiger, *The Gospel Working Up: Progress and the Pulpit in Nineteenth-Century Virginia* (New York: Oxford University Press, 2000).

6. Morris Sheppard, *Fraternal and Other Addresses* (Omaha, Neb.: Beacon Press, 1910), 281–301; "Anti-Rum Army at Capitol," *New York Times*, December 11, 1913; *Dallas Morning News*, December 10–11, 1913; Morris Sheppard, *National Prohibition and States Rights* (Washington, D.C.: Government Printing Office, 1914).

7. It took only three weeks for Mississippi to become the first state to ratify the amendment. The next three states to ratify, Virginia, Kentucky, and South Carolina, followed soon thereafter. George Brown Tindall, *The Emergence of the New South, 1913-1945* (Baton Rouge: Louisiana State University Press, 1967), 220. By 1907, grassroots activists had long since dried up most of the former Confederacy through "local option" campaigns—by 1907 New York City had more saloons than the entire American South. William A. Link, *The Paradox of Southern Progressivism, 1880-1930* (Chapel Hill: University of North Carolina Press, 1992), 96; John Corrigan, "The Prohibition Wave in the South," *American Review of Reviews* 36 (September 1907): 328–334.

8. *Congressional Record*, vol. 57 (Washington, D.C.: Government Printing Office, 1919), 1502; *New York Times*, January 17, 1919, 4.

9. Robert Wuthnow, *Rough Country: How Texas Became America's Most Powerful Bible-Belt State* (Princeton, N.J.: Princeton University Press, 2014), 5. For the sheer scope of religion in Texas, see Pew Forum on Religion and Public Life, "U.S. Religious Landscape Survey" (Washington, D.C.: Pew Research Center: 2008); Barry A. Kosmin and Ariela Keysar, *American Religious Identification Survey (ARIS) 2008* (Hartford, Conn.: Trinity College, March 2009).

10. Lewis L. Gould, *Progressives and Prohibitionists: Texas Democrats in the Wilson Era* (Austin: University of Texas Press, 1973), 26, citing *Dallas Morning News* (August 10, 1916). Also see, for instance, W. R. Buyauh to Oscar Branch Colquitt, May 16, 1910, Oscar Branch Colquitt Papers, 1873–1941, Dolph Briscoe Center for American History, University of Texas at Austin.

11. History is of course messy, and historical change proceeds haltingly, unevenly, and with multitudes of exceptions that spill over the narrow categories we assign it. Historian James Kloppenberg, for instance, warned against "the perils of using static categories for slippery historical phenomena." James Kloppenberg, *Uncertain Victory: Social Democracy and Progressivism in European and American Thought, 1870-1920* (New York: Oxford University Press, 1986), 300. The *Oxford English Dictionary* defines *anticlericalism* as "opposed to clericalism," which it defines as "clerical principles; clerical rule or influence; clerical partisanship." See *Oxford English Dictionary*, 2nd ed., s.vv. "anticlericalism," "clericalism." For an introduction to some of the many nuances of historical anticlericalism, see especially, Jose Sanchez, *Anticlericalism* (Notre Dame, Ind.: University of Notre Dame Press, 1972); Rene Remond. "Anticlericalism: Some Reflections by Way of Introduction," *European Studies Review* 13 (1983): 121–26; and Rene Remond, *L'anticlericalisme en France de 1815 a nos jours* (Paris: Fayard, 1976).

12. Richard Coke told Texans to "scourge" political preachers in 1885. *Galveston Daily News*, August 30, 1885. Two years later, in a debate with Baptist minister B. H. Carroll, senator Roger Q. Mills pointed to the preacher and said, "Hell was full of such political preachers—so full that their legs are hanging out of the windows." A. M. Perry to B. H. Carroll, January 11, 1892, Benajah Harvey Carroll Collection, Archives, Southwestern Baptist Theological Seminary, Fort Worth, Texas.

13. Anticlerical attitudes, Isaac and Hatch argued, fostered a flexible democratic faith unburdened by bureaucratic hierarchy or concentrated power. Rhys Isaac, *The Transformation of Virginia, 1740-1790* (Chapel Hill: University of North Carolina Press, 1982), 145–147, 155–157, 181–183; Nathan O. Hatch, *The Democratization of American Christianity* (New Haven, Conn.: Yale University Press, 1989), 44–46, 170–179.

14. The doctrine of spirituality has long been a target for southern historians. Scholars can't help but note the stark hypocrisy of white preachers who proclaimed the apolitical doctrine of spirituality while bolstering the Confederacy, attacking Reconstruction, and sanctifying white supremacy. In his study of antebellum southern theology, E. Brooks Holifield called spirituality a "protective posture during

the slavery controversy." Brooks Holifield, *The Gentleman Theologians: American Theology in Southern Culture, 1795-1860* (Durham, N.C.: Duke University Press, 1978), 154; Emphasizing the antebellum proslavery work of leading Presbyterian theologians, Jack P. Maddex called the doctrine of spirituality a postbellum invention, a theological contortion necessary to perpetuate white supremacy in a post-Confederate world. Jack P. Maddex, "From Theocracy to Spirituality: The Southern Presbyterian Reversal on Church and State," *Journal of Presbyterian History* 54, no. 4 (Winter 1976): 438–457.

15. Historians most often associate anticlericalism with Western Europe and Latin America, areas where the realities of institutionalized Catholicism kept the issue most salient. It is no accident that southerners so often referred to Protestant "priesthoods" and "Romish" plots, but as the sources of such epithets suggest, anticlericalism could thrive in mostly Protestant countries as well, adapted to the demands of religious disestablishment and evangelical religion.

16. Alan Wolfe, "The Culture War That Never Came," in *Is There a Culture War? A Dialogue on Values and American Public Life*," ed. James Davison Hunter and Alan Wolfe (Washington, D.C.: Pew Research Center and the Brookings Institution Press, 2006), 41–73.

17. As historians have explored the region's many faiths, they have yet to take seriously the region's many *un*faiths. Samuel Hill's exhaustive *Encyclopedia of Religion in the South*, for example, as historian Art Remillard first noted, contains no entries for "irreligion," "atheism," "skepticism," "free thought," or "anticlericalism." Art Remillard, "What about Southern Irreligion?," *Religion in American History: A Group Blog on American Religious History and Culture*, February 26, 2010, http://usreligion.blogspot.com/2010/02/what-about-southern-irreligion.html.

18. Samuel S. Hill, *Southern Churches in Crisis Revisited* (Tuscaloosa: University of Alabama Press, 1999), xiii, xv.

19. See especially Hill, *Southern Churches in Crisis*, and John Lee Eighmy, *Churches in Cultural Captivity: A History of the Social Attitudes of Southern Baptists* (Knoxville: University of Tennessee Press, 1972). Joe Coker has recently applied this approach to the study of southern prohibition by emphasizing the movement's capitulation to southern prejudices. Coker, *Liquor in the Land*. Some scholars, captivated by northern movements and refusing to surrender southern churches to Menckenesque scorn, discovered strains of a southern social gospel., see especially J. Wayne Flynt, "Dissent in Zion: Alabama Baptists and Social Issues," *Journal of Southern History* 35 (November 1969): 523–542; John Patrick McDowell, *The Social Gospel in the South: The Woman's Home Mission Movement in the Methodist Episcopal Church, South, 1886-1930* (Baton Rouge: Louisiana State University Press, 1982); Randal L. Hall, *William Louis Poteat: A Leader of the Progressive-Era South* (Lexington: University Press of Kentucky, 2000); and, in Texas, John Storey, *Texas*

Baptist Leadership and Social Christianity, 1900-1980 (College Station: Texas A&M University Press, 1986).

20. In the creation of a Lost Cause religion, Charles Reagan Wilson writes that "the culture was a captive of the churches." Charles Reagan Wilson, *Baptized in Blood: The Religion of the Lost Cause, 1865-1920* (Athens: University of Georgia Press, 1980), 12. Paul Harvey suggests the same in *Redeeming the South*, 4.

21. It has been nearly two decades, for instance, since Beth Barton Schweiger urged southern historians to abandon the term "evangelicalism," in Donald Mathews, et al., "Forum: Southern Religion," *Religion and American Culture* 8 (Summer, 1998): 147–177.

22. In recent years, for instance, robust new historiographies have developed around Colonial Anglicans, Appalachian Protestants, and southern Pentecostals.

23. As Harry Stout and Robert Taylor put it, "[H]istorians are swimming alone in their own particularities." Harry S. Stout and Robert M. Taylor, "Studies of Religion in American Society: A State of the Field," in *New Directions in American Religious History*, ed. Harry S. Stout and D. G. Hart (New York: Oxford University Press, 1998), 32. See also Stephen J. Stein, "American Religious History: Decentered with Many Centers," *Church History* 71 (June 2002): 374–379. Thomas Bender notably pled for historical synthesis over a quarter of a century ago in the pages of the *Journal of American History*. Thomas Bender, "Wholes and Parts: The Need for Synthesis in American History," *Journal of American History* 73 (June 1986): 120–136.

24. Paul Harvey offered one model for a black-white synthesis in *Redeeming the South*. Scholars such as Amanda Porterfield and John Modern, meanwhile, have been busy breaking down barriers between "religion" and "the world" in the history of early America. Amanda Porterfield, *Conceived in Doubt: Religion and Politics in the New American Nation* (Chicago: University of Chicago Press, 2012); John Lardas Modern, *Secularism in Antebellum America* (Chicago: University of Chicago Press, 2011).

25. Harry Yandell Benedict and John Avery Lomax, *The Book of Texas* (New York: Doubleday, Page & Company, 1916), 58.

26. Gregg Cantrell quoted in John Nova Lomax, "Is Texas, Western, or Truly a Lone Star?" *Texas Monthly*, March 3, 2015. For Texas's southern identity, see especially Walter L. Buenger, "Texas and the South," *Southwestern Historical Quarterly* 103 (January, 2000): 308–324; Buenger, *The Path to a Modern South: Northeast Texas between Reconstruction and the Great Depression* (Austin: University of Texas Press, 2001); and Randolph B. Campbell, *An Empire for Slavery: The Peculiar Institution in Texas, 1821-1865* (Baton Rouge: Louisiana State University Press, 1989).

27. See especially Alwyn Barr, *Reconstruction to Reform: Texas Politics, 1876-1906* (Austin: University of Texas Press, 1971).

28. Henry Adams, *The Education of Henry Adams: An Autobiography* (Boston: Houghton Mifflin Company, 1918), 379–391.

29. Morris Sheppard, *Congressman Sheppard Is for Prohibition* (Fort Worth: Statewide Prohibition Amendment Association Headquarters, 1911), 8.

30. Beth Barton Schweiger, Paul Harvey, Ted Ownby, and Gaines Foster have all specifically identified the embrace of prohibition as a revolutionary moment. Schweiger, *Gospel Working Up*, 193; Ownby, *Subduing Satan*, 170; and Foster, *Moral Reconstruction*, 6, 46, 221, 224.

31. Sheppard, *Fraternal and Other Addresses*, 284.

32. Michael S. Patterson, "The Fall of a Bishop: James Cannon Jr. versus Carter Glass, 1909-1934," *Journal of Southern History* 39, no. 4 (1973): 493–518, 493.

33. Wayne Flynt, *Cracker Messiah: Governor Sidney J. Catts of Florida*, (Baton Rouge: Lousiana Ssate University Press, 1977). Tindall, *Emergence of the New South*, 25–26.

34. Edwin Mouzon to Clarence Ousley, January 15, 1913, Edwin D. Mouzon Papers, Archives, Center for Methodist Studies at Bridwell Library, Perkins School of Theology, Southern Methodist University, Dallas, Texas.

CHAPTER I

1. Quoted Tindall, *Emergence of the New South*, 210.

2. See, for instance, Charles H. Lippy, ed., *Bibliography of Religion in the South* (Macon, Ga: Mercer University Press: 1985), 23; James C. Cobb, *Away Down South: A History of Southern Identity* (New York: Oxford University Press, 2005), 114; and Paul Harvey, "Religion in the American South since the Civil War," in *A Companion to the American South*, ed. John B. Boles (Malden, Mass.: Blackwell Publishing, 2004), 387.

3. Stowell, *Rebuilding Zion*.

4. U. S. Census Office, *Seventh Census of the United States: 1850*, vol. 1 (Washington, D.C.: Government Printing Office, 1854); U. S. Census Office, *Eighth Census of the United States: 1860* (Washington, D.C.: Government Printing Office, 1864).

5. William H. Jack, quoted in Homer Thrall, *History of Methodism in Texas* (Houston: E. H. Cushing, Publisher, 1872), 180.

6. *Texas Christian Advocate*, January 27, 1887.

7. In 1850, 1860, and 1870, federal census workers enumerated the number of places of worship, the value of church property, and the total seating capacity for religious organizations in each state: they did not enumerate specific data on church membership. Nevertheless, in 1986 Roger Finke and Rodney Stark leveraged mathematical regression models against available data and confirmed the probability of drastically low religious adherence. Roger Finke and Rodney Stark, "Turning Pews into People: Estimating Nineteenth-Century Church Membership," *Journal for the Scientific Study of Religion* 25 (June 1986): 180–192. See also Rodney Stark, "The Reliability of Historical United States Census Data on Religion," *Sociological Analysis* 53 (Spring 1992): 91–95.

8. U. S. Census Office, *Eleventh Census of the United States: 1890*, vol. 9 (Washington, D.C.: Government Printing Office, 1894).

9. *Texas Siftings*, June 27, 1885.

10. Carry A. Nation, *The Use and Need of the Life of Carry A. Nation* (Topeka, Kans.: F. M. Steves & Sons, 1908), 91.

11. Ibid., 70–74; Fran Grace, *Carry A. Nation: Retelling the Life* (Bloomington: Indiana University Press, 2001), 66.

12. Nation, *Use and Need*, 74.

13. Carry Amelia Nation Diary and Scrapbook, 1870–1900, October 24, 1880, Carry Amelia Nation Papers, 1870–1961, Kansas Historical Society, Kansas Memory, http://www.kansasmemory.org.

14. Nation, Diary, August 15, 1879.

15. Nation, *Use and Need*, 84. "Mr. Nation," Carry wrote, "said that up to this year I had been a good wife."

16. According to one biographer, she believed in "visions, dreams, and ecstasies." Grace, *Carry A. Nation*, 80.

17. Nation, *Use and Need*, 86, 117.

18. "An event has happened," she wrote on July 24, 1879. "I have had a dream, a vision of the night . . . an event of darkness and silence." On August 15, she reported "raptuously [*sic*] contemplated the goodness of God." Nation, Diary. See also Grace, *Carry A. Nation*, 71.

19. For the fire, see Nation, *Use and Need*, 87. According to Nation's autobiography, in March 1889 she received a warning from God of an impending fire and the next day a fire broke out in the city. When it threatened her hotel, a sheriff asked Nation if it was insured. She looked at the sheriff, pointed to the sky, and said it was. Her hotel was spared. Her biographer, Fran Grace, found that Nation's account of the fire clashed with contemporary reports. Grace, *Carry A. Nation*, 84. On praying for rain, see Nation, *Use and Need*, 94; Grace, *Carry A. Nation*, 85. Years later, Carry claimed it then rained for three days. She called it "nothing short of a miracle."

20. Nation, *Use and Need*, 84.

21. Grace, *Carry A. Nation*, 79.

22. Nation, *Use and Need*, 91.

23. Quoted in Grace, *Carry A. Nation*, 85.

24. Nation, *Use and Need*, 100

25. Ibid., 84–85. She formed her own interracial, nondenominational Sunday school in her National Hotel and attracted several dozen children. Grace, *Carry A. Nation*, 83.

26. Grace, *Carry A. Nation*, 71.

27. Quoted in Daniel Okrent, *Last Call: The Rise and Fall of Prohibition* (New York: Simon and Schuster, 2010), 24.

28. Charles Postel, *The Populist Vision* (New York: Oxford University Press, 2009), 243.

29. Ibid., 244.

30. S. S. McKay and Doug Johnson, "Dohoney, Ebenezer Lafayette," in *Handbook of Texas Online* (Austin: Texas State Historical Association) http://www.tshaonline. org/handbook/online/articles/fdoo7 (accessed April 08, 2012).

31. Ibid.

32. *Dallas Morning News*, September 15, 1897.

33. See especially R. Laurence Moore, *In Search of White Crows: Spiritualism, Parapsychology, and American Culture* (New York: Oxford University Press, 1977).

34. Ivy, *No Saloon in the Valley*, 1.

35. "In Camp: The Day with the Spiritualists at Oak Cliff," *Daily Times Herald*, September 1, 2, 4, and 6, 1896, cited in Charles Postel, "The Populist Context: Texas Cotton Farmers and Religious Conflict, 1880-1900," Agrarian Studies Colloquium, Yale University, January 29, 2010; *Dallas Morning News*, September 15, 1897.

36. Quoted in Keith Lynn King, "Religious Dimensions of the Agrarian Protest in Texas, 1870-1908" (PhD diss., University of Illinois, 1985), 163.

37. Catherine Nugent, ed., *Life Work of Thomas L. Nugent* (Stephenville, Tex.: C. Nugent, 1896), 161; Postel, 254.

38. Harry Leon McBeth, *Texas Baptists: A Sesquicentennial History* (Dallas: Baptistway Press, 1998), 65. "If Texans had a state religion," *Time* mused in 1947, "it would probably be Baptist." At the end of the nineteenth century, no possibility seemed more distant. "Religion: In Texas," *Time*, November 24, 1947.

39. See especially Hatch, *Democratization of American Christianity*; and Gregory A. Wills, *Democratic Religion: Freedom, Authority, and Church Discipline in the Baptist South, 1785-1900* (New York: Oxford University Press, 1997).

40. B. F. Riley, *History of the Baptists of Texas: A Concise Narrative of the Baptist Denomination in Texas, from the Earliest Occupation of the Territory to the Close of the Year 1906* (Dallas: B. F. Riley, 1907), 261.

41. Ibid., 234.

42. Ibid., 261–262.

43. Ibid., 249.

44. Joseph E. Early, *A Texas Baptist Power Struggle: The Hayden Controversy* (Denton: University of North Texas Press, 2005), 21.

45. Early, *Texas Baptist Power Struggle*, vii; McBeth, *Texas Baptists*, 65–66. The organizations were the Baptist State Convention, the Baptist General Association, the East Texas Baptist Convention, the North Texas Missionary Baptist Convention, and the Central Texas Baptist Convention; the universities were Waco University and Baylor University (in Independence); and the two papers were iterations of the *Texas Baptist and Herald* and the *Baptist Standard*. Riley, *History of the Baptists*, 247.

46. Quoted in McBeth, *Texas Baptists*, 66.

47. Early, *Texas Baptist Power Struggle*, 7–11. Riley, *History of the Baptists*, 250–251. Buckner's faction challenged Link's membership, Buckner claimed that his faction had adhered to church principles and that his rivals, by rushing Link's membership, had not. Appealing to precedent, Buckner argued that his bloc represented

the one true First Baptist Church. He published his claims and fifty-nine members signed their support. For this, Pastor Curry and his supporters purged the would-be usurpers from the church. See Early, *Texas Baptist Power Struggle*, 7–11.

48. Early, *Texas Baptist Power Struggle*, 20; *Texas Baptist Herald*, March 4, 1880, quoted in Early, *Texas Baptist Power Struggle*, 19.

49. *Texas Baptist Herald*, March 4, 1880, quoted in Early, *Texas Baptist Power Struggle*, 20.

50. Early, *Texas Baptist Power Struggle*, 12, 21; Riley, *History of the Baptists*, 250–251.

51. Riley, note 40, 249.

52. Ibid., 255.

53. "An Appeal for Peace & Reconciliation," undated manuscript, Rufus Columbus Burleson Papers, Texas Collection, Carroll Library, Baylor University, Waco, Texas.

54. Burleson, "An Appeal," Rufus Columbus Burleson Papers.

55. Riley, *History of the Baptists*, 219.

56. Early, *Texas Baptist Power Struggle*, 115.

57. Ibid., 57–62, 65–66, 74–75.

58. J. B. Cranfill, *Courage and Comfort; or, Sunday Morning Thoughts* (Nashville, Tenn.: Southwestern Company, 1908), 445.

59. Riley, *History of the Baptists*, 372.

60. Early, *Texas Baptist Power Struggle*, 51–56; Riley, *History of the Baptists*, 15.

61. "Dr. Carroll's Sermons," undated manuscript, Benajah Harvey Carroll Collection, Southwestern Baptist Theological Seminary Archives, Fort Worth, Texas.

62. In 1890, alongside 2,318 Southern Baptist bodies and their 129,734 members, there were eight Freewill Baptist churches, claiming 261 members; 257 Primitive Baptist churches, claiming 7,032 members, and fourteen bodies of what the Census Bureau called "Other Baptists," claiming 358 members. Bureau of the Census, *Eleventh Census of the United States, 1890*, vol. 9, "Report on the Statistics of Churches in the United States," "Statistics of Churches," 2.

63. Riley, *History of the Baptists*, 397–398.

64. William Clark Griggs, *Parson Henry Renfro: Free Thinking on the Texas Frontier* (Austin: University of Texas Press, 1994), 118.

65. Ibid., 124, 126, 123.

66. Ibid., 130.

67. *Independent Pulpit* 2 (May 1884): 34.

68. Griggs, *Parson Henry Renfro*, 131, 134, 135, 136.

69. For Martinism, see McBeth, *Texas Baptists*, 113–115; Early, *Texas Baptist Power Struggle*, 53–55; Karen O'Dell Bullock, "Martin, Matthew Thomas," in *Handbook of Texas Online* (Austin: Texas State Historical Association), http://www.tshaon-line.org/handbook/online/articles/fmads (accessed July 18, 2012).

70. J. M. Carroll, *A History of Texas Baptists: Comprising a Detailed Account of Their Activities, Their Progress, and Their Achievements* (Dallas: Baptist Standard Publishing Company, 1923), 735–736.

71. Riley, *History of the Baptists*, 311, 368.

72. Ibid., 312.

73. *Dallas Morning News*, July 19, 1889; Carroll, 735–736.

74. J. M. Carroll, *History*, 735.

75. Early, *Texas Baptist Power Struggle*, 53–54; Riley, *History of the Baptists*, 311–312, 368.

76. B. F. Fuller, *History of Texas Baptists* (Louisville, Ky.: Baptist Book Concern, 1900), 398.

77. *Minutes of Ex Parte Council Held at the Call of the Minority of the First Baptist Church, Paris, Texas, February 11 & 12, 1896* (Paris: P. H. Bennett, Printer, 1896), quoted in Early, *Texas Baptist Power Struggle*, 151.

78. For Fortunism, see Carroll, 736–738; and Fuller, *History of Texas Baptists*, 398–407.

79. *Fort Worth Gazette*, August 1, 1883.

80. *Dallas Weekly Herald*, August 30, 1883.

81. *Dallas Morning News*, October 11, 1889.

82. Quoted in Blake W. Barrow, "Freethought in Texas: J. D. Shaw and the *Independent Pulpit*" (master's thesis, Baylor University, 1983).

83. George McCulloch, *History of the Holiness Movement in Texas, and the Fanaticism Which Followed* (Aquilla, Tex.: J. H. Padgett, 1886), 1–4.

84. Barry W. Hamilton, "The Corsicana Enthusiasts: A Pre-Pentecostal Millennial Sect," *Wesleyan Theological Journal* 39 (Spring 2004): 173–193.

85. McCulloch, note 84, 1–6.

86. Charles Brougher Jernigan, *Pioneer Days of the Holiness Movement in the Southwest* (Kansas City, Mo.: Pentecostal Nazarene Publishing House, 1919), 94–96.

87. McCulloch, note 84, 19–25.

88. Ibid., 41–42.

89. Ibid., 27.

90. *Texas Christian Advocate*, November 15, 1879; Walter N. Vernon, *Methodism Moves across North Texas* (Dallas: North Texas Methodist Historical Society, 1967), 144–146; *Texas Christian Advocate*, November 15, 1879. Anxious preachers pled for the denomination to "stop this craze" before it engulfed them. *Texas Christian Advocate*, November 29, 1879.

91. McCulloch, *History of the Holiness Movement in Texas*, 37–39; Jernigan, *Holiness Movement in the Southwest*, 150–151. McCulloch recalls that Haynes succumbed to exposure on the way to the tank and was taken home before he could be dunked; Jernigan says he was dunked and rendered "unconscious from the dunking and the chill of the cold" and was hurried home.

92. William B. Godbey, *Autobiography of W. B. Godbey* (Cincinnati, Ohio: God's Revivalist Office, 1909), 353–354, quoted in Barry W. Hamilton, "William Baxter Godbey: Apostle of Holiness," *Wesleyan Theological Journal* 36 (Fall 2001): 144–163.

93. Bureau of the Census, *Eleventh Census of the United States, 1890*, vol. 9, 11. Alongside 1,076 Southern Methodist bodies (and 139,347 members) were 346 bodies (and 27,453 members) of the Methodist Episcopal Church; 31 bodies (and 5,536 members) of the Methodist Protestants; and 25 bodies (and 1,236 members) of what the Census Bureau called "Other Methodists," which included the Holiness churches of the Free Methodists and Congregational Methodists. Owing in part to these intractable divisions, it was in these turbulent decades that Methodists lost the Lone Star field to the Baptists.

94. Early, *Texas Baptist Power Struggle*, 5–6.

95. B. H. Carroll, "My Infidelity and What Became of It," Benajah Harvey Carroll Collection.

96. Glen E. Lich and Dona B. Reeves, eds., *German Culture in Texas* (Boston: Twayne, 1980). See also Glen E. Lich, *The German Texans* (San Antonio: University of Texas Institute of Texan Cultures, 1981).

97. Allan O. Kownslar, *The European Texans* (College Station: Texas A&M University Press, 2004), 112.

98. Griggs, *Parson Henry Renfro*, 122.

99. For Shaw, see especially Barrow, "Freethought in Texas."

100. J. B. Cranfill, *Dr. J. B. Cranfill's Chronicle: A Story of Life in Texas* (New York: Fleming H. Revell Company, 1916), 316.

101. Carroll blasted the "infidel tide which pushes its chilling waves over the earth." *Gatesville Advance*, June 1884, quoted in Postel, "Populist Context," 14.

102. Virginia H. Ming, "Religious and Benevolent Association," in *Handbook of Texas Online* (Austin: Texas State Historical Association), http://www.tshaonline.org/handbook/online/articles/ixr01 (accessed April 8, 2012).

103. See Steven R. Butler, "Freethinkers: Religious Non-Conformity in Dallas, 1879-1904," *Legacies: A History Journal for Dallas and North Central Texas* 24 (Fall 2012): 16–29.

104. *Dallas Morning News*, June 7, 1894; March 23, 1891.

105. Ibid., March 8, 1886.

106. Ibid., September 26, 1898.

107. Ibid., January 28, 1895; January 31, 1898.

108. Ibid., March 23, 1891.

109. Ibid., November 1, 1897, August 27, 1894.

110. Ibid., October 24, 1898.

111. Ibid., September 19, 1894; September 30, 1895.

112. Samuel Porter Putnam, *400 Years of Freethought* (New York: Truth-Seeker Company, 1894), 554.

113. *Dallas Morning News*, March 1, 1897.

114. Ibid., January 15, 1886; *Fort Worth Gazette*, April 8, 1891.

115. This was actually the second stint for the *Iconoclast*. He had briefly published his personal paper in Austin in 1891 or 1892 before failing financially. He sold his

press to William Sydney Porter—the noted short story writer O. Henry. Charles Carver, *Brann and the Iconoclast* (Austin: University of Texas Press, 1957), 28.

116. *Iconoclast*, December 1897, quoted in Roger N. Conger, "Waco: Cotton and Culture on the Brazos," *Southwestern Historical Quarterly* 75 (July 1971): 60.

117. Cranfill, *Cranfill's Chronicle*, 429.

118. Bureau of the Census, *Eleventh Census of the United States, 1890*, vol. 9, "Report on the Statistics of Churches in the United States," "Statistics of Churches," 159.

119. Carver, *Brann and the Iconoclast*; Gary Cleve Wilson, "Bane of the Baptists," *Texas Monthly*, January 1986, 122.

120. William Cowper Brann, *The Complete Works of Brann, the Iconoclast*, vol. 12 (New York: Brann Publishers, Inc., 1919), 278.

121. Ibid.

122. Brann, *Complete Works*, vol. 8, 3.

123. Brann, *Complete Works*, vol. 12, 278–279.

124. Susan Jacoby, *The Great Agnostic: Robert Ingersoll and American Freethought* (New Haven, Conn.: Yale University Press, 2013).

125. Susan Jacoby, *Freethinkers: A History of American Secularism* (New York: Metropolitan Books, 2005), 177–178; *Dallas Morning News*, February 2, 1896.

126. Jacoby, *Freethinkers*, 177–178.

127. Cecil Harper Jr., "Redwater, TX," in *Handbook of Texas Online* (Austin: Texas State Historical Association), http://www.tshaonline.org/handbook/online/articles/hlr08 (accessed April 8, 2012).

128. *Dallas Morning News*, September 26, 1898.

CHAPTER 2

1. B. H. Carroll, *Prohibition: Dr. B. H. Carroll's Reply to Senator Coke* (Austin: J. B. Link, 1887?), n.p.

2. For overviews of the politics of prohibition in the South, see Dewey Grantham, *Southern Progressivism: The Reconciliation of Progress and Tradition* (Knoxville: University of Tennessee Press, 1983), 160–177; and Link, *Paradox of Southern Progressivism*, 31–57.

3. *Galveston Daily News*, August 30, 1885; *Dallas Weekly Herald*, September 3, 1885.

4. According to much historiography on southern religion, a sitting southern senator should not have been able to say what Coke had said. Historians have said the Bible Belt had its "beginnings" and its "origins" nearly a century earlier. Evangelical revivals had long since burned through much of the country, a proslavery Christianity bolstered the region's antebellum social order, ministers advocated secession, preachers bolstered Confederate nationalism, and religious leaders fashioned a new southern civil religion to deal with defeat and "redeem" the region from Reconstruction. See, for instance, Boles, *Great Revival*; Heyrman,

Southern Cross; Charles Irons, *The Origins of Proslavery Christianity: White and Black Evangelicals in Colonial and Antebellum Virginia* (Chapel Hill: University of North Carolina Press, 2008); Eugene Genovese and Elizabeth Fox-Genovese, *The Mind of the Master Class: History and Faith in the Southern Slaveholders' Worldview* (Cambridge: Cambridge University Press, 2005); Mitchell Snay, *Gospel of Disunion: Religion and Separatism in the Antebellum South* (1993; Chapel Hill: University of North Carolina Press, 1997); Drew Gilpin Faust, *The Creation of Confederate Nationalism: Ideology and Identity in the Civil War South* (Baton Rouge: Louisiana State University Press, 1988); and Wilson, *Baptized in Blood*.

5. *Fort Worth Telegram*, January 10, 1908; *Dallas Morning News*, January 8, 1908.

6. See especially Isaac, *Transformation of Virginia*, 145–147, 155–157, 181–183; and Hatch, *Democratization of American Christianity*, 44–46, 170–179.

7. An earlier generation of southern religious historians wrote of southerners' other-worldly "doctrine of spirituality." See especially Hill, *Southern Churches in Crisis*; and Eighmy, *Churches in Cultural Captivity*.

8. Thrall, *History of Methodism*, 5.

9. Thrall, *History of Methodism*, 5.

10. George W. Truett, "The Coming of the Kingdom in America," in Baptist World Alliance, *Second Congress, Philadelphia, June 19-25, 1911: Record of Proceedings* (Philadelphia, Pa., Harper & Brother Company, for the Philadelphia Committee, 1911), 421–429.

11. *New York Times*, May 3, 1873.

12. *Dallas Morning News*, October 24, 1886.

13. Ibid., October 16, 1885; October 16, 1885. Baird cites 2 Corinthians 10:4.

14. Quoted in *Baptist Standard*, March 31, 1892.

15. *Baptist Standard*, March 31, 1892.

16. Susan Jacoby, *Freethinkers: A History of American Secularism* (New York: Metropolitan Books, 2005), 1.

17. *Reynolds v. United States*, 98. U.S. 145 (1878).

18. James Ward Lee, *Texas, My Texas* (Denton: University of North Texas Press, 1993), 80.

19. Thrall, *History of Methodism*, 49, 51, 180.

20. Over the course of the nineteenth century, thirteen American states constitution-ally forbade clergy from holding political office. Of the thirteen, only Delaware and New York were not in the South or the Border South. Of the eleven Confederate states, only Alabama, Arkansas, and Florida elected not to exile their clergy from government. The rest chose to lump ministers with duelists and perjurers—and African American males and all women—as classes unfit for political office. Tennessee and Maryland maintained the exclusions until 1978. William Silverman, "The Exclusion of Clergy from Political Office in American States: An Oddity in Church-State Relations," *Sociology of Religion* 2 (Summer 2000): 223–230. Thomas Jefferson advocated such limits in his 1783 draft of the constitution of Virginia

and later reflected, "Even in 1783 we doubted the stability of our recent measures for reducing them [the clergy] to the footing of other useful callings." Thomas Jefferson to Jeremiah Moor, August 14, 1800, Barbara B. Oberg, ed., *The Papers of Thomas Jefferson*, vol. 32, *1 June 1800–16 February 1801* (Princeton, NJ: Princeton University Press, 2005), 102–103.

21. Daniel Parker, an antimissionary Baptist leader, was elected to the Congress of the Republic of Texas and took his seat on November 11. He was removed by November 14. The House Committee of Privileges and Elections unanimously ruled that Parker "is a minister of the gospel, and as such is not entitled to a seat in this house." See Dan B. Wimberly, "Daniel Parker: Pioneer Preacher and Political Leader" (PhD diss., Texas Tech University, 1995), 244.

22. Thrall, *History of Methodism in Texas*, 27.

23. *Texas Christian Advocate*, July 16, 1881; *Dallas Weekly Herald*, July 28, 1881.

24. In 1908, on the heels of the clerical triumph, the state supreme court ruled, in *Church v. Bullock*, 109 S.W. 115 (Tex. 1908), that schools could lead students in readings from the Bible and recitations of the Lord's Prayer. These were judged to not be sectarian but to be essential supports for students' moral development.

25. William Seagle, "The Moral Law," *American Mercury*, December 1926, 451.

26. *Columbus Daily Enquirer*, September 8, 1881.

27. Ibid.

28. Ibid.

29. *Columbus Daily Enquirer*, September 8, 1881.

30. See Robert T. Handy, "Protestant Theological Tensions and Political Styles in the Progressive Period," in *Religion and American Politics: From the Colonial Period to the Present*, ed. Mark A. Noll and Luke E. Harlow (New York: Oxford University Press, 2007), 239. For a typical representation of this argument, see "The Parson in Politics," *Macon (Ga.) Telegraph and Messenger*, April 24, 1883.

31. *Dallas Morning News*, June 25, 1894.

32. Ibid., May 10, 1894.

33. Ibid., July 19, 1897.

34. Willam Cowper Brann, *The Writings of W. C. Brann*, vol. 1 (Waco: Herz Brothers, 1911), 169. See also Carver, *Brann and the Iconoclast*.

35. *Fort Worth Gazette*, April 8, 1891. Bondie married the daughter of Baylor University president William Carey Crane. She later sued for divorce, citing Bondie's religious infidelity. *Dallas Morning News* January 15, 1886.

36. *Dallas Morning News*, December 4, 1895.

37. Ibid., February 12, 1889; September 6, 1889.

38. Ibid., September 6, 1889.

39. Ibid., February 12, 1889.

40. "Temperance Resolutions of the First Baptist Church of Waco, TX." December, 1873, Benajah Harvey Carroll Collection, Archives, Southwestern Baptist Theological Seminary.

41. H. W. Stanton, "A Criticism of the Waco Baptist Church," (newspaper clipping, n.d.), Benajah Harvey Carroll Collection.

42. See Alan J. Lefever, *Fighting the Good Fight: The Life and Work of Benajah Harvey Carroll* (Austin: Eakin Press, 1994).

43. J. M. Carroll, *Dr. B. H. Carroll, the Colossus of Baptist History: Pastor, First Baptist Church, Waco, Texas and First President of S.W.B.T. Seminary* (Fort Worth: J. W. Crowder, 1946).

44. Lefever, *Fighting the Good Fight*.

45. J. M. Carroll, *A History of Texas Baptists: Comprising a Detailed Account of their Activities, Their Progress, and Their Achievements* (Dallas: Baptist Standard Publishing Company, 1923), 915.

46. For the 1885 contest, see especially James Ivy's brief but informative *No Saloon in the Valley*, 25–45.

47. J. D. Shaw, "The Local Option Contest," *Independent Pulpit* 3, September 1885, 79.

48. Ibid.

49. B. H. Carroll, *Prohibition*, n.p.

50. *Dallas Weekly Herald*, September 3, 1885.

51. See, for instance, Riley, *History of Texas Baptists*, 302; and Cranfill, *Cranfill's Chronicle*, 365.

52. *Waco Daily Examiner*, October 2, 1885

53. *Texas Siftings*, November 21, 1885.

54. *Galveston Daily News*, August 26, 1885; August 30, 1885; August 20, 1885.

55. Shaw, "Local Option Contest," 79.

56. *Dallas Morning News*, May 21, 1911.

57. Ormond Paget to Bertrand Adoue, "Report for the Month of August, 1907." Alexander Dienst Collection, 1784–1929, Dolph Briscoe Center for American History, University of Texas at Austin.

58. J. O. Terrell, "Speech of Senator Terrell on the Importation, Manufacture and Sale of Alcoholic Liquors within the State," Texas Collection, Carroll Library, Baylor University, Waco, Texas.

59. Peter Radford and W. D. Lewis, *Down with the Bosses* (Fort Worth: Farmers' Educational and Cooperative Union, May 25, 1914).

60. Peter Radford and W. D. Lewis, *Regulating Political Preachers* (Fort Worth: Farmers' Educational and Cooperative Union, June 1, 1914).

61. *Dallas Morning News*, May 21, 1911.

62. D. R. Wallace, "Christianity vs. Secularization as a Factor in Nineteenth Century Civilization," *Independent Pulpit* 4, March 1886, 3.

63. J. D. Shaw, "Prohibition," *Independent Pulpit* 5, April 1887, 40.

64. H. W. Stroter to O. B. Colquitt, January 30, 1910, Oscar Branch Colquitt Papers, 1873–1941, Dolph Briscoe Center for American History, University of Texas at Austin.

65. Wallace, "Christianity vs. Secularization," 4.

66. *Dallas Morning News*, May 21, 1911.
67. B. P. Hintze, "Liquor and Law," speech delivered in San Antonio, January 15, 1909, Oscar Branch Colquitt Papers, 1873–1941.
68. R. Q. Mills, "Speech of the Hon. R. Q. Mills before the United Anti-Prohibition clubs of Corsicana, Texas, Saturday, May 21, 1887," Texas Collection.
69. Hintze, "Liquor and Law."
70. J. D. Shaw, "Politics and Religion," *Independent Pulpit* 4, July 1886, 119.
71. See, for instance, Justin Nordstrom, *Danger on the Doorstep: Anti-Catholicism and American Print Culture in the Progressive Era* (Notre Dame, Ind.: University of Notre Dame Press, 2006).
72. See especially the April 2009 special issue of the *Americas* on "Personal Enemies of God: Anticlericals and Anticlericalism in Revolutionary Mexico, 1915-1940," in *Americas*, April 2009, 467–559.
73. Oscar Colquitt, untitled speech delivered at Palestine, Texas, on July 13, 1911, Oscar Branch Colquitt Papers, 1873–1941.
74. Terrell, "Speech of Senator Terrell."
75. H. L. Mencken, *Prejudices: Fifth Series* (New York: A. A. Knopf, 1926), 253.
76. W. J. Cash, *The Mind of the South* (New York: A. A. Knopf, 1941), 17.
77. Terrell, "Speech of Senator Terrell."
78. Radford and Lewis, *Regulating Political Preachers*.
79. *Galveston Daily News*, August 20, 1885, quoted in J. Ivy, *No Saloon in the Valley*, 39. See also Joseph Locke, "Conquering Salem: The Triumph of the Christian Vision in Turn-of-the-Twentieth-Century Texas," *Southwestern Historical Quarterly* 114 (January 2012): 232–257.
80. Oscar Colquitt, untitled speech delivered at Palestine, Texas, on July 13, 1911. Colquitt Collection.
81. Carroll, *Reply to Senator Coke*, n.p.
82. B. H. Carroll, *Prohibition*, n.p.
83. Cranfill, *Cranfill's Chronicle*, 341.
84. Ibid., 341.
85. *Dallas Morning News*, July 22, 1887.
86. In his *Path to a Modern South*, Walter Buenger argued, "The 1887 prohibition election badly needs study, and, despite the turmoil it created, is not even mentioned in the best textbook history of Texas." Buenger, *Path to a Modern South*. For work on the 1887 contest, see especially Barr, *Reconstruction to Reform*, 85–93; and J. Ivy, *No Saloon in the Valley*, 45–103.
87. Cranfill, *Cranfill's Chronicle*, 343.
88. B. H. Carroll, Personal Notebook of B. H. Carroll, Benajah Harvey Carroll Collection.
89. Quoted in J. Ivy, *No Saloon in the Valley*, 47–48.

90. Cranfill, *Cranfill's Chronicle*, 347.

91. Terrell, "Speech of Senator Terrell," 6.

92. J. D. Shaw, "The Prohibition Campaign," *Independent Pulpit* 5, September 1887, 163.

93. Ibid.

94. Quoted in J. Ivy, *No Saloon in the Valley*, 54.

95. Roger Q. Mills, *Speech of the Hon. R. Q. Mills before the United Anti-Prohibition clubs of Corsicana, Saturday, May 21, 1887* (Corsicana, Tex.: Corsicana Daily Courier, May 1887), 24.

96. *Dallas Morning News*, October 28, 1892. See also Macum Phelan, *The Expansion of Methodism in Texas* (Dallas: Mathis, Van Ort & Company, 1937), 268.

97. *Dallas Morning News*, May 21, 1887.

98. J. Ivy, *No Saloon in the Valley*, 74.

99. Riley, *History of the Baptists of Texas*, 308.

100. In his home state of Mississippi, he publicly scolded prohibitionist and Methodist Bishop Charles Betts Galloway, who, Davis said, never "should have left the pulpit and the Bible to mount the political rostrum and plead the higher law of prohibitionism." Davis to Lubbock, July 20, 1887, in William J. Cooper, ed., *Jefferson Davis: The Essential Writings* (New York: Random House, 2004), 435. Varina Davis, *Jefferson Davis: Ex-President of the Confederate States of America*, 890–892; partially quoted in William J. Cooper, *Jefferson Davis, American* (New York: Alfred A. Knopf, 2000), 694–695. See also Coker, *Liquor in the Land*, 80–82.

101. *Dallas Morning News*, May 5, 1887.

102. J. Ivy, *No Saloon in the Valley*, 45–87.

103. Roughly 66 percent of the electorate voted in the general election of 1886. In the special prohibition election the following year, with no candidates on the ballot, 72 percent of eligible voters turned out. Ibid., 92.

104. Barr, *Reconstruction to Reform*, 88–92.

105. Shaw, "Prohibition Campaign," 163.

106. *Dallas Morning News*, July 22, 1887.

107. Ibid.

108. J. D. Shaw, "Church and State," *Independent Pulpit*, November 1888, 230.

109. Cranfill, *Cranfill's Chronicle*, 351.

110. "It is generally understood," Shettles claimed, "that the brewerys [*sic*] and distilleries outside the state brought on the election that they might with more security make investments." Elijah Shettles, "The Recollections of a Long Life," unfinished manuscript, Elijah L. Shettles Papers, 1792–1940, Dolph Briscoe Center for American History, University of Texas at Austin.

111. J. Ivy, *No Saloon in the Valley*, 94, 100–102.

CHAPTER 3

1. Robert Wiebe, *The Search for Order, 1877–1920* (New York: Hill and Wang, 1967), 76.

2. Some simply surrendered to nervous tension. Historian Jackson Lears identified neurasthenia as the epidemic of the age. A wave of fatigue, anxiety, depression, and a thousand other related symptoms seemed to suddenly crash over the American people. Leading neurologists associated it with the frenetic new pace of American life and William James called it "Americanitis." It was supposed to be the physical manifestation of the new age of anxiety. The diagnosis exploded among the middle and upper classes and afflicted some of the leading lights of the emerging clerical movement in Texas. The Baptist luminary J. B. Cranfill complained of life-long bouts of nervousness, or what he called "neurasthenic diathesis." He suffered from severe panic attacks. "If I had been a woman," he confessed, "I would have sometimes been called hysterical." He reported waking at night, feeling suffocated, and fearing death. He said he experienced this a thousand times. Other nights Cranfill lay awake, alone with his anxieties, hoping for sleep that would never come. "I have counted all the sheep in the universe," he wrote. He often retired early "to take every advantage to get mental rest and to get quietude for my nerves, or I am unfit for the next day's tasks." He tried everything. He gave up tobacco and coffee. He became a functioning vegetarian. He chewed his food deliberately. He took cold baths daily. He exercised regularly. He avoided trains and factories and mills as best he could. And, in general, Cranfill abated his symptoms, although he never banished them. He accepted neurasthenia as a condition of life. But despite the occasionally exacting physical toll wrought by turn-of-the-century anxiety, a broader unease drifted over the country and over Texans. A full-blown spiritual crisis transcended the nervous exhaustion of neurasthenic bodies, infected the spiritual confidence of religious leaders, and reoriented the world of religion. Jackson Lears, *Rebirth of a Nation: The Making of Modern America, 1877–1920* (New York: Harper Collins, 2009), 7; Cranfill, *Cranfill's Chronicle*, 111.

3. For general anxieties in the New South, see Edward L. Ayers, *The Promise of the New South* (New York: Oxford University Press, 1992); for specifically religious anxieties, and their relationship to moral reform, see especially Schweiger, *Gospel Working Up*; Ownby, *Subduing Satan*; and Harvey, *Redeeming the South*.

4. Ayers, *Promise of the New South*, viii.

5. Ownby, *Subduing Satan*, 1.

6. *Dallas Morning News*, November 24, 1900.

7. U. S. Census Office, *Religious Bodies: 1906*, parts I and II (Washington, D.C.: Government Printing Office, 1910).

8. Henry King Carroll, *The Religious Forces of the United States Enumerated, Classified, and Described; Returns for 1900 and 1910 Compared with the Government Census of 1890: Condition and Characteristics of Christianity in the United States* (New York: C. Scribner's Sons, 1912), lxvi.

9. For the most direct questioning along these lines, see Beth Barton Schweiger, "How Would Jesus Vote? The Prehistory of the Christian Right," *Reviews in American History* 32 (March, 2004): 49–57.

10. Truett, "Coming of the Kingdom," 421–429, 422.

11. *Minutes of the Eighteenth Annual Session of the Northwest Texas Conference of the Methodist Episcopal Church, South* (Galveston: Shaw & Blaylock, 1883), 28; *Minutes of the Twentieth Annual Session of the Northwest Texas Conference of the Methodist Episcopal Church, South* (Galveston: A. W. & Co., 1885), 26.

12. *Minutes of the Eighteenth Annual Session*, 28.

13. Ibid., 32.

14. *Minutes of the Twenty-Second Annual Session of the Northwest Texas Conference, of the Methodist Episcopal. Church, South* (Waxahachie, Tex.: Enterprise Book and Job Print, 1888), 32, 33.

15. *Minutes of the Twenty-Third Annual Session of the Northwest Texas Conference, of the Methodist Episcopal Church, South* (Dallas: Ewing B. Bedford, 1888), 30.

16. Ibid., 51–54.

17. Morris Sheppard, "His Eloquent Words on the Influences of The Epworth League," Speech Delivered in San Antonio, 1896, Morris Sheppard Papers, 1894–1953, Center for American History, University of Texas at Austin.

18. Ayers, *Promise of the New South*, 163.

19. Schweiger, *Gospel Working Up*, 169–180; Ayers, *Promise of a New South*, 163.

20. See Paul Allen Carter, *The Spiritual Crisis of the Gilded Age* (Dekalb: Northern Illinois University Press, 1971).

21. Quoted in Schweiger, *Gospel Working Up*, 180.

22. Josiah Strong, *Our Country: Its Possible Future and Present Crisis* (New York: Baker & Taylor Co., 1885), v.

23. Truett, "Coming of the Kingdom," 424.

24. Schweiger, *Gospel Working Up*; Stowell, *Rebuilding Zion*. On the era's ambiguous uses of antimodern rhetoric, also see, for instance, T. J. Jackson Lears, *No Place of Grace: Antimodernism and the Transformation of American Culture, 1880-1920* (New York: Pantheon, 1981).

25. Quoted in J. D. Shaw, "The Decay of Church-Going," *Independent Pulpit* 4, August 1886, 138.

26. Lee to Shettles, N. D., Elijah L. Shettles Papers, Dolph Briscoe Center for American History, University of Texas at Austin.

27. Quoted in Shaw, "Decay of Church-Going," 138.

28. *San Antonio Evening Light*, February 17, 1883.

29. *Minutes of the Thirty-Third Annual Session*, 30.

30. *Palestine Daily Herald*, February 19, 1904.

31. *Dallas Morning News*, August 16, 1908.

32. Cranfill, *Courage and Comfort*, 241.

33. George C. Rankin, *The Story of My Life; or, More Than Half a Century as I Have Lived It and Seen It Lived* (Nashville: Smith & Lamar, 1912), 315.

34. Shaw, "Decay of Church-Going," 138.

35. Shaw, "Prohibition Campaign," 163.

36. *Dallas Morning News*, May 12, 1907.

37. Cranfill, *Courage and Comfort*, 245

38. E. B. Fleming, *Early History of Hopkins County, Texas: Biographical Sketches and Incidents of the Early Settled Families* (n.p.: 1902), 35–36.

39. J. B. Gambrell, "Evangelization of the Rural Districts," Baptist World Alliance, *Second Congress, Philadelphia, June 19–25, 1911: Record of Proceedings* (Philadelphia, Pa., Harper & Brother Company, for the Philadelphia Committee, 1911), 203–207, 204.

40. *Dallas Morning News*, May 12, 1907.

41. Gambrell, "Evangelization," 204.

42. Travis L. Summerlin, "Crane, William Carey," *Handbook of Texas Online* (http://www.tshaonline.org/handbook/online/articles/fcro6), accessed April 09, 2012. Published by the Texas State Historical Association; William Carey Crane Papers, Texas Collection, Carroll Library, Baylor University, Waco, Texas.

43. See entries in for March and June 1863 in Crane Diary, William Carey Crane Papers.

44. Stowell, *Rebuilding Zion.*

45. E. Bruce Thompson, "William Carey Crane and Texas Education," *Southwestern Historical Quarterly* 58 (January 1955): 409.

46. Crane Diary, March 17, 1880, William Carey Crane Papers.

47. Ibid., June 12, 1886, William Carey Crane Papers.

48. Ibid., March 17, 1864, William Carey Crane Papers.

49. Ibid., June 18, 1876, William Carey Crane Papers.

50. Ibid., March 17, 1865, William Carey Crane Papers.

51. Ibid., February 4, 1864, and March 7, 1865, William Carey Crane Papers.

52. Ibid., March 17, 1876, William Carey Crane Papers.

53. Ibid., January 16, 1885, William Carey Crane Papers, quoted in E. Thompson, "Crane and Texas Education," 421.

54. Ibid., March 7, 1865. William Carey Crane Papers.

55. Mark Chaves, "Secularization as Declining Religious Authority" *Social Forces* 72 (March 1994): 749–774. Generations of social scientists and scholars gave themselves over to studying the consequences of "secularization." Religion, it was commonly assumed, could never survive the onslaughts of modernity and cultural pluralism. As various social institutions were unmoored from religious bearings, scholars assumed religious belief would crumble. And yet, rather than retreat, religious adherence advanced. This realization shook common assumptions about secularization and scholars scrambled to reorient research the beyond the realm of personal belief and social structure. See Phillip Gorski, "Historicizing the Secularization Debate," *American Sociological Review* 65 (February 2000): 138–167.

56. See especially Mark Chaves, "Secularization as Declining Religious Authority," *Social Forces* 72 (March 1994): 749–774.

57. Wiebe, *Search for Order*, 76.

58. B. H. Carroll, Personal Notebook.

59. George W. Truett, "Coming of the Kingdom," 424.

60. J. B. Cranfill, "Looking Backward," Lecture delivered by J. B. Cranfill at YMCA Hall, Waco, Texas, April 21, 1893. James Milton Carroll Collection, Southwestern Baptist Theological Seminary, Fort Worth, Texas.

61. Ibid.

62. Ibid.

63. Morris Sheppard, "His Eloquent Words," Morris Sheppard Papers, 1894–1953.

64. Ibid.

65. Ibid.

66. Shaw, "Prohibition Campaign," 163.

67. Rankin, *Story of My Life*, 321.

68. Cranfill, *Cranfill's Chronicle*, 490.

69. See R. Laurence Moore, *Religious Outsiders and the Making of Americans* (New York: Oxford University Press, 1986) for the interplay of "outsiderhood" and "deliberate differentiation." For the statistical reality of this phenomenon in contemporary evangelicalism, see Christian Smith and Michael Emerson, et al., *American Evangelicalism: Embattled and Thriving* (Chicago: University of Chicago Press, 1998).

70. Schweiger, *Gospel Working Up*, 194.

71. Sheppard, *Congressman Sheppard Is for Prohibition*, 8.

72. Ayers, *Promise of the New South*, ix–x.

73. John Boles, "Evangelical Protestantism in the Old South: From Dissent to Dominance," in *Religion in the South: Essays*, ed. Charles Reagan Wilson (Jackson, Miss.: University of Mississippi Press, 1985).

74. Hatch, *Democratization of American Christianity*, 193; Schweiger, *Gospel Working Up*, 6.

CHAPTER 4

1. Sumner B. Callaway, "Chief Elements of Church Strength," essay delivered by Sumner B. Callaway before Minister's Conference in Belton, Texas, April 2, 1885. J. M. Carroll Collection.

2. Scrap, *Texas Baptist Herald*, January 8, 1874, B. H. Carroll Collection.

3. B. H. Carroll, Personal Notebook.

4. Samuel H. Blackwell to Elijah L. Shettles, October 16, 1907. Elijah L. Shettles Papers, 1792–1940, Dolph Briscoe Center for American History, University of Texas at Austin.

5. Cranfill, *Cranfill's Chronicle*, 32, 246, 266.

6. Rankin, *Story of My Life*, 315.

7. Scrap, "Final Action of the First Baptist Church at Waco, on the Temperance Resolutions, as Published in the Herald," B. H. Carroll Collection.

8. Ibid.

9. Ownby, *Subduing Satan*, 208. Another historian, Gaines Foster, called this the "antebellum moral polity": a system of voluntarism and moral suasion, not coercion. Foster, *Moral Reconstruction*, 9–26.

10. Ownby, *Subduing Satan*, best captures the menacing look of recreation and amusement to evangelical eyes.

11. For the majority of the nineteenth century, these bodies only formally existed in those fleeting moments when messengers met and reported. During the 1890s, clerical leaders reinterpreted several of these notions in the Baptist General Convention and maneuvered to grant the body a more permanent and coercive influence. See especially Riley, *History of the Baptists*, 372

12. W. F. McMurry to Elijah L. Shettles, April 16, 1907, Elijah L. Shettles Papers.

13. See especially Schweiger, *Gospel Working Up*.

14. *Dallas Morning News*, June 10, 1906.

15. C. E. Simpson to Elijah L. Shettles, October 21, 1907, Shettles Papers.

16. I. F. Betts to Elijah L. Shettles, November 23, 1910, Shettles Papers.

17. Samuel H. Blackwell to Elijah L. Shettles, October 16, 1907, Shettles Papers.

18. G. E. Cameron to Chas F. Smith, August 6, 1905, August 24, 1905, Shettles Papers.

19. I. Z. T. Morris, to Elijah L. Shettles, January 8, 1910, Shettles Papers.

20. C. A. Tower to Elijah L. Shettles, November 18, 1909, Shettles Papers.

21. Jesse Lee to Elijah L. Shettles, May 13, 1910, Shettles Papers.

22. Rankin, *Story of My Life*, 340–342.

23. Edwin D. Mouzon to Elijah L. Shettles, November 14, 1907, Shettles Papers.

24. Cranfill, *Cranfill's Chronicle*, 363–364.

25. See Barry Hankins, *God's Rascal: J. Frank Norris & the Beginnings of Southern Fundamentalism* (Lexington: University Press of Kentucky, 1996), 124.

26. James L Leloudis, *Schooling the New South: Pedagogy, Self, and Society in North Carolina, 1880-1920* (Chapel Hill: University of North Carolina Press, 1996), describes education as the way station to larger religious activism. Charles Israel integrates the two in his *Before Scopes: Evangelicalism, Education, and Evolution in Tennessee, 1870-1925* (Athens: University of Georgia Press, 2004).

27. *Texas Christian Advocate*, October 23, 1913.

28. J. M. Carroll, "Our School and Its Part in the Greater Awakening of Our People & the Further Upbuilding of Our Cause," lecture notes (n.d.), J. M. Carroll Collection.

29. *Texas Christian Advocate*, July 16, 1881.

30. J. M. Carroll, "Christian Education: It's Importance and Necessity," lecture notes (n.d.), J. M. Carroll Collection.

31. During these years, Texas claimed two major Baptist colleges: Baylor University, in Independence, and Waco University, in Waco. The two schools consolidated after

the 1885–1886 formation of the Baptist General Convention of Texas and became Baylor University in Waco.

32. Rufus Burleson and T. E. Muse, "Schools & Education," undated manuscript, Rufus Columbus Burleson Papers, Texas Collection, Carroll Library, Baylor University, Waco, Texas.

33. William Carey Crane, "Should the Higher Education of Youth Be Committed to the State?," undated manuscript, Crane Papers.

34. Ibid.

35. For a similar progression in Tennessee, see Israel, *Before Scopes.*

36. B. H. Carroll, *Christian Education: A Sermon Preached at San Antonio, Texas, Sunday, January 28, 1900* (Waco: Kellner Printing Company, 1900), B. H. Carroll Collection.

37. J. L. Massey, to Rev. Nathan Powell, February 13, 1913, Shettles Papers.

38. See Jerome A. Moore, *Texas Christian University: A Hundred Years of History* (Fort Worth: Texas Christian University Press, 1974).

39. See Marshall Terry, *"From High on the Hilltop . . .": A Brief History of SMU* (Dallas: Southern Methodist University Press, 1993).

40. Lefever, *Fighting the Good Fight,* 98–117.

41. Carroll, "Our School and Its Part," J. M. Carroll Collection.

42. Cranfill, *Cranfill's Chronicle,* 161–62.

43. Ibid., 429, 452.

44. Ibid., 459.

45. Ibid., 465.

46. *Baptist Standard,* September 14, 1911.

47. For the industry of evangelical nostalgia, see especially Schweiger, *Gospel Working Up,* 174, 196.

48. C. C. Cody to Elijah L. Shettles, March 10, 1911, Elijah L. Shettles Papers.

49. Thrall, *History of Methodism in Texas,* 3.

50. Z. N. Morrell, *Flowers and Fruits from the Wilderness; or, Thirty-Six Years in Texas and Two in Honduras* (Boston: Gould and Lincoln, 1872), v–vi.

51. Morrell, *Flowers and Fruits,* vii.

52. William Carey Crane, *Centennial Address Embracing the History of Washington County, Texas, at the Fair Grounds in Brenham, July 4, 1876* (Galveston: News Steam Job Printing Office, 1876).

53. Ibid.

54. For the concept of "historical memory" in Texas, see especially Gregg Cantrell and Elizabeth Hayes Turner, eds., *Lone Star Pasts: Memory and History in Texas* (College Station: Texas A&M University Press, 2007).

55. Rev. John H. McLean, "Introduction," *Texas Methodist Historical Quarterly* 1 (July 1909): 4–5.

56. Senator Sheppard, "Religion and the American Republic," speech delivered at State Line Methodist Church, Texarkana, on September 2, 1934, Morris Sheppard

Papers, 1894-1953, Dolph Briscoe Center for American History, University of Texas at Austin.

57. H. A. Ivy, *Rum on the Run in Texas: A Brief History of Prohibition in the Lone Star State* (Dallas: Temperance Pub. Co., 1910), 68.

58. Shepard to Dear Madam, September 30, 1912, Morris Sheppard Papers, 1894-1953.

59. "Address issued by Dr. Gambrell," February 1, 1914, Oscar Branch Colquitt Papers, 1873–1941.

60. J. B. Gambrell, "The Problem of Baptist Progress," Lee L. Campbell Papers, 1890–1919, Dolph Briscoe Center for American History, University of Texas at Austin.

61. "Address Issued by Dr. Gambrell," Colquitt Papers.

62. Senator Sheppard, "Religion and the American Republic."

63. It was a northern Presbyterian minister and prohibitionist who attacked Democrats in 1884 as the party of "rum, Romanism, and rebellion." That charge, as far as the first two labels were concerned, may have hit too close to home for religious southerners: a generation later they led the southern exodus from the Democratic, Catholic, antiprohibitionist Al Smith in the presidential election of 1928.

64. *Dallas Morning News*, May 15, 1894.

65. Ibid., July 9, 1906.

66. Ibid.

67. Address of Dr. Rufus C. Burleson, on the One Hundredth Anniversary of the Birth of Gen. Sam Houston, and the Fifty-Seventh of the Independence of Texas, Delivered in the Hall of the House of Representatives, at Austin, Texas, March 2, 1893. By invitation of the House of Representatives. Printed by Ben C. Jones & Co., printers, Austin, Texas, Burleson Papers.

68. See James L. Haley, *Sam Houston* (Norman: University of Oklahoma Press, 2004); and Ernest C. Shearer "Sam Houston and Religion," *Tennessee Historical Quarterly* 20 (March 1961), 38–50. For quotations, see Haley, *Sam Houston*, 333.

69. See Gregg Cantrell, "The Bones of Stephen F. Austin: History and Memory in Progressive-Era Texas," in Cantrell and Turner, *Lone Star Pasts*, 39–74.

70. Truett, "Coming of the Kingdom," 421.

71. Shepard to Dear Madam, September 30, 1912, Morris Sheppard Papers, 1894–1953.

72. Robert Pierce Shuler, *The New Issue; or, Local Booze Government: Being a Collection of Articles on "Prohibition"* (Temple, Tex.: Temple Printing and Office Appliance Co., 1911).

73. Shuler, *New Issue*.

74. Thrall, *History of Methodism in Texas*, 4.

75. Charles Betts Galloway, *Great Men and Movements: A Volume of Addresses* (Dallas: Smith & Lamar, 1914), 36.

76. Morris Sheppard, *Congressman Sheppard Is for Prohibition*, 8.

77. Morris Sheppard, *National Prohibition and States Rights* (Washington, D.C.: Government Printing Office: 1914).

78. Gould, *Progressives and Prohibitionists*, 32–33.

79. Samuel P. Brooks, "At the Prohibition Mass Meeting," 1885, Samuel Palmer Brooks Papers, Texas Collection, Carroll Library, Baylor University, Waco, Texas.
80. Senator Sheppard, "Religion and the American Republic."
81. H. L. Mencken, editorial, *American Mercury*, November 1924.

CHAPTER 5

1. *Baptist Standard*, March 17, 1892.
2. Edwin D. Mouzon to Elijah L. Shettles, February 22, 2012, Elijah L. Shettles Papers, 1792–1940, Dolph Briscoe Center for American History, University of Texas at Austin.
3. T. M. Bronwlee to Elijah L. Shettles, February 3, 1909, Shettles Papers.
4. *Dallas Morning News*, June 10, 1906.
5. Taken from Romans 11:13: "For I speak to you Gentiles, inasmuch as I am the apostle of the Gentiles, I magnify mine office."
6. B. H. Carroll, "An Office Magnified," Sermon, 1898, Benajah Harvey Carroll Collection, Archives, Southwestern Baptist Theological Seminary, Fort Worth, Texas.
7. Samuel Palmer Brooks, "Real Religion," undated manuscript, Samuel Palmer Brooks Papers, The Texas Collection, Carroll Library, Baylor University, Waco, Texas; Samuel Palmer Brooks, "Social Duties," undated manuscript, Brooks Papers.
8. *Dallas Morning News*, June 10, 1896.
9. Fuller, *History of Texas*, 3.
10. I. Z. T. Morris to Elijah L. Shettles, July 8, 1907, Shettles Papers.
11. *Dallas Morning News*, June 10, 1896.
12. *Fort Worth Morning Register*, December 18, 1900.
13. Ayers, *Promise of the New South*, 169.
14. Methodist Episcopal Church, South, General Conference, *Journal*, 1898, (Nashville, Tenn., n.d.), 19, quoted in Kenneth K. Bailey, *Southern White Protestantism in the Twentieth Century* (New York: Harper & Row, 1964), 38.
15. Presbyterian Church in the United States, General Assembly, *Minutes*, 1902 (Richmond, Va.: 1902), 297–298, quoted in Bailey, *Southern White Protestantism*, 36.
16. *Dallas Morning News*, May 16, 1898.
17. Christopher Long, "Caro, TX," *Handbook of Texas Online* (http://www.tshaonline.org/handbook/online/articles/hlc12), accessed March 1, 2011. Published by the Texas State Historical Association.
18. C. N. Morton to Elijah L. Shettles, April 25, 1907, Shettles Papers.
19. Ormond Paget to Bertrand Adoue, Esq., "Report for the Month of August, 1907," Alexander Dienst Collection, 1784–1929, Dolph Briscoe Center for American History, University of Texas at Austin.
20. Jesse Lee to Elijah L. Shettles, October 1, 1907, Shettles Papers.

21. For southern religious history, see especially Ownby, *Subduing Satan*, 2–3. For contemporary evangelicals and sociological theory, see particularly Smith and Emerson, *American Evangelicalism*.

22. C. N. Morton to Elijah L. Shettles, May 8, 1907, Shettles Papers.

23. *Dallas Morning News*, June 10, 1896.

24. Cranfill, *Cranfill's Chronicle*, 386.

25. Truett, "Coming of the Kingdom," 421–429.

26. Rankin, *Story of My Life*, 343

27. Rankin, *Story of My Life*, 343.

28. *Dallas Morning News*, January 8, 1902.

29. Cranfill, *Cranfill's Chronicle*, 89–93.

30. J. B. Turrentine to Elijah L. Shettles, May 25, 1908, Shettles Papers.

31. *Dallas Morning News*, August 9, 1908.

32. Ibid., May 12, 1907.

33. The Disciples of Christ, vastly outnumbered by the Baptists and Methodists, accounted for perhaps 6 percent of all religiously affiliated Texans in 1906. US Census Office, *Religious Bodies: 1906*, parts I and II (Washington, D.C.: Government Printing Office, 1910).

34. Eugene C. Barker, *A History of Texas and Texans*, vol. 4 (Chicago: American Historical Society, 1914), 1786–1788.

35. Cadwell Walton Raines, *Year Book for Texas, 1901* (Austin: Gammel Book Company, 1902), 44.

36. Barker, *Texas and Texans*, 1788.

37. *Dallas Morning News*, August 9, 1897.

38. J. Stuart Holden, *The Price of Power* (New York: Fleming H. Revell Company, 1908), 9.

39. Jesse Lee to Elijah L. Shettles, January 19, 1909, Shettles Papers.

40. Southern Baptist Convention, *Annual*, 1888 (Atlanta, 1888), 3, 33–34, quoted in Bailey, *Southern White Protestantism*, 35

41. Methodist Episcopal Church, South, General Conference, *Journal*, 1894 (Nashville: n.d.), 34–35, in Bailey, *Southern White Protestantism*, 35.

42. George Truett, "The Subject and Object of the Gospel (annual sermon preached before the Southern Baptist Convention at Louisville, Ky., May 12, 1899," in George Truett, *We Would See Jesus, and Other Sermons*, ed. J. B. Cranfill (New York: Fleming H. Revell Company, 1915), 206.

43. Truett, "Subject and Object of the Gospel," 212.

44. *Texas Presbyterian*, May 4, 1894.

45. While he built up the Austin School of Theology, he served as the chair of mental and moral philosophy at the University of Texas. For Dabney, see Sean Michael Lucas, *Robert Lewis Dabney: A Southern Presbyterian Life* (Philipsburg, N.J.: P&R Publishing, 2005).

46. Robert Lewis Dabney, *Sacred Rhetoric: or, a Course of Lectures on Preaching* (Richmond, Va.: Presbyterian Committee of Publication, 1870), 42–45.

47. Dabney, *Sacred Rhetoric*, 40–41.

48. *Temple Daily Telegram*, October 31, 1912.

49. *Dallas Morning News*, June 10, 1896.

50. *Baptist Standard*, March 16, 1911.

51. A. Y. Old to Edwin D. Mouzon, January 4, 1913, Edwin Mouzon Papers, Bridwell Library, Perkins School of Theology, Southern Methodist University, Dallas, Texas.

52. J. T. Smith to Elijah L. Shettles, September 4, 1907, Shettles Papers.

53. T. D. Cobbs to B. H. Carroll, July 24, 1911, Benajah Harvey Carroll Collection.

54. Clarence Ousley to Edwin D. Mouzon, January 11, 1913, Mouzon Papers.

55. *Baptist Standard*, April 20, 1911.

56. *Dallas Morning News*, May 13, 1910.

57. *Temple Daily Telegram*, October 31, 1912.

58. *Dallas Morning News*, November 15, 1905.

59. Ibid., February 5, 1907.

60. *Baptist Standard*, February 18, 1909, quoted in Storey, *Texas Baptist Leadership*, 25.

61. *Dallas Morning News*, January 26, 1909.

62. *Baptist Standard*, April 2, 1908, quoted in Storey, *Texas Baptist Leadership*, 26.

63. *Dallas Morning News*, July 18, 1910.

64. *Baptist Standard*, February 10, 1910, quoted in Storey, *Texas Baptist Leadership*, 26.

65. *Dallas Morning News*, February 23, 1909.

66. *Fort Worth Star-Telegram*, November 15, 1908.

67. Ibid.

68. Quoted in Harvey, *Redeeming the South*, 216.

69. For the politics of prohibition in the South, see especially Dewey Grantham, *Southern Progressivism*, 160–177.

70. Quoted in Gould, *Progressives and Prohibitionists*, 28.

71. *Victoria Advocate*, July 18, 1911.

72. *Fort Worth Star-Telegram*, July 9, 1909.

73. *Dallas Morning News*, February 5, 1907.

74. *Fort Worth Star-Telegram*, July 9, 1909.

75. *Texas Christian Advocate*, January 2, 1913.

76. Edwin D. Mouzon to J. D. Barbee Jr., December 28, 1912, Mouzon Papers.

77. J. D. Barbee Jr. to Edwin D. Mouzon, December 30, 1912, Mouzon Papers.

78. *Texas Christian Advocate*, January 2, 1913.

79. Frank M. Thomas to Edwin D. Mouzon, January 8, 1913, Mouzon Papers.

80. Allen Tooke to Edwin D. Mouzon, January 1913, Mouzon Papers.

81. I. Z. T. Morris to Edwin D. Mouzon, December 6, 1910, Mouzon Papers.

82. James Kilgore to Edwin D. Mouzon, January 2, 1913, Mouzon Papers.

83. *Dallas Morning News*, May 13, 1910.
84. Ibid., April 2, 1898.
85. Truett, "Coming of the Kingdom," 427.

CHAPTER 6

1. Morris Sheppard, "His Eloquent Words on the Influences of The Epworth League," Speech Delivered in San Antonio, 1896, Morris Sheppard Papers, 1894-1953, Center for American History, University of Texas at Austin.
2. For examples of rhetoric in the Deep South, see, for instance, Ownby, *Subduing Satan*, 172.
3. Coker, *Liquor in the Land*, 2–3.
4. Beth Barton Schweiger, in her account of nineteenth-century evangelical Virginians, rightly concluded only that "ambiguity suggests the complexity of race and religion even in the caustic atmosphere of Jim Crow." Schweiger, *Gospel Working Up*, 176.
5. The proportion of African Americans in Texas diminished after the war to numbers unseen among the former Confederate states. By 1910, African Americans accounted for only 17.7 percent of the Texas population, the smallest percentage among any of the former Confederate states. In 1910, only 8 of 217 Texas counties had black majorities. In some parts of West Texas, such as Lubbock, Amarillo, and Abilene—places where, incidentally, the Bible Belt would thrive—black populations were almost nonexistent. J. Morgan Kousser, *The Shaping of Southern Politics: Suffrage Restriction and the Establishment of the One-Party South, 1880-1910* (New Haven, Conn.: Yale University Press, 1974), 197.
6. Mexican immigration peaked in the 1910s and 1920s just as white evangelical moral judgments became politicized and bound up with preconceptions of race and ethnicity. The clerics taught Anglo Texans to perceive mounting Mexican migration through a particularly moral and racialized lens: white missionaries and evangelical moral reformers often used the politics of prohibition and moral reform as the means to judge the state's surging Hispanic population. See, for instance, H. Ivy, *Rum on the Run in Texas*, 35; and Rankin, *Story of My Life*, 334–336. On Anglo attitudes toward Mexicans and Mexican Americans, see especially David Montejano, *Anglos and Mexicans in the Making of Texas, 1836-1986* (Austin: University of Texas Press, 1987); Arnoldo De León, *They Called Them Greasers: Anglo Attitudes toward Mexicans in Texas, 1821-1900* (Austin: University of Texas Press, 1983); and Neil Foley, *The White Scourge: Mexicans, Blacks, and Poor Whites in Texas Cotton Culture* (Berkeley: University of California Press, 1997).
7. On the "southernness" of Texas, see especially Buenger, *Path to a Modern South*; and Campbell, *Empire for Slavery*. Observers since regional political scientist V. O. Key have suggested that some Lone Star racial dynamics hinted at divergence. V.

O. Key, *Southern Politics in State and Nation* (New York: A. A. Knopf, 1949), 254–260, 646–675.

8. The frequency and ferocity of racial violence aligned Texas with other southern states. Texas trailed only Mississippi and Georgia in the number of lynchings. Buenger, *Path to a Modern South*, 3, 19–20.

9. *Texas Baptist Herald*, August 14, 1872.

10. *Baptist Standard*, June 15, 1893.

11. Baptist General Convention of Texas, *Proceedings of the Fifty-Fourth Annual Baptist General Convention of Texas* (Dallas: Texas Baptist Publishing House, 1902), 55; *Baptist Standard*, February 5, 1903. See also Storey, *Texas Baptist Leadership*, 96.

12. *Baptist Standard*, July 13, 1893.

13. William T. Tardy, *The Man and the Message* (Marshall, Tex.: Mrs. W. T. Tardy, 1920), 186.

14. *Dallas Morning News*, December 19, 1893.

15. *Baptist Standard*, May 11, 1899.

16. Ibid., November 23, 1893.

17. Not all historians have agreed. After studying several counties in northeastern Texas, for instance, historian Walter Buenger noted the overlap of some lynchings with moral crusades and their "demands for sobriety, order, and good government." He concluded that "lynching and reform wrapped together." But moral reform did not only contribute to lynching, lynching—and the associated perception of moral lawlessness—contributed to moral reform. Prohibitionists consistently blamed liquor for inciting white violence just as they blamed it for inciting black misdeeds. Buenger, *Path to a New South*, 25.

18. *Baptist Standard*, May 11, 1899.

19. Joe Coker writes, "The specter of racism and race relations overarches and embraces every aspect of the story of southern prohibition," and Lee Willis cites Central Floridians' fears of newly emancipated African Americans for prohibition's rising success. Coker, *Liquor in the Land*, 232; Lee L. Willis, *Southern Prohibition: Race, Reform, and Public Life in Middle Florida, 1821-1920* (Athens: University of Georgia Press, 2011), 82–101.

20. Tardy, *Man and the Message*, 184.

21. C. Vann Woodward, *Origins of the New South, 1877-1913* (Baton Rouge: Louisiana State University Press, 1951), 390.

22. "Whiteness" studies, such as Grace Elizabeth Hale's excellent account of the New South, helpfully remind us that race cuts in more than one direction, but moral reformers built something bigger still. Grace Elizabeth Hale, *Making Whiteness: The Culture of Segregation in the South, 1890-1940* (New York: Pantheon, 1998).

23. Many studies of race and reform in the South suggest the prevalence of a better-and-worse-sort worldview. Historian Glenda Gilmore discovered that gendered and class-based identities allowed for limited interracial alliances in North

Carolina. She noticed that black and white elites cultivated a "best" or "better class" identity that they cast against the lesser masses of their respective races. The discovery was not hers alone. Janette Thomas Greenwood's study of race relations in Charlotte depicted a similar core of upwardly mobile blacks struggling to distinguish themselves as a class apart from poorer African Americans. Greenwood detailed how prohibition split a biracial "better class" from a "worse sort" of working-class whites and blacks. What Greenwood discovered in North Carolina aligns with what happened in the Lone Star State. Glenda Gilmore, *Gender and Jim Crow: Women and the Politics of White Supremacy in North Carolina, 1896-1920* (Chapel Hill: University of North Carolina Press, 1996); Janette Thomas Greenwood, *Bittersweet Legacy: The Black and White "Better Classes" in Charlotte, 1850-1910* (Chapell Hill: University of North Carolina Press, 1994).

24. Francis W. Johnson, *A History of Texas and Texans*, vol. 3 (Chicago: American Historical Society, 1914), 1389.
25. *Baptist Standard*, May 6, 1909.
26. B. F. Riley, *The White Man's Burden: A Discussion of the Interracial Question with Special Reference to the Responsibility of the White Race to the Negro Problem* (Birmingham, Ala.: B. F. Riley, 1910), 195–196.
27. *Baptist Standard*, May 11, 1899.
28. Ibid., June 15, 1893.
29. Riley, *White Man's Burden*. Harvey, *Redeeming the South*, 230–231.
30. *Baptist Standard*, June 15, 1893.
31. Ibid., May 6, 1909. Headquartered in Dallas before it moved to Birmingham, the federation was largely led and funded by whites, but Riley demonstrated a profound willingness to work with black prohibitionists, and like most white Texas evangelical leaders, he rejected race-based arguments for prohibition. Paul Harvey argues that "Riley's refusal to fan the fires of racism in this way was rare even among the southern religious progressives," but the experience of Texas prohibitionists suggests otherwise—even those who rejected Riley's relatively liberal racial views nevertheless resisted crass race-baiting. Harvey, *Redeeming the South*, 218.
32. *Baptist Standard*, May 6, 1909.
33. Tardy, *Man and the Message*, 186.
34. Johnson, *History of Texas*, 1389.
35. *Baptist Standard*, January 5, 1911, quoted in Storey, *Texas Baptist Leadership*, 23–24.
36. *Baptist Standard*, May 6, 1909.
37. Thrall, *History of Methodism*, 140.
38. See John B. Boles, *Masters and Slaves in the House of the Lord: Race and Religion in the American South, 1740-1870* (Lexington: University Press of Kentucky, 1988); and Stowell, *Rebuilding Zion*, 153.

39. Alwyn Barr, *Black Texans: A History of African Americans in Texas, 1528-1995* (Norman: University of Oklahoma Press), 166.

40. *Dallas Morning News*, August 24, 1903; *Colorado Springs Gazette*, September 13, 1903.

41. Lawrence Goodwyn's landmark recovery of a biracial Populist coalition, for instance, grew out of his research in Texas. Lawrence Goodwyn, *Democratic Promise: The Populist Moment in America* (New York: Oxford University Press, 1976).

42. Ayers, *Promise of the New*, 180.

43. Benajah Harvey Carroll to Benjamin Franklin Riley, May 3, 1909, Benajah Harvey Carroll Collection.

44. *Fort Worth Weekly Gazette*, July 8, 1887.

45. Barr, *Black Texans*, 113.

46. Hicks Scrapbook, quoted in Chandler Davidson, *Race and Class in Texas Politics*, (Princeton, N.J.: Princeton University Press, 1990), xxiii.

47. See especially Paul H. Thompson Jr., *A Most Stirring and Significant Episode: Religion and the Rise and Fall of Prohibition in Black Atlanta, 1865-1887* (DeKalb: Northern Illinois University Press, 2013).

48. *Dallas Morning News*, December 1, 1906.

49. Ibid.

50. Buenger, *Path to a Modern South*, 22.

51. Ibid., 25.

52. For such a dynamic operating elsewhere in the American South, see especially P. Thompson, *Most Stirring and Significant Episode*, 119–153.

53. Barr, *Black Texans*, 113.

54. Rayner had earlier offered his support to prohibitionists. In fact, in 1887 a private letter of his advising B. H. Carroll how best to reach black voters—and asking for cash to do the same—was made public and further damaged that year's prohibition campaign. Gregg Cantrell, "'Dark Tactics': Black Politics in the 1887 Texas Prohibition Campaign," *Journal of American Studies* 25 (April 1991): 85–93.

55. J. B. Rayner to S. T. Morgan, September 19, 1907, quoted in *The Brewers and Texas Politics*, vol. 2 (San Antonio: Passing Show Print Company, 1916), 732.

56. Douglas Hales, *A Southern Family in White and Black: The Cuneys of Texas* (College Station: Texas A&M University Press, 2003), 84.

57. Stowell, *Rebuilding Zion*, 151.

58. *Dallas Morning News*, May 5, 1887.

59. Ibid., May 5, 1887.

60. Jared Paul Sutton, "Ethnic Minorities and Prohibition in Texas, 1887–1919" (master's thesis, University of North Texas, 2006).

61. Benajah Harvey Carroll to Benjamin Franklin Riley, May 3, 1909, Benajah Havey Carroll Collection.

62. Barr, *Black Texans*, 113.

63. Quoted in Kousser, *Shaping of Southern Politics*, 202. See also Lewis L. Gould, *Alexander Watkins Terrell: Civil War Soldier, Texas Lawmaker, American Diplomat* (Austin: University of Texas Press, 2004).

64. Buenger, *Path to a New South*, 88; Michael Perman, *Struggle for Mastery: Disfranchisement in the South, 1888-1908* (Chapel Hill: University of North Carolina Press, 2001), 275.

65. Quoted in Patrick L. Cox and Michael Phillips, *The House Will Come to Order: How the Texas Speaker Became a Power in State and National Politics* (Austin: University of Texas Press, 2010), 22.

66. "Reformers more than any other faction led the way to segregation," wrote Walter Buenger. Buenger, *Path to a New South*, 29.

67. In 1903, the state's Democratic executive committee decreed participation for "all races except negroes." *Texas Almanac and State Industrial Guide for 1904* (Galveston: Clarke & Courts, 1904), 35.

68. The laws imposed a noncumulative poll tax, a secret ballot, and allowed counties to implement a white primary. Political scientist V. O. Key called such restrictions a fait accompli, a simple codification of an already realized disfranchisement wrought by violence, fraud, and disorganization. Historian J. Morgan Kousser and others, however, have pointed to substantial black political participation in the years leading up to the restrictions. Regardless, voting restrictions crippled political participation. Kousser, *Shaping of Southern Politics*, 208.

69. The meeting paralleled a whites-only meeting in progress at the Fort Worth Auditorium. *Dallas Morning News*, June 6, 1911.

70. *Dallas Morning News*, June 9, 1911.

71. *Baptist Standard*, July 30, 1914, quoted in Lewis L. Gould, "Progressives and Prohibitionists: Texas Democratic Politics, 1911-1921," *Southwestern Historical Quarterly* 75 (July 1971): 5–18.

72. *Dallas Morning News*, July 24, 1912.

73. Barr, *Black Texans*, 113.

74. "Whisky is a powerful agency in overcoming race prejudices, especially before elections," the *News* wrote. *Dallas Morning News*, February 16, 1886.

75. Oscar Paget, Report, January 7, 1909, in *Brewers and Texas Politics*, 611.

76. R. L. Autrey, January 15, 1913, in *Brewers and Texas Politics*, 310.

77. H. M. Broyles to H. Prince and H. Hamilton, December 7, 1911, in *Brewers and Texas Politics*, 1523.

78. Otto Warmund to O. Paget, March 15, 1911, in *Brewers and Texas Politics*, 648.

79. O. Paget to John E. Weeden, September 23, 1911, in *Brewers and Texas Politics*, 957

80. Oscar Paget, Report, August 1908, sent September 2, 1908, in *Brewers and Texas Politics*, 37, 262.

81. J. B. Rayner to Otto Wahrmund, July 9, 1912, in *Brewers and Texas Politics*, 68.

82. Over the last several decades, an avalanche of scholarship has uncovered lost women's worlds and probed the changing uses and meanings of gender in southern society. Recent works pay particular attention to the pivotal role women played in the temperance and prohibition movements and depict the nuanced ways in which gender shaped male and female moral reformers. Commonly cited works include Anne Firor Scott, *The Southern Lady: From Pedestal to Politics, 1830-1930* (Chicago: University of Chicago Press, 1970); Gilmore, *Gender and Jim Crow*; Jacquelyn Dowd Hall, *Revolt Against Chivalry: Jessie Daniel Ames and the Women's Campaign against Lynching* (New York: Columbia University Press, 1979).

83. See especially Scott, *Southern Lady;* Jean E. Friedman, *The Enclosed Garden: Women and Community in the Evangelical South, 1830-1900* (Chapel Hill: University of North Carolina Press, 1985), 111–120; and, nationally, Catherine Gilbert Murdock, *Domesticating Drink: Women, Men, and Alcohol in America, 1870-1940* (Baltimore: Johns Hopkins University Press, 2001).

84. For Texas women and churches, see especially Judith N. McArthur, *Creating the New Woman: The Rise of Southern Women's Progressive Culture in Texas, 1893-1918* (Urbana: University of Illinois Press, 1998); Elizabeth Hayes Turner, *Women, Culture, and Community: Religion and Reform in Galveston, 1880-1920* (New York: Oxford University Press, 1997); and Patricia Martin, "Hidden Work: Baptist Women in Texas, 1880-1920 (PhD dissertation, Rice University, 1982).

85. *Baptist Standard*, October 15, 1914.

86. Martin, "Hidden Work," xi.

87. *Dallas Morning News*, July 21, 1891.

88. *Journal of the Forty-Third Annual Session, Northwest Texas Conference, Methodist Episcopal Church, South* (Belton: Embree Printing Co.: 1908), 57.

89. *San Antonio Daily Express*, March 1, 1903.

90. *Fort Worth Telegram,* November 27, 1907.

91. Quoted in McArthur, *Creating the New Woman*, 78.

92. *Home and State*, January 24, 1914

93. Coker, *Liquor in the Land*, 200.

94. See especially Edward J. Blum, *Reforging the White Republic: Race, Religion, and American Nationalism, 1865-1898*, 174–208; and Ian Tyrell, *Woman's World, Woman's Empire: The Woman's Christian Temperance Union in International Perspective, 1880-1930.*

95. Ownby, *Subduing Satan*, 171.

96. For Willard's Texas tours, see especially James D. Ivy, "'The Lone Star State Surrenders to a Lone Woman': Frances Willard's Forgotten 1882 Texas Temperance Tour," *Southwestern Historical Quarterly* 102 (July 1998): 44–61.

97. J. Ivy, *No Saloon in the Valley*, 21.

98. McArthur, *Creating the New Woman*, 8.

99. Quoted in J. Ivy, *No Saloon in the Valley*, 19–21.
100. McArthur, *Creating the New Woman*, 7.
101. Ibid., 6–8.
102. Ibid., 9.
103. Ibid., 7, 8, 21.
104. Turner, *Women, Culture, and Community*, 277.
105. McArthur, *Creating the New Woman*, 78.
106. J. Ivy, *No Saloon*, 10.
107. See especially Martin, "Hidden Work."
108. Harry Leon McBeth, "The Role of Women in Southern Baptist History," *Baptist History and Heritage* 12 (January 1977): 25.
109. *Baptist Standard*, June 5, 1902.
110. Ibid., January 16, 1913.
111. J. Ivy, *No Saloon*, 31, 101.
112. According to Judith McArthur, when suffrage began to gain traction, the new generation of suffragists "only marginally included the WCTU." McArthur, *Creating the New Woman*, 116.
113. At the height of the state's prohibition agitation, they had 10,000 members, or four times the numbers of the state's WCTU. By 1914 it had only 2,600 members, fewer than it had a decade earlier. McArthur, *Creating the New Woman*, 15, 117.
114. McArthur, *Creating the New Woman*, 104.
115. *Galveston Daily News*, November 29, 1897.
116. *Dallas Morning News*, July 21, 1891.
117. "Reform in Galveston was engendered by elite women from nonevangelical congregations who responded to the urban conditions peculiar to that city between the 1870s and 1920." Turner, *Women, Culture, and Community*, 9.
118. McArthur, *Creating the New Woman*, 15.
119. As Turner says of Galveston, a gulf separated suffragists from WCTU members: In 1915, no leadership overlapped. "The truth is in Galveston suffragists and WCTU members moved in different circles bound by religion and economic status." Turner, *Women, Culture, and Community*, 8.
120. Of the twenty identifiably affiliated officers, nine were Episcopalians and four were Presbyterians. Turner, *Women, Culture, and Community*, 272–273.
121. The most common characteristics of female reformers were their husband's upper-class status as wealthy merchants, doctors, lawyers, and businessmen. Turner, *Women, Culture, and Community*, 272.
122. During World War I she volunteered in the patriotic public life wrought by World War I and opposed James Ferguson's wars against the University, prohibition, and women's suffrage. She helped spearhead state suffrage efforts. She wrote weekly columns in the local newspaper from 1917 to 1919, and in 1929 she published a work of history: a recovery of the accounts of colonial women. In the 1920s she lobbied with the Women's Joint Legislative Council and supported Dan

Moody's campaign against Governor Miriam Ferguson. She was rewarded with a position as the Texas secretary of state. She stayed active in public life until her death in 1957. Janet H. Humphrey, *A Texas Suffragist: Diaries and Writings of Jane Y. McCallum* (Austin: Ellen C. Temple, 1988).

123. See especially Judith N. McArthur and Harold L. Smith, *Minnie Fisher Cunningham: A Suffragist's Life in Politics* (New York: Oxford University Press, 2005).

124. McArthur and Smith, *Cunningham*, 284.

125. See Carry A. Nation, *The Use and Need of the Life of Carry A. Nation* (Topeka, Kan.: F. M. Steves & Sons, 1908); and Fran Grace, *Carry A. Nation: Retelling the Life* (Bloomington: Indiana University Press, 2001).

126. Sam Woolford, "Carry Nation in Texas," *Southwestern Historical Quarterly* 63 (April 1960): 554–566.

127. The classic work on southern honor is Bertram Wyatt-Brown, *Southern Honor: Ethics and Behavior in the Old South* (New York: Oxford University Press, 1982).

128. See especially Coker, *Liquor in the Land*, 175–198.

129. George W. Truett, "The Preacher in the Pulpit," Lewis Holland Lectureship, Southwestern Baptist Theological Seminary, Fort Worth, Texas, February 25, 1914, James Milton Carroll Collection; Truett, "Coming of the Kingdom," 424.

130. Morris Sheppard to Dear Madam, September 30, 1912, Morris Sheppard Papers, 1894–1953, Dolph Briscoe Center for American History, University of Texas at Austin.

131. Ownby, *Subduing Satan*, 11.

132. J. B. Cranfill, "Prohibition Orators in the South," clipping, January 14, 1886, Benajah Harvey Carroll Collection, Archives, Southwestern Baptist Theological Seminary, Fort Worth, Texas.

133. W. F. Packard, *The Saloon vs. The Home* (Houston and Fort Worth: Statewide Prohibition Amendment Headquarters, 1911).

134. Gambrell, *Ten Years in Texas*, 214.

135. J. B. Cranfill, "Looking Backward," Lecture delivered at YMCA Hall, Waco, Texas, April 21, 1893. J. M. Carroll Collection, Archives, Southwestern Baptist Theological Seminary, Fort Worth, Texas.

136. Morris Sheppard, *National Prohibition and States Rights* (Washington, D.C.: Government Printing Office: 1914).

CHAPTER 7

1. For the emergence of prohibition within Texas progressive politics, see Gould, *Progressives and Prohibitionists*, esp. 43–45.

2. W. W. Ballew to G. C. Pendleton, September 17, 1907, Alexander Dienst Collection, Center for American History, University of Texas at Austin.

3. As Ted Ownby wrote, "Evangelicalism, so long a vital part of Southern private life, had by early in the twentieth century become central to the public life of the region." Ownby, *Subduing Satan*, 210–211. Speaking specifically to southern prohibitionists, Joe L. Coker wrote that "evangelicals turned increasingly outward in orientation," and "increased [their] involvement in the realm of secular politics." Coker, *Liquor in the Land*, 37, 56.

4. *Dallas Morning News*, October 31, 1909.

5. "Roman civilization did not die a natural death. It was assassinated." Andre Piganiol, *L'Empire Chrétien (325–395)* (Paris: Presses universitaires de France, 1947), 422.

6. *Houston Daily Post*, November 14, 1901.

7. *Dallas Morning News*, February 5, 1907.

8. *Dallas Morning News*, January 26, 1909.

9. Dallas *Morning News*, October 13, 1908.

10. Ibid.

11. Ibid.

12. G. C. Pendleton to P. J. Sury, January 19, 1909. Dienst Collection.

13. *Dallas Morning News*, February 23, 1909

14. Goodwyn, *Progressives and Prohibitionists*. Also see, for instance, W. R. Buyauh to Oscar Branch Colquitt, May 16, 1910, Oscar Branch Colquitt Papers, 1873–1941, Dolph Briscoe Center for American History, University of Texas at Austin.

15. "Prohibition Rally Program," undated, Dienst Collection.

16. *Minutes of the Forty-third Annual Session of the North Conference of the Methodist Episcopal Church South* (n.p.: R. G. Mood, 1909).

17. *Dallas Morning News*, July 21, 1910.

18. *Baptist Standard*, March 18, 1911.

19. *Dallas Morning News*, May 13, 1910.

20. *Fort Worth Star-Telegram* June 5, 1911.

21. *Baptist Standard*, February 23, 1911.

22. *Dallas Morning News*, February 2, 1912.

23. *North Texas Conference Minutes*, 1909.

24. Cranfill, *Cranfill's Chronicle*, 489.

25. *Dallas Morning News*, May 9, 1910.

26. Ibid., May 13, 1910.

27. Ibid., May 15, 1910.

28. R. O. Braswell to Colquitt, April 26, 1910, Oscar Branch Colquitt Papers.

29. *Dallas Morning News*, April 8, 1910, and March 26, 1910.

30. Ibid., May 13, 1910.

31. Ibid., January 9, 1910.

32. Two other candidates, Robert Vance Davidson and William Poindexter, also ran. Poindexter championed a more moderate prohibition message in a less overtly religious campaign. In a tight race for second place, he narrowly topped Johnson's vote total. Davidson, on the other hand, believed he could rise above the prohibition

issue. "The future story and greatness of this State," he declared in May of 1910, "ought not to be made to revolve around a whisky bottle . . . Reclamation, irrigation, drainage, agriculture, public education, the building of railroads, the penitentiary question, the care of our Confederate Veterans, judicial reform—these are the main questions which candidates for state offices should discuss." Davidson was too late. A governor, he argued, "should not be selected because he is in favor of prohibition—a worthy belief—nor because he is an anti-prohibitionist—an honorable belief." By then, it was abundantly clear that this would in fact be the case: prohibition would decide the election, whether in the form of support or opposition to the issue or the reformers promulgating it. Davidson failed to gain traction. *Dallas Morning News*, May 29, 1910.

33. W. R. Buyauh to Colquitt, May 16, 1910, Oscar Branch Colquitt Papers.

34. *Dallas Morning News*, January 9, 1910.

35. *North Texas Conference Minutes*, 1909.

36. S. M. King to Oscar Branch Colquitt, April 28, 1910, Oscar Branch Colquitt Papers.

37. C. W. Simpson to Oscar Branch Colquitt, April 23, 1910; A. W. Campbell to R. M. Colquitt, May 4, 1910; G. W. Walthall to Oscar Branch Colquitt, May 2, 1910; S. M. King to O. B. Colquitt, April 28, 1910, Oscar Branch Colquitt Papers.

38. *Dallas Morning News*, July 21, 1910.

39. Ibid., July 23, 1910.

40. J. T. Trezevant to Oscar Branch Colquitt, January 26, 1910, Oscar Branch Colquitt Papers.

41. P. W. Templeton to Oscar Branch Colquitt, January 13, 1910, Oscar Branch Colquitt Papers.

42. D. A. Griffitts to Oscar Branch Colquitt, January 10, 1910, Oscar Branch Colquitt Papers.

43. A. W. Campbell to R. M. Colquitt, May 4, 1910, Oscar Branch Colquitt Papers.

44. Jos. O. Boehmer to Oscar Branch Colquitt, February 10, 1910, Oscar Branch Colquitt Papers.

45. Walter A. Nelson, "A Texan's Soliloquy: How Must I Vote?" undated manuscript, Martin Crane Papers, Center for American History, University of Texas at Austin.

46. L. C. Rummel to Oscar Branch Colquitt, January 24, 1910, Oscar Branch Colquitt Papers.

47. Untitled Poem, June 14, 1910, Oscar Branch Colquitt Papers.

48. *Dallas Morning News*, May 22, 1910; Sterling P. Strong to Elijah L. Shettles, January 1, 1909, Elijah L. Shettles Papers, 1792–1940, Dolph Briscoe Center for American History, University of Texas at Austin.

49. Sterling P. Strong to Elijah L. Shettles, January 1, 1909, Elijah L. Shettles Papers.

50. J. B. Gambrell to Elijah L. Shettles, June 21, 1910, Elijah L. Shettles Papers.

51. *Dallas Morning News*, May 18 and 22, 1910.

52. Ibid., January 3, 1910.

53. Ibid. July 16, 1910.

54. Ibid., May 31, 1910.
55. *Baptist Standard*, July 28, 1910.
56. A. W. Walker to Benajah Harvey Carroll, March 20, 1911, Benajah Harvey Carroll Collection, Archives, Southwestern Baptist Theological Seminary, Fort Worth, Texas.
57. *Dallas Morning News*, June 9, 1911.
58. Ibid.
59. Ibid.
60. Ibid.
61. Ibid.
62. *Baptist Standard*, May 18, 1911.
63. *New York Times*, June 4, 1911.
64. *Dallas Morning News*, July 15, 1911; *New York Times*, July 15, 1911.
65. Edwin D. Mouzon to Clarence Ousley, January 15, 1913, Edwin Mouzon Papers, Bridwell Library, Perkins School of Theology, Southern Methodist University, Dallas, Texas.
66. *New York Times*, May 29, 1911.
67. The Texas & Pacific ran one such special from El Paso; it had ten coaches and an estimated 500 passengers. *Fort Worth Star-Telegram*, June 5, 1911.
68. *Fort Worth Star-Telegram*, June 5, 1911.
69. Ibid.
70. Ibid.
71. Ibid.; *Dallas Morning News*, June 5, 1911.
72. *Fort Worth Star-Telegram*, June 5, 1911.
73. Anti-State-wide Prohibition Organization of Texas, *State-wide Prohibition by Questions and Answers* (San Antonio: Anti-State-wide Prohibition Organization of Texas, 1911), n.p.
74. *Dallas Morning News*, May 21, 1911.
75. Ibid., July 14, 1911.
76. *Dallas Morning News*, July 5, 1911.
77. *New York Times*, May 29, July 15, 1911.
78. *Dallas Morning News*, July 15, 1911.
79. S. R. Carruth to Oscar Branch Colquitt, January 17, 1910, Oscar Branch Colquitt Papers.
80. *Fort Worth Star-Telegram*, June 5, 1911.
81. S. M. King to O. B. Colquitt, April 28, 1910, Oscar Branch Colquitt Papers.
82. *Fort Worth Star-Telegram*, July 17, 1911.
83. *Victoria Advocate*, July 18, 1911; *Forth Worth Star-Telegram*, July 17, 1911.
84. *Dallas Morning News*, July 25, 1911.
85. *Texas Christian Advocate*, January 11, 1912.
86. Gould, *Progressives and Prohibitionists*, 89–91.

87. *Temple Daily Telegram*, October 31, 1912. Shuler would later solidify his position as a leading belligerent and national figure while tending his fundamentalist Southern California fiefdom in the 1920s.
88. *Baptist Standard*, June 4, 1914.
89. Radford and Lewis, *Regulating Political Preachers*.
90. Richard Hofstadter, *The Age of Reform: From Bryan to FDR* (New York: A. A. Knopf, 1955), 290.
91. See especially Roger Finke and Rodney Stark, *The Churching of America, 1776-1990: Winners and Losers in Our Religious Economy* (New Brunswick, N.J.: Rutgers University Press, 1992); Peter Berger, ed., *The Desecularization of the World* (Grand Rapids, Mich.: W. B. Eerdmans, 1999); and R. Stephen Warner, *A Church of Our Own: Disestablishment and Diversity in American Religion* (New Brunswick, N.J.: Rutgers University Press, 2005).
92. Ayers, *Promise of the New South*, ix–x. See also Schweiger, *Gospel Working Up*; and Harvey, *Redeeming the South*.
93. Samuel S. Hill, *Religion and the Solid South* (Nashville, Tenn.: Abingdon, 1972), 37; Ayers, *Promise of the New South*, 499.
94. Ayers, *Promise of the New South*, 162; Harvey, *Redeeming the South*, 199.
95. Schweiger, *Gospel Working Up*, 130–133.
96. Beth Schweiger termed the clerical elite the "ministerial aristocracy." Schweiger, *Gospel Working Up*, 130.
97. Harvey, *Redeeming the South*, 7.
98. This chasm, as historian William Link has written, strained the larger progressive movement in the South. Link, *Paradox of Southern Progressivism*.
99. Dohoney, in fact, authored the local-option clause of the state during the 1875 constitutional convention. Later, in the 1880s, he hosted Frances Willard, president of the Woman's Christian Temperance Union, in Paris, Texas. Dohoney's wife was a prominent member of the organization. He pushed the Greenbackers to endorse the cause, toured the state in support of the 1887 amendment, and pushed the issue among Populists. Buenger, *Path to a Modern South*, 7.
100. Buenger, *Path to a Modern South*, 14.
101. John Lee Eighmy long ago noted that "Baptist spokesmen, for the most part, expressed attitudes that were more Bourbon than Populist." Eighmy, 43; Buenger compared prohibition support in 1877 to Populist support in 1894. Buenger, *Path to a Modern South*, 9.
102. As noted in chapter 1, historian Charles Postel best captured the heterodox religious beliefs of American Populists—especially in Texas—during the late nineteenth century. Postel, *Populist Vision*, 243.
103. Quoted in Keith Lynn King, "Religious Dimensions of the Agrarian Protest in Texas" (PhD diss., University of Chicago, 1973), 110–111.

104. Dean M. Kelley, *Why Conservative Churches Are Growing* (New York: Harper & Row, 1973), 53.

105. Jesse Lee to Elijah L. Shettles, January 19, 1909, Elijah L. Shettles Papers, 1792–1940, Dolph Briscoe Center for American History, University of Texas at Austin.

106. *Baptist Standard*, June 8, 1893, quoted in Harvey, *Redeeming the South*, 79–80.

107. "To the Boys on Southern Farms," undated address, Samuel Palmer Brooks Papers, Texas Collection, Carroll Library, Baylor University, Waco, Texas.

108. J. B. Gambrell, "Evangelization of the Rural Districts," in The Baptist World Alliance, *Second Congress, Philadelphia, June 19–25, 1911: Record of Proceedings* (Philadelphia, Pa., Harper & Brother Company, for the Philadelphia Committee, 1911), 203–207.

109. "Texas Citizenry," undated address, Samuel Palmer Brooks Papers, Southwestern Baptist Theological Seminary.

110. Gould, *Progressives and Prohibitionists*, 127.

111. Connie L. Lester, *Up from the Mudsills of Hell: The Farmers' Alliance, Populism, and Progressive Agriculture in Tennessee, 1870–1915* (Athens: University of Georgia Press, 2006).

112. *Fort Worth Star-Telegram*, February 17, 1914.

113. W. R. Buyauh to the Editors of the Home and State, May 16, 1910, Oscar Branch Colquitt Papers.

114. Hames Gilford Browning to Oscar Branch Colquitt, April 23, 1910, Oscar Branch Colquitt Papers.

115. *Dallas Morning News*, May 14, 1910.

116. Ibid., July 23, 1910.

117. Ibid., April 8, 1910.

118. Radford and Lewis, *Regulating Political Preachers*.

119. *State Topics*, May 30, 1914; see also Radford and Lewis, *Down with the Bosses*.

120. Peter Radford and W. D. Lewis, *Back to the Soil with Legislation* (Fort Worth: Farmers' Educational and Cooperative Union, 1914).

121. Radford and Lewis, *Regulating Political Preachers*.

122. "Samuel Palmer Brooks before the Southern Sociological Congress," speech delivered in New Orleans, Louisiana, April 12, 1916, Samuel Palmer Brooks Papers.

123. Horace Bishop to Elijah L. Shettles, August 10, 1914, Elijah L. Shettles Papers.

124. J. B. Cranfill, "Looking Backward," Lecture delivered by J. B. Cranfill at YMCA Hall, Waco, Texas, April 21, 1893, James Milton Carroll Collection, Southwestern Baptist Theological Seminary, Fort Worth, Texas.

125. *Corsicana Daily Sun*, May 29, 1914.

126. For the politics of the 1914 campaign, see especially Gould, *Progressives and Prohibitionists*, 120–149.

127. Horace Bishop to Elijah L. Shettles, August 10, 1914, Elijah L. Shettles Papers.

128. B. Y. Cummings, "The Relation of Landlord and Tenant in Texas," speech delivered in Itasca, Tex., April 25, 1914, Alexander Dienst Collection, 1784–1929, Center for American History, University of Texas at Austin.

129. *New York Times*, August 3, 1914.

130. Quoted in Gould, "Progressives and Prohibitionists," 13.

131. W. H. Basden to W. P. Hobby, June 23, 1918, Dienst Collection.

132. Gould, *Progressives and Prohibitionists*, 125.

133. *Corsicana Daily Sun*, May 29, 1914, in Colquitt Papers.

134. Elijah L. Shettles to Alexander Dienst, July 18, 1914, Elijah L. Shettles Papers.

135. *Dallas Morning News*, July 17, 1914.

136. Q. U. Watson to John G. McKay, June 26, 1914, Alexander Dienst Collection.

137. Kevin C. Motl, "Under the Influence: The Texas Business Men's Association and the Campaign against Reform, 1906-1915," *Southwestern Historical Quarterly*, 109, no. 4 (2006): 494–529.

138. John S. Morris to Elijah L. Shettles, August 11, 1914, Elijah L. Shettles Papers.

139. Radford and Lewis, *Down with the Bosses*.

140. *New York Times*, December 20, 1914.

CHAPTER 8

1. George W. Truett, "Preacher in the Pulpit."

2. Ibid.

3. Ibid.

4. *Baptist Standard*, June 9, 1910.

5. *Dallas Morning News*, July 18, 1910.

6. *Baptist Standard*, July 9, 1914.

7. *Baptist Standard*, July 9, 1914.

8. *Baptist Standard*, June 4, 1914

9. Cranfill, *Cranfill's Chronicle*, 490.

10. *Baptist Standard*, July 9, 1914.

11. Baptist General Convention of Texas, *Proceedings* (n.p., n.d.), 26–27, quoted in Storey, *Texas Baptist Leadership*, 36. Storey attributed the creation of the committee to the power of a "social Christianity," if not necessarily a social gospel.

12. *Texas Christian Advocate*, July 31, 1913.

13. *Dallas Morning News*, March 6, 1911

14. Ibid., July 18, 1910.

15. Ibid., October 31, 1909.

16. Morris Sheppard, *Congressman Sheppard Is for Prohibition*, 8.

17. *Dallas Morning News*, January 30, 1913; Texas House of Representatives, *Journal of the House of Representatives of the Regular Session of the Thirty-Third Legislature of Texas* (Austin: Von Boeckmann-Jones, 1913), 224–263.

18. "Anti-Rum Army at Capitol," *New York Times*, December 11, 1913; *Fort Worth Star Telegram*, December 10, 1913; *Dallas Morning News*, December 10–11, 1913.

19. Samuel S. Hill, *Southern Churches in Crisis Revisited* (Tuscaloosa: University of Alabama Press, 1999), 16.

20. John Fea, *Was America Founded as a Christian Nation: A Historical Introducing* (Louisville, Ky.: Westminster John Knox Press, 2011), 22.

21. Morris Sheppard, *National Prohibition and States Rights* (Washington, D.C.: Government Printing Office, 1914).

22. *Bob Shuler's Free Lance*, March 1919, 55.

23. Hankins, *God's Rascal*, 1–11. Marsden, 237.

24. Hankins, *God's Rascal*, 17–18. First Baptist has been called "America's first megachurch," not only for becoming among the nation's largest, but because the church also contained a rec center with a pool and gymnasium. David Stokes, *Apparent Danger: The Pastor of America's First Megachurch and the Texas Murder Trial of the Decade in the 1920s* (Minneapolis, Mn.: Bascom, 2010).

25. J. Frank Norris, *Inside History of First Baptist Church, Fort Worth and Temple Baptist Church, Detroit: Life Story of Dr. J. Frank Norris* (New York: Garland, 1988), 42.

26. *Bob Shuler's Free Lance*, January 1917, 36.

27. Randolph B. Campbell, *Gone to Texas: A History of the Lone Star State* (New York: Oxford University Press, 2003), 354; *New York Times*, August 29, 1916.

28. Chris Cappozola, *Uncle Sam Wants You: World War I and the Making of the Modern American Citizen* (New York: Oxford University Press, 2008).

29. Gould, *Progressives and Prohibitionists*, 226–227.

30. *Bob Shuler's Free Lance*, October 1917, 260.

31. *Dallas Morning News*, February 14, 1918.

32. Baptist General Convention of Texas, *Annual of the Baptist General Convention of Texas* (Dallas: Texas Baptist Book House, 1917), 138.

33. Ibid., 19.

34. *Bob Shuler's Free Lance*, May 1918, 149.

35. *New York Times*, August 29, 1916.

36. Gould, *Progressives and Prohibitionists*, 177–181.

37. *New York Times*, August 27, 1916.

38. Gould, *Progressives and Prohibitionists*, 227.

39. Ibid., 228.

40. *Dallas Morning News*, September 11, 1917, 1. Reported vote totals were 10,351 for and 8,486 against, for a dry margin of 1,865 votes. *Dallas Morning News*, October 20, 1917.

41. *Bob Shuler's Free Lance*, November 1917, 282.

42. Ibid., 279–280.

43. *Dallas Morning News*, October 27, 1917, 12.

44. Texas House of Representatives, *Journal of the House of Representatives of the Second Called Session of the Thirty-Fifth Legislature of Texas*, vol. 35, part 2 (Austin: Von Boeckmann-Jones Co., 1917), 325–328.

45. Campbell, *Gone to Texas*, 351. Ferguson would publicly object to Vinson on religious grounds. In his testimony before the Texas House of Representatives, he said, "He is also a sectarian preacher, and not only makes no denial of such fact, but since the elevation to the presidency of the institution has regularly and often continued to preach under the auspices of his particular religious denomination." He said it violated the religious qualifications clause of the university code? Law? Charter? And religious liberty clauses of the Texas constitution. Texas House of Representatives, *Journal of the House of Representatives of the Second Called Session of the Thirty-Fifth Legislature of Texas*, vol. 35, part 2 (Austin: Von Boeckmann-Jones Co., 1917), 326. Ferguson was grilled during the impeachment proceedings on accusations of anti-religious bias. Hee was asked, "Q. Did you have any prejudice against him because he was a minister? / A. None whatever. / Q. Any prejudice against ministers? / A. None whatever." Texas House, *Journal*, 589.

46. Campbell, *Gone to Texas*, 351.

47. This coincided with regional trends. See Dewey W. Grantham, "The Contours of Southern Progressivism," *American Historical Review* 86 (December 1981): 1051–1052. The political aspirations of Texas women were generally fostered outside of the evangelical churches. While defending "the home" and proclaiming the virtues of pure womanhood, Lone Star clerics demonstrated a sustained ambivalence toward public roles for women. The public enfranchisement of women was generally cultivated within secular women's clubs and elite, mainline churches. See especially McArthur, *Creating the New Woman*; and Turner, *Women, Culture, and Community*.

48. Jane Y. McCallum, "Activities of Women in Texas Politics," in *Texas Democracy*, ed. Frank Carter Adams (Austin: Democratic Historical Association, 1937), 474–476.

49. Campbell, *Gone to Texas*, 353. See Lewis L. Gould, "The University Becomes Politicized: The War with Jim Ferguson, 1915-1918," *Southwestern Historical Quarterly* 86 (October 1982): 255–276; and Ralph W. Steen, "Ferguson's War on the University of Texas," *Southwestern Social Science Quarterly* 35 (March 1955): 356–362.

50. See, for instance, *Dallas Morning News*, September 26, 1917.

51. *Bob Shuler's Free Lance*, October 1917, 249.

52. Gould, *Progressives and Prohibitionists*, 227.

53. *Dallas Morning News*, February 14, 1918.

54. *Bob Shuler's Free Lance*, January 1918, 32.

55. *Dallas Morning News*, March 18, 1917.

56. Gould, *Progressives and Prohibitionists*, 228–229, 242–248. The Texas Constitution dictates that the Texas legislature convenes for no more than 140 calendar days beginning in January in odd-numbered years. Texas therefore only has a legislature

in regular session about one-fifth of the time. But the governor may call the legislature back for a thirty-day special session, and prohibitionists pressured Hobby to
call one as soon as possible.

57. Baptist General Convention of Texas, *Annual of the Baptist General Convention of Texas* (Dallas: Texas Baptist Book House, 1917), 139.

58. *Bob Shuler's Free Lance*, November 1917, 273.

59. Gould, *Progressives and Prohibitionists*, 228–231

60. *Dallas Morning News*, October 10, 1917.

61. *Bob Shuler Free Lance*, November 1917, 273.

62. *Dallas Morning News*, January 29, 1918.

63. Gould, *Progressives and Prohibitionists*, 230–31.

64. *Dallas Morning News*, October 10, 1917.

65. Ibid., November 18, 1917.

66. *San Antonio Express*, January 21, 1918, 4, 6.

67. Gould, *Progressives and Prohibitionists*, 232.

68. *Dallas Morning News*, February 14, 1918.

69. Ibid., March 22, 1918; Gould, *Progressives and Prohibitionists*, 232–233, 242–248.

70. *Dallas Morning News*, March 22, 1918.

71. Ibid., March 27, 1918.

72. Ibid., July 27, 1918.

73. *Bob Shuler's Free Lance*, September 1918, 238.

74. *Brownwood Bulletin*, August 10, 1918; *Bob Shuler's Free Lance*, September 1918, 239.

75. *Texas Mesquiter*, August 9, 1918.

76. *Bob Shuler's Free Lance*, September 1918, 239.

77. Gould, *Progressives and Prohibitionists*, 247.

78. *Baptist Standard*, September 12, 1918.

79. *Dallas Morning News*, September 4, 1918.

80. *Fort Worth Star-Telegram*, November 25, 1918.

81. P. A. Baker, "An Appeal to the Pastors and Churches," undated manuscript, Benajah Harvey Carroll Collection, Archives, Southwestern Baptist Theological Seminary, Fort Worth, Texas.

82. Quoted in *Bob Shuler's Free Lance*, May 1918, 123.

83. Speaking of the sudden string of victories in 1918, Lewis Gould wrote, "More than any other cause, the war decided the outcome of the 1918 contest and produced the dry victory." He added that, "In Texas, the conflict swept away most of the barriers in the way of the dry progressives and established them as the dominant faction within the party. Their supremacy was secure." Gould, *Progressives and Prohibitionists*, 248.

84. *Bob Shuler's Free Lance*, August 1918, 215.

85. Baptist General Convention of Texas, *Annual of the Baptist General Convention of Texas* (Dallas: Texas Baptist Book House, 1919), 162.

86. *Fort Worth Star-Telegram*, January 17, 1919.

87. *Dallas Morning News*, January 17, 1919; *Fort Worth Star-Telegram*, January 18, 1919.

88. *Dallas Morning News*, January 18, 1919.

89. "First Baptist Church and Sunday School Give Senator Silver Service," *Fort Worth Star-Telegram*, July 31, 1919, 8; Hankins, *God's Rascal*, 47.

90. The newly seated Governor William P. Hobby acceded to the times. Realizing that he could not stand in the way of prohibition, he relented. He had delayed as long as he could, but in February 1918 he called a special session of the state legislature to pass a state prohibition law. It passed overwhelmingly and with little controversy. The state legislature meanwhile ratified the national prohibition amendment and made an effort to amend the state constitution in a similar manner. The prohibition measures all passed that year. Gould, *Progressives and Prohibitionists*, 242–248.

91. *Dallas Morning News*, October 25, 1918.

92. *Baptist Standard*, quoted in *Tulia Herald*, May 2, 1919.

93. Gould, *Progressives and Prohibitionists*, 253.

94. R. Harper Kirby, *An Appeal to the Patriotic Voters of Texas* (Austin: Statewide Prohibition Campaign Headquarters, 1919), n.p.

95. *Bob Shuler's Free Lance*, June 1919, 125.

96. *Dallas Morning News*, April 18, 1919.

97. Kirby, *Appeal to the Patriotic Voters*.

98. *Bob Shuler's Free Lance*, May 1919, 102.

99. *Dallas Morning News*, April 26, 1919.

100. Kirby, *Appeal to the Patriotic Voters*.

101. *Bob Shuler's Free Lance*, June 1919, 117.

102. Gould, *Progressives and Prohibitionists*, 255.

103. Presumably only Texas's Independence Day would reign ahead of it. *Lubbock Avalanche*, June 26, 1919.

104. *Fort Worth Star-Telegram*, August 10, 1920.

105. *Bob Shuler's Free Lance*, September 1918, 239.

106. Baptist General Convention of Texas, *Annual of the Baptist General Convention of Texas* (Dallas: Texas Baptist Book House, 1920), 162.

107. Tardy, *Man and the Message*, 185.

108. Methodist Episcopal Church, South, *Journal of the Central Texas Conference, Fifty-Fourth Annual Session* (Corsicana: A. D. Porter, 1919), 71.

EPILOGUE

1. James N. Gregory, *The Southern Diaspora: How The Great Migrations of Black and White Southerners Transformed America* (Chapel Hill: University of North Carolina Press, 2005).

2. Darren Dochuk, *From Bible Belt to Sunbelt: Plain-Folk Religion, Grassroots Politics, and the Rise of Evangelical Conservatism* (New York: W. W. Norton, 2011), xvii, xix.

3. For the importance of such questions, see Beth Barton Schweiger, "How Would Jesus Vote? The Prehistory of the Christian Right," *Reviews in American History* 32 (March 2004): 49–57.

4. Lisa McGirr, *Suburban Warriors: The Origins of the New American Right* (Princeton, N.J.: Princeton University Press, 2001), 31, 241; Gregory, *Southern Diaspora*, 225–227.

5. Hankins, *God's Rascal*; Stokes, *Apparent Danger*.

6. *New York Times*, March 26, 1922.

7. Hankins, *God's Rascal*; David R. Stokes, *The Shooting Salvationist: J. Frank Norris and the Murder Trial That Captivated America* (Hanover, N.H.: Steerforth, 2011).

8. Senator Morris Sheppard, "Religion and the American Republic," speech delivered at State Line Methodist Church, Texarkana, on September 2, 1934, Morris Sheppard Papers, 1894-1953, Dolph Briscoe Center for American History, University of Texas at Austin.

9. Pat M. Neff, *Speeches Delivered by Pat M. Neff, Governor of Texas, Discussing Certain Phases of Contemplated Legislation* (Austin: Von Boeckmann-Jones Co., 1923), 57.

10. Ibid., 60.

11. On Neff, see Norman D. Brown, *Hood, Bonnet, and Little Brown Jug: Texas Politics, 1921-1928* (College Station: Texas A&M University Press, 1984); and Mark Stanley, "Portrait of a southern Progressive: The Political Life and Times of Governor Pat M. Neff of Texas, 1871–1952" (PhD diss., University of North Texas, 2011).

12. See especially Nancy MacLean *Behind the Mask of Chivalry: The Making of the Second Ku Klux Klan* (New York: Oxford University Press, 1994); and Kelly J. Baker, *Gospel According to the Klan: The KKK's Appeal to Protestant America, 1915-1930* (Lawrence: University Press of Kansas, 2011); and Brown, *Hood, Bonnet, and Little Brown Jug*.

13. Charles C. Alexander, *The Ku Klux Klan in the Southwest* (Lexington: University of Kentucky Press, 1965), xvii.

14. Brown, *Hood, Bonnet, and Little Brown Jug*, 6.

15. *Fort Worth Star-Telegram*, August 20, 1922.

16. See Hankins, *God's Rascal*.

17. McGirr, *Suburban Warriors*, 31; Gregory, *Southern Diaspora*, 225–227.

18. David Stricklin, "Fundamentalism," *Handbook of Texas Online* (http://www.tshaonline.org/handbook/online/articles/itf01), accessed April 10, 2012. Published by the Texas State Historical Association.

19. Michael Phillips, *White Metropolis: Race, Ethnicity, and Religion in Dallas, Texas, 1841-2001* (Austin: University of Texas at Austin, 2006), 47–56.

20. Stricklin, "Fundamentalism."

21. Brown, *Hood, Bonnet, and Little Brown Jug*, 254.

22. *Tulia Herald*, February 14, 1929.

23. Hankins, *God's Rascal;* Keith E. Durso, *Thy Will Be Done: A Biography of George W. Truett* (Macon, Ga.: Mercer University Press, 2009)

24. Dick J. Reavis, "The Politics of Armageddon," *Texas Monthly*, October 1984, 162–166. See also David Stricklin, *A Genealogy of Dissent: Southern Baptist Protest in the Twentieth Century* (Lexington: University Press of Kentucky, 1999).

25. Steven P. Miller, *Billy Graham and the Rise of the Republican South*, (Philadelphia: University of Pennsylvania Press, 2009).

26. *Life*, June 30, 1972, 40–45; John G. Turner, *Bill Bright and Campus Crusade for Christ: The Renewal of Evangelicalism in Postwar America* (Chapel Hill: University of North Carolina Press, 2008), 139–146;

27. Blake Ellis, "An Alternative Politics: Texas Baptists and the Rise of the Christian Right, 1975-1985," *Southwestern Historical Quarterly* 112 (April 2009): 361–386.

28. Darren K. Williams, *God's Own Party: The Making of the Christian Right* (New York: Oxford University Press, 2010).

29. George W. Bush, *A Charge to Keep: My Journey to the White House* (New York: Harper Collins, 1999), 45.

30. H. L. Mencken, *Prejudices: Fifth Series* (New York: A. A. Knopf, 1926), 111.

Bibliography

MANUSCRIPT COLLECTIONS

Samuel Palmer Brooks Papers. The Texas Collection, Carroll Library. Baylor University. Waco, Texas.

Rufus Columbus Burleson Papers. Texas Collection, Carroll Library. Baylor University. Waco, Texas.

Benajah Harvey Carroll Collection. Archives. Southwestern Baptist Theological Seminary. Fort Worth, Texas.

James Milton Carroll Collection. Archives. Southwestern Baptist Theological Seminary. Fort Worth, Texas.

Oscar Branch Colquitt Papers, 1873–1941. Dolph Briscoe Center for American History. University of Texas at Austin. Austin, Texas.

Richard Coke Scrapbook. Dolph Briscoe Center for American History. University of Texas at Austin.

Martin McNulty Crane Papers, 1834–1973. Dolph Briscoe Center for American History. University of Texas at Austin. William Carey Crane Papers. Texas Collection, Carroll Library. Baylor University. Waco, Texas.

J. B. Cranfill Papers, 1844–1941. Dolph Briscoe Center for American History. University of Texas at Austin. Alexander Dienst Collection, 1784–1929. Dolph Briscoe Center for American History. University of Texas at Austin. James Edward Ferguson Collection, 1911–1936. Dolph Briscoe Center for American History. University of Texas at Austin.

Roger Quarles Mills Papers, 1813–1938. Dolph Briscoe Center for American History. University of Texas at Austin.

Edwin D. Mouzon Papers, 1869–1937, Archives, Center for Methodist Studies, Bridwell Library, Perkins School of Theology. Southern Methodist University. Dallas, Texas.

Carry Amelia Nation Papers, 1870–1961. Kansas Memory, www.kansasmemory.org (accessed March 20, 2012). Kansas Historical Society. Topeka, Kansas.

Morris Sheppard Papers, 1894–1953. Dolph Briscoe Center for American History. University of Texas at Austin. Elijah L. Shettles Papers, 1792–1940. Dolph Briscoe Center for American History. University of Texas at Austin.

George W. Truett Collection. Archives. Southwestern Baptist Theological Seminary. Fort Worth, Texas.

NEWSPAPERS

American Mercury (New York)
Baptist Standard (Dallas)
Bob Shuler's Free Lance (Temple, Texas)
Columbus Daily Enquirer
Colorado Springs Gazette
Corsicana Daily Sun
Dallas Morning News
Dallas Weekly Herald
Fort Worth Gazette
Fort Worth Morning Register
Fort Worth Star-Telegram
Galveston Daily News
The Iconoclast (Waco)
Independent Pulpit (Waco)
New York Times
Palestine Daily Herald
San Antonio Evening Light
Temple Daily Telegram
Texas Baptist Herald (Dallas)
Texas Christian Advocate (Dallas)
Texas Presbyterian (Austin)
Texas Siftings (Austin)
The Tulia Herald
Victoria Advocate
Waco Daily Examiner

PUBLISHED PRIMARY SOURCES

Anti-Saloon League. *The Brewers and Texas Politics*, 2 vols. San Antonio: Passing Show Print Company, 1916.

Adams, Henry. *The Education of Henry Adams: An Autobiography*. Boston: Houghton Mifflin Company, 1918.

Anti-State-wide Prohibition Organization of Texas. *State-wide Prohibition by Questions and Answers*. San Antonio: Anti-State-wide Prohibition Organization of Texas, 1911.

Baptist World Alliance. *Second Congress, Philadelphia, June 19-25, 1911: Record of Proceedings*. Philadelphia: Harper & Brother Company, 1911.

Barker, Eugene C. *A History of Texas and Texans*. Vol. 4. Chicago: American Historical Society, 1914.

Brann, William Cowper. *The Complete Works of Brann, the Iconoclast*. New York: Brann Publishers, 1919.

———. *The Writings of W. C. Brann*. Vol. 1. Waco: Herz Brothers, 1911.

Burleson, Rufus. *Address of Dr. Rufus C. Burleson, on the one Hundredth Anniversary of the Birth of Gen. Sam Houston, and the Fifty-Seventh of the Independence of Texas, Delivered in the Hall of the House of Representatives, at Austin, Texas, March 2, 1893*. Austin: Ben C. Jones & Co., 1893.

Carroll, B. H. *Christian Education: a Sermon Preached at San Antonio, Texas, Sunday, January 28, 1900*. Waco: Kellner Printing Company, 1900.

———. *Evangelistic Sermons*, ed. J. B. Cranfill. New York: Fleming H. Revell, 1913.

Carroll, J. M. *A History of Texas Baptists: Comprising a Detailed Account of Their Activities, Their Progress, and Their Achievements*. Dallas: Baptist Standard Publishing Company, 1923.

———. *Dr. B. H. Carroll, the Colossus of Baptist History: Pastor, First Baptist Church, Waco, Texas and First President of S.W.B.T. Seminary*. Fort Worth: J. W. Crowder, 1946.

Crane, William Carey. *Centennial Address Embracing the History of Washington County, Texas, at the Fair Grounds in Brenham, July 4, 1876*. Galveston: News Steam Job Printing Office, 1876.

Cranfill, J. B. *Courage and Comfort; or, Sunday Morning Thoughts*. Nashville, Tenn.: Southwestern Company, 1908.

———. *Dr. J. B. Cranfill's Chronicle: A Story of Life in Texas*. New York: Fleming H. Revell Company: New York, 1916.

Dabney, Robert Lewis. *Sacred Rhetoric: or, a Course of Lectures on Preaching*. Richmond, Va.: Presbyterian Committee of Publication, 1870.

Fleming, E. B. *Early History of Hopkins County, Texas: Biographical Sketches and Incidents of the Early Settled Families*. n.p., 1902.

Fuller, B. F. *History of Texas Baptists*. Louisville, Ky.: Baptist Book Concern, 1900.

Godbey, William B. *Autobiography of W. B. Godbey*. Cincinnati, Ohio: God's Revivalist Office, 1909.

Holden, J. Stuart. *The Price of Power*. New York: Fleming H. Revell Company, 1908.

Ivy, H. A. *Rum on the Run in Texas: A Brief History of Prohibition in the Lone Star State*. Dallas: Temperance Publishing Company, 1910.

Jernigan, Charles Brougher. *Pioneer Days of the Holiness Movement in the Southwest*. Kansas City, Mo.: Pentecostal Nazarene Publishing House, 1919.

Johnson, Francis White. *A History of Texas and Texans*. Vol. 3. Chicago: American Historical Society, 1914.

Radford, Peter, and W. D. Lewis. *Back to the Soil with Legislation*. Fort Worth: Farmers' Educational and Cooperative Union, 1914.

———. *Down with the Bosses*. Fort Worth: Farmers' Educational and Cooperative Union, 1914.

———. *Regulating Political Preachers*. Fort Worth: Farmers' Educational and Cooperative Union, 1914.

McCallum, Jane Y. "Activities of Women in Texas Politics." In *Texas Democracy*, edited by Frank Carter Adams, 467–487. Austin: Democratic Historical Association, 1937.

McCulloch, George. *History of the Holiness Movement in Texas, and the Fanaticism Which Followed*. Aquilla, Tex.: J. H. Padgett, 1886.

McLean, Rev. John H. "Introduction." *Texas Methodist Historical Quarterly* 1 (July 1909): 4–5.

Mencken, H. L. *Prejudices: Fifth Series*. New York: A. A. Knopf, 1926.

Methodist Episcopal Church, South. *Minutes of the Twenty-Second Annual Session of the Northwest Texas Conference of the Methodist Episcopal Church, South*. Dallas: Ewing R. Bedford, 1888.

Mills, Roger Q. *Speech of the Hon. R. Q. Mills before the United Anti-Prohibition clubs of Corsicana, Saturday, May 21, 1887*. Corsicana, Tex.: Corsicana Daily Courier, May 1887.

Morrell, Z. N. *Flowers and Fruits from the Wilderness; or, Thirty-Six Years in Texas and Two in Honduras*. Boston: Gould and Lincoln, 1872.

Nation, Carry A. *The Use and Need of the Life of Carry A. Nation*. Topeka, Kan.: F. M. Steves & Sons, 1908.

Neff, Pat M. *Speeches Delivered by Pat M. Neff, Governor of Texas, Discussing Certain Phases of Contemplated Legislation*. Austin: Von Boeckmann-Jones Co., 1923.

Nugent, Catherine, ed. *Life Work of Thomas L. Nugent*. Stephenville, Tex.: C. Nugent, 1896.

Phelan, Macum. *A History of Early Methodism in Texas, 1817-1866*. Nashville, Tenn.: Cokesbury Press, 1924.

Putnam, Samuel Porter. *400 Years of Freethought*. New York: Truth-Seeker Company, 1894.

Raines, Cadwell Walton. *Year Book for Texas, 1901*. Austin: Gammel Book Company, 1902.

Radford, Peter. *Radford's Views*. Fort Worth: Farmers' Educational and Cooperative Union, 1914.

Rankin, G. C. *The Story of My Life: or, More than Half a Century as I Have Lived It and Seen It Lived*. Dallas: Smith & Lamar, 1912.

Riley, Benjamin Franklin. *History of the Baptists of Texas: A Concise Narrative of the Baptist Denomination in Texas, from the Earliest Occupation of the Territory to the Close of the Year 1906*. Dallas: B. F. Riley, 1907.

———. *The White Man's Burden: A Discussion of the Interracial Question with Special Reference to the Responsibility of the White Race to the Negro Problem*. Birmingham, Ala.: B. F. Riley, 1910.

Sheppard, Morris. *Congressman Sheppard Is for Prohibition*. Fort Worth: Statewide Prohibition Amendment Association Headquarters, 1911.

——. *National Prohibition and States Rights*. Washington, D.C.: Government Printing Office: 1914.

——. *Fraternal and Other Addresses*. Omaha, Neb.: Beacon Press, 1910.

Shettles, Elijah L. *Recollections of a Long Life*. Edited by Archie P. McDonald. Nashville, Tenn.: Blue & Gray Press, 1973.

Tardy, William T. *The Man and the Message*. Marshall, Tex.: Mrs. W. T. Tardy, 1920.

——. *Trials and Triumphs: An Autobiography*. Marshall, Tex.: Mrs. W. T. Tardy, 1919.

Shuler, Robert Pierce. *The New Issue, or, Local Booze Government: Being a Collection of Articles on "Prohibition."* Temple, Tex.: Temple Printing and Office Appliance Co., 1911.

Strong, Josiah. *Our Country: Its Possible Future and Present Crisis*. New York: Baker & Taylor Co., 1885.

Texas House of Representatives, *Journal of the House of Representatives of the Regular Session of the Thirty-third Legislature of Texas*. Austin: Von Boeckmann-Jones, 1913.

Thrall, Homer. *History of Methodism in Texas*. Houston: E. H. Cushing, Publisher, 1872.

Truett, George. *We Would See Jesus, and Other Sermons*. Edited by J. B. Cranfill. New York: Fleming H. Revell Company, 1915.

Weeks, William F. *Debates of the Texas Convention*. Houston: J. W. Cruger, 1846.

SECONDARY SOURCES

Alexander, Charles C. *The Ku Klux Klan in the Southwest*. Lexington: University of Kentucky Press, 1965.

Arreola, Daniel. *Tejano South Texas: A Mexican American Cultural Province*. Austin: University of Texas Press, 2002.

Ayers, Edward L. *The Promise of the New South: Life after Reconstruction*. New York: Oxford University Press, 1992.

Bailey, Kenneth K. *Southern White Protestantism in the Twentieth Century*. New York: Harper & Row, 1964.

Baker, Kelly J. *Gospel according to the Klan: The KKK's Appeal to Protestant America, 1915-1930*. Lawrence: University Press of Kansas, 2011.

Barr, Alwyn. *Black Texans: A History of African Americans in Texas, 1528-1995*. Norman: University of Oklahoma Press, 1996.

——. *Reconstruction to Reform: Texas Politics, 1876-1906*. Austin: University of Texas Press, 1971.

Barrow, Blake W. "Freethought in Texas: J. D. Shaw and the Independent Pulpit." Master's thesis, Baylor University, 1983.

Bender, Thomas. "Wholes and Parts: The Need for Synthesis in American History." *Journal of American History* 73 (June 1986): 120–136.

Bernstein, Patricia. *The First Waco Horror: The Lynching of Jesse Washington and the Rise of the NAACP.* College Station: Texas A&M University Press, 2005.

Blocker, Jack S., Jr. *Retreat from Reform: The Prohibition Movement in the in the United States, 1890-1913.* Westport, Conn: Greenwood Press, 1976.

Boles, John B. "Evangelical Protestantism in the Old South: From Dissent to Dominance." In *Religion in the South,* edited by Charles Reagan Wilson, 13–34. Jackson: University of Mississippi Press, 1985.

———. *The Great Revival, 1787-1805: The Origins of the Bible Belt.* Lexington: University Press of Kentucky, 1972.

———. *The Irony of Southern Religion.* New York: Peter Lang, 1995.

———. *Masters and Slaves in the House of the Lord: Race and Religion in the American South, 1740-1870.* Lexington: University Press of Kentucky, 1988.

Boyer, Paul S. *When Time Shall Be No More: Prophecy Belief in Modern American Culture.* Cambridge, Mass.: Harvard University Press, 1992.

Brown, Norman D. *Hood, Bonnet, and Little Brown Jug: Texas Politics, 1921-1928.* College Station: Texas A&M University Press, 1984.

Buenger, Walter L. "Texas and the South." *The Southwestern Historical Quarterly* 103 (January 2000): 308–24.

———. *The Path to a Modern South: Northeast Texas between Reconstruction and the Great Depression.* Austin: University of Texas Press, 2001.

Butler, Jon. "Jack-in-the-Box Faith: The Religion Problem in Modern American History." *Journal of American History* (March 2004): 1357–1378.

Butler, Steven R. "Freethinkers: Religious Non-Conformity in Dallas, 1879-1904." *Legacies: A History Journal for Dallas and North Central Texas* 24 (Fall 2012): 16–29.

Campbell, Randolph B. *An Empire for Slavery: The Peculiar Institution in Texas, 1821-1865.* Baton Rouge: Louisiana State University Press, 1989.

Cantrell, Gregg. "'Dark Tactics': Black Politics in the 1887 Texas Prohibition Campaign." *Journal of American Studies* 25 (April 1991): 85–93.

———. *Kenneth and John B. Rayner and the Limits of Southern Dissent.* Urbana: University of Illinois Press, 1993.

———. *The People's Revolt: Populism in Texas.* New Haven: Yale University Press, Forthcoming.

Cantrell, Gregg, and Elizabeth Hayes Turner, eds. *Lone Star Pasts: Memory and History in Texas.* College Station: Texas A&M University Press, 2007.

Carwardine, Richard J. *Evangelicals and Politics in Antebellum America.* New Haven, Conn.: Yale University Press, 1993.

Carter, Paul Allen. *The Spiritual Crisis of the Gilded Age.* Dekalb: Northern Illinois University Press, 1971.

Carver, Charles. *Brann and the Iconoclast.* Austin: University of Texas Press, 1957.

Cash, W. J. *The Mind of the South.* New York: A. A. Knopf, 1941.

Chaves, Mark. "Secularization as Declining Religious Authority." *Social Forces* 72 (March 1994): 749–774.

Clark, Norman H. *Deliver Us from Evil: An Interpretation of American Prohibition.* New York: W. W. Norton, 1976.

Cohen, Stanley. *Folk Devils and Moral Panic: 30th Anniversary Edition.* New York: Routledge, 2002.

Coker, Joe L. *Liquor in the Land of the Lost Cause.* Lexington: University Press of Kentucky, 2007.

Conger, Roger N. "Waco: Cotton and Culture on the Brazos." *Southwestern Historical Quarterly* 75 (July 1971): 54–76.

Cooper, William J. *Jefferson Davis, American.* New York: A. A. Knopf, 2000.

———, ed. *Jefferson Davis: The Essential Writings.* New York: Random House, 2004.

Creech, Joe. *Righteous Indignation: Religion and the Populist Revolution.* Urbana: University of Illinois Press, 2006.

Crunden, Robert Morse. *Ministers of Reform: The Progressives' Achievement in American Civilization, 1889-1920.* New York: Basic, 1982.

Davidson, Chandler. *Race and Class in Texas Politics.* Princeton, N.J.: Princeton University Press, 1990.

De León, Arnoldo. *They Called Them Greasers: Anglo Attitudes toward Mexicans in Texas, 1821-1900.* Austin: University of Texas Press, 1983.

———. "Rancheros, Comerciantes, and Trabajadores in South Texas, 1848-1900." In *Reflections of the Mexican Experience in Texas,* edited by Margarita Melville and Hilda Castillo Phariss, 98–105. Houston: University of Houston, 1979.

Dochuk, Darren. *From Bible Belt to Sunbelt: Plain-Folk Religion, Grassroots Politics, and the Rise of Evangelical Conservatism.* New York: W. W. Norton, 2011.

Durso, Keith E. *Thy Will Be Done: A Biography of George W. Truett.* Macon, Ga.: Mercer University Press, 2009.

Early, Joseph E. *A Texas Baptist Power Struggle: The Hayden Controversy.* Denton: University of North Texas Press, 2005.

Eighmy, John Lee. *Churches in Cultural Captivity: A History of the Social Attitudes of Southern Baptists.* Knoxville: University of Tennessee Press, 1972.

Ellis, Blake. "An Alternative Politics: Texas Baptists and the Rise of the Christian Right, 1975-1985." *Southwestern Historical Quarterly* 112 (April 2009): 361–386.

Emerson, Michael O., and Christian Smith. *American Evangelicalism: Embattled and Thriving.* Chicago: University of Chicago Press, 1998.

———. *Divided by Faith: Evangelical Religion and the Problem of Race in America.* New York: Oxford University Press, 2000.

Farish, Hunter Dickinson. *The Circuit Rider Dismounts: A Social History of Southern Methodism, 1865-1900.* Richmond, Va.: Dietz, 1938.

Faust, Drew Gilpin. *The Creation of Confederate Nationalism: Ideology and Identity in the Civil War South.* Baton Rouge: Louisiana State University Press, 1988.

Finke, Roger, and Rodney Stark. *The Churching of America, 1776-1990: Winners and Losers in Our Religious Economy.* New Brunswick, N.J.: Rutgers University Press, 1992.

———. "Turning Pews into People: Estimating Nineteenth-Century Church Membership." *Journal for the Scientific Study of Religion* 25 (June 1986): 180–192.

Flynt, Wayne. *Alabama Baptists: Southern Baptists in the Heart of Dixie.* Tuscaloosa: University of Alabama Press, 1998.

———. "Dissent in Zion: Alabama Baptists and Social Issues." *Journal of Southern History* 35 (November 1969): 523–542.

Foley, Neil. *The White Scourge: Mexicans, Blacks, and Poor Whites in Texas Cotton Culture.* Berkeley: University of California Press, 1997.

Foster, Gaines. *Moral Reconstruction, Christian Lobbyists and the Federal Legislation of Morality, 1865-1920.* Chapel Hill: University of North Carolina Press, 2002.

Fox-Genovese, Elizabeth, and Eugene D. Genovese. *The Mind of the Master Class: History and Faith in the Southern Slaveholders' Worldview.* Cambridge: Cambridge University Press, 2005.

Gilmore, Glenda. *Gender and Jim Crow: Women and the Politics of White Supremacy in North Carolina, 1896-1920.* Chapel Hill: University of North Carolina Press, 1996.

Goodwyn, Lawrence. *Democratic Promise: The Populist Moment in America.* New York: Oxford University Press, 1976.

Gould, Lewis L. *Alexander Watkins Terrell: Civil War Soldier, Texas Lawmaker, American Diplomat.* Austin: University of Texas Press, 2004.

———. *Progressives and Prohibitionists: Texas Democrats in the Wilson Era.* Austin: University of Texas Press, 1973.

———. "Progressives and Prohibitionists: Texas Democratic Politics, 1911–1921." *Southwestern Historical Quarterly* 75 (July 1971): 5–18.

Grantham, Dewey W. *Southern Progressivism: The Reconciliation of Progress and Tradition.* Knoxville: University of Tennessee Press, 1983.

Grace, Fran. *Carry A. Nation: Retelling the Life.* Bloomington: Indiana University Press, 2001.

Gregory, James. *The Southern Diaspora: How the Great Migrations of Black and White Southerners Transformed America.* Chapel Hill: University of North Carolina Press, 2005.

Griggs, William Clark. *Parson Henry Renfro: Free Thinking on the Texas Frontier.* Austin: University of Texas Press, 1994.

Hale, Grace Elizabeth. *Making Whiteness: The Culture of Segregation in the South, 1890-1940.* New York: Pantheon, 1998.

Harper, Keith. *The Quality of Mercy: Southern Baptists and Social Christianity, 1890-1920.* Tuscaloosa: University of Alabama Press, 1996.

Hales, Douglas. *A Southern Family in White and Black: The Cuneys of Texas.* College Station: Texas A&M University Press, 2003.

Haley, James L. *Sam Houston.* Norman: University of Oklahoma Press, 2004.

Hamilton, Barry W. "The Corsicana Enthusiasts: A Pre-Pentecostal Millennial Sect." *Wesleyan Theological Journal* 39 (Spring 2004): 173–193.

Hankins, Barry. *God's Rascal: J. Frank Norris and the Beginnings of Southern Fundamentalism.* Lexington: University Press of Kentucky, 1996.

Harvey, Paul. *Freedom's Coming: Religious Culture and the Shaping of the South from the Civil War through the Civil Rights Era*. Chapel Hill: University of North Carolina Press, 2005.

———. *Redeeming the South: Religious Cultures and Racial Identities among Southern Baptists, 1865-1925*. Chapel Hill: University of North Carolina Press, 1997.

———. "Religion." In *The South*, edited by Rebecca Mark and Robert Vaughn, 407–438. Westport, Conn.: Greenwood Publishing Group, 2004.

Hatch, Nathan O. *The Democratization of American Christianity*. New Haven, Conn.: Yale University Press, 1989.

Heyrman, Christine Leigh. *Southern Cross: The Beginnings of the Bible Belt*. New York: A. A. Knopf, 1997.

Higginbotham, Evelyn Brooks. *Righteous Discontent: The Women's Movement in the Black Baptist Church, 1880-1920*. Cambridge, Mass.: Harvard University Press, 1993.

Hill, Samuel S. *Religion and the Solid South*. Nashville, Tenn.: Abingdon, 1972.

Hill, Samuel S., Jr. *The South and the North in American Religion*. Athens: University of Georgia Press, 1980.

Hill, Samuel S. *Southern Churches in Crisis Revisited*. Tuscaloosa: University of Alabama Press, 1999.

Hofstadter, Richard. *The Age of Reform: From Bryan to FDR*. New York: A. A. Knopf, 1955.

Hohner, Robert A. *Prohibition and Politics: The Life of Bishop James Cannon, Jr.* Columbia: University of South Carolina Press, 1999.

Hollinger, David A. "The Secularization Question in the United States in the Twentieth Century." *Church History* 70 (March 2001): 132–143.

Irons, Charles. *The Origins of Proslavery Christianity: White and Black Evangelicals in Colonial and Antebellum Virginia*. Chapel Hill: University of North Carolina Press, 2008.

Isaac, Paul E. *Prohibition and Politics: Turbulent Decades in Tennessee, 1885-1920*. Knoxville: University of Tennessee Press, 1965.

Isaac, Rhys. *The Transformation of Virginia, 1740-1790*. Chapel Hill: University of North Carolina Press, 1982.

Israel, Charles. *Before Scopes: Evangelicalism, Education, and Evolution in Tennessee, 1870-1925*. Athens: University of Georgia Press, 2004.

Ivy, James D. *No Saloon in the Valley: The Southern Strategy of Texas Prohibitionists in the 1880s*. Waco: Baylor University Press, 2003.

Jacoby, Susan. *Freethinkers: A History of American Secularism*. New York: Metropolitan, 2005.

———. *The Great Agnostic: Robert Ingersoll and American Freethought*. New Haven, Conn.: Yale University Press, 2013.

Kelley, Dean M. *Why Conservative Churches Are Growing*. New York: Harper & Row, 1973.

Key, V. O. *Southern Politics in State and Nation*. New York: A. A. Knopf, 1949.

King, Keith Lynn. "Religious Dimensions of the Agrarian Protest in Texas, 1870-1908." PhD diss., University of Illinois, 1985.

Kousser, J. Morgan. *The Shaping of Southern Politics: Suffrage Restriction and the Establishment of the One-Party South, 1880-1910*. New Haven, Conn.: Yale University Press, 1974.

Kownslar, Allan O. *The European Texans*. College Station: Texas A&M University Press, 2004.

Lears, T. J. Jackson. *No Place of Grace: Antimodernism and the Transformation of American Culture, 1880-1920*. New York: Pantheon, 1981.

———. *Rebirth of a Nation: The Making of Modern America, 1877-1920*. New York: Harper Collins, 2009.

Lee, James Ward. *Texas, My Texas*. Denton: University of North Texas Press, 1993.

Lefever, Alan J. *Fighting the Good Fight: The Life and Work of Benajah Harvey Carroll*. Austin: Eakin Press, 1994.

Leloudis, James L. *Schooling the New South: Pedagogy, Self, and Society in North Carolina, 1880-1920*. Chapel Hill: University of North Carolina Press, 1996.

Lester, Connie L. *Up from the Mudsills of Hell: The Farmers' Alliance, Populism, and Progressive Agriculture in Tennessee, 1870–1915*. Athens: University of Georgia Press, 2006.

Lich, Glen E., and Dona B. Reeves, eds. *German Culture in Texas*. Boston: Twayne, 1980.

Lich, Glen E. *The German Texans*. San Antonio: University of Texas Institute of Texan Cultures, 1981.

Link, William A. *The Paradox of Southern Progressivism, 1880-1930*. Chapel Hill: University of North Carolina Press, 1992.

Loveland, Anne C. *Southern Evangelicals and the Social Order, 1800-1860*. Baton Rouge: Louisiana State University Press, 1980.

Lucas, Sean Michael. *Robert Lewis Dabney: A Southern Presbyterian Life*. Philipsburg, N.J.: P&R Publishing, 2005.

MacLean, Nancy. *Behind the Mask of Chivalry: The Making of the Second Ku Klux Klan*. New York: Oxford University Press, 1994.

Marsden, George. *Fundamentalism and American Culture: The Shaping of Twentieth-Century Evangelicalism, 1870-1925*. New York: Oxford University Press, 1980.

McArthur, Judith N. *Creating the New Woman: The Rise of Southern Women's Progressive Culture in Texas, 1893-1918*. Urbana: University of Illinois Press, 1998.

McBeth, Leon. *Texas Baptists: A Sesquicentennial History*. Dallas: Baptistway Press, 1998.

McCarty, Jeanne Bozzell. *The Struggle for Sobriety: Protestants and Prohibition in Texas, 1919-1935*. El Paso: Texas Western Press, 1980.

McDowell, John Patrick. *The Social Gospel in the South: The Woman's Home Mission Movement in the Methodist Episcopal Church, South, 1886-1930*. Baton Rouge: Louisiana State University Press, 1982.

McGirr, Lisa. *Suburban Warriors: The Origins of the New American Right*. Princeton, N.J.: Princeton University Press, 2001.

Miller, Randall M., Harry S. Stout, and Charles Reagan Wilson, eds. *Religion and the American Civil War*. New York: Oxford University Press, 1998.

Miller, Steven P. *Billy Graham and the Rise of the Republican South*. Philadelphia: University of Pennsylvania Press, 2009.

Modern, John Lardas. *Secularism in Antebellum America*. Chicago: University of Chicago Press, 2011.

Montejano, David. *Anglos and Mexicans in the Making of Texas, 1836-1986*. Austin: University of Texas Press, 1987.

Moore, Jerome A. *Texas Christian University: A Hundred Years of History*. Fort Worth: Texas Christian University Press, 1974.

Moore, R. Laurence. *In Search of White Crows: Spiritualism, Parapsychology, and American Culture*. New York: Oxford University Press, 1977.

Montgomery, William E. *Under Their Own Vine and Fig Tree: The African-American Church in the South, 1865-1900*. Baton Rouge: Louisiana State University Press, 1993.

Motl, Kevin C. "Under the Influence: The Texas Business Men's Association and the Campaign against Reform, 1906-1915." *Southwestern Historical Quarterly* 109 (April 2006): 494–529.

Noll, Mark A., and Luke E. Harlow, eds. *Religion and American Politics: From the Colonial Period to the Present*. New York: Oxford University Press, 2007.

Nordstrom, Justin. *Danger on the Doorstep: Anti-Catholicism and American Print Culture in the Progressive Era*. Notre Dame, Ind.: University of Notre Dame Press, 2006.

Okrent, Daniel. *Last Call: The Rise and Fall of Prohibition*. New York: Simon and Schuster, 2010.

Orozco, Cynthia. *No Mexicans, Women, or Dogs Allowed: The Rise of the Mexican American Civil Rights Movement*. Austin: University of Texas Press, 2009.

Ownby, Ted. *Subduing Satan: Religion, Recreation, and Manhood in the Rural South, 1865-1920*. Chapel Hill: University of North Carolina Press, 1990.

Pegram, Thomas R. "Temperance Politics and Regional Political Culture: The Anti-Saloon League in Maryland and the South, 1907–1915." *Journal of Southern History* 63 (February 1997): 57–90.

Perman, Michael. *Struggle for Mastery: Disfranhisement in the South, 1888-1908*. Chapel Hill: University of North Carolina Press, 2001.

Phillips, Michael. *White Metropolis: Race, Ethnicity, and Religion in Dallas, 1841-2001*. Austin: University of Texas Press, 2006.

Porterfield, Amanda. *Conceived in Doubt: Religion and Politics in the New American Nation*. Chicago: University of Chicago Press, 2012.

Postel, Charles. *The Populist Vision*. New York: Oxford University Press, 2009.

Remond, Rene. "Anticlericalism: Some Reflections by Way of Introduction." *European Studies Review* 13 (1983): 121–126.

Remond, Rene. *L'anticlericalisme en France de 1815 a nos jours*. Paris: Fayard, 1976.

Sallee, Shelley. *The Whiteness of Child Labor Reform in the New South*. Athens: University of Georgia Press, 2004.

Sanchez, Jose. *Anticlericalism*. Notre Dame, Ind.: University of Notre Dame Press, 1972.

Shearer, Ernest C. "Sam Houston and Religion." *Tennessee Historical Quarterly* 20 (March 1961): 38–50.

Schweiger, Beth Barton. *The Gospel Working Up: Progress and the Pulpit in Nineteenth-Century Virginia*. New York: Oxford University Press, 2000.

———. "How Would Jesus Vote? The Prehistory of the Christian Right." *Reviews in American History* 32 (March 2004): 49–57.

Sehat, David. *The Myth of American Religious Freedom*. New York: Oxford University Press, 2011.

Silverman, William. "The Exclusion of Clergy from Political Office in American States: An Oddity in Church-State Relations." *Sociology of Religion* 61, no. 2 (Summer 2000): 223–230.

Smith, H. Shelton. *In His Image, But . . .: Racism in Southern Religion, 1780-1910*. Durham, NC: Duke University Press, 1972.

Snay, Mitchell. *Gospel of Disunion: Religion and Separatism in the Antebellum South*. Chapel Hill: University of North Carolina Press, 1993.

Spain, Rufus B. *At Ease in Zion: A Social History of Southern Baptists, 1865-1900*. Nashville, Tenn.: Vanderbilt University Press, 1967.

Stanley, Mark. "Portrait of a Southern Progressive: The Political Life and Times of Governor Pat M. Neff of Texas, 1871-1952." PhD diss., University of North Texas, 2011.

Stark, Rodney. "The Reliability of Historical United States Census Data on Religion." *Sociological Analysis* 53 (Spring 1992): 91–95.

Stephens, Randall. *The Fire Spreads: Holiness and Pentecostalism in the American South*. Cambridge, Mass.: Harvard University Press, 2008.

Stokes, David R. *The Shooting Salvationist: J. Frank Norris and the Murder Trial That Captivated America*. Hanover, N.H.: Steerforth, 2011.

Storey, John W. *Texas Baptist Leadership and Social Christianity, 1900-1980*. College Station: Texas A&M University Press, 1986.

Stowell, Daniel W. *Rebuilding Zion: The Religious Reconstruction of the South, 1863-1877*. New York: Oxford University Press, 1998.

Stricklin, David. *A Genealogy of Dissent: Southern Baptist Protest in the Twentieth Century*. Lexington: University Press of Kentucky, 1999.

Sutton, Jared Paul. "Ethnic Minorities and Prohibition in Texas, 1887-1919." Master's thesis, University of North Texas, 2006.

Szymanski, Ann-Marie. "Beyond Parochialism: Southern Progressivism, Prohibition, and State-Building." *Journal of Southern History* 69 (February 2003): 107–136.

Terry, Marshall. *"From High on the Hilltop . . .": A Brief History of SMU*. Dallas: Southern Methodist University Press, 1993.

Thompson, E. Bruce. "William Carey Crane and Texas Education." *Southwestern Historical Quarterly* 58 (January 1955): 405–421.

Thompson, Paul H., Jr. *A Most Stirring and Significant Episode: Religion and the Rise and Fall of Prohibition in Black Atlanta, 1865-1887*. DeKalb: Northern Illinois University Press, 2013.

Timberlake, James H. *Prohibition and the Progressive Movement, 1900-1920*. Cambridge, Mass.: Harvard University Press, 1963.

Tindall, George Brown. *The Emergence of the New South, 1913-1945*. Baton Rouge: Louisiana State University Press, 1967.

Turner, Elizabeth Hayes, *Women, Culture, and Community: Religion and Reform in Galveston, 1880-1920*. New York: Oxford University Press, 1997.

Turner, John G. *Bill Bright and Campus Crusade for Christ: The Renewal of Evangelicalism in Postwar America*. Chapel Hill: University of North Carolina Press, 2008.

Tweedie, Stephen W. "Viewing the Bible Belt." *Journal of Popular* Culture 11 (Spring 1978): 865–876.

Vernon, Walter N. *Methodism Moves across North Texas*. Dallas: North Texas Methodist Historical Society, 1967.

Warner, R. Stephen. *A Church of Our Own: Disestablishment and Diversity in American Religion*. New Brunswick, N.J.: Rutgers University Press, 2005.

Wiebe, Robert. *The Search for Order, 1877-1920*. New York: Hill and Wang, 1967.

Williamson, Joel. *The Crucible of Race: Black-White Relations in the American South since Emancipation*. New York: Oxford University Press, 1984.

Willis, Lee L. *Southern Prohibition: Race, Reform, and Public Life in Middle Florida, 1821-1920*. Athens: University of Georgia Press, 2011.

Wills, Gregory A. *Democratic Religion: Freedom, Authority, and Church Discipline in the Baptist South, 1785-1900*. New York: Oxford University Press, 1997.

Wilson, Charles Reagan. *Baptized in Blood: The Religion of the Lost Cause, 1865-1920*. Athens: University of Georgia Press, 1980.

———. "The Bible Belt." In *Encyclopedia of Religion in the South,* edited by Samuel S. Hill. Macon, Ga.: Mercer University Press, 2005.

Wilson, Charles Reagan, and Mark Silk, eds. *Religion and Public Life in the South: In the Evangelical Mode*. Walnut Creek, Calif: Alta Mira, 2005.

Wimberly, Dan B. "Daniel Parker: Pioneer Preacher and Political Leader." PhD diss., Texas Tech University, 1995.

Woodward, C. Vann. *Origins of the New South, 1877-1913*. Baton Rouge: Louisiana State University Press, 1951.

———. *The Strange Career of Jim Crow*. New York: Oxford University Press, 2002.

Wuthnow, Robert. *Rough Country: How Texas Became America's Most Powerful Bible-Belt State*. Princeton, N.J.: Princeton University Press, 2014.

Index

CPSIA information can be obtained
at www.ICGtesting.com
Printed in the USA
BVHW031614280620
582405BV00004B/6